DRUNK ON GENOCIDE

DRUNK ON GENOCIDE

Alcohol and Mass Murder in Nazi Germany

EDWARD B. WESTERMANN

PUBLISHED IN ASSOCIATION WITH THE
UNITED STATES HOLOCAUST MEMORIAL MUSEUM

CORNELL UNIVERSITY PRESS
ITHACA AND LONDON

A volume in the series
BATTLEGROUNDS: CORNELL STUDIES IN MILITARY HISTORY
Edited by David J. Silbey
Editorial Board: Petra Goedde, Wayne E. Lee,
Brian McAllister Linn, and Lien-Hang T. Nguyen

A list of titles in this series is available at cornellpress.cornell.edu.

Copyright © 2021 by Cornell University

The assertions, arguments, and conclusions contained herein are those
of the author or other contributors. They do not necessarily reflect the
opinions of the United States Holocaust Memorial Museum.

Photographs are courtesy of the United States Holocaust Memorial
Museum, Collection 1999.99.3.

First published 2021 by Cornell University Press

Printed in the United States of America

ISBN 978-1-5017-5419-7 (hardcover)
ISBN 978-1-5017-5421-0 (pdf)
ISBN 978-1-5017-5420-3 (epub)

Library of Congress Control Number: 2020950259

For my friends and survivors George Fodor, Susi Jalnos,
Anna Rado, Zev Weiss, and Rose Williams

CONTENTS

Illustrations begin on page 121.

Acknowledgments

Given the subject matter, this has been a difficult book to research and to write. Researching the Holocaust is a dark journey at the best of times; however, the intersection of alcohol, masculinity, and atrocity reveals some of the most horrific manifestations of human behavior and violence that one can imagine, and these actions will be difficult for many to read. Still, I believe that this is an important topic that has much to reveal not only about the events of the Shoah, but also about other cases of mass atrocity and genocide. Like any book project, this effort is not only the work of the author, but involves the research and assistance of many different institutions and individuals. In fact, the interest and enthusiasm shown by my friends, colleagues, and students have been a great source of inspiration in helping me to bring this book to press.

First, I would like to thank several institutions that supported my research into the relationship of alcohol and acts of violence and atrocity, including the staffs of the William P. Clements Center for Southwest Studies and the DeGolyer Library at Southern Methodist University during a research travel grant in 2017. The generosity and expertise shared by Andy Graybill, Ruth Ann Elmore, and Russell Martin as I looked at the role of alcohol and violence in the US West is not a part of this work, but it certainly helped to inform my thinking on this project. Likewise, I would like to thank the United States Holocaust Memorial Museum in Washington, DC, for awarding me a J. B. and Maurice C. Shapiro fellowship in the spring of 2019 in support of this project. During my time at the Jack, Joseph, and Morton Mandel Center for Advanced Holocaust Studies, I was able to work with some of the finest archivists and library professionals in the world, including Liviu Carare, Judy Cohen, Nancy Hartman, Kassandra LaPrade-Seuthe, Megan Lewis, Vincent Slatt, Suzy Snyder, Caroline Waddell, and Elliot Wrenn. Their expertise and friendly assistance are greatly appreciated. Finally, I would like to thank the College of Arts and Sciences at Texas A&M–San Antonio for providing an internal research grant to support my research, and especially the support shown to me by the university provost, Mike O'Brien, as well as that of the university president, Cynthia Teniente-Matson, in allowing me to take a period of developmental leave to complete the manuscript. The Texas A&M–San Antonio library staff, especially Sarah Timm and Emily Bliss-Zaks, assisted me in finding and acquiring key sources, and I greatly appreciate their efforts. I also would like to thank the department chair Bill Bush, all my history colleagues, and my students for their interest and support of this project. In the case of the last, I now have the answer to my students' question on when the book will finally be published—it's here.

Second, I would like to express my appreciation to the number of persons who read either all or parts of the manuscript and offered their insights and contributions. My mentor Gerhard Weinberg read and commented on the entire manuscript with his usual perspicuity and keen analytical ability. Likewise, the manuscript readers, Waitman Beorn and Björn Krondorfer, provided important suggestions and insights for improving the manuscript while also generously sharing additional sources for the project. In turn, my friend and a leading scholar in the field of Holocaust studies, Jürgen Matthäus, not only read the entire manuscript, but spent a number of hours discussing my findings and conclusions and as always proved invaluable in helping me find additional sources related to the project. Likewise, my friend and colleague Billy Kiser read the manuscript with an unfaltering sense of judgment and a valuable editorial hand. In addition to these individuals, Richard Breitman, Ovi Creanga, Hilary Earl, Geoffrey Giles, Dagmar Herzog, Thomas Pegelow-Kaplan, Thomas Kühne, Carolin Lange, and Amy Porter read and commented on chapters or earlier articles related to this project, and each has made a contribution to my thinking on this topic. Portions of the introduction and chapters 1 and 4 were previously published, in a different form, in "Stone Cold Killers or Drunk with Murder? Alcohol and Atrocity in the Holocaust," *Holocaust and Genocide Studies* 30 (2016): 1–19; "Drinking Rituals, Masculinity, and Mass Murder in Nazi Germany," *Central European History* 51 (2018): 367–89; and "Tests of Manhood: Alcohol, Sexual Violence, and Killing in the Holocaust," in *The Holocaust and Masculinities: Critical Inquiries into the Presence and Absence of Men*, ed. Björn Krondorfer and Ovidiu Creanga (Albany: SUNY Press, 2020), 147–69. I thank Cambridge University Press, Oxford University Press, and SUNY Press for allowing me to reprint these materials.

Third, I have benefited over the last five years by the generosity and expertise of a number of colleagues who have provided invitations to speak on this subject at their institutions or who have shared their thoughts in fellowship and research forums. For example, I would like to thank all of the academic year 2018–19 fellows at the United States Holocaust Memorial Museum, especially Steve Baumann, Jennie Burnet, Bettina Brandt, Marilyn Campeau, Paula Chan, Anna Duensing, Amos Goldberg, Yosef Goldstein, Gabrielle Hauth, Yurii Kaparulin, Carolin Lange, Abby Lewis, Miriam Schulz, and Nick Warmuth. In particular, Steve Baumann, Bettina Brandt, and Carolin Lange provided key insights to this project during my time in Washington, DC. In addition, I would like to thank the following researchers and staff members at the museum: Suzanne Brown-Fleming, Rebecca Carter-Chand, Jennifer Chiappone, Jennifer Ciardelli, Jo-Ellyn Decker, Steven Feldman, Michael Gelb, Neal Guthrie, Mel Hecker, Andrew Kloes, Michael Kraus, Jan Lambertz, Alexandra Lohse, Geoff Megargee, Katarzyna Pietrzak, Katie Saint John, and Gretchen Skidmore. I owe a specific debt to Betsy Anthony, who introduced me to the International Tracing Service database and helped me negotiate this valuable source. Likewise, I am delighted that the Holocaust Memorial Museum agreed to copublish this work, and I want to thank Robert Ehrenreich, Lisa Leff, and Claire Rosenson for their efforts in championing my project.

Additionally, I would like to thank the following individuals for either providing me with source materials or for sharing their insights as I researched this topic: Kimberly Allar, Truman Anderson, Patrice Bensimon, Doris Bergen, Patrick Bernhard, Jeremy Black, Chris Browning, Maya Camargo-Vermuri, Winson Chu, David Crew, Sarah Cushman, Jeffrey Burds, John Delaney, Curran Egan, Lorena Fontaine, Tomasz Frydel, Francis Galan, Chad Gibbs, Dorota Glowacka, Mary Ann Grim, Wolf Gruner, Carlos Haas, Valerie Hébert, Jeffrey Herf, Alexis Herr, Jason Johnson, Stefan Klemp, Thomas Köhler, Piotr Kosicki, Jan Láníček, Tatjana Lichtenstein, Jay Lockenour, Nancy Love, Wendy Lower, Vojin Majstorović, Sonya Michel, Yves Müller, Sylvia Naylor, Sandy Ott, Gregg and Michelle Philipson, Carson Phillips, Ian Rich, Jeff Rutherford, Eli Sacks, Andrew Sanders, Adam Seipp, David Shneer, Kevin Simpson, Christoph Spieker, Gerald Steinacher, Angelique Stevens, Don Stoker, Greg Urwin, Melissa Weininger, Sara Winger, and Jamie Wraight. From the list of names above, it is evident that I owe a great debt of thanks to many individuals, and, for those whom I may have inadvertently missed, I am grateful for the insights you provided.

I owe a debt of gratitude to the entire team at Cornell University Press. Emily Andrew was an early and enthusiastic supporter of this project and an expert adviser. As series editor, David Silbey provided valuable suggestions and support for publication. Additionally, Susan Specter and Alexis Siemon offered timely and expert assistance in the production of the manuscript, and Glenn Novak proved to be a sophisticated and sensitive copy editor on a very dark subject. I also want to thank Brock Schnoke and the entire marketing team for their efforts on my behalf.

Finally, I would like to thank my wife, Brigitte, and our daughters, Sarah and Marlies, for their understanding and support as I worked on the book, an effort that came at the expense of time spent together.

DRUNK ON GENOCIDE

INTRODUCTION

It was a cold Tuesday morning in January 1942 as a group of senior Nazi administrators arrived for a meeting at a lakeside villa on the Wannsee on the outskirts of Berlin. The participants represented the highest echelons of power from within the SS, the Justice Ministry, the Foreign Ministry, and the Interior Ministry, as well as senior representatives from the occupied eastern territories. They came in response to an invitation by the SS general Reinhard Heydrich, the head of the Security Police and the Security Service and the right-hand man of Heinrich Himmler, the Reich leader of the SS and chief of the German Police. The meeting involved top-secret deliberations concerning the implementation of the "Final Solution to the Jewish Question," or, in plain speech, the annihilation of the European Jews, a mission that had been entrusted to Heydrich.[1] The SS lieutenant colonel Adolf Eichmann, the head of the Gestapo office in charge of Jewish affairs, was charged with arranging the meeting, including preparing the invitations and editing multiple drafts of Heydrich's opening remarks.[2] The effort associated with Heydrich's opening speech reflected his desire to establish the right tone for the meeting and to gain the support of these administrators for his leadership in the process of mass murder, a crucial requirement in a regime characterized by bureaucratic infighting and internecine contests for power.[3]

To the surprise and delight of Heydrich, the attendees not only enthusiastically supported his direction of the efforts, but also provided specific recommendations for implementing these plans. Eichmann subsequently observed, "These State Secretaries, in rare unanimity and *joyful* agreement, demanded accelerated action."[4] In fact, the deliberations concerning the destruction of the European Jews took less than two hours, a tangible expression of the group's consensus and a clear affirmation of Heydrich's principal role in the process. After the meeting, the Nazi potentates gathered in small groups for personal discussions before heading back to their offices in central Berlin.[5] A clearly ebullient Heydrich, despite the early hour, invited Eichmann and Heinrich Müller, head of the Gestapo (Secret State Police), to join him near the fireplace for cigars and cognac to celebrate the success of the meeting. Eichmann remembered that it was the first time he had seen Heydrich "take any alcoholic drink in years," but it would not be the last time, as at some point in the following months he joined Heydrich for a "friendly get-together of the Security Service [SD] where . . . we sang a song, we drank, we climbed up on a chair and drank again, and then onto the table and down again, and so on—a type of merrymaking I had not known."[6]

The picture of Heydrich and Eichmann, the key agents of annihilation, drinking, singing, and celebrating their work while standing on a table provides a vivid image of one way in which alcohol and celebratory ritual became incorporated into the process of mass murder by the perpetrators as they rejoiced in their accomplishments. Indeed, any subsequent meeting after Wannsee between the two men, especially based on Eichmann's role as junior subordinate, could have had only one purpose, and that would have been to update his boss on the progress toward achieving the destruction of the European Jews. In this sense, the news must have been very good if it led to these SS comrades singing drunkenly from the top of a table. This behavior was all the more remarkable as Heydrich carefully cultivated an image of "inner composure, masculinity, and strength" in which he avoided drinking in public, especially in uniform.[7]

Over the course of the Third Reich (1933–1945), scenes involving alcohol consumption and revelry among the SS and police would become a routine part of rituals of humiliation in the camps, ghettos, and killing fields of Eastern Europe. Such celebrations were not anomalous events and extended from meetings of top SS and police leaders to the rank and file celebrating at the graves of the victims. For example, SS colonel Karl Jäger, the commander of a special killing detachment, *Einsatzkommando 3* (EK 3), proudly reported to Berlin on December 1, 1941, that "I can determine today that the goal of solving the Jewish problem in Lithuania has been accomplished by EK 3."[8] In fact, Jäger and the men under his command had been responsible for the murder of almost 140,000 people since late June 1941, and despite the difficulty in gaining transportation and leave approvals, he would assemble his lieutenants for a weekend reunion celebration a year later in order to carouse and swap stories of their murderous accomplishment.[9] Likewise, Franz Stangl, the SS commandant at the Treblinka killing center, retired to his bed each night with a glass of cognac, a reward for a hard day's work of mass murder.[10]

SS and policemen involved with the destruction of the European Jews experienced a twofold feeling of intoxication. First, these men went east in an imperial campaign of mass murder during which they exercised power over life and death, a heady feeling of psychological supremacy over conquered and "inferior" subject populations. For many Germans, an "almost intoxicating feeling of superiority" accompanied the process of conquest and eastern colonization.[11] Second, the occupiers integrated drinking rituals into their daily routines in order to commemorate and celebrate masculine virtues of camaraderie and shared violence. Under National Socialism, intoxication in both a literal and metaphorical sense became part of a "hypermasculine" ideal and "constellations of violence" in which manhood and male group solidarity were established and reaffirmed by the perpetrators in rituals of celebration and mass murder.[12] In the case of Eichmann, his drinking bouts and prolific "sexual escapades" became both a manifestation of the SS ideal of masculinity and a reflection of the "intoxication of power" (*Machtrausch*) expressed by his control over the life and death of millions.[13] As one Polish Jewish survivor testified after the war, this "intoxication of power and arrogance" was a trait shared by many SS men, who used it to justify their murder of "completely innocent people."[14] The effects of such intoxication were not limited, however, to the perpetrators alone, but also found expression in the feelings and actions of the Nazi Party and the "Aryan" German population as a whole that experienced these feelings as part of a people's community bound together by ties of racial superiority, comradeship, and a colonial mission of conquest and ultimately genocide.[15]

Power and Intoxication

In a diary entry of June 4, 1942, Victor Klemperer described National Socialism as evoking a "literal blood lust with which these people [the Germans] became *intoxicated.*" He continued, "all of them are somehow *drunk*, obsessed, [and] dangerously delirious."[16] Klemperer, an accomplished scholar who, because of his Jewish heritage, lost his university teaching position after the Nazi seizure of power, was an astute observer of German society. His linkage of the concept of drunkenness with "blood lust" offers an apt perspective related to the connection between psychological feelings of intoxication and manifestations of aggression aimed at the Third Reich's putative enemies. Interestingly, the Red Army correspondent Ilya Ehrenburg, writing from the battlefront a month earlier, described German soldiers within the Soviet Union as "not only drunk on schnapps" but "drunk with the blood of Poles, Frenchmen, and Serbs."[17]

Hans Bernd Gisevius, a senior police official and a future member of the German resistance, shared Klemperer's observations of a German public in a "state of permanent intoxication" as "day after day the people sang and marched themselves into ever-madder states of intoxication."[18] Gisevius also remarked on the key role played by the paramilitary SA or storm troopers, whose intoxication emerged from the "possession of power" and found public expression "with their own bloodthirsty songs."[19] For Nazi paramilitaries, the concepts of aggression, violence, and intoxication became intertwined with conceptions of masculinity in which the experience of war and combat became the ideal of German manhood, a sentiment encapsulated in Ernst Jünger's description of impending battle: "The air was charged to overflowing with manliness, so that every breath was an intoxication."[20] Over the course of the Second World War, such feelings of intoxication and bloodlust epitomized the actions of the members of Heinrich Himmler's SS and police empire in their "growing elation stemming from repetition [of murder], from the ever-larger numbers of the killed others."[21]

Klemperer, Ehrenburg, Gisevius, and Jünger were not the only contemporary observers to make the association between intoxication and acts of violence. Walter Tausk, a German Jew living in Breslau, noted "blood drunk" storm troopers as they terrorized his coreligionists on the streets of Breslau and celebrated the invasion of Poland in September 1939.[22] Friedrich Kellner, a bureaucrat in the small town of Laubach, recorded similar thoughts by describing his fellow citizens as "intoxicated" by the success of the German army in Poland. In his diary on June 14, 1940, Kellner reflected on the impending fall of France: "The National Socialists' intoxication with victory will be of an unrestrained nature . . . [for] those who plan the premeditated murder of mankind."[23] As Kellner's words reveal, feelings of intoxication and acts of atrocity became inextricably intertwined under the Third Reich. Until his final entry of May 17, 1945, Kellner not only frequently commented on a German public "intoxicated" with military victories and Nazi propaganda slogans, but he repeatedly remarked on the crimes and atrocities committed by the regime in the occupied eastern territories, including "the final goal of extermination" of the Jews.[24] The intoxication with visions of victory was not merely limited to the German home front but extended to the most senior ranks of the German army. In his postwar memoir, General Heinz Guderian recalled the "high spirits" of the Army High Command (OKH) who were "drunk with the scent of victory" in the fall of 1941 even as an exhausted army struggled to reach Moscow before the onset of winter.[25]

The promotion of a metaphorical *intoxication* among the German populace extended to traditional holidays and to massive Nazi rallies, parades, and ceremonies that served as rituals and public spectacles for generating popular support for the regime. A pre-Lenten 1938 carnival parade float in Nuremberg featured four Jewish effigies hanging from a spinning windmill, a public spectacle in which tipsy spectators could laugh, cheer, celebrate, and ultimately conceptualize the idea of lynched Jews.[26] Gisela Apel, a young German girl whose parents opposed the regime, still recalled seven decades later the emotional effects of mass Nazi spectacles, "The wonderful aspect of such a a [sic] mass assembly, which I experienced as intoxication [*Rausch*]. That's something one can hardly escape from, you know."[27] Similarly, Bella Fromm, a Jewish socialite, described the 1934 Nuremberg party rally in her diary as a "powerful drug" whose "psychological results on the mass mind are really shattering . . . in fact especially revolting, the fits of hysterical rapture among the women."[28] The creation among the public of a sense of intoxication and power created by thousands of men marching in serried ranks and thundering Nazi anthems was followed by literal "drinking bouts" among the men of the SA and SS in which the ideal of martial masculinity was transferred from the streets into the confines of male-dominated bars and taverns.[29]

While the German home front experienced euphoria in military victories and mass public spectacles, the term *Ostrausch* (intoxication of the East) emerged as a description of the "imperial high" that characterized the behavior and actions of those participating in the National Socialist conquest of Eastern Europe, a campaign in which "hedonism and genocide went hand in hand."[30] For the army of Nazi Party bureaucrats, the men of the SS and police, and for female auxiliaries who set about the task of conquering and "civilizing" the occupied territories, *Ostrausch* constituted both a feeling and a justification for German rule. While German forces traveled east to participate in conquest, the feelings of colonial entitlement also reflected elements of a militarized and hypermasculine ethos among the conquerors, who "became addicted to the intoxication of the East and became drunk with power [*machttrunken*]."[31] While the expression "drunk on power" served a symbolic purpose, the use of alcohol among the perpetrators was a very real and prevalent fact of life and constituted an important ritual in the preparation, implementation, and celebration of acts of mass killing in the East.

Willy Peter Reese, a German soldier in Russia, recorded his sense of "intoxication" (*Rausch*) as he and his comrades sang and engaged in drunken revelry around a campfire while smearing the breasts of a Russian woman with boot polish and forcing her to dance naked for their amusement.[32] Similarly, a Polish waitress testified about the "intoxicated" state of the SS and SA men who gathered for "drinking bouts" in her restaurant to sing, dance, and to stage races by pushing one another around the room in chairs in the wake of weekly mass killings.[33] During the occupation of the East, SS and policemen routinely gathered together for "nightly drinking bouts" of celebratory ritual, drinking sessions commonly following mass killings and often accompanied by acts of additional physical violence aimed not only at the occupied, but in some cases fellow Germans.[34]

Creating a Geography of Violence

Recent scholarship in the field of Holocaust studies has focused on the geographic and spatial elements of mass murder. The Yale historian Timothy Snyder described Eastern Europe less as a "political geography" and more as a "human geography of victims." He argued, "The bloodlands were no political territory, real or imagined; they are simply where Europe's most murderous regimes did their most murderous work."[35] Another historian described the occupied territories under German control as "zones of exception" in which "laws simply did not apply as they did at home [i.e., within Germany proper]." In this sense, the occupied East became a colonial space of "unbridled, unaccountable power . . . where human beings could be abused in the extreme."[36] Within these areas, the local populations, and especially Jews, became "free game," subject to acts of humiliation, physical and sexual abuse, as well as victims of murder in which the proscriptions of the center could often be ignored or manipulated by the perpetrators on the periphery.

In one respect, the East also was a gendered geography in which the "masculine battlefront" distinguished itself from the "feminine home front" by the actions of hardened soldiers and SS and policemen, a geography where acts of violence, atrocity, and mass killing could be justified as a preventive measure to protect one's women from the sexual danger posed by Russian "hordes."[37] The "wild East" was a geography freed of traditional moral and ethical boundaries in which the occupiers and their auxiliaries could transgress against rules and prohibitions that applied within Germany proper. The work of subjugating the eastern territories that encompassed the enslavement of local populations, widespread acts of physical abuse, and the routine conduct of mass killing essentially created a colonial mentality among the perpetrators in which new, expanded norms of behavior reigned supreme.

The excessive use of alcohol exemplified one of these expanded norms, where high alcohol consumption became an acceptable and, in some locations, a daily practice among the German occupiers.[38] Writing home from the East in August 1944, one soldier remarked, "The way it's whored and guzzled here is incredible."[39] In fact, SS and police daily orders in the East include numerous references to prohibitions on drinking during duty hours, including one order requiring that this prohibition be repeated to all policemen "*every week.*"[40] These repeated prohibitions also can be found in the daily orders issued to SS personnel at Auschwitz and in the occupied territories. However, it is exactly the ubiquity of such prohibitions that exposes the widespread practice of alcohol consumption and its horrific consequences for the conquered peoples.[41] While habitual drunkenness on duty by SS and policemen within the "old Reich" transgressed organizational norms and was punished,[42] the testimonies by witnesses, accomplices, and bystanders are filled with stories of perpetrators in the East who routinely drank on duty and whose brutality noticeably increased after their intoxication.

The commander of the First Company of Police Battalion (PB) 61, Erich Mehr, a man who took noticeable pleasure in the killing of Jews, was described by one of his subordinates as "always intoxicated" and as "an animal" when he was drunk. When the battalion was assigned to guard duty in the Warsaw ghetto, Mehr not only beat Jews with his pistol until they "looked horrible," but also regularly fired wildly in the ghetto, killing Jews.[43] Similarly, an SS guard at the Gusen concentration camp described a fellow guard, Karl Chmielewski, as a "heavy drinker" and asserted, "When Chmielewski was drunk, he was not human anymore, but rather a raging beast. Everything horrible that you can imagine, he invented."[44] The correlation between intoxication and brutality was not merely limited to members of the SS and police, as can be seen in the example of First Lieutenant Fritz Glück, a Wehrmacht company commander. Glück was described by his men as a "Jew-hater," a "fanatic National Socialist," and a habitual drunk. One soldier in his unit recalled an incident during which an inebriated Glück "dragged two Jews out of a house and shot them," while another testified that "not a day went by that he didn't stagger around the *Kaserne* [military base] courtyard in a very drunken state, firing wildly with his pistol."[45] Likewise, Nazi Party administrators had free rein to abuse the subject populations, as in Poland, where a Nazi official "was known as the greatest sadist in all the district, he got drunk every day, shot at the mirrors and the paintings, and used his whip on all who waited on him."[46] In these cases, the linkage between alcohol, violence, and murder expressed the perpetrators' intoxication with their colonial authority and the power they enjoyed over life and death.

The effect of alcohol in escalating violent behavior also can be seen in the actions of German auxiliaries in the East. Alcohol dramatically affected the behavior of Semion Serafimowicz, the head of a Belorussian auxiliary police detachment, whose unit was routinely involved in the killing of Jews. Oswald Rufeisen, a Jew living undercover who served as the unit's translator, called Serafimowicz "uneducated" but still "intelligent." He noted, however, that when he drank, "he became cruel and unmanageable."[47] Rufeisen also described a German gendarme, Karl Schultz, as an alcoholic and "a beast in the form of a man" whose "drinking merely increased his cruelty."[48] As these examples demonstrate, duty for many men in the East provided them an opportunity to exercise unrestrained power and to engage in violence aimed at conquered and "inferior" peoples, a process in which alcohol consumption could and often did play a major role.

The Uses and Abuses of Alcohol

Despite the perpetrators' widespread use of alcohol, intoxication was neither a necessary nor sufficient condition for promoting acts of physical and sexual brutality and killing. Rather, alcohol functioned in a number of roles. In his widely acclaimed study of SS doctors, the psychologist Robert J. Lifton noted that alcohol proved "central to a pattern of male bonding," but he also emphasized its use in a process of "group numbing" that served to "shape the [perpetrator's] emerging Auschwitz self."[49] Similarly, a more recent study of SS and police occupation activities argued that alcohol "mainly had a desensitizing effect and was intended to help people forget their own terrible deeds" as part of a post hoc ritual used by the perpetrators to cope with their actions.[50] In turn, some perpetrators during postwar investigations sought to use excessive drinking as a defense strategy for their actions by claiming that the killings were "only bearable when drunk."[51] Michael Musmanno, the chief judge during the trial of the members of the *Einsatzgruppen* or SS death squads in 1947, remarked on SS men who allegedly reached for a bottle of schnapps as a means for overcoming their inhibitions to kill the innocent.[52]

While alcohol played a role for some perpetrators in coping and disin-hibition, it is clear that post-killing drinking behaviors were not limited to coping but also reflected elements of performative masculinity, social bonding, and celebration.

A letter by Elkhanan Elkes, a physician and head of the Jewish Council in the Kovno ghetto, to his son and daughter in October 1943 provides one eyewitness perspective on the ritual of mass murder and celebration conducted in the East by the perpetrators:

> The Germans killed, slaughtered, and murdered us with peace and with inner calm. I saw them, and I was standing near them when they sent many thousands of men and women, infants and unweaned children to be killed. How they ate then their morning bread and butter with appetite while laughing and ridiculing our holy martyrs. I saw them returning from the Valley of Slaughter, dirty from head to toe with the blood of our loved ones. In high spirits they sat down at the table, ate and drank and listened to light music on the radio. Professional executioners![53]

Elkes's letter offers several interesting insights into the process of mass murder. First, he notes the "inner calm" and "inner peace" of the killers who could eat their breakfast while engaged in slaughter. Second, he re-marks on the ridicule and the laughter of the perpetrators who had humil-iated and then murdered men, women, and children. Third, although they returned from the grave sites literally covered in the blood of their victims, they did so in high spirits and sat down to drink, eat, and enjoy music and song. In another respect, the behavior of the Germans described in the let-ter also epitomizes the ideal propagated within the SS and police of mass murder as a fraternal responsibility that was both shared and celebrated among one's comrades.

As envisioned by the head of the SS Heinrich Himmler, the moder-ate consumption of alcohol by SS and policemen, especially in the wake of mass executions, was a method for promoting social bonding and camaraderie within the confines of "fellowship evenings" rather than a means for losing control of one's mental faculties.[54] And while alcohol promoted psychological disinhibition, allowing men to pull their triggers in order to murder men, women, and children, it also acted as an enabler or accelerant for brutal behaviors that often reached beyond disinhibition. In addition, alcohol, a luxury good during the war, was used in many cases as an incentive or reward for participation. Perhaps most importantly, this study demonstrates the ways in which the men of the Nazi Party's paramilitary arms and the German police embraced drinking as a ritual that was linked to "a pattern of male bonding" and the National Socialist conception of masculinity. Furthermore, I explore the perpetrators' incorporation of alcohol consumption as a key part of celebratory ritual conducted prior to, during, and after mass killings.[55]

Based on the multiple roles played by alcohol among the perpetrators, it is clear that these uses were not mutually exclusive and that individual killers at different times and places may have reached for the bottle based on several of these factors. This study offers valuable insights into not only the use of alcohol by perpetrators in the Shoah, but also reveals clues on the role of alcohol in the conduct of other atrocities. Most significantly, alcohol use by the killers and the sites where and ways in which it was consumed reveal the mentalities of those participating in genocide.

"Blitzed" or Buzzed: Neither Necessary nor Sufficient for Mass Murder

In his controversial *Blitzed: Drugs in the Third Reich*, the journalist Norman Ohler argued, "Methamphetamine bridged the gaps [between the rhetoric and reality of Nazi society], and the doping mentality spread into every corner of the Reich. Pervitin allowed the individual to function in the dictatorship. National Socialism in pill form."[56] In Ohler's view, drug use is a way of explaining the participation of citizens, soldiers, and the political leadership in the Nazi genocidal mission. In his review of the book, the British historian Richard Evans contested Ohler's conclusions and remarked, "This sweeping generalisation about a nation of 66 to 70 million people has no basis in fact. . . . What's more, it is morally and politically dangerous. Germans, the author hints, were not really responsible for the support they gave to the Nazi regime, still less for their failure to rise up against it. This can only be explained by the fact that they were drugged up to the eyeballs."[57] In a similar critique, Dagmar Herzog, reviewing the book in the *New York Times*, warned, "Ohler frequently identifies causation where there is only correlation," and she perceptively commented, "Ohler says nothing about the well-documented link between Nazi genocide and alcohol abuse."[58] With respect to the SS and police, Himmler issued multiple directives and prohibitions related to excessive drinking, but in the research for this book, I did not find one such directive by the Reich leader of the SS related to drug use, a key point of distinction between the issues of drug and alcohol abuse by these men.

As the criticisms of Ohler's work reveal, there is a danger in creating a historical explanation in which cause and effect are reduced to the effect of a single factor or, in this case, a single drug. As stated previously, alcohol functioned in a number of roles for the perpetrators and was neither necessary nor sufficient for explaining genocide. Nevertheless, drinking ritual and perceptions of masculinity were both important factors in the development of camaraderie among the men who shared a bottle and a communal role in mass murder. The genocidal community of the killers expressed itself most clearly in celebratory rituals that took place in bars, canteens, barracks, and restaurants and in their songs, their jokes, their boasts, and their games. In social science parlance, acts of murder became the "central activity" dominating the perpetrators' social setting, in which drinking became a key ritual accompaniment to these acts.[59]

Alcohol and Aggression

In one important respect, the use of alcohol in facilitating mass atrocity is not surprising, based on the long-established connection between the abuse of alcohol and drugs and the frequency of violent crime and homicide. Several studies from the field of criminology have highlighted the close relationship between violent crime, particularly murder, and substance abuse. At the individual level, one study in the field of psychology found that "alcohol intoxication [among men] resulted in more aggression."[60] Another study confirmed the relationship between alcohol use and violence among gang members and concluded, "Because alcohol is an integral and regular part of socializing within gang life, drinking works as a social lubricant . . . but also to affirm masculinity and male togetherness."[61]

While these studies from the social sciences link alcohol use and aggression, they also highlight the importance of social cohorts and psychological predispositions related to conceptions of masculinity, including qualities such as toughness, brutality, and the readiness to engage in violent acts. In fact, these were exactly the "masculine" traits promoted within Nazi paramilitary and police formations, as well as within the German army over the course of the Third Reich, a case in which "comradeship signified community within the group and violence outside of the group."[62] The concept of gang behavior can be applied to the activities of the storm troopers and the SS as evidenced in the diary descriptions of Walter Tausk concerning the wanton brutality and extralegal actions of these groups after the Nazi seizure of power.[63] The historian Sven Reichardt emphasized the "gang mentality" of the SA and highlighted the demand for "total commitment" among its members, a demand shared by participants within contemporary gang culture.[64]

The correlation between alcohol consumption and acts of physical violence also extends to the use of lethal force. One study of criminal homicide in the US found that alcohol was a factor in over 60 percent of these cases.[65] The close correlation between alcohol and criminal homicide is not merely limited to the US. One comparative analysis found that between 1959 and 1998, "the role of alcohol in homicide seems to be larger in Russia than in the United States," with an astounding 73 percent of homicides during this period in the former being "attributable" to alcohol.[66] Another study, focused on the Udmurt Republic in western Russia, found that 84 percent of those committing homicides between 1989 and 1991 were intoxicated. This study also identified a clear connection between alcohol, sexual violence, and murder in which "murders committed by men against women often involved sexual violence in addition to the presence of alcohol."[67]

Without doubt, alcohol and violence were both manifest in the killing fields of Eastern Europe, even if the SS and police ideal stylized its members as stone-cold killers rather than drunken murderers. The role of alcohol and celebratory ritual in the Nazi genocide of European Jews offers an important perspective on the intersection between masculinity, drinking ritual, and mass murder. In this sense, it is certainly true that "timing, frequency, and above all, [the] company of drinkers can tell us a great deal about sociability and shared values," especially among SS and police perpetrators.[68] While numerous studies from the social sciences have demonstrated the links between drinking, homicide, and sexual violence, the connection between mass murder and alcohol is underresearched.

In the field of Holocaust studies, explanations of perpetrator motivation embrace a variety of instrumental and affective factors, ranging from "ordinary men" propelled by peer pressure, obedience to authority, and personal ambition, to "willing executioners" imbued with antisemitism and racial ideology; however, alcohol consumption facilitated acts of murder and atrocity whether by ordinary men or true believers. In contrast, the relationship between drinking rituals, violence, and perceptions of masculinity among the perpetrators has received much less attention and constitutes the focus of this work.

Alcohol, Germany, and SS "Virtues"

Despite a state-sponsored campaign to address the "drinking question" (*Getränkefrage*) and Adolf Hitler's description of drinking as a vice and "harmful to humanity," the Nazi Party's ascension to power in January 1933 coincided with a significant rise in alcohol consumption.[69] In a country in which beer had been described as "liquid bread," efforts at controlling drinking based on health and economic grounds faced a stiff test within the *Volksgemeinschaft* (people's community) even if championed in the words and the example of an abstemious führer.[70] Between 1933 and the start of the war in September 1939, the consumption of beer increased by 25 percent, wine consumption almost doubled, and the intake of champagne increased by 500 percent.[71] A National Socialist health bulletin from February 1939 noted that alcohol use had nearly doubled, from 10.5 million gallons in 1933 to a whopping 20.1 million gallons in 1939.[72] Another study estimated that 6.7 percent of an individual's salary was spent on purchasing alcohol in 1935, while a total of 9 percent of Germany's national income was spent on alcohol in the first years of the Nazi regime. With the start of the war on September 1, 1939, the demand for alcohol "steadily rose," a fact in part explained by the classification of beer as a "foodstuff."[73]

As might be expected, rising consumption was accompanied by an increase in the number of alcoholics, estimated at three hundred thousand in 1938.[74] Being labeled a habitual drunk not only risked public shaming by the listing of one's name in the local newspaper or incarceration in prison or a concentration camp, but the Law for the Prevention of Hereditarily

Diseased Progeny introduced in July 1933 included the provision for the forced sterilization of "chronic alcoholics."[75] In such cases, a panel of two doctors and one judge reached a verdict after a presentation in which no medical or biological evidence was necessary and where "vague indications of alcohol abuse sufficed."[76] In fact, of 301 applications for sterilization of inmates by prison officials in the state of Bavaria, fifty-three (18 percent) of this sample were based on the diagnosis of alcoholism alone.[77] Over the course of the Third Reich, one historian estimates that doctors under the Nazi regime forcibly sterilized between twenty and thirty thousand individuals on the basis of chronic alcoholism.[78]

While Nazi health authorities waged their own war on alcohol and tobacco use, Himmler addressed the role of alcohol within the black and green legions of the SS and the police. For Himmler, alcohol, especially beer, was not to be used as an inebriant, but rather as a means for social bonding, and the *Kneipe* (bar) served as a site for camaraderie rather than debauchery. Tellingly, on his induction in 1923 into a nationalist student fraternity, a group known for its hard drinking, Himmler was able to consume only two tankards of beer and was eventually "granted a beer dispensation" by his fraternity based on his low tolerance for alcohol.[79]

Throughout his time as Reich leader of the SS, Himmler took an active role in addressing sobriety or, more correctly, cases of alleged insobriety within the SS. Prior to the start of the war, Himmler frequently punished cases of public drunkenness among SS men by instituting a ban on the consumption of alcohol for the affected individual. He justified this action by noting, "If anyone is unable to handle alcohol and treats it as would a small child, I take it away from him. Just as one takes away a pistol from a small child because he does not know how to use it properly."[80] Himmler's infantilizing of men who were unable to hold their liquor offers an insight into one way in which masculinity was tied to an individual's ability to drink. Additionally, Himmler's conflation of alcohol and firearms is significant, as the ability to use both was primarily reserved for men under the Third Reich, and both were tied to conceptions of masculinity.[81]

Despite Himmler's repeated warnings about the abuse of alcohol and firearms indiscipline, both behaviors became a routine part of German occupation. In fact, the number of cases of SS and policemen brandishing or even firing their weapons while intoxicated during *social* occasions emerged as a persistent problem that eventually led to Himmler's intervention and his order of October 24, 1942, warning of severe consequences for the offenders. Discussing these incidents, he noted, "These usually occur in group fellowship and under the influence of alcohol and especially in the eastern territories."[82] Such incidents also occurred on duty, as in the case of a member of the Auschwitz command staff who visited a sub-camp under the influence and shot and killed an unidentified person and was subsequently referred to an SS and police court for disciplinary proceedings.[83] In a speech to Nazi Party leaders in October 1943, Himmler informed his audience that "unfortunately very often alcohol abuse and similar matters caused 'old Fighters' to come off the rails." However, he assured them that such men would not be abandoned by him, but rather were given the chance to "prove their manhood" (*sich als Mann zu rehabilitieren*) at the front, a case in which a weapon and the willingness to use it could reestablish an individual's masculinity and fitness for duty in the eyes of the Reich leader of the SS.[84]

For his part, Himmler favored the moderate consumption of alcohol, especially in the wake of mass executions, as a method for promoting social bonding and for "teaching the men about the political necessity of these measures."[85] He explicitly warned against such occasions becoming a "drunk fest" (*Saufabend*) and provided several guidelines on the organization of fellowship evenings, including the requirement for the participants to eat before drinking and the limiting of beer to one-half or one liter for each man. He also discussed moderating tobacco use and called for the integration of singing, music, or poetry into the event to promote camaraderie among the participants. Furthermore, he made it the personal responsibility of unit leaders that "not a single man should become drunk" during these celebrations.[86] Himmler's guidelines may have established his expectations, but they would prove largely illusory within the SS and police corps in the eastern territories, a case in which the actors in the field established their own standards of celebratory ritual.

In truth, three factors—situation, chronology, and geography—would be crucial in determining the appropriate use of alcohol among members of the SS and the police, especially after the start of the war. In the case of the first, Himmler, perhaps as a function of his own experience in a student fraternity, placed a great deal of emphasis on the situation or context in which alcohol consumption occurred. For example, SS general Friedrich Jeckeln was able to avoid disciplinary action despite a drunken joyride through the German countryside on the evening of June 23, 1939. When confronted by Himmler about the incident, Jeckeln admitted to having consumed four or five glasses of wine, three or four shots of schnapps, and another three glasses of beer. Jeckeln argued, however, that these drinks, consumed over the course of the day, occurred in an "intimate lunch" gathering in order "to maintain good social relations and comradeship."[87] Based on this explanation, Himmler dropped the matter. In this case, it appears that the amount of alcohol consumed was less important than the context in which it occurred.

In a similar manner, chronology and geography emerged as mitigating factors in the consumption of alcohol among SS and policemen. The start of the war on September 1, 1939, signaled an early relaxation of the strictures on alcohol use. Already in a speech in June 1936, Himmler referenced the connection between "booze" and combat among veterans of World War I, and, after the invasion of Poland, he adopted a more lenient attitude toward drinking by rescinding existing drinking bans, thus opening the door to greater abuse.[88] In the case of place or geography, the same dynamics that made the East a zone of exception were reflected in a lowering of prohibitions on alcohol consumption and increased brutality associated with its use. Prior to the war, the concentration camps within Germany, also a place of exception, had in part become sites in which drinking became a facilitator and accelerant for acts of cruelty and murder.[89] Similarly, alcohol in the "bloodlands" of Eastern Europe emerged as an important lubricant in mass murder.

Punishing Drunken Transgressions?

It is important to note that Himmler made a distinction between drunken acts of violence between members of the SS and the police and such acts committed by SS and policemen against the regime's racial and political enemies. To be sure, instances involving excessive drinking and resulting violence between policemen, along with concerns about cases of alcoholism, became a subject of discussion within the Prussian police administration by 1930.[90] This trend within the police appears to have accelerated after the Nazi seizure of power, and Himmler devoted special attention to incidents involving intoxication and violence among SS or policemen. In a speech on November 12, 1938, he addressed the case of a drunken SS man who had attacked a fellow SS member with his ceremonial SS dagger. On this occasion, the offending SS man was given a choice of resigning or giving his word of honor to abstain from alcohol for three years. In addition, the man's entire SS unit lost its privilege to wear their ceremonial daggers for one year for allowing the altercation to occur.[91]

In another example, SS major Karl Künstler was disciplined by his superiors for a drunken incident with two fellow SS guards at Dachau in December 1938. SS general Theodore Eicke expressed his anger at Künstler's "disgraceful behavior" and warned, "Whoever succumbs to alcohol is unreliable and will lose his Death's Head insignia."[92] Still, Eicke, himself a prodigious drinker, gave Künstler a second chance, and the latter eventually rose to command the Flossenbürg concentration camp, where he was known to the inmates for his brutality and drunkenness. As one historian notes, "Such behaviour was tolerable in dealings with prisoners" but unacceptable in the leadership of one's SS subordinates.[93] Indeed, abusive behavior while under the influence often was allowed or ignored when directed at the regime's political and racial enemies; however, intoxication resulting in loss of control among or violence against one's comrades, especially before the war, violated the norms of the SS brotherhood and comradeship.[94] In a similar sense, drunken behavior among party members was often overlooked but could be punished severely when it brought the reputation of the party into public disrepute.[95]

In addition to acts of drunken violence against one's SS comrades, Himmler also took a personal interest in "correct" relations between SS men and members of the female SS auxiliary corps (*SS-Helferinnenkorps*).[96] Formed in 1942, the female SS auxiliary corps conducted a variety of clerical and administrative duties in support of SS and Order Police (*Ordnungspolizei* or Orpo) forces and also included four thousand women serving in the concentration camps and killing centers. In the case of the last group, female camp guards had been recruited as early as 1937 for service at the Lichtenburg concentration camp, but wartime demands and the expanding SS terror network witnessed a major increase in female auxiliaries up to 1945.[97] Their duties within the Reich and in the occupied territories alongside their male SS and police colleagues created ample opportunity for professional and social interaction. Although recognizing the racial "advantages" to be gained in sexual relationships between

SS men and these female auxiliaries, Himmler declared that these women should be treated as "daughters or sisters" by their male counterparts. As a result, Himmler and senior SS leaders took strong disciplinary measures in cases involving perceived inappropriate contacts between the sexes, especially when these interactions involved alcohol, dancing, or parties. In one example, a female SS auxiliary received a reprimand and a transfer after she was found drunk in an SS barrack at a troop training area within Germany in September 1943. In contrast, the SS men involved in the incident were placed under arrest.[98]

The outcome of this case, and Himmler's policy with respect to the correct relationship between SS men and female auxiliaries, are instructive in several respects. First, they highlight his paternalistic concept of the appropriate relationship between male and female SS colleagues. Second, they display the Reich leader's own perspective on masculinity and the dominant role of the men by placing the burden for "protecting" the woman's honor on these men, and did so by punishing them more severely. Third, they once again highlight the belief that heavy alcohol consumption by women transgressed SS norms, even if such behavior was rampant among males, especially in the East by this time in the war. Once again, drunken behavior that sullied the self-image of the SS, the ideal of German womanhood, and the perception of correct behavior between the sexes, at least within the old Reich, could be punished.

In a similar way, drunken violence that threatened the image of the police within the occupied territories could result in disciplinary measures, as in the example of an intoxicated police official who without justification attacked and killed a Pole and received a sixteen-month prison sentence. The length of the sentence resulted less from the act and more from the court's finding that the policeman had "severely damaged the image of the German rural police" and "created great unrest among the Polish population."[99] Another example of such concerns can be found in a July 18, 1942, daily order issued by police colonel Erik von Heimburg, commander of the Order Police in Belorussia. Heimburg declared, "The irreproachable behavior of the Order Police in the occupied territories is an expression of German power and strength." He warned against actions that "undermine the honor and the image of the German police," including "excessive alcohol consumption" and overfamiliarity with the local population.[100] In a more egregious example of the growing indiscipline within police ranks due to excessive drinking, the commander of the First Gendarmerie Battalion stationed in Lublin remarked in a daily order in March 1943 on the increasing number of incidents involving intoxicated policemen "on their own authority" and "off duty" forcing their way into the homes of Polish citizens to conduct house searches and interrogations of the inhabitants, a situation that resulted in the shooting death of one drunk policeman by a sober colleague who sought to intervene in the unauthorized action.[101] In this instance, it is clear that alcohol served to facilitate the abuse of the local population, as these policemen, after a bout of off-duty drinking, made the decision to act beyond the limits of their authority.

By the middle of the war, while drinking was widespread among SS men, disciplinary proceedings based on drunkenness remained statistically a minor issue.[102] For example, SS courts tried a total of 16,567 cases in 1943, with 359 persons convicted for drunkenness, a mere 2 percent of the total. From this sample, the most severe sentences included one jail term of between five and ten years and four sentences for up to five years. In comparison, over three hundred of those convicted received a sentence of less than one year, while another thirty-two (9 percent of the total) received "light disciplinary penalties." Based on this report, the historian Jonathan Lewy concluded, "Nazis tolerated alcohol; drunkenness was frowned upon, and alcoholism was treated by force."[103] Unfortunately, these statistics are not broken down by region and therefore ignore the important role of geography in the charging and punishment of SS men for alcohol-related offenses. To be sure, the extensive and heavy use of alcohol by SS and policemen was reflected in increased acts of brutality after the outbreak of war and came to Himmler's attention. In fact, he addressed allegations of atrocities committed in Poland during a speech on February 29, 1940. He conceded, "I am well aware that in the East some excesses have occurred, shootings when people were drunk, cases where people may well have deserved to be shot but shouldn't have been shot by persons who were drunk . . . [individuals] from every conceivable agency and by every conceivable person in every conceivable uniform."[104]

Despite his knowledge of such incidents, Himmler appeared to accept such atrocities as simply part of the price of war in the East. It is with this premise in mind that one should weigh against Himmler's own actions his rhetoric and his admonition to "avoid" alcohol as one of the nine virtues of the SS man. During his notorious speech in Posen on October 4, 1943, he cautioned his SS and police leaders, "We really need waste no words on the subject of alcohol. . . . With the hundreds of thousands of men that we're losing in the war, we can't afford to lose still more men, physically or morally, through addiction to alcohol and self-destruction." He then warned, "Here as well, the best comradeship which you can extend to your subordinates is the greatest, most merciless severity. Crimes committed under the influence of alcohol must be punished twice as severely. Leaders who allow their subordinates to hold drinking parties in their companies will be punished."[105] On its face, Himmler's statement seemed to offer a strong condemnation of the use, and especially the abuse, of alcohol, but it is telling that he finished this discussion by "requesting" and not "ordering" that these instructions be implemented by his senior leadership corps. On the one hand, Himmler clearly knew that wartime losses, especially among the Waffen-SS and the police battalions, were increasingly difficult to replace from within Germany proper. On the other hand, he equally was aware of the widespread use of alcohol among his SS and police forces in the occupied East, a situation that could hardly be stopped by fiat, especially in the midst of a collapsing eastern front.

One study of the German occupation of the Polish General Government not only noted the widespread use of alcohol among SS and policemen, but also highlighted that the majority of related offenses were punished by warnings, reprimands, or drinking bans. More than half of such offenses involved "altercations," including a case in which an off-duty security policeman hit a Pole and another where an SS man slapped a Reich German for "not standing at attention" when they met.[106] These instances once again not only illustrate the connection between drinking and physical violence, but also demonstrate that such acts were often ignored or minimized in the East. Furthermore, while some SS men were punished for drunkenness, the senior leadership corps remained relatively immune from prosecution, as Himmler preferred "moral condemnations" and "educative means" rather than disciplinary punishments in the majority of cases.[107] In fact, in 1941 the Reich leader of the SS had created a rehabilitation home at the Buchenwald concentration camp for SS men with severe alcohol problems. Despite its location, he viewed the facility's purpose as a means to "create an exemplary compulsory recovery home, in which the inmates would be weaned off alcohol" while pursuing sports and being educated on the benefits of a healthy lifestyle.[108]

Without doubt heavy alcohol consumption among SS and policemen did have grave personal negative effects for some individuals. For example, deaths from alcohol poisoning occurred on occasion in the wake of binge drinking bouts, as well as for those who consumed bootleg spirits containing methyl alcohol.[109] In the killing center at Sobibor, one SS guard, Ferdl Grömer, received a disciplinary transfer because of his excessive drinking; not surprisingly, he also was described as "a drunk who frequently resorted to violence."[110] Intoxication also resulted in violence among SS and policemen, as in the case of two police medical personnel who became so drunk that they engaged in a pistol duel outside their quarters in Russia. Luckily for the two men, their aim was so impaired by alcohol that they failed to hit each other, and both passed out in the snow.[111] This last case reflected a broader problem involving the repeated link between firearm indiscipline and drinking, a point addressed by Himmler in his October 1942 order concerning the "misuse of firearms" among SS and policemen, particularly in the occupied East.[112]

Himmler's statement on the lack of firearm discipline is revealing in four respects. First, the willingness of SS and policemen to draw their weapons in social settings outside their usual duties points to the normalization of weapons use among these men and their casual indifference to using their firearms. Second, the use of firearms in the company of other men constituted an act of male bravado or performative masculinity in which the weapon itself reflected the individual's strength or potency. Third, the ubiquity of alcohol in these gatherings facilitated violent acts and frequently led to killing expeditions into ghettos or camps. Finally, the fact that the majority of these cases occurred in the East underlines this "privileged geography" as a zone of exception in which the traditional rules or prohibitions were often ignored by the perpetrators.

Tracing the Roots of Manliness and Intoxication

Prior to Hitler's ascension to power, the storm troopers constituted the template for the Nazi Party's ideal of a "masculine martial community." The activities of the SA during the so-called time of struggle (*Kampfzeit*) also demonstrate the ways in which drinking, song, celebration, and violence became defining characteristics of the nascent regime's paramilitary forces prior to the Third Reich. In this sense, the SA provides the incubus for evaluating the role and importance of racial and ideological violence within the hypermasculine ideal established under National Socialism and a prism for viewing how the political soldiers of the SS and police later translated these rituals in the camps, ghettos, and killing fields.

1

ALCOHOL AND THE MASCULINE IDEAL

During the Third Reich, alcohol served as both a literal and metaphorical lubricant for creating camaraderie and contributing to acts of violence and atrocity by the men of the SA, the SS, and the police, and its use and abuse among the perpetrators have been documented extensively in the historical record. In contrast, the relationship between drinking rituals, violence, and perceptions of masculinity among the perpetrators has received much less attention and constitutes the focus of this chapter. From the earliest days of the National Socialist movement, drinking ritual played a visible and important role in acts of violence aimed at the Nazi Party's putative enemies, whether on the streets of Berlin and Hamburg by storm troopers before the "seizure of power," in the concentration camps by members of the SS as they prepared for and celebrated their brutalization of prisoners, or in the occupied East by SS and policemen at unit bars on the fringes of Jewish ghettos and in the killing fields. Hjalmar Schacht, the president of the Reich Bank under the Nazi regime, described "drunkenness as a constituent part of Nazi ideology" during his testimony at the International

Military Trials of the major war criminals at Nuremberg after the war.[1] While such utterances in the dock should be weighed with care, Schacht's comment does offer an insight into the widespread use and the important role of drinking within the movement.[2] Indeed, one Berlin-based newspaper lampooned Munich as "the dumbest city in Germany" and attributed "Hitlerism" and the rise of right-wing ideologies in the Bavarian capital to "500 liters of beer."[3] In this sense, the popular association of Nazi organizations with "beer drinkers" was not without some merit, but such contemporary assertions must be set within the framework of traditional regional antipathies and the role of drinking ritual within specific party organizations.[4]

The use of alcohol as a manifestation of masculine strength and shared community was not simply a product of the Third Reich but drew upon a much older Germanic "legacy" that prized the "desire for intoxication" and a "culture of alcohol consumption among a broad majority of the population."[5] In early twentieth-century German culture, the Nazi ideologue Alfred Rosenberg remarked critically that the "highest manifestation of masculinity" had been one's ability "to drink everyone else under the table," with one's "endurance at the bar [*Biertisch*]" serving "as a record of masculine upbringing."[6] For his part, Alfons Heck, a former Hitler Youth leader, perfectly expressed the connection between heavy drinking and masculinity with his boast that in the Rhineland, "men were expected to get drunk."[7] While Heck laid his claim under the banner of German regional particularism, such assertions could have been made by Bavarians, Saxons, or Frisians as well. However, as documented in numerous studies from the social sciences, the act of getting "drunk" carries implications beyond the mere process of consumption and into the realm of specific actions. This chapter explores connections between the perpetrators' consumption of alcohol, their acts of violence, and the use of celebratory ritual as expressions of camaraderie and manifestations of masculinity.

It is important to note that the connection between drinking ritual, violence, and masculinity was not a specific German phenomenon, but in truth a broader manifestation of European and US culture. One study from the social sciences noted that within Western culture, drinking is viewed as "a key component of the male sex role" and that "men are encouraged to drink, and in so doing are perceived as masculine."[8] In her study of drinking in the US between 1870 and 1940, Catherine Gilbert Murdock argued that drinking "remained a potent badge of masculine identity" and closely tied to the concept of "virility."[9] The same was true in colonial Spain, where drinking served as a "warrior's rite of passage," with an expectation of men "being able to 'hold' their liquor without losing control."[10] For working-class men in New York City in the 1930s and 1940s, neighborhood bars became primarily male spaces and sites of heavy drinking in which the ability to hold one's liquor was prized equally with the aptitude to use one's fists.[11] In some respects, these beliefs continued into the twenty-first century, as one US-focused study concluded, "The use of alcohol and the license to drink to intoxication are deeply rooted in expectations of male behavior."[12] On the one hand, drinking became an act of male prowess in which "heavy drinking" and "greater consumption is equated with greater masculinity."[13] On the other hand, another study found, "alcohol-related violence perpetrated by men may help to establish and maintain a gendered identity," and concluded, "Violence and alcohol use simultaneously embodied an image of the masculine. Commitment to aggressive and violent practices as a means of establishing a masculine reputation in a peer group context was evident."[14]

Among the SA, the SS, and the police, the consumption of alcohol was part of a ritual that bound the perpetrators together and became a key ingredient in acts of "performative masculinity," a type of masculinity expressly linked to acts of physical and sexual violence.[15] In this sense, performative masculinity refers to a set of male behaviors that establish an ideal for comparing oneself to other men, a practice that may involve the quantity of alcohol one can consume, the number of one's sexual "conquests," or one's aptitude with one's fists. Among the SA during the Weimar Republic (1919–1933), drinking rituals also served as a means of male bonding and for creating group solidarity that often led to acts of political violence. The emphasis on physical fitness and martial sports (*Kampfsport*) such as boxing or jujitsu within the Nazi Party's paramilitary organizations was intended to create a "disciplined masculine fighter" and to prepare these men for confrontations with their political opponents in the streets and in the beer halls.[16] Similarly, the pages of the *Black Corps*, the weekly SS newspaper, celebrated boxing as a means of inculcating "masculine hardness" and preventing the emergence of a "soft gender" (*weiches Geschlecht*).[17]

One contemporary described the stakes of SA battles fought in beer halls during this period as "the fight for the soul of the German man and the new Germany . . . [a battle involving] fists and chair legs in order . . . to drive out the racially alien 'leaders' and their bodyguards."[18] In Munich's egalitarian beer halls, "frequent brawls and riots" accompanied political rallies during which "heavy earthenware steins, emptied of their liquid bliss, became dangerous weapons."[19] The political policeman Hans Bernd Gisevius described the ideal of an SA man at the time as one who "tested his biceps at the bloody brawls that were part of the routine of every political meeting."[20] After the outbreak of war, the exaltation of martial skills within the SS remained an important marker of masculine prowess. For example, Franz Schalling, a policeman attached to the *Einsatzgruppen*, remembered boxing and jujitsu training at Pretzsch in preparation for the invasion of Russia in June 1941.[21]

In his survey of comradeship in the Wehrmacht, Thomas Kühne remarked, "Excessive drinking, tales of sexual adventures, misogynistic rhetoric, rowdyism, even collective rape—all this gained its social momentum from being 'celebrated'—practiced, reported, or applauded—*together*."[22] What was true for the German armed forces, a demographically diverse group of some eighteen million men in total, proved even more valid for the much smaller and largely self-selected men of the Nazi Party's paramilitary arms and the German police, as the consumption of alcohol became "central to a pattern of male bonding" among the perpetrators and a key part of celebratory ritual conducted prior to, during, and after mass killings.[23] Indeed, along with alcohol use, membership in paramilitary organizations like the SS, the SA, and the police "shape[d] and inform[ed] masculinity constructs."[24] Heavy drinking as a manifestation of masculinity may have found its apotheosis under the Third Reich, but the connection between the consumption of alcohol and perceptions of manliness predated the Nazi seizure of power.

Within Imperial Germany, the departure of the "boy" from his home and his enlistment as a soldier into the all-male community of barracks life entailed a belief in the loss of youthful innocence and the acquisition of masculine identity. Based on his own experience, Hitler reflected on this process and described the German army as the "institution that educated our people into manhood."[25] For many German males, their entry into the ranks began in a pub in which drinking and physical "excesses" became a "ritual of farewell." The connection between alcohol, martial identity, and entry into manhood was anchored in "leave-taking rituals" in which military recruits would solicit donations from the local community prior to their departure, with these monies being turned into a "farewell drink" or "drinking bout."[26]

These practices continued in Weimar Germany as paramilitary groups from both ends of the political spectrum battled one another in the streets and engaged in acts of performative masculinity by drinking and fighting.[27] On the right, the *Freikorps*, mostly groups of demobilized soldiers, battled against Red Guards with a brutality that facilitated acts of atrocity on both sides. For these foot soldiers of the nascent fascist movement, "Fantasies of violence—which were, of course, frequently acted out—were a means by which the 'soldierly man' . . . could find release."[28] In the words of Ernst von Salomon, "We saw red: we roared out our songs and threw grenades after them. We no longer had anything of human decency left in our hearts. The land where we had lived groaned with destruction." He concluded, "And so we returned, swaggering, drunken, laden with plunder."[29] In Salomon's testimony, he and his fellow combatants were "intoxicated on glory and valor" and established camaraderie through heavy drinking that promoted vocal and physical aggression and masculine swagger as men "sung over the tenth [mug of beer]" expressing their martial, nationalist, and ideological beliefs.[30] In fact, such "songs of revolt" became an instrument for expressing verbal aggression among parties of both the left and the right under Weimar.[31]

In Munich, alcohol consumption combined with political extremism led to politically motivated murder in the spring of 1919. In one case, twelve men were taken at night from their homes in the Bavarian town of Perlach and transported to Munich's Hofbräuhaus, where they were "leisurely shot in pairs" that evening as the killers drank mugs of beer between the executions. In another instance, a witness recalled the beating deaths of fourteen men in the town of Gerlach, as "the soldiers, some of them drunk, trampled the prisoners." After the killings, two of the participants "slung their arms around each other . . . [and] began an Indian warrior dance next to the corpses. They shouted and howled."[32] In the first example, alcohol consumption and male camaraderie were integrated into a fraternal ritual of murder. The second case exposes triumphant ritual in the form of a "war dance" as part of the humiliation of the deceased and the celebration of the perpetrators' act, a practice also adopted by SS guards at Sachsenhausen who integrated an "Indian victory dance" into a communal beating of a prisoner in March 1940.[33] In both cases, drinking accompanied these acts as part of a ritual of shared purpose and comradeship among the killers.

The experiences of the *Freikorps* and other right-wing groups found continued expression under Weimar within the SA in their "celebration of a heroic and martial masculinity" and their renown as the "heroes of bar-room brawls."[34] In fact, it was in beer halls and SA taverns that the nascent Nazi movement's paramilitary forces were formed and won their infamy as the saviors of the "new Germany." One witness, Friedrich Klaehn, described the entry of an SA unit into a meeting hall in messianic terms: "The music boomed out. . . . Here marched the new Germany. Here ancient Germany was reawakening. They are the men who will save us, who are our future."[35] Another observer of a Nazi Party rally in the *Löwenbräukeller* recalled "the hot breath of hypnotic mass enthusiasm" and the "special battle songs, their own flags, symbols and greetings."[36] The beer-soaked tables of these sites became the seedbeds of revolutionary fervor, action, and martyrdom in one. For his part, Hitler, in a speech of January 27, 1932, honored the "sacrifice" of hundreds of thousands of SA and SS men who fought in the streets and in beer halls to defend their führer and his message of national redemption.[37]

For these men, the salvation of Germany was linked in a very real sense with their own conceptions of masculinity and the reappropriation of their virility. Hitler waged a dual battle for the "'Aryan' victory over the Jew and male triumph over the emancipated woman."[38] The chief of the SA, Ernst Röhm, complained in his autobiography that under Weimar, "female lamentation" had replaced "virile hate," and it was only the latter in the hands of a soldier that would lead the "Fatherland out of wretchedness and shame to freedom and honor."[39] In this way paramilitary groups on both the right and the left believed that "their sense of *impotence* could be assuaged by a resort to force."[40] The men of the SA were "fascinated" by Hitler, but "even more so by the atmosphere of virile and resentful solidarity that reigned in the SA inns."[41]

The glorification of martial virtues and violence as "the highest manifestation of manhood" emerged as defining characteristics of the National Socialist ideal of hypermasculinity, especially within the SS and the police complex.[42] With respect to the Third Reich, numerous historians have used the term "hypermasculinity" to refer to the Nazi male gender ideal, whether in regard to prowess in impregnating German women or linked to the longer-standing tradition of Prussian militarism.[43] Indeed, Himmler emphasized procreation as a political and biological imperative within the SS and the police, with large families serving as a visible symbol of the individual SS man's virility, but more importantly as the "life cell of the German Volk" in which the field of battle included both the cradle and the front lines.[44] Likewise, the *Black Corps* newspaper, read by the SS and the police, emphasized that "war was the father of all things . . . and from it come all manly virtues."[45] This intersection between procreation, power, war, and masculinity reflected the "troubling relationship between power and masculinity, between absolute power and hypermasculinity—cultivated by the SS" during the Third Reich.[46]

The linkage between hypermasculinity and militarism was critical in two respects. First, it promoted a concept of martial masculinity or an exaggerated belief in the necessity for merciless brutality against one's enemies.[47] This conviction in hardness and ruthlessness as manifestations of masculinity permeated SS ranks, from the prewar concentration camps into the wartime killing fields.[48] In a letter to his wife, Karl Kretschmer, a member of the *Einsatzgruppen* in the Soviet Union, expressed this belief: "We have to be hard out here otherwise we will lose the war. Compassion in any form is out of place."[49] Second, this concept of hypermasculinity was itself radicalized by the practice of racial war, as the SS and the police emerged as "uncompromising" agents of annihilation in the East, where the regime's putative enemies, especially the Jews, became "free game" and targets of humiliation, brutalization, and ultimately mass murder.[50]

In contrast to "hypermasculinity," the concept of "hegemonic masculinity" has been used by other scholars to describe the interplay between the factors of gender, power, and community that create a dominant, if contested and malleable, paradigm of masculinity within a given social and cultural context.[51] While accepting the premise of hegemonic masculinity, this work adopts the term hypermasculinity in describing the Nazi masculine ideal by framing this term within the discourse of National Socialism that established a specific racial, biological, and gender ideal with respect to both masculinity and femininity. In this regard, "race and sex became the predominant social markers" in the creation of a "hierarchy of masculinities" tied to a belief in superior virility.[52] Likewise, the concept of militarized masculinity has been tied to the "hyper-masculine qualities" of the soldier and "represented a process whereby the manly conquered the unmanly."[53] Ultimately, it was this concept of hypermasculinity incorporating extreme conceptions of militarized masculinity within a rigid patriarchal racial hierarchy that linked sexuality, racism, and the practice of racial war with the ideal of German manhood.[54]

Regardless of the term used to define masculinity in the Third Reich, the manner in which masculinity emerged as a cultural ideal within political and social organizations, and the way in which this ideal created expectations and influenced behaviors, would become most important, especially with respect in the conduct of war and genocide. Right-wing groups under the Weimar Republic not only contributed to the brutalization of daily life, but also to the creation of a belief in which politics itself became viewed as a "battle," a conflict to be waged by a "new race of [soldierly] men . . . men of steel" who had survived the hecatombs of World War I and who exalted the warrior as "the paradigm of manliness."[55] It is in this sense that one must understand Adolf Hitler's assertion, "War is eternal, war is universal. . . . War is life. . . . War is the origin of all things."[56]

Combining Hitler's view of war with his own vision of masculinity, the German academic Ewald Banse argued, "War is a purifying bath of steel from which new impulses arise, and war is an infallible test of fitness for manhood."[57] Such appeals, whether found in Banse's book *Wehrwissenschaft* (Military science) or in more popular forms, including Ernst Jünger's best-selling memoir *In Stahlgewittern* (*Storm of Steel*), were intended to create an indissoluble linkage between war, masculinity, and comradeship in the minds of the reader.[58] Similarly, under National Socialism, great efforts were exerted to link the concepts of the martial with the masculine and to define the people's community as primarily a "masculine martial community" (*maskuline Kampfgemeinschaft*) in order to infuse the regime's archetype among its soldiers.[59]

Masculinity and Alcohol in Germany

The connection between concepts of masculinity, whether martial or otherwise, and heavy drinking extends into antiquity and can be found in the writings of the Roman philosopher Seneca.[60] Likewise, the tie between masculinity and a man's ability to hold his liquor predated the Third Reich and was a "class-cutting phenomenon" within German society during the *Kaiserreich* (1871–1918).[61] In Imperial Germany, taverns became both sites of heavy drinking and locations of social and political ritual, a trend exemplified in the drinking practices and ceremonies of the *Burschenschaften* (student fraternities), in which the annual consumption by members of a thousand liters of beer was not exceptional.[62] In a similar way, drinking among members of the nineteenth-century working class was "an essential ingredient of masculine sociability" and served both physiological and psychological functions, with the tavern emerging as an important locus of social and political interaction.[63]

In the city of Hamburg, bars usually capable of seating ten to twenty people became identified not only by the class or occupation of their customers, but also with specific political parties, especially those on the left and those devoted to antisemitic agitation.[64] For patrons of these establishments, the tavern remained a location of male contestation, political discourse, and social bonding. In addition, drinking establishments by their very nature are "high-risk locations for alcohol-related violence especially for aggression [verbal or physical] by men towards other men."[65] The politicization of such spaces thus tied their clientele together as political rhetoric became entwined with, and manifested in, acts of public violence.

By the late nineteenth century, taverns in major urban centers such as Hamburg and Berlin emerged as "crucial institution[s] of the labor movement" and places in which workers could "discuss their aspirations and grievances."[66] A leading German socialist, Georg Käferstein, went so far as to argue, "Without alcohol, without customary drinking practices . . . the labor movement in those years would have had to find another way to achieve its political and economic goals."[67] Yet taverns were also exclusionary. Despite the opportunity for broader participation in the socialist movement and the absence of an expressed prohibition on women entering the premises, "the tavern, like politics itself, was part of the masculine cultural sphere."[68]

The precedent of nineteenth-century taverns as sites of political exhortation and mobilization and masculine identity continued into the Weimar Republic and embraced parties across the political spectrum.[69] For the

National Socialists and their paramilitary arm, the SA, political theater, alcohol, and violence were intrinsic elements of public meetings held in beer halls throughout the country, from Munich to Hamburg. *"Saal-schutz"* (meeting or hall protection) served a defensive and an offensive role, but both were tied explicitly to the use of force. One Berlin storm trooper remembered an attack on a communist meeting in which SA members in the crowd unsuccessfully tried to shout down the speaker before changing tactics and using folding chairs as weapons and launching beer mugs to break up the event.[70] Reflecting on these political bar fights, Victor Klemperer observed that the nature of wounds received by the participants could be used to identify the political affiliation of the combatants.[71] Indeed, the Nazis' widespread use of the image of the wounded storm trooper with his head wrapped in white bandages but still ready for combat represented not only the concept of sacrifice for the movement, but also an idealized vision of masculinity in which the dressings became a symbol of martyrdom and a badge of honor among his fellow men.[72]

In the case of the mass meetings in beer halls, the act of attempting to shout down one's opponent was itself a reflection of a contest for vocal dominance, a battle that was in no small part fueled by the alcohol consumed by spectators during hours-long gatherings with interminable speeches. Within the SA, these gatherings reflected a "deeply rooted masculine culture of beer-hall hooliganism" in which alcohol consumption was conjoined with acts of physical violence.[73] In these settings, it was the dominant male or "the most brutal comrade [who gained] the greatest respect."[74] As the historian Richard Bessel observed, these acts of political violence were "an expression of *male* politics" in which "toughness, readiness to stand one's ground and 'never quit the field' . . . were values associated with manliness."[75] As they marched into battle on the streets or within the beer hall, SA men used "songs of triumph and hate" to threaten their enemies with broken bones and to assert their masculinity through the ability to physically dominate their opponents.[76]

For contemporary observers, the presence of massed formations of uniformed men, combined with the aural onslaught of song and music, created an extraordinary effect. Abraham Plotkin, an American labor organizer, attended a Nazi Party rally in Berlin on December 16, 1932, and recorded his impression in a diary entry: "The double file of Nazi uniforms behind them, the band took up a martial air and the hall was filled with a volume of music that made every rafter in the huge building shake." He remarked, "It made an impressive show of force."[77] Similarly, the Berlin-based American journalist Howard K. Smith remarked on his impression of a Nazi march as a force of nature, "a broad undulating river of ten, twenty thousand men in uniform, stamping in unison down the cobble-stone street below, flooding the valley between the houses with a marching song so loud the windows rattled and so compelling your very heart adopted its military rhythm."[78] One German youth recalled the power of such formations: "The crashing tread of the feet . . . the flickering light from the torches on the faces and the songs with melodies that were at once aggressive and sentimental. . . . I longed to hurl myself into this current, to be submerged and borne along by it."[79]

For German Jews, these public spectacles were threatening, if not terrifying.[80] A twelve-year-old Josef Stone remembered "their [Nazi] big parades in the evening, their flags, their music, and torchlight parades at night. . . . Nobody went outside. No one felt secure, no one."[81] For her part, Bella Fromm remembered the "dreaded stamping of boots" of a group of SA men and their chants of "'To hell with the Jews! Shameful death to the Jews! We won't have any more Jews'" during the April 1933 boycott of Jewish businesses.[82] When one considers these slogans and the lyrics to popular SA and SS songs with phrases such as "Stand the Jews, stand the bosses on the wall" and "When Jewish blood spurts from the knife," it is hardly surprising that German Jews felt endangered when engulfed by such public and thunderous expressions of hatred and violence.[83]

The connection between drinking, masculinity, and expressions of antisemitism was not simply limited to the army or party paramilitary units under Weimar or in the Third Reich but also found resonance among the millions of members of German gun clubs (*Schützenvereine*). In the district (*Gau*) of Westphalia there were over two hundred thousand members alone, and these gun clubs became early and ardent supporters of Hitler and the Nazi regime in a process of "self-coordination" in which the members expelled Jews de jure or de facto.[84] These gun clubs reached across Germany into villages and towns and were famous for their annual shooting competitions (*Schützenfeste*), during which marksmen competed literally for the patriarchal crown of the king. For these men, the conceptions of masculinity, athleticism, and martial values bound the members to the group. The clubs' gender-specific practices of coffee for women and heavy alcohol consumption among the men, the use of fellowship evenings, and the incorporation of Nazi Party songs after 1933 created an environment in which these associations, along with their membership, merged with the regime both organizationally and through the growing number of Nazi Party and SA members within their ranks. In a psychological sense, the shooting clubs fused with the Nazi state through a shared discourse and an embrace of the regime's ideal of the martial and the masculine.[85]

In the Weimar period, stadiums, shooting festivals, and beer halls and taverns all emerged as locations for shows of force dominated by "male politics" and became way points for political mobilization and exhortations to violence.[86] These locales served as SA and SS assembly sites and places for recruitment, planning, and propaganda distribution, and the launching point for "bloody political acts."[87] Albert Krebs, a district leader (*Gauleiter*) in Hamburg from 1923 to 1933, described the importance of the movement's first mass meetings on the city's SA membership in the mid-1920s: "Individual Nazis periodically needed the stimulus of a mass meeting in which their secret wishes, hopes, and dreams would be openly expressed and their courage, sense of comradeship, and willingness to sacrifice would be enhanced." Likewise, he obliquely mentioned the specter of violence at these events by discussing the need for "protection against disturbances." Such precautions proved especially important when mass meetings were held in working-class areas, as such assemblies often resulted in "pitched battles with Communist harassment squads."[88]

As previously noted, taverns under Weimar became sites of political mobilization in both a theoretical and a practical sense. The political materials exchanged and the alcohol consumed combined to fuel tirades among the members, but this invective was not intended to be confined to the barroom alone. Instead, such discussions were intended, in the words of one SA publication, to result in the creation of an "SA man, who also had the faculty for revolutionary combat."[89] Participation created an environment in which personal identity was linked to acts of political violence resulting in the creation of a "culture of violence" and the formation of a normative "militarized identity."[90] In fact, violence was a constitutive element of the party's paramilitary groups and even a form of "recreation" for men whose athletic training had been intended to turn their bodies into "a weapon."[91] Despite the self-serving nature of his testimony at the Nuremberg trials, Hjalmar Schacht admitted, "Hitler did nothing to put a stop to the excesses of individual Party members or Party groups. . . . [He] let the SA have its fling for once . . . as a means of recreation, so to speak, behavior which is absolutely incompatible with good order in the State."[92] This conjoining of political mobilization and aggression embraced several elements of masculine identity, including male camaraderie, rituals involving alcohol and song, and the creation of a space saturated with verbal ferocity only waiting for an opportunity to find release in acts of physical violence.

These SA sites became "exclusive male communities" and served as places where the individual could demonstrate his masculinity through his knowledge of weapons, his ability with his fists, or his prowess in drinking.[93] The historian Christopher Dillon remarked, "Vast consumption of alcohol could fuel an intense, fiercely emotional camaraderie within local *Stürme* [SA units]," as "banter and masculine horseplay came to the fore." He continues, "Heavy drinking sessions might spill over into 'punitive expeditions' to working-class enclaves and thence public violence."[94] In this regard, the barroom became more than just a site for political rhetoric, but more importantly a realm of political mobilization and radicalization where words would be turned into violent deeds. "Unleashing brutality in bar brawls, fighting together furiously in the streets and committing murder together," according to Thomas Kühne, not only proved a mechanism for social bonding and male comradeship, but such "ruthless violence guaranteed public attention and established community."[95] Men involved in such acts measured themselves against their comrades, whether in their martial bearing and political activism or their ability to drink and fight.

During Weimar, the growing reliance on acts of political violence was reflected in the activities of Nazi storm troopers, highlighted by their physical training regimen, land marches, and field exercises, and an increasing emphasis on political indoctrination and public demonstrations in the tavern.[96] The martial and partisan focus of such efforts led to the decline of "cultural events" and a growing reliance on "fellowship evenings" for promoting group bonding within the SA.[97] These fellowship evenings centered on the consumption of alcohol, male bravado, and song, and they would emerge after 1939 as important rites for celebrating the masculinity of the individual and communal acts of performative violence in the camps, the ghettos, and the killing fields.

Fellowship Evenings, Alcohol, and Violence

Jürgen Matthäus was one of the first historians to emphasize the importance of fellowship evenings within the National Socialist Order Police and to highlight the role of these activities as formal rituals designed to promote internal group cohesion in the wake of mass killing operations in the East.[98] Further study of fellowship evenings and their use by various party and police organizations prior to and during the war offers additional insights into the important ceremonial nature, as well as the psychological and social functions, of such gatherings within the National Socialist terror apparatus. As previously noted, the use of fellowship evenings had originated among the storm troopers from the earliest years of the Nazi movement, and these activities would be extended to SS personnel within the concentration camp system and among SS and police units involved in the prosecution of racial policy throughout the occupied eastern territories during the war.[99]

Within the SA, during the "time of struggle" before Hitler's ascension to the post of Reich chancellor in 1933, taverns became ritualistic bonding sites and often served as the first and last stop of the day for these men. For unemployed SA men with families, these taverns became sites for reasserting their masculinity away from the "guilt inducing stares of any dependent family members [or for that matter neighbors] who might be lurking at home."[100] In addition to hosting social functions, the SA taverns and SA *Heime* (homes) served as meeting sites, with all members required to appear twice a week to receive orders and to attend a fellowship evening.

Despite an official prohibition against drinking during duty hours, in practice such prohibitions could be quietly ignored, at least with regard to the consumption of beer.[101] In his analysis of the SA, Andrew Wackerfuss noted, "Contemporary reports and letters from Stormtroopers often mentioned comrades' extreme drunkenness, saying they had imbibed on the way to the tavern or that those eating supper in the back room drank with their meal, but in fact the line between being on or off duty rarely existed for men living such an all-encompassing lifestyle."[102] In this respect, the ability to drink large amounts of alcohol and to "hold one's liquor," without demonstrating visible effects of intoxication, served as one marker of the individual's masculinity, especially for those suffering from the psychological emasculation of unemployment caused by the failure of the head of the household to provide for his family.[103] In such cases, the object was not to drink oneself into a stupor or to lose control of one's faculties, but rather to demonstrate, as a visible sign of superior manliness, the ability to continue to function despite one's heavy alcohol consumption, a trait that reached into the senior ranks of the SS. For example, a former military superior of Reinhard Heydrich remarked that as a young naval officer, the future senior SS leader sought "to shine everywhere, [including] at work, in front of his superiors, his comrades, and his subordinates, at sport, in fellowship, and at the bar."[104] Likewise, Arthur Greiser, a future SS general, district leader of the Wartheland, and a key player in mass murder in Poland, displayed an early "passion for weapons and hunting" and a "fondness for drink"—a man who would demonstrate not only ruthlessness in eliminating racial "enemies" but also an ability to "hold his own during drinking sprees."[105]

For SS leaders such as Greiser and Friedrich Jeckeln, fellowship evenings provided a powerful mechanism for a demonstration of masculinity among comrades, but also for weaving together communities of violence. Organized around specific political themes, these events incorporated martial ceremony with the military formation of the members, roll call, uniform inspections, and the announcement of orders. The next portion of the program might involve a guest speaker, including testimonies by veterans of World War I. The recitation of heroic combat narratives served to underline the connection between war, masculinity, and comradeship. Concluding rituals included the singing of SA and Nazi Party songs and an emphasis on male bonding. In the words of the historian Peter Longerich, "These training objectives make it apparent, that National Socialist depictions of the time of struggle testify to raw masculinity as the ideal of the SA and to robust carousing, while a combative nature dominated the scene."[106] Once again, the ability to hold one's alcohol and the willingness to fight emerged as the hallmarks of male virtue within the SA organization. Not coincidentally, SA taverns became male-dominated sites, and female "visitors" were expressly prohibited from engaging in these masculine demonstrations and were limited to soft drinks (*Limonade*) or water, a clear reflection of segregated gender norms and an expectation that extended into the Third Reich with the belief that "good" German girls and women neither smoked nor drank.[107]

During Weimar, music became a key ritual element for parties across the political spectrum, and communal singing served as "a means of unification and strategy, to create a sense of coherence among their members."[108] At SA meetings, song became an important mechanism for political mobilization and an instrument for inciting violent acts. Songs that rejected the "wages of gold" tossed from "Jewish thrones" or called national comrades to "arms" to face a looming threat in the East underlined the antisemitic beliefs of these men as well as their willingness to fight for their ultranationalist ideals.[109] Not only songs, but Prussian military marches proved "stirring" to those who heard them. One clear indicator of the authorities' recognition of the power of music during Weimar can be found in local police prohibitions forbidding singing by groups of SA men.[110] Similarly, the effort by SS and police forces to regulate song after Hitler's ascension to power, both within Germany and the occupied territories, offers another indication of the Nazis' obsession with the use and control of music.[111]

The Intoxication of Violence

For the SA men gathered in their taverns, song and drinking ritual served as powerful reinforcing mechanisms for increasing feelings of hostility, as well as for creating masculine camaraderie.[112] In this sense, Sven Reichardt argued, "through their violent actions, the unit's members could confirm the meaning of comradeship." He continued, "To that extent the community forming violence was a premise for ideological integration: through his actions, the individual became successively more entangled in the SA, which operated as a closed community in which security and violence, hierarchy and solidarity were closely interwoven."[113] SA units in Berlin in the early 1930s routinely partied in home taverns and then launched attacks at members of paramilitaries of the left using knives and firearms.[114] Specific types of SA violence represented overt manifestations of gender power as well, including genital beatings and whipping the naked buttocks of captured political opponents, acts emphasizing the emasculation of the victim.[115] In some cases, wives taken hostage with their husbands were forced to witness these beatings, a further humiliation for the "man of the house" and a visible sign of the loss of the male's traditional authority.[116]

While the "Night of the Long Knives" on June 30, 1934, resulted in the purge of the SA leadership and signaled the waning of SA power relative to the SS and the German armed forces, SA violence still continued, and the "dangerous combination of ideology, personal frustration, and alcohol" led to a multitude of individual attacks by SA members against German Jews, such as an incident on October 10, 1935, during which a drunken storm trooper bullied Alice Meyer, a Jewish woman, at her apartment in Berlin with the threat to "crush the small of her back."[117] Prior to the war, SA men continued their reign of terror and humiliation on the streets even as many of their numbers received "mass appointments to municipal and state offices," including positions in the police—appointments that would contribute to spreading their ideals and attitudes into the administrative structure of the Nazi state.[118] Likewise, these SA men remained "coercive instruments of violence" until the last days of the Third Reich and key actors in the regime's efforts at domestic social control and as agents of imperial conquest.[119]

Kristallnacht, November 9, 1938

The events of *Kristallnacht* or the "Night of Broken Glass" starting on November 9, 1938, enacted "the single instance of large-scale public, and organized physical violence against the Jews inside Germany before the Second World War."[120] The resulting violence spearheaded by SA units in hundreds of communities represented a public spectacle that exemplified the interweaving of drinking ritual, male camaraderie, song, and rituals of humiliation. The shooting of a German diplomat, Ernst vom Rath, in Paris by a Jewish man and vom Rath's death on the fifteenth anniversary of the Nazi "holy day" marking the failed Beer Hall Putsch of 1923 created a pretext and an especially propitious moment for Hitler to unleash a pogrom against the nation's Jewish population, as SA leaders and units gathered throughout Germany in fellowship evenings to commemorate the party's "martyrs."[121] In a diary entry of November 8, 1938, Willy Cohn, a German Jew living in Breslau, correctly predicted that the shooting of vom Rath would unleash a "thirst for vengeance" (*Rachedurst*) among the Nazi Party's paramilitary arms.[122]

As orders for the pogrom reached SA leaders late on the evening of November 9, many units had gathered hours earlier at SA pubs and beer halls to commemorate and celebrate the organization's role in establishing the Nazi regime. In his history of the November pogroms, the historian Alan Steinweis asserts, "The keyed-up and drunken state of some Storm Troopers helps explain why in certain instances the violence intensified beyond the bounds stipulated by the Nazi leadership . . . reaching the level of murder, rape, and the widespread theft of Jewish property."[123] Furthermore, the attacks allowed the men of the SA, still smarting from the organization's symbolic castration during the Night of the Long Knives four years earlier, a chance at rehabilitating the SA's damaged reputation through the "proven methods of direct terror" and to reassert its importance as a "relevant and violent organization, particularly on the local and regional levels."[124] The opportunity to once again claim the streets of Germany and to inflict "interpersonal violence" also manifested the members' own need to reestablish their claim to a masculine identity, "particularly as the SA man's self-image was to a substantial degree based on his ability to impose himself on others physically."[125]

As groups of SA men left their pubs and meeting sites, they embarked on numerous expeditions of systematic ritual humiliation of Jews. Not surprisingly, many of these acts took place in front of synagogues, symbolizing both the desecration of the Jewish faith and the degradation of the individual. In Bensheim, for example, the entire Jewish community was forced to dance around the city's burning synagogue; in Laupheim, the local SA unit made Jewish men kneel before the flames of the synagogue; and in a town in Ostfriesland, SA men ordered Jews to sing "obscene" songs as they stood in their pajamas amid the smoke and fire engulfing their place of worship.[126] In Berlin, the journalist Howard K. Smith recalled how SA men ordered a jazz band in a café to play louder for the enjoyment of spectators watching a nearby synagogue burn.[127] One German witness to these events also remarked on the inclusion of song into these acts of brutality and ridicule: "SA men with torches. *Völkisch* songs. Roaring. Devastation of Jewish shops and flats. Men beaten and jeered at."[128] Werner Holz, a fourteen-year-old Jewish boy living in Krefeld, recalled walking through the city "all night long" and the "many horrible things" he witnessed, including the destruction of Jewish homes and property and the burning of the synagogue. Holz commented, "They [the perpetrators] were all drunk."[129] The forty-four-year-old Hugo Moses described the SA in Oppenheim as "a horde of drunken animals," and he smelled "a wave of alcohol" as a group of intoxicated SA men barged into and ransacked his home, fired shots, and hit him so hard on the head with a walking stick that the swelling was still visible two weeks later.[130]

The actions of an SA unit in Neidenburg, East Prussia, on the night of November 9–10 illustrate the combination of alcohol, song, celebratory ritual, and violence that culminated in attacks against German Jews. In this case, the local SA unit gathered for a fellowship evening following the town's official commemoration of the failed 1923 putsch. At the bar, a group of newly promoted SA men invited their comrades to join them for a keg of free beer. Over the course of the promotion party, approximately thirty SA men not only finished the keg of beer, but at least three bottles of schnapps as well. The men continued to drink and sing until two o'clock the next morning, when the Nazi Party county leader (*Kreisleiter*) Liedl* arrived at the bar and began a confidential discussion with the town's senior SA leader, SA major Brandt*. In response to orders transmitted from the district party headquarters, Brandt instructed the assembled SA men to prepare for action against the town's small Jewish population.[131]

With the SA men gathered around him, Liedl exclaimed, "You all know where the Jews live. I don't need to say anything else; you are SA men. You don't need to handle the Jews too gently!"[132] One SA man gave vent to the group's anger by exclaiming, "Blood has flowed, blood must flow!" and several others pulled their SA daggers from their sheaths and sang the refrain, "Whet the long knives on the sidewalk!"[133] At this point, Liedl and Brandt left the pub to go to the local Gestapo headquarters, but not before Brandt told the SA men to remain there until he returned with further orders. After Liedl's and Brandt's departure, the men remained at the pub drinking until someone arrived and yelled that the synagogue was on fire. Taking this as the signal for the start of the action, two groups of SA men left the bar in search of Jews. One group forced their way into the home of the fifty-six-year-old Minna Zack, stabbed her to death, and wounded three of her sons before returning to the bar to resume drinking. Another group of three SA men also had ventured out after vowing to "kill" (*kaltmachen*) a Jew and proceeded to the apartment of Julius Naftali.[134] Finding the apartment empty, the men continued on to Naftali's brother's home and forced their way inside by stabbing the person who opened the door. They then confronted Naftali and stabbed him to death.[135]

Based on the events in Neidenburg and other eyewitness reports, it appears that alcohol consumption in many cases facilitated or even accelerated acts of violence and destruction by the perpetrators, and some of these men chose to end their nights by returning to the pub to drink in celebration of their actions.[136] Still, it seems that the "intoxication" experienced by most of these men was reflected most profoundly, in a psychological sense, in the power that they had been given over their Jewish neighbors and in their ability to exercise violence. Once again, the perpetrators' figurative intoxication of power intersected with drinking and celebratory ritual with lethal results.

During the pogrom, the male SA members expressed their collective power by roaring out songs and conducting acts of physical and sexual humiliation, allowing them to lay claim to their masculine identity while effeminizing their victims through communal violence.[137] What is perhaps most interesting about the attacks is that despite the fact that the Nazi leadership had not issued specific instructions on rituals of humiliation, "such actions nevertheless occurred in a great number of cases."[138] *Kristallnacht* more than any event from the prewar period not only shows the manner in which violence served as a reflection of a hypermasculine ideal within the SA, but also reveals the function of violence as "an integral component of the identity of fascist movements."[139]

Setting the Stage for War and Genocide

In his study of the SA, the historian Peter Longerich argued that *Kristallnacht* was the organization's "last large 'wild action.'" He continued, "The terror exerted in the Third Reich now went completely and finally over to the responsibility of the disciplined and calculating SS."[140] In truth, the prewar activities and rituals of both the SA and the SS created a model for the actions of the Nazi Party's paramilitary and police forces after 1939, many of which incorporated similar rites of abuse. While *Kristallnacht* integrated horrific acts of cruelty and systematic ritual humiliation, these events in many respects simply reflected the prewar apotheosis of a pattern of masculine behaviors involving alcohol consumption, violence, and celebratory ritual that would be further radicalized during the war. The existence of the SA homes and taverns as "pure masculine communities" and as sites for celebrating one's violent exploits against the movement's enemies, for demonstrating one's ability to handle a weapon, or for consuming large quantities of alcohol created a "lifestyle" that persisted beyond the existence of the SA as a major political force.[141] Ultimately, the SA was both a symptom and a product of National Socialism, whose members epitomized the Nazi concept of masculinity, but even more so reflected the intrinsic values of the regime itself, values that would be maintained within the SA and transferred to other groups over the course of the Third Reich.

During World War II, the "community violence" pioneered by the SA found expression in killing actions by SS and police units in the occupied East in which murder became a rite of passage for new members to demonstrate their hardness and toughness as "real men."[142] Likewise, drinking ritual, verbal and musical aggression, public humiliation, and deeds of physical and sexual abuse found expression in the actions of SS and policemen guarding camps within the Reich or stationed outside its borders. In the case of the latter, the outbreak of war created a new political reality and "new" geographical spaces that freed the perpetrators from traditional limitations and moral restraints, a process promoted by two factors. First, many of the SA's "hard-core members were transferred to other killing institutions" upon the outbreak of the war.[143] Second, and perhaps most importantly, the masculine ideal celebrated within the SA mirrored the Nazi movement's vision of the political soldier both at home and abroad.

As the historian Detlev Peukert identified, the exaltation of the "'soldierly' man, with an inner hardness," would find its ultimate "fulfillment in acts of terror and mass slaughter."[144] This concept of "hardness" and of being "unconditionally tough" or "tough and determined men" was a defining feature of masculinity within the Nazi Party's paramilitary organizations and extended into the entire SS and police complex, a trait that became especially pronounced after the outbreak of the war.[145] These expectations existed for SS and policemen involved in mass murder in the East as well as for SS personnel in the concentration camps.

In the case of the former, a member of an *Einsatzkommando* during the invasion of Poland testified that his superior justified the reprisal killings of Poles and exclaimed, "In this action, anyone can prove he's a real man."[146] In the case of the latter, the historian Angelika Benz contended that within the camps, "masculinity, defined through strength, control, determination and an iron hand, were demonstrated and experienced in acts of power . . . and unyielding toughness as well as the willingness to do things that were too difficult for others."[147] Ultimately, these acts of power would be integrated into rituals of humiliation aimed at the physical, psychological, and spiritual annihilation of the victims.

2

RITUALS OF HUMILIATION

Ritual and symbolism were integral to the construction and manifestation of power under National Socialism, ranging from the mammoth party rallies at Nuremberg to the universal displays of the swastika on flags, pins, and armbands and the ubiquitous use of "Heil Hitler" as the standard greeting of the Third Reich. The anthropologist David Kertzer underlined the importance of such practices under the Nazi regime: "Although all political movements became known through their rituals and symbols, the identification of politics with ritual is perhaps nowhere more graphic than in the case of Nazism." He also contended that the creation of Nazi power "was accomplished in no small measure by the use of ritual."[1] In fact, ritual in the Third Reich served as an expression of "social power" that extended into virtually all aspects of German society.[2] In a diary entry of June 8, 1933, discussing the ubiquity of Nazi revelry, Willy Cohn exclaimed, "Every week there is a celebration!"[3] Likewise, Hans Gisevius asserted that National Socialism "got drunk at its own victory celebrations."[4]

These celebratory events of Nazi power involved daily acts of verbal or physical humiliation of Jews, communists, and socialists, as well as organized and exemplary episodes of abusive behavior. For example, the boycott of Jewish businesses on April 1, 1933, was an act of psychological terror and intimidation, but also included torture, as in the case of one SA unit that kidnapped a Jewish livestock trader, beat him with rubber batons, shaved his head, and cut a swastika into his flesh.[5] For these SA men, humiliation and physical abuse were acts of "theater" that not only effaced the identity of the victim but also bound "the perpetrators to a collectivity and reinforce[d] their [masculine] solidarity."[6] Likewise, deeds of physical abuse allowed one to demonstrate his strength and toughness among his colleagues in feats of performative masculinity, especially within the camps where "it was the custom for the executioners [i.e., SS guards] to compete with each other in perfecting the means of torture."[7] From the earliest days of the party and into the war years, the symbiotic relationship between violence, competition, and male comradeship became manifest in the actions, rituals, and celebratory practices of Nazi paramilitary organizations, especially within the SA and the SS, through acts of humiliation by SS and policemen on the streets, in the concentration camps, and in the killing fields.

Rituals of Humiliation

Some of the best-known images of the Nazi era before the start of World War II include pictures of road signs or placards with the phrase "Jews are not welcome," park benches painted with the phrase "only for Aryans," and photographs of Jews forced to clean streets and sidewalks with rags and brushes after the annexation of Austria in March 1938. Ritual humiliation also found its expression in the "welcome beatings" administered to prisoners upon their entry into the concentration camps, acts that often were merely a prelude to further abuse and "drunken night-time chicanery" by SS guards.[8] Likewise, the public degradation of targeted groups constituted a key ritual in the occupied East. In the conquest of the East, SS and policemen routinely forced local Jewish populations into demeaning acts. In one example, twenty Jewish professionals from Lvov were ordered to "wash" seven flights of stairs with their tongues and then to gather garbage in the building's garden with their lips as German forces entered the city in July 1941.[9] All these examples point to the role and importance of rituals of humiliation against Jews and other putative enemies of the Nazi regime. Under Nazism, these acts of violence were "no longer regarded as instrumental but rather raised to the status of a self-justifying, self-referential."[10] Ultimately, these acts of degradation bound the perpetrators together, demonstrated their toughness, delegitimized the victims, and served as tangible expressions of the intoxication of power enjoyed by the conquerors.

After the start of the war, such ritualistic humiliation would become an integral part of German occupation policies in the East, best captured in the many pictures of policemen and soldiers who staged and posed for photographs as they abused their victims.[11] The frequency of descriptions of such abuse in witness statements is understandable not only because of the horrifying nature of these experiences, but also since, for many, these acts constituted their first encounter with German forces. One onlooker recalled, "The beards of old [Jewish] men were cut off, and the young were forced to eat the hair," and another detailed the men of PB 309 plundering alcohol stores as they entered the city of Bialystok, burning the beards of Jews and forcing their victims to dance.[12] During the invasion of Poland, German forces literally tore off the beards of Jewish men or shaved them with knives "till they were bleeding, with pieces of flesh almost coming off."[13] Paula Biren recalled the "constant fear," especially on the part of Jewish men, of being "shamed in the street," "an everyday occurrence" in the Łódź ghetto.[14] The custom of targeting the beards of observant Jews was not simply an act of abuse, but an expression of the emasculation of the victim in a culture in which facial hair served as a visible manifestation of manhood. This practice continued during the invasion of the Soviet Union, as one Jewish survivor testified to numerous instances of Germans cutting off the beards of devout Jewish men with knives and bayonets, with "pieces of skin" still attached, in the Galician town of Kosów in June 1941.[15]

From survivor and perpetrator accounts, it is evident that Jewish and other religious leaders were often the victims of special rituals of humiliation. For example, a rabbi with a long beard and in traditional Orthodox clothing arrived at the Mauthausen camp in June 1943. He was led to the center of the camp, where a number of SS guards, along with the camp commandant Franz Ziereis, had assembled. The rabbi was forced to undress and stand naked on a table brought to the site by one of the guards. The SS men then began to "amuse" themselves, noting the man's "oddly formed toenails." At this point Ziereis ordered that photographs be made of the rabbi by one of the guards, while another SS man brought a pair of garden shears and proceeded to cut the man's toenails. A prison barber was ordered to shave off all the rabbi's hair. Ziereis then instructed that instead of a camp uniform, the man be given only a pair of underwear and a shirt. After enduring this sadistic ritual, the rabbi was led to the camp's notorious quarry and shot.[16] In a similar example, SS sergeant Josef Schwammberger targeted a popular and devout rabbi, named Frenkel, for abuse and execution on Yom Kippur 1942 in the forced labor camp of Rozwadów. Aware of the respect enjoyed by Frenkel among his fellow prisoners, Schwammberger expressly chose the most holy of Jewish observances as the time to accuse the rabbi of sabotage by not having worked during the day. As Frankel pleaded for his life, Schwammberger executed him in front of the assembled prisoners.[17]

The events involving Ziereis and Schwammberger offer examples of choreographed rituals of humiliation that expressed the perpetrators' intent to seek both the physical and spiritual destruction of their victims. At Mauthausen, Ziereis used the torture and murder of the rabbi as a form of entertainment and to build comradeship among his men. For Schwammberger, the exercise of power took place at a more personal level and on a continual basis. A witness in a postwar investigation noted that "hardly a day went by" during which Schwammberger did not shoot one or more persons. This witness also stated that Schwammberger usually "smelled of alcohol" and after each execution would exclaim, "Another shooting!"[18] One former prisoner testified that Schwammberger told him, "I am your God, when I want, you live, when I want, you die."[19] For these SS men, it was the intoxication of power, often accompanied by recreational drinking, and the ability to demonstrate their "hardness" among their subordinates, their peers, or to themselves, that served as the ultimate measure of their masculinity.

While alcohol consumption played a role in Schwammberger's actions, he was not alone, as other perpetrators also integrated drinking into their rituals of humiliation. An eyewitness recalled, "One day, for their own amusement, some drunken Nazi prison guards led out two Jewish prisoners and forced them at gunpoint to crawl on all fours and to bark like dogs or meow like cats. The Germans were standing there, laughing sadistically."[20] By making prisoners act as pets, the guards exhibited their power through the dehumanization of the victims. Some rituals of humiliation were overtly sexual, as was the case for a Jewish woman from the Polish town of Nasielsk who was forced to dance naked before a crowd in the initial days of the German occupation.[21] In a similar example, the teenaged Mary Berg recalled how the SS forced Jewish women from the Warsaw ghetto to clean their headquarters by removing their underwear and using it to scrub the floors and windows.[22] Acts of profane humiliation also took place in Auschwitz-Birkenau against a Catholic nun who was forced to strip naked while the SS guards donned her habit and "performed obscene dances in her presence."[23] At the Skarżysko-Kamienna forced-labor camp, these acts of humiliation crossed over from voyeurism to rape. The camp's SS commandant, Kurt Krause, had a "weakness for beautiful women" and expressed "rites of manhood" among the SS personnel through "orgies of drunkenness and gang rapes of Jewish girls."[24]

Power and Humiliation

Regardless of the sobriety or intoxication of the perpetrators, acts of humiliation inflicted physical and psychological trauma on the victims. The scholar Elaine Scarry described a threefold rationale for the perpetrators' imposition of pain on the victim. She asserts, "First, pain is inflicted on a person in ever-intensifying ways. Second, the pain . . . is objectified, made visible to those outside the person's body. Third, the objectified pain is denied as pain and read as power."[25] In short, rituals of humiliation accomplished several objectives, including physical and psychological injury, but even more so these acts constituted a public manifestation of the perpetrator's absolute control over the victim. In these public spectacles, not only were the victim's humanity denied and the perpetrator's authority declared, but the presence of witnesses or bystanders to this process served as an indirect affirmation of both the reality and rightness of this relationship. Finally, it is important to note that the many initial acts of abuse were part of a broader process that presaged increasing levels of brutality and torture.

Under National Socialism, mockery and humiliation permeated the entire process of Jewish persecution, from the earliest caricatures published in the Nazi press, on to the camps, and into the killing fields. In this sense, "killings often characterized by sadistic mockery commingled with obsessive anger and horrible violence" that also "betrayed a sense of anxiety over the presence of Jews in the world" among the perpetrators.[26] The mixture of sadistic mockery and horrific violence was present in the Kelbasin camp near Grodno, where SS sergeant Karl Rintsler "forced the prisoners to eat excrement, to clean a huge square with toothbrushes, [and] to clear away snow with teaspoons."[27] Mary Berg recalled "bored" German guards at the entrance to the Warsaw ghetto who "arrange[d] entertainments for themselves" by randomly forcing Jews to throw themselves face down into the snow before tearing off the men's beards until the snow was "red with blood."[28] Likewise, the common practice in the camps of ordering prisoners to move piles of rocks from one spot and then to return the same rocks to their original positions highlighted the use of hard labor as a means of perverse amusement and torture.[29]

In Auschwitz, SS guards continued a "violent ritual" that had originated in German camps by designing "amusements" at the expense of the prisoners, amusements that included drunken and abusive nighttime forays into prisoner barracks as a form of entertainment.[30] Emilio Jani, an Italian Jewish survivor of Auschwitz, asserted that the "pet pastime" for SS guards was "beating up a Jew," and in particular he recalled the practice of one regularly drunk SS guard, Kaduk, who "used to greet me affably enough, but on leaving me and going on his way, would administer me his usual punch," a blow that left Jani's cheek "smart[ing] for hours."[31] Kaduk's brutality toward Jani typified the former's use of physical force as a method to both humiliate his victim and to demonstrate his "strength" to his fellow guards, a frequent practice in the camps. For example, one SS man "tested his strength by crushing children's heads," and another SS guard, "Gomersky, a boxer from Berlin, [on a bet] would chop through a man's arm or leg at one blow."[32]

The ritualistic humiliation of Jews and other targeted groups served as an expression of both social power and masculinity among the perpetrators, while acts of abuse as demonstrations of an individual's physical strength were clear manifestations of performative masculinity among one's peers. In another respect, acts of humiliation are "richly gendered as feminine," and for male victims such abuse served to emphasize their metaphorical emasculation. In the case of female victims, acts of humiliation often were "intimately connected to vulgar views of the sexual act" in which male power is exerted through the control and dominance over the female body.[33] At times, such control and dominance transgressed the boundaries of human sexuality, as in the case of a policeman who forced two Jewish girls, a ten-year-old and a fourteen-year-old, to engage in sex acts with a police dog before executing them.[34] In this especially sickening case, the girls were denied their fundamental humanity through a forced act of sexual torture.

For male victims, humiliation and physical violence at times focused on abuse aimed at the anatomical manifestation of one's biological sex, especially for those accused of homosexuality. In one case, an SS sergeant at Dachau first "greeted" an inmate charged with homosexuality with a blow to the face before "he brought his knees up hard" into the man's groin.[35] In another example, a male homosexual prisoner was castrated, and as he lay in bed recovering from the operation, the SS commandant "walked in triumphantly and held up a glass" before announcing, "'You can have one more look at your balls, but as a conserve.'"[36] In this last case, symbolic and physical emasculation were conjoined with an act of vicious mockery. During extended roll calls at Gusen, drunk SS guards wandered down the ranks and arbitrarily beat prisoners with "pizzles [dried ox penises] and other tools."[37] Similarly, SS guards at Dachau also beat prisoners with pizzles to inflict pain, but also as a symbolic demonstration of the perpetrator's superior virility to his victim.[38]

Profaning Faith

Acts involving verbal, physical, or sexual abuse by Germans and local collaborators are recurrent themes in survivors' testimonies. Verbal mockery and rituals of humiliation often incorporated a grotesque parody of Jewish religious practices. For example, some members of the *Einsatzgruppen* forced their victims to recite the phrase "I want to go to the Promised Land" prior to their execution.[39] Similarly, SS camp guards at Treblinka dressed prisoners as rabbis with cowbells around their necks and forced them to supervise the latrines and respond to the question "How's it going with the shit?"[40] At Treblinka, the front wall of the building housing the gas chambers was adorned with a Star of David and a curtain taken from a synagogue with the Hebrew sentence, "This is the gate through which the righteous pass."[41]

In some cases, the perpetrators went so far as to create ritual religious parodies as "ceremonial mockeries" of their victims' Jewish faith. One witness in the Ukrainian town of Chudnov described the Germans' use of one such "ceremonial mockery" in which the town's eighty-seven-year-old rabbi was forced to don his religious garments and was led by two women carrying candles to the execution site. Escorted by a German with a rubber whip, "the old women were forced to sing, walking through the whole shtetl [village] until they reached the garden. . . . They were killed and buried in the same pit right there in the garden, and a cross was put over their grave."[42] During mass killings in Minsk, SS and police forces organized a "ceremony" on Saturdays (the Sabbath) that included Jewish musicians playing arias from the opera *The Jewess* and "Kol Nidre," the opening sung prayer of the Yom Kippur service.[43] These acts were not only intended as a humiliation of the individual, but also to ridicule Judaism itself. By incorporating song, prayers, and religious artifacts into the killing process, the perpetrators appropriated their victims' rituals while symbolically repudiating their Jewish faith, an act made explicit with the placing of the cross over the mass grave in Chudnov.

The incorporation of music, song, or dance into the ritual of humiliation was in fact a common practice. At the Kelbasin camp, one of the "inventions" of SS sergeant Kurt Rintsler included morning rituals in which "relatives bore the bodies of the dead from the barracks. . . . [Rintsler] forced them to throw the dead on the ground, to stand around the bodies and sing and dance." In another case, a "dunce cap made of a tin plate with bells on it" was placed on the head of the respected Jewish lawyer Isaac Gozhansky, and a violinist stood near him during a mass shooting in December 1942 as his fellow prisoners "were forced to sing and dance along their way to death."[44] In Auschwitz, Wiesław Kielar remembered being ordered by a kapo to perform a rapid sequence of physical exercises or "sport" while he and his fellow sufferers were forced to learn and sing a song titled "Here in Auschwitz I must stay."[45] Similarly, SS guards in Sobibor demanded that prisoners be taught to sing German songs as they marched to work, a measure intended to entertain their German tormentors and to represent a linguistic extension of the perpetrators' control over their victims.[46]

The infliction of humiliation also crossed gender lines, as illustrated in the case of a female SS guard nicknamed "the gray mouse" by prisoners at Bergen Belsen. In her memoir of the camp, Hanna Levy-Hass detailed her tormentor's "specialty" of delivering a hard blow for minor infractions during her daily inspections, with the "sole aim" of the inspections being "to intimidate, persecute, and humiliate us."[47] Similarly, female SS guards at Majdanek routinely flogged the women prisoners as a manifestation of their authority that emphasized the subjugation and humiliation of their victims.[48] According to the prisoner Olga Lengyel, Irma Griese, the notorious head female SS guard at Auschwitz-Birkenau, "made liberal use of her whip. . . . Our shrieks of pain and our spurts of blood made her *smile*."[49] In another especially grotesque act of humiliation, Jewish women tasked with burying the victims at a killing site in the Galician town of Schodnica had to lick the blood-spattered forest to the sounds of laughing Germans and the singing of drunken Ukrainians.[50]

Victims faced humiliation and mockery not only at the hands of the Germans, but also from some of their neighbors and acquaintances. Blyuma Bronfin escaped with her son from a killing site, only to be turned in to the local Ukrainian police by a neighbor. As she was being escorted to the town's jail, a female Russian acquaintance mockingly inquired if she was being taken to the "women's section," before bursting into laughter while winking at the policeman. At that moment, the policeman used his gun butt to deliver "two powerful blows" to the back of Bronfin's head. Upon arrival at the jail, she was beaten and thrown into a cell, and "every ten minutes the local police and the Germans would turn up and take people out to work, shouting 'Come out, you kike!'" Bronfin recalled, "They would go into the cell, set up a phonograph, and put on a popular Jewish tune, and they made people run around a table to this music where policemen were standing with rubber whips. They beat them unconscious."[51]

Whipping as Ritual

Bronfin's mention of whipping in the torture and murder of Jews in the East raises an important point concerning the types of instruments used in rituals of humiliation. Witness testimonies are replete with descriptions of the use of whippings as a "favorite" punishment method by the perpetrators, especially within the concentration camp system, and such abuse was a standard part of "welcome beatings."[52] From the victims' perspective, these punishments were terrifying and painful ordeals, and accounts of these incidents often included particulars on the type of whip used, many of which they described as specially designed for the purpose. One former prisoner described a customized whip with lead balls encased in leather and attached to chains wrapped in barbed wire, while another recalled an SS captain named Kiefer who beat prisoners with clubs "specially detailed for the purpose."[53] In fact, descriptions by witnesses on the variety of whips used by the SS demonstrate in part the agency of these men and women and their own malice aforethought in administering such torture.[54] From the viewpoint of the victim, such detail is understandable, as the act of whipping is fundamentally demeaning and dehumanizing and was in many cases fatal. Throughout history, including in early America, whipping served as part of a spectacle of public humiliation for punishing transgressions of religious and civil mores.[55] Likewise, the use of public whipping for disciplining African slaves throughout the Western Hemisphere is well known.[56]

At one level, the SS guards used whippings as a means of asserting control and stripping away the dignity of the victim.[57] Horsewhips or riding crops carried by SS and party officials who never rode a horse served as symbols of power and authority.[58] Whipping and beatings within the concentration camps were performative acts that not only emphasized the individual guard's own "hardness" but also served as a measure for comparing one's own masculine qualities to those of fellow guards. A former camp inmate, Paul Neurath, described how SS guards watched one another as they mistreated the prisoners. He observed, "That gives a great deal of publicity to each act—and this publicity seems to play a large role in the amount of mistreatment or teasing which the sentinels accord the prisoners." He continued, "Apparently the individual guards want to show off to their friends and colleagues . . . and to prove what tough guys they are."[59] Similarly, a survivor of Dachau recalled the beating of seven prisoners with a rod, as the SS guards competed with one another to "impress" the new commandant with their ability to administer such punishments.[60] The beatings of camp inmates also offered an opportunity to

establish community among the perpetrators. At the work camp at Rade-
berg, SS guards positioned themselves at the corners of the barracks and
beat prisoners as they ran around the building, a routine evening practice
described by one of the victims as "sadistic orgies" that brought "visible
pleasure" to the guards.[61] These practices emphasized the creation of male
camaraderie through communal punishment and reflected the organizational expectations established at the "Dachau school" under Theodore
Eicke. In fact, Eicke, in his role as commandant of Dachau and head of the
concentration camp system, set the example for his men by threatening
to remove any inmate's "Lenin beard" (i.e., facial hair) with his whip.[62]

At another level, however, the Nazi practice of whipping prisoners—
especially Jews—like the use of flogging in slavery, reflects the racial aspect
of both belief systems in which the objects of such punishments were portrayed as beasts or subhumans. One of the tragic facts of the Third Reich
is that animals and pets had more legal protections than Slavs or Jews.[63]
For example, the area surrounding Auschwitz-Birkenau was a hunting
preserve with its own SS game warden, and while the camp's personnel
required a license to hunt game in the area, they needed only a pretext to kill
a prisoner.[64] Heinz Doering, a German administrator serving in occupied
Poland, noted this paradox as he watched a German guard flog a forced
laborer down a street in Cracow in September 1942. In a letter to his
mother, Doering confided, "I am in complete agreement with the extermination of the European Jews, but this sadistic abuse is rather awful."
He continued, "There are laws against tormenting stock animals. In my
opinion, one should eliminate the Jews in a similar way, but not torture
them for fun."[65] Despite Doering's reservations about torturing Jews "for
fun," a police court investigating "sadistic" interrogation methods found
"there is no ban on policemen for hitting Poles . . . due to their racial and
national traits. . . . They have to feel the whip."[66]

SS and policemen made regular use of specially designed or improvised
whips in the camps and in the killing fields. In the case of the former, a
member of *Einsatzkommando* 10a reflected on beatings administered at
a killing site to "victims who didn't do as they were told." He explained,
"I particularly remember a red-haired SD man who had a length of cable
on him with which he used to beat the people when the action was not
going as it should."[67] Likewise, German precinct policemen in the Polish
city of Kolomea routinely used horsewhips to beat the ghetto's Jewish

inhabitants while shouting "Jewish swine" or "Jewish pig."[68] In this case, verbal abuse that dehumanized the victims offered a natural complement to these acts of physical abuse. Similarly, Franz Wolf, an SS guard at Sobibor, enjoyed whipping female prisoners while shouting "Hurry, hurry, my ladies, work makes life sweet!"[69] In his death cell memoir, Rudolf Höss, a former commandant at Auschwitz, explained these actions by asserting that some SS guards "looked upon the flogging of prisoners as a welcome spectacle, a kind of entertainment."[70]

In addition to its sadistic nature, whipping at times represented the sexual humiliation of the victim. One British prisoner of war, Arthur Dodd, recalled Auschwitz SS guards with "coiled whips," and a specific incident involving the flogging by an SS officer of a young Jewish female prisoner who was "naked above the waist." The girl, kneeling before the officer, pleaded for mercy, while her tormentor "laughed out loud and shouted across to two of the guards" as he continued "mercilessly whipping her across the head and shoulders."[71] Mosze Lifschüftz testified about an SS man, Hermann, who enjoyed making men and women from a camp in Tarnopol strip naked and lie on a bench, before beating them with a riding crop "until the blood sprayed."[72] Similarly, Thomas Blatt, a survivor of Sobibor, recalled the "long whips" and the daily floggings after the final roll call as "prisoners took down their pants" and "screamed out the numbers, until they reached the number of lashes they had been sentenced to."[73]

At times, such abuse also crossed traditional gender roles. For example, female SS guards joined in these brutal punishments. Eugenia Lipinska, a survivor of Majdanek, recalled SS guard Rosa Reischl, who ordered woman prisoners to lift their skirts as "she administered 25 blows on our buttocks, along with a 26th blow, to our head, using the metal grip of the whip."[74] In some cases, the floggings even served as sexual gratification for some perpetrators. Arne Lie, a Norwegian prisoner at the Natzweiler concentration camp, detailed a case in which a German kapo "unlimbered his leather whip. . . . As they [the prisoners] cower he starts to croon, '*Schweine* [pigs], *Schweine*.'. . . Lashes and *Schweine*, faster and faster. Hermann's eyes glaze, he's gasping now panting. I realize I am watching the capo [*sic*] quite literally 'whipping himself off.'" Lie concludes, "He jerks and whips and quivers to his climax."[75]

The ubiquitous use of staged whippings within the camps offers an insight into the way in which rituals of humiliation were transformed into public spectacles. This type of "spectacular violence" involving ritual and torture was itself a method for proclaiming "racial dominance and superiority" by the perpetrators and for the onlookers.[76] At Majdanek, whippings constituted the most common form of corporal punishment, and "official whippings" followed a predetermined sequence. First, an SS guard or functionary reported the alleged offense to Division III in the camp's chancery, and it was this office that determined the punishment. In the case of public whippings, the prisoner was held face down on a specially designed table commonly known as the *Bock* (ram), as one or two SS men administered blows to the buttocks and the back while forcing the prisoner to call out the number of each stroke.[77] In cases where two SS men participated, it should be noted that delivering twenty-five, fifty, or even one hundred strokes with a whip or belt was a physically demanding exercise, and the division of this duty provides another example of the communal bonds of violence shared among some perpetrators.[78] The physical exertion associated with such brutality, which often left the perpetrators exhausted from their efforts, should also be emphasized, as it highlights their commitment to inflicting such abuse.[79] It also must be stressed that whippings of twenty-five to fifty lashes frequently led to permanent injury or the death of the victim.[80]

As noted above, flogging was inflicted by both men and women, and female SS guards often joined in this ritual, as in the case of an "official" whipping for a female prisoner at Majdanek accused of stealing turnips and sentenced to twenty-five lashes at roll call. An SS male guard initiated the flogging, but after several blows, Hildegard Lächert, a female SS guard, "grabbed the whip out of his hand and began whipping with all the strength she could muster."[81] Lächert's actions are reminiscent of another female perpetrator, Erna Petri, the wife of an SS officer stationed in Ukraine who killed groups of Jews on two separate occasions. Petri declared, "I lived only among SS men who carried out executions of Jews." She then justified her murders by asserting, "In order not to be inferior to the SS men and to show them that I as a woman could act just like them, I shot the four Jews and the six Jewish children."[82] One female SS guard recalled her training at the Neuengamme concentration camp and her instructor's admonition to "remain hard or become hard."[83] For these women at least, their willing participation in rituals of physical abuse and killing represented entry and acceptance within the masculine domain.

More importantly, these women not only acted in a "manly fashion," but they were appropriating, if only for a short time, the hypermasculine standard of their male colleagues as their own.

Musical Humiliation?

The integration of music, dance, and song into acts of humiliation and physical abuse was a common occurrence that reflected the perpetrators' sense of domination over their victims and revealed the enjoyment perpetrators experienced at the suffering of their victims. In Dachau, Hugo Burkhard recalled the SS guards singing the refrain "When the Jew's blood spurts from the knife, ah then it is a wonderful time!" as the customary prelude to pending acts of abuse against the camp's Jewish inmates.[84] Not only did songs and music serve as instruments of domination, but "[concentration camp] guards often abused music, using it as an instrument of torture, as a means of violence and sadism, and as a symbol of their 'absolute power.'"[85] The inclusion of alcohol and music in rituals of physical abuse occurred in Dachau in the first months of the camp's existence. Hans Beimler, an imprisoned German communist, recalled the "dance of death" involving the guards' celebratory ritual in the wake of the horrific beating of a fellow prisoner in an adjoining cell. Beimler offered a detailed description of the events.

> They were two S.A. "nurses"; their duty was to "care for" Comrade [Fritz] Dressel. . . . I jumped; the beasts were beginning to play music in their room. From the tone I could distinguish a zither, a guitar and an accordion. There was insane yelling, wild whooping. Gay, drunken songs were sung, accompanied by music. I was no longer surprised that they had drunk heavily at the same time, that was part of their "joviality." My thought was only, "What will Fritz do? How it must hurt him in that condition; he is being tortured with musical instruments instead of with blows!"[86]

The guards' incorporation of alcohol, music, and song during prisoner punishments offers an insight into the way in which violence was normalized, legitimized, and even celebrated within the camp. For his part, Beimler understandably explained the guards' intoxication as a means to "numb their senses," since such acts of brutal "joviality" lay beyond his understanding of human nature or perpetrator behavior.[87] The abuse of prominent prisoners who were "'greeted' with songs of ridicule and mocking welcoming ceremonies" also exposes the importance of music in acts of ritual humiliation.[88] Physical torture combined with the drinking and "joviality" reflects what the sociologist Klaus Theweleit described as the "two sides" of torture, which "destroys the victim and enlivens the torturer."[89]

The precedents established in Dachau later found expression in camps in the East. In the Płaszów camp, the notorious Amon Göth and his SS subordinates invented numerous rituals for humiliating and torturing the camp's Jewish prisoners. One SS guard, Franz Grün, nicknamed the "ape" by the prisoners for his rolling gait, would make prisoners dance before he shot them. For his part, Göth was famous for his "drinking bouts" and his alcohol-fueled parties replete with music provided by Jewish prisoners.[90] During one such "party," SS lieutenant Anton Scheidt had several Jewish women strip naked while he and his colleagues chased them with whips around the banquet tables.[91] In a similar example at Treblinka, the intoxicated SS doctor Irmfried Eberl forced a Jewish female dancer to undress and "dance naked in the kitchen."[92] In these last cases, the location of this drunken behavior is revealing, since both occurred at locations of revelry and communal activity involving food and alcohol, sites that underline the celebratory ritual involved in the sexual humiliation of the victim on the one hand while exposing the sexual titillation of the perpetrator on the other. While alcohol was not a prerequisite for such acts, drinking and listening to music within this celebratory setting appear to have stimulated the men's desire to exert their domination over the female prisoners. In this case, the intersection between the metaphorical intoxication of power enjoyed by the perpetrators over their victims and their literal intoxication through drink is apparent.

It also should be noted that the perceived sobriety of individual camp guards was an important factor in the way in which prisoners responded to the presence of these men or women. A prisoner at the Janowska camp described it as a "playground for young SS men" and stated, "More than anything did we fear the drunken orgies of the SS."[93] Another former prisoner, Anna Pawełczyńska, observed, "If a drunken SS man who was known for his cruelty appeared on the camp premises, his arrival touched off the prisoners' warning signals. . . . Thus one man became a source of acute danger for all prisoners, and it was difficult to anticipate the direction his aggression would take."[94] Such caution also proved to be prudent in dealing with SS auxiliary guards. One survivor noted that the Ukrainian guards "were often drunk, which made them eager to shoot at the Jewish prisoners."[95] In a similar case, some female prisoners at Auschwitz discussed the brutality of a female kapo who made liberal use of her "cudgel," especially when drunk.[96] One unintended but welcome consequence of SS drunkenness for the prisoners involved instances of SS men becoming so intoxicated that they injured themselves as "they stumbled around the camp."[97]

An incident involving Amon Göth highlights the relationship between drinking ritual, masculinity, and killing that clearly demonstrates the influence of the SS culture of masculinity on other individuals. During one of his frequent drinking bouts at Płaszów, Göth and his SS colleagues began ridiculing Karlheinz Bigell, a German civilian working at the camp. In a postwar deposition, Oskar Schindler stated, "They were making fun of Bigell, saying he didn't have the guts to knock off a Jew." In response, a drunken Bigell sent for a Jewish family who were personal acquaintances and proceeded to shoot the husband, wife, and two children "as a test of courage."[98] In this example, Göth used the ritual of sharing alcohol combined with the willingness to kill to establish the standard of performative masculinity expected by members of the group. For his part, Bigell reacted to the questioning of his manhood by demonstrating his "courage" and "toughness" through cold-blooded murder.

Ritual humiliation of Jews and other groups involving song was not unique to the German occupiers but also extended to the actions of local collaborators under their command. One witness recalled that Lithuanian auxiliaries "found entertainment in tormenting and abusing the Jews by sending them to do humiliating tasks and in between, forcing them to do strange calisthenics and to dance or sing religious and Soviet songs." In this case, the auxiliaries often held these torture sessions on Sundays in order to allow families from the surrounding villages to attend and "enjoy the satanic humiliation of their Jewish acquaintances," an act that once again highlights the community-forming purpose of racial domination as spectacular violence.[99] Similarly, in the Lithuanian village of Reynyay in July 1941, the local Gestapo officer devised a special ritual known as the "devils' dance." German and Lithuanian auxiliaries formed Jewish male prisoners into a circle while the Gestapo officer "'explained' to them the meaning of different commands: 'Run! Fall down! Run fast, turn right, turn left' and so on, and the 'gymnastics' started." After a few minutes the pace of the exercises increased while the policemen rained blows on the Jews and laughed. One witness remembered that the "dance" continued for three hours until the exhausted and bloodied men "could no longer stand on their feet."[100] In these cases, the conduct of punitive exercise as a form of sport or what I describe as "recreational violence" for the perpetrators is apparent.

Despite the perpetrators' efforts to incorporate music into the humiliation of their victims, Jews and Gentiles at times used song as a means of defiance and resistance, to boost their morale, or to recapture some small joy even as they approached their deaths.[101] During the final liquidation of the Jewish ghetto in the Polish town of Dąbrowa Tarnowska in September 1942, German policemen escorted a group of Jews to the execution site. One survivor of the action stated, "The victims were brought to the cemetery, where they linked their arms, and sang Hillel [Hallel]" before the gendarmes forced them to the ground and purposefully "shot them through the mouth."[102] On rare occasions, the use of song and prayer by the victims could even elicit a type of reluctant admiration from the perpetrators, as in the case of a German gendarme who testified on "how calmly most of them climbed down into the pit. Some of them prayed, others sang."[103] In Auschwitz, song and music also could be used as means for improving one's chances of survival. Because of her beautiful voice, Zofia Posmysz was named "the Singer" and received some additional privileges by singing German songs for SS guards during work breaks. Similarly, the Italian prisoner and professional singer Emilio Jani credited his survival at Auschwitz to the "privileged" treatment he received because of his voice.[104]

Killing as Public Spectacle

The staging of acts of torture and mass killing as a public spectacle for the German occupiers or the local population was not an isolated occurrence and offers another insight into the larger purpose of such events. On the one hand, the public nature of such measures joined, at least spatially, perpetrators and onlookers in the ritual of abuse. Similarly, the "almost carnivalesque atmosphere" of these events manifested the celebratory nature of acts of humiliation and murder for some witnesses and participants.[105] In one example, S. Krivoruchko, a Jew confined to the Kharkov ghetto, recalled the amusement that bystanders took in the plight of their Jewish neighbors during a German police action on January 2, 1942, in which a group of Jews were being led to a nearby killing site. Krivoruchko stated, "Along the way, we met many Germans who had run out of their homes to see us on our way with laughs and malicious smiles."[106]

One aspect of the mass killings that illustrates the carnivalesque nature of some of these actions was the use of public spaces, a practice that transformed murder into group ritual that allowed for spectator participation in both a psychological and, at times, a practical sense. After the war, a former policeman testified about witnessing his first mass killing: "It could have been around October to November in Bobruisk [Belorussia] as we three, out of curiosity, went *to the place that was generally known* as where the Jews were shot." He continued, "Approximately 200 Wehrmacht soldiers and groups from other organizations stood at the execution site."[107] Standing only some twenty yards from the open grave site, this policeman and his friends watched as Jews in groups of ten were taken from trucks to the ditch and shot. During the execution the crowd had the opportunity to participate not only vicariously in the process, but actively as well. The former policeman recalled how a young Jewish boy attempted to escape but was captured by a soldier after running about four hundred yards. Returned to the execution pit, the boy was about to be forced into the ditch when a policeman stopped him and cynically commented, "First you get your reward [for trying to escape]," whereupon he picked up a shovel and beat the boy to death before throwing the body in the grave. In his testimony, the witness added that he had heard from his police colleagues that children were used as "clay pigeons" at the site and thrown in the air to be shot.[108] Another policeman from the same unit recalled "hearing about" a murder spot in Rowno near the highway to Kiev where "curiosity seekers" from his platoon went to watch executions. He then admitted that one of his police colleagues had shown him a photo from the killings, a picture that showed "a naked woman and two naked children, as they went to the execution site."[109]

The postwar testimonies of these men, some of whom were still serving in the police, demonstrate the general knowledge among soldiers and policemen of the mass killings of Jews and reveal that some sites were public and permitted spectators to observe the killings. In fact, the US Holocaust Memorial Museum website contains rare film footage of a mass shooting conducted by an *Einsatzkommando* in Liepāja, Latvia, in August 1941 that clearly reveals hundreds of spectators in various uniforms around a mass grave, some casually smoking, as they watched the execution of Jews.[110] These testimonies further show that a number of curiosity seekers went to these sites to watch the murders, and in some cases even became active participants. It also should be noted that the witnesses at Rowno came from the Third Company of Reserve Police Battalion 69, a unit whose policemen "took part in a number of murder actions" soon after their arrival in the East in September 1941.[111] In other words, despite the excuse of being "curious," those who went to these sites knew exactly what to expect and were there because they *wanted* to watch the killings. Finally, the taking of photos as keepsakes of the killings, especially the pornographic nature of the picture of a naked woman and naked children, points not only to indirect participation in the event, but also to a desire to revisit it and to share it with one's colleagues.

During the twentieth century, racially based killing as a public exhibition with groups of spectators taking and posing for photographs was certainly not unique to Nazi Germany, as the history of lynching in the United States, accompanied in some cases with the production of postcards, shows. While such atrocities in both countries shared elements of racial hatred and transgressive violence, the scale of such murders in the Nazi East was staggering, especially within the limited time period they occurred, and was the product of a state-sanctioned genocide.[112] Still, both historical cases demonstrate the importance among the perpetrators and the onlookers of documenting their acts with a photographic souvenir, which was in fact common practice in the occupied East.

3

Taking Trophies and Hunting Jews

The taking of trophies from an enemy during wartime, like the conduct of atrocity, has been a recurrent practice throughout history. The types of trophies or prizes taken normally included the opponents' weapons, ships, food supplies, wealth, and in many cases women and children, who were either enslaved or taken into the families of the conquerors. The ubiquity of such practices stretches from antiquity, as exemplified in the actions of the Athenians who upon the surrender of the Melians in 416 BC slaughtered the colony's male population, took possession of the land, and "sold the women and children for slaves."[1] Likewise, the Comanche of the US West created an "empire" that ranged from the Southern Plains deep into Mexico based on their martial prowess and expert and often brutal military campaigns involving large-scale raids for livestock, the routine execution of men, and the taking of women and children as hostages or slaves; only the growth of US federal power in the last third of the nineteenth century finally overwhelmed them and subdued the tribes of the Southern Plains.[2] Trophy taking in the form of scalps or body parts by some native tribes, settlers, and US Army and Mexican army soldiers was a fact of life for many parties involved in the battle for control over these North American borderlands, even if the cultural, economic, or spiritual significance of such artifacts varied greatly among these groups.[3]

In the borderlands of Eastern Europe during World War II, however, the practice of trophy taking, dispossession, and atrocity reached a staggering scale that distinguishes these actions from other historical precedents. Here, the act of trophy taking assumed numerous forms, including snapping photographs, plundering personal effects, and confiscating the teeth or hair of the victims. Throughout the East, the perpetrators' creation of killing games and the integration of hunting rituals offer insights into the ways in which racial ideology became intertwined with conceptions of masculinity and acts of mass murder. This process not only exposes the ways in which the victims were dehumanized by the killers, but also reveals a mentality that facilitated and normalized mass murder.

"Trophy Photos"

Within Nazi Germany, photography and graphic images became important propaganda instruments for documenting the Aryan ideals of masculinity and femininity, as well as creating the image of the dangerous "other." During the war, official German magazines published images of Wehrmacht troops that portrayed "a vibrant German masculinity" in stark comparison to "the dejected, dirty, and weak male Soviet POWs but particularly to the women who fought in the Red Army."[4] In a similar manner, a Nazi propaganda unit armed with movie cameras entered the Warsaw ghetto in May 1942 to document "daily life," a process that included ordering a group of Jews "to make a Hasidic dance around a basket full of naked corpses" in the ghetto cemetery.[5] In these cases, photography and film were intended for public consumption and served the regime's goals of demonstrating the depravity of the Jewish enemy. In addition to official propaganda units, millions of soldiers, SS and policemen, and German civilians traveled east with their own cameras to document their role in the process of subjugation and conquest of the land and its peoples, a process that revealed "mentalities, behaviors, and practices" of occupation through the lens of the conquerors.[6]

Perhaps one of the clearest indications of the pride some of the perpetrators took in their acts of humiliation and killing involved the photographing of these events. As the historian Christopher Browning observed, "Germans in Poland often conducted rituals of humiliation and staged trophy photos of their exploits."[7] Similarly, the Polish historians Jan and Irena Gross noted, "Like hunters who photograph themselves with the game they shot, Nazi murderers took photos of Jews at execution sites." They continued, "German soldiers photographed themselves laughing heartily as terrified Jews cut each other's beards or performed other humiliating exercises."[8] Another witness recalled a mass execution by Belorussian policemen during which three SS men "got up close to the ditch" to take photos and then hung their cameras on nearby bushes in order to drink and smoke with local police auxiliaries in the wake of the murders.[9] These photographs, kept in the wallets and blouse pockets of soldiers and policemen, served as tangible expressions "of the power of the German war heroes and the supposed superiority of the master race."[10] In fact, it appears that many men carried these "atrocity photos" on their persons, like the medals and decorations that they wore, as testaments to their activities and ready artifacts that could be shared with pride among one's comrades on the battlefront or with friends while home on leave.[11] This practice continued in some cases even several months after the war ended. US military police captured one former SS man who continued to carry a photo of a naked Jew hanging from a meat hook as a "memento" of his service.[12]

In addition to photos carried by individuals, scrapbooks and photo albums served as repositories for huge numbers of photographs, both official and private, taken by SS and policemen after the occupation of Poland. The albums juxtaposed idyllic landscapes with pictures of atrocity, including many showing the brutalization of Jews and Poles. This practice also extended into the campaign in the Soviet Union. Samuel Belous, a survivor, described the Jewish population of Mariupol being marched to an execution site near the city on October 8, 1941. Belous remembered cars full of German officers along the route who "would jump out of the vehicles with cameras in their hand."[13] These photos were intended to celebrate the conquerors' "achievements" while fostering "a strong self-image and sense of collective solidarity."[14] The importance of such photographic records to the perpetrators is evident in numerous examples, including the work of the photo department at the Buchenwald concentration camp, which designed "splendid photo albums for SS members"; the so-called Auschwitz album made by SS personnel detailing the destruction of Hungarian Jews in 1944; and the photo album of an SS camp commandant of Treblinka, Kurt Franz, with the title "The Most Beautiful Years of my Life."[15]

The actions of *Einsatzkommando* 2 stationed in Liepāja, Latvia, provide another example of the integration of photography into the process of mass murder. During a three-day massacre from December 15 to December 17, 1941, the men of EK 2, the Order Police, and local auxiliaries killed 2,746 Jewish men, women, and children.[16] As part of the unit's largest mass murder action, SS lieutenant Wolfgang Kügler, the commander of EK 2, not only hosted high-ranking SS and Wehrmacht officials from Riga at the execution site, but also allowed photos to be taken of the killing process, photographs that were reproduced and shared among the members of the unit after the event. In fact, both the photographing of mass killings and the subsequent exchange of photographs of these atrocities were not uncommon, which once again offers an important insight into the way the perpetrators thought about such actions and reveals their own desire for keepsakes and souvenirs of these events.[17]

The Liepāja killings also involved drinking ritual, as "milk cans" full of vodka were transported to the site in order to provide refreshment to the large number of killers.[18] After the war, a Jewish female former worker for the SD, Nikolajewna Adler, testified to watching SS sergeant major Hans Baumgartner, a member of EK 2, and other policemen herding the victims into trucks for transport to the killing site using their batons to beat the victims. She also recalled Baumgartner returning one morning from the killing site "tipsy" (*angetrunken*), with blood on his uniform and boots.[19] When returning from these actions, Baumgartner and his fellow policemen normally would toss their blood-soaked clothes at the feet of the unit's Jewish cleaning women for them to wash.[20] Afterward, Baumgartner and his SS colleagues engaged in "nightly raucous carousing" and openly discussed the killings in the presence of their Jewish servants. Additionally, the men kept pictures of the executions, including those of naked female victims, in their rooms.[21] From Baumgartner's postwar testimony, it can be inferred that the reason for taking the photographs was connected to the size and scale of the killings, as these men had conducted numerous smaller-scale killings, not similarly documented, in the preceding months. In other words, for the men of EK 2, the December massacre was a significant event in the unit's history, complete with visiting Nazi and Wehrmacht dignitaries, and it was an occasion that they wanted to document and remember.

In a similar example, a platoon from PB 91 shot 364 Jewish men, women, and children for alleged arson in the Polish town of Ostrów on November 11, 1939. At least one of these policemen chose to record the killings by taking photographs of victims kneeling in front of mass graves just prior to their execution. In this case, these atrocity photos served two purposes. First, they demonstrated the battalion's sense of pride in their "accomplishment." Second, these photos were passed among new members of the unit, an act of socialization that normalized such killings and established expectations for the new arrivals.[22] In another case, SS lieutenant Max Täubner took photos of his unit's murder of Jews, including a shot of a partially clad Jewish woman, described by an SS court-martial as "shameless and nauseating." Täubner had no qualms, however, in sending the film home to Germany to be privately developed and shared with his wife and friends.[23] Indeed, while such practices were expressly forbidden, SS and policemen and soldiers repeatedly ignored the prohibition in their letters home to family and friends.[24] In a similar fashion, the many extant photographs showing SS and policemen smiling or singing as they gathered in pubs or barracks celebrating among bottles of beer, wine, and schnapps, after a day of occupation duty that routinely involved acts of brutality and murder, document in part the intersection of alcohol, celebration, and commemoration for these individuals and their units.[25]

The use of photographs as celebratory keepsakes and tools of socialization extended to the established killing centers. Oskar Berger, a Polish Jewish merchant, on his arrival at Treblinka, was selected to clean the train cars and help dispose of the bodies of the victims. After the war, he testified, "The work was supervised by SS men who held a pistol or truncheon in one hand, whiskey bottle in the other. Even now my memory stands aghast at the picture of small children seized by their feet and dashed against tree trunks." Berger then remarked, "There were [SS] sergeants, incidentally, who carried photographs of such scenes as souvenirs."[26] In a similar example, a witness in the Ukrainian village of Chudnov detailed the actions of German perpetrators at a mass killing in October 1941: "One of the butchers took the three-week old child, tossed it up by the leg like a football, and shot it in midair. This sort of stunt and others were photographed by the German fiends."[27]

In some cases, picture taking had sexual connotations. For example, German forces incorporated photography into courting rituals to impress their girlfriends. Simon Wiesenthal, a survivor and famous Nazi hunter, noted, "SS leaders and army officers would arrive [at the Lwów ghetto], with some women, in their big cars, and they would watch us and laugh and take photographs of the strange species of sub-humans."[28] In a more explicit sense, the large numbers of photographs of women, both dead and alive, in various stages of dress demonstrate the prevalence of the male sexual gaze, and these images served as pornographic souvenirs for soldiers, policemen, and SS alike.[29] In one particularly grotesque case, a group of fifteen Wehrmacht soldiers, including one man who, smiling at the camera, straddles a woman's body in a simulated act of intercourse, gather around grinning and laughing while the female "prop" in the photograph lies inert, and perhaps lifeless, with her face turned toward the camera.[30] In this last case, sexual transgression itself was normalized, with the photograph serving as both a reminder and proof of the physical and sexual domination of the male conqueror over the occupied and a tribute to the men's shared bonds of comradeship.

The existence of atrocity trophy photographs is important for another reason. Despite a strict prohibition, Himmler had to issue repeated orders banning the practice, one clear indication of the widespread practice among SS and policemen of taking such pictures.[31] In his study of the killing process, Patrick Desbois remarked on the many families in Germany "who received a snapshot, a trophy from their beloved criminal." He continues, "The question only grows more insistent: how can a mass crime that is openly displayed and exhibited like a scene at a fair, and so often photographed, remain so little known?"[32] Desbois's comparison of the killing sites with a "fair" highlights the act of mass murder as a type of public spectacle in which the perpetrators documented, commemorated, and celebrated their role in genocide. The mass execution at Liepāja in December 1941 offers but one of many examples in which the killers recorded their murders in souvenirs of atrocity as a testament to their actions and a tangible reminder of their hardness and power.

Sadistic Amusements

One of the clearest indications of the mind-set of the perpetrators can be seen in the way that the killers "carried out their duties by thinking up individual little *amusements* which fulfilled a sadistic need."[33] From the perspective of the victims, these "amusements" involving pointless acts of labor inflicted on them or gratuitous violence exercised by their persecutors made little sense, and led Primo Levi to declare that "the first words of wisdom in the Lager" were "'not trying to understand.'"[34] However, such acts did in fact serve a purpose for the perpetrators as a demonstration of the dominance and power they enjoyed over their victims. They also were an important ritual, present since the concentration camp system had been created, a widespread abusive practice initiated in Dachau in 1933 that continued in the occupied East.[35]

The term "amusement" is in fact appropriate for many of these punishments, as they reflected not only the perpetrators' warped sense of humor but also their very real sense of pride and enjoyment in these acts. Charlotte Delbo, a survivor, notes at several points in her memoir the enjoyment taken by SS men in torturing prisoners.[36] Benjamin Goldsztejn remembered the Germans entering his town in September 1939 and firing wildly at windows and wounding a young girl. The girl's mother ran out of the house and "fell at the feet of a German officer pleading to be allowed to fetch the doctor. . . . The officer and the other Germans standing around watching this 'spectacle' shook with laughter."[37] Another witness recalled that one senior police NCO in the Polish town of Sosnowiec "was known as a notorious sadist who *enjoyed* torturing Jews of both sexes," a killer who was especially proud of his nickname "the shooter."[38]

Reflecting on the perpetrators' sense of gratification in killing, the psychologist Johannes Lange wrote, "Nazism's passionate exclusionary, arrogant form of pride made its adherents capable of unspeakable violence." He continued, "The joy of self-esteem and the pleasure of belonging helped forge strong affective bonds between the perpetrators, just as arrogant pride served to prevent such bonds from forming between the perpetrators and their victims."[39] Furthermore, the pride and enjoyment experienced by the killers were themselves a manifestation of the hypermasculine ideal of *hardness* celebrated within the SS and police complex, a trait that served as the justification for brutality and abuse. It is in this sense that one must understand the many references by victims and witnesses to the perpetrators' visible pleasure in their abasement.

Symcha Poliakewicz, one of the few survivors of Treblinka, reminisced on the enjoyment of drunken SS guards performing their duties at the camp. He discussed their brutality upon his arrival and commented, "Death does not come easy. The murderers love the sadistic bloody games they play with their victims."[40] In some cases, Germans recorded the pride expressed by their fellow countrymen in the conduct of atrocity, as did Heinz Rothmann, who described how a "Nazi, radiant with joy," recounted the mass murder of twenty thousand Jews in Romania.[41] In another example, the former driver for an SS camp commander testified that his boss "amused himself" through the daily act of killing and beating prisoners.[42] In much the same way, a survivor of the Chełmno killing center testified that, during the building of cremation furnaces at the site, SS guards "sometimes killed [Jewish laborers] for entertainment."[43] Dark humor and sadistic amusements served as an expression of power, and they provide an important insight into the mentality of the killers.

The numerous accounts of SS and policemen who became more violent when drunk reveal another key point about the ritual of abuse. For example, a group of drunken policemen at the Gestapo prison at the notorious Fort VII at Poznań entered the cells at night and forced a group of half-naked prisoners to the SS canteen. At this site of SS revelry, a place of communal eating and drinking, the SS men made the prisoners sing and slap each other in the face to the amusement of their intoxicated torturers.[44] In a similar way, SS guards at Gusen used the camp's canteen as a site for celebration and routinely ventured into the camp at night after drinking, to beat and harass the prisoners.[45] In these examples, communal alcohol consumption within the canteen provided a preparatory stage for men embarking on acts of brutal and perverse entertainment. The types of activities became in fact a form of recreational violence for the perpetrators in which the metaphorical intoxication of control over the life and bodies of the victims was conjoined with and facilitated by celebratory drinking. Likewise, the communal nature of these sites allowed individual SS men to perform and compete against their fellow guards as a public demonstration of their masculine toughness.

In fact, beatings by SS men in the camps at times constituted a form of male competition among the SS guards. Richard Glazar, a survivor of

Treblinka, remarked that when an SS man witnessed a colleague beating a prisoner, the other would often join in the brutality, and both would attempt to "outdo the other in order to demonstrate that he was 'better' than the other."[46] Likewise, "'Tough and determined men,' who kept their 'weapons loaded,'" epitomized the model of masculinity among the SS camp guards.[47] Some SS guards held "shooting competitions" in which they sought to demonstrate their marksmanship to their colleagues or to engage in a deadly display of their own masculine prowess. One SS guard at Auschwitz accepted a bet for a bottle of schnapps that he could kill a prisoner with a neck shot at fifty paces using his pistol, while Kurt Franz, an SS officer in Treblinka, sought to impress his colleagues with his "specialty" of "shooting Jews in the eyes."[48] In reference to this practice, Abraham Bomba, a prisoner at Treblinka, commented, "The biggest pleasure for them [the SS] was to kill, to shoot at a special place they had in their mind. . . . When they succeeded they were just happy."[49] SS men in the Janowska camp aimed at the noses or fingertips of the prisoners as they carried stones around the camp.[50] In another version of this "game," the SS forced a prisoner to hold a glass of water. "If the glass was hit, the person was allowed to live," Michael Wind testified. "If the bullet hit his [the prisoner's] hand, he was killed on the pretext that he was no longer capable of working."[51] Among these SS men, the ability to drink more than one's colleague, to inflict a better beating, or to outshoot him became markers of superior manliness.

The organization of these deadly "games" provides another clear indication of the enjoyment taken by some SS men in the performance of their duties and their shared bonds established through group violence. In Dachau, SS guards christened a fishpond "the Red Sea" and forced Jewish prisoners into the water during work details. The guards then hit the inmates with poles as they surfaced or shot at their heads for target practice.[52] In one example of how the brutal precedents created in the camps later found expression in the East, Valya Yurkevich, a young boy, recalled the transportation of Jews to a ghetto in boats across the Dvina River. Valya described the scene: "The bank was encircled by Germans. Before our eyes, they loaded the boats with old people, children, towed them to the middle of the river, and overturned them. . . . The fascists hit them with their paddles, laughing. They hit them here, they would resurface somewhere else; they would catch up with them and hit them again." Clearly traumatized by what he was witnessing, Valya remembered, "Suddenly . . . laughter rang out. Such young belly laughter. . . . Young Germans were standing nearby, watching it all and laughing."[53] Once again spectacular violence in the form of mass murder became a method for demonstrating domination over the racial other and for bonding groups of German perpetrators and onlookers as they reveled in the conquest of the East.

The integration of excrement into some of these celebratory rituals provided another method by which control over others was emphasized. In Buchenwald, drunken SS guards supervised Russian prisoners in a manure-carrying detail on May 1, 1943, as part of a cynical "celebration" of this traditional workers' holiday. As prisoners collapsed under their loads, SS guards set dogs upon the fallen men. Two prisoners had the misfortune of spattering the uniform of SS corporal Fritz Schulz, who immediately shot one of the men and then "trampled" the other prisoner to death with his hobnailed boots.[54] The transformation of a day of celebration for workers into a day of designated humiliation of Russian prisoners of war and other political prisoners, by forcing them to carry excrement from one place to another in a meaningless exercise, points to the calculated malice of the SS. In this case, alcohol seems to have been an important part of the SS ritual, as a celebratory preface to the day's activities. At Majdanek, SS guards also employed feces as a prop in acts of humiliation by forcing prisoners into the camp's cesspools or into the manure pits of the camp's farm. SS guards administered such punishments seemingly at a whim, either for real or alleged offenses or for no offense at all.

"Immersing Jews in excrement in all compounds for the sole reason that they were Jews was a frequent occurrence," according to one historian.[55] Such practices existed from the early days of the camp system, and Hugo Burkhard, a Jewish prisoner at Dachau, recalled how SS guards beat and forced a fellow inmate to eat his own feces during a work detail in January 1934. Burkhard observed, "In my entire life, I will never forget the horrible appearance of a tortured man and the satanic grinning SS scoundrels who once again had satisfied their sadistic desires."[56] In another case, an SS guard ordered the chief rabbi of Sered, Slovakia, into a pool of excrement, an act designed both to humiliate the community's spiritual representative and to ridicule his faith. Indeed, acts of cleaning and depictions of filth harked back to Nazi prewar rituals of humiliation involving the forced cleaning of streets and buildings.

During the war, SS and police units incorporated the metaphor of "cleansing" into deeds of humiliation and into the language of annihilation. In the case of the former, German soldiers, after entering the Ukrainian town of Matzeev in the summer of 1941, ordered the town's Jewish population to clean the streets and to make the cobblestones "shine."[57] In the case of the latter, SS and police reports often employed the phrase "cleansing operations" (*Säuberungsaktionen*) to describe mass killings.[58] Against the semantic specter of imminent biological danger evoked by terms such as "pestilence," "plague," and "epidemic," the term "cleansing" provided the perpetrators with the perfect linguistic complement to combat this biologically prescribed threat.[59] This language constituted both a rationale and a solution for mass murder aimed at those allegedly threatening the health and vitality of the German corpus.

Playing Murder Games

After the invasion of Poland in 1939, the rhetoric of killing also found expression in killing as a game or type of sport. One Jewish survivor witnessed a German military policeman shoot his neighbor "on the street merely for sport."[60] Another witness, Mieczysław Garfinkel, described Hans Pienkowski, the SS commander of a work camp in Zamość, as a man who made "fun out of killing." In order to impress an SS buddy, Pienkowski, a notorious drinker, created a killing game based on geometrical progression by shooting one Jewish man and then ordering two men to bury him; he then shot these two men and commanded four others to bury them, and so on. Pienkowski continued his "numbers game" until he single-handedly had murdered over two hundred men. For this profligate waste of Jewish labor, an SS court ordered Pienkowski confined to quarters for a week, a punishment that he passed by forcing the Jewish community to deliver him a bottle of schnapps each day.[61] In another case, SS killers incorporated performative feats of male strength into a killing game, with alcohol as a reward: A survivor recalled how an SS unit took a group of Jews, including children, from the Kirillovka concentration camp near Kiev to an execution site in the Golosayev woods in October 1941.

"I heard one German officer explain to the soldiers how the game was to be played." He continued, "From a distance of twelve meters [about forty feet], they were to toss the children in such a manner that their heads would strike the trunk of the tree. For every cracked skull they would receive a glass of schnapps."[62]

How closely these survivors' recollection corresponded with the reality of the SS killers can be found in the words of Franz Stangl, the SS commandant at Treblinka who recalled his conversation with other SS men during a visit to the officers' canteen. Stangl noted, "They [the SS men] said they had great fun; shooting [Jews] was 'sport.'"[63] In another example, Josef Blösche and an SS colleague received orders to enter the Warsaw ghetto looking for Jews who failed to appear for a work detail and to "make a little ruckus [*Remidemi*] and shoot a couple of Jews."[64] According to Blösche, these operations in the ghetto occurred every two to three weeks, during which he would hide at the entrances to buildings and in doorways to catch or to shoot Jews, much like a hunter waiting quietly for his quarry.[65] The teenaged Mary Berg remembered these regular "man hunts" and specifically recalled the actions of one German, nicknamed Frankenstein, who, "raging through the ghetto, one day he kills ten persons, another day five."[66]

The conduct of killing as a type of game or contest tied to masculine exploits of drinking ritual and mass murder appears in numerous survivor testimonies. SS lieutenant Kurt Wiso was in charge of the Grodno ghetto and "loved to have a good time." One method of entertainment involved heavy drinking, after which "he would come to the ghetto with his friends and organize a 'hunt' for Jewish girls and boys."[67] In a similar vein, the readiness of some guards to make use of their weapons was encouraged by the concentration camp leadership through the distribution of rewards for the shooting of prisoners in so-called escape attempts, with incentives that included special leaves, salary bonuses, or rapid promotion. These inducements led some at Buchenwald to create a game in which a guard would take a prisoner's cap and throw it past the sentry point. The prisoner would then be ordered to retrieve the cap, and "if the prisoner innocently ran after it, he was shot down for 'attempted escape.'"[68] Such "pranks" also occurred in Auschwitz. Wiesław Kielar, a Polish prisoner in the camp, recalled an SS guard who snatched the cap from a prisoner, threw it, and then ordered the man, "Go and fetch your cap." As the prisoner bent down to retrieve his cap, the SS guard shot him. When a nearby SS officer rode over to investigate, he questioned Kielar, who reported that the prisoner had been shot, whereupon the SS officer corrected him: "He was shot while attempting to escape. Understood?"[69]

The games of some SS guards at Majdanek incorporated feats of performative masculinity involving physical prowess with one's fists. SS sergeant Groffman specialized in patrolling prisoner ranks during roll call and "aimed his hand at the place which he intended to strike, and next, with a single blow at the stomach, the liver, the heart or ear, knocked the prisoner down." Not to be outdone by his colleague, Anton Thumann, described as the "greatest murderer in Majdanek's history," prided himself on his ability to "knock down, with a single blow at the face, even the strongest of prisoners."[70] Similarly, Franz Suchomel, an SS guard at Treblinka, mentioned a fellow guard who would make prisoners stand at attention in order to practice his "knock-out punch," a blow normally followed by the execution of the victim.[71]

The fact that several guards in various camps took pride in their ability to knock down prisoners with a single blow offers a strong indication that these guards not only intended to demonstrate their superior strength and masculinity, but were taking part in a type of contest with their SS comrades. In fact, Rudolf Höss remarked on the practice of SS guards at Auschwitz who "all tried to outdo one another with better 'methods' [of brutality]."[72] Felix Weinberg, a survivor of Auschwitz, attributed such contests to SS men who "fancied themselves" in the role of the fiction writer Karl May's character "Old Shatterhand," famed for "his ability to knock out any opponent with a single blow to the head."[73] As noted previously, being good with one's fists was part of the SS and SA's masculine ideal from the earliest days of the movement.[74] In such contests of performative masculinity among SS guards, heavy drinking was often involved and led not only to a "complete loss of inhibitions" but also to quarrels among the perpetrators as they vied for individual dominance.[75] The competition itself was "the main vehicle of masculine socialization and gender performance" among SS guards.[76]

The use of beatings as means for impressing one's colleagues was not limited to male guards. Hilde Zimmerman, a female prisoner at

Ravensbrück, recalled a group of female SS guards who "beat the prisoners like crazy, especially when a man was watching." She continued, "I still remember it quite clearly: the way they first would fawn over the SS man, and then . . . go after the prisoners, berating and beating them, showing how brutal they could be, in order to please him." Zimmerman concluded, "The *Aufseherinnen* [female camp guards] flirted by showing the men they could behave in an equally masculine fashion, beating the prisoners half to death; they wanted to show what kind of a 'fellow' they were, so to speak."[77] From this account, it appears that these women appropriated SS virtues of "hardness" and "toughness" as part of a bizarre and brutal courting ritual with their male colleagues and perhaps even, like the men, to demonstrate their own superiority over their female counterparts.

The preparation for and the variety of methods used in the killings reflect the expanded boundaries of police behavior that normalized and justified murder. For example, attempts to either leave or enter the ghetto along the barbed wire boundary provided policemen with "legitimate" grounds for the use of deadly force based on German police edicts. However, it is also clear that some policemen used the pretense of escape attempts to shoot individuals walking near the wire. In postwar testimony, a policeman from PB 61 recalled one incident in the Warsaw ghetto during which a colleague on sentry duty set up a position outside the ghetto and waited for a Jew to cross his line of fire. The witness remembered hearing a shot and then seeing a dead Jew lying inside the ghetto boundary.[78] Furthermore, the use of chicanery and humiliation was a normal part of some killings. In the Łódź ghetto, a woman suffering from mental illness begged the sentry to shoot her; the sentry obliged, but not before demanding that the woman perform "a little dance."[79] In another example, a policeman in the Warsaw ghetto stopped a Jew and ordered him to patch an opening in the ghetto wall. As the Jew examined the opening, a colleague of the policeman on the other side of the wall shot him.[80] In a similar incident, a Jewish laborer was shot dead by a Lithuanian auxiliary as he worked to repair a fence in the Kovno ghetto.[81] The gratuitous nature of these killings in which the victims were "played with" provides an insight into the metaphorical intoxication of the killers as they designed rituals of abuse to exercise their power over the life and death of the victims.

The Ritual of the Hunt

The use of staged hunts by the perpetrators provides another perspective into the ways in which acts of performative masculinity combined with drinking, male competition, and celebratory ritual. Indeed, the hunt, an act in itself traditionally invested with manliness and masculine strength, frequently served as a supporting rite to celebratory killing.[82] The incorporation of recreational drinking applied to stalking of both man and beast. One Polish witness commented, "They [the Germans] hunted lots," during which "they had huge amounts of vodka."[83] As they stalked their prey, hunters competed against each other for the most kills, and these kills in turn were symbolized by "trophies," especially when such acts involved taking the body parts of the victims.

The social anthropologist Simon Harrison observed, "Expeditionary trophy-taking seems to occur only in societies in which . . . hunting is understood as an iconically male pursuit." He further argued that such acts conducted during warfare are limited to "certain categories of enemies [who] are strongly dehumanized or depersonalized, and represented as animal quarry."[84] The use of *Treiberkommandos* (beater detachments) by the police for driving the Jews to execution sites offers one manifestation of the language of the hunt being applied to mass murder.[85] In a like case, an SS officer "for the sake of amusing his subordinates" organized "man hunts [*Treibjagd*] ending at the camp limits with the shooting of the human quarry."[86] In Auschwitz, SS guards routinely conducted "real hunts of prisoners" assigned to the grass-cutting detail in which the total killed sometimes reached sixteen per day.[87] Likewise, the formation of "hunting platoons" (*Jagdzüge*) within the German police provided another linguistic expression of this phenomenon, as these were units designed specifically to track, engage, and destroy Jews, communists, and partisans.[88] Similarly, the SS Dirlewanger Brigade, a unit known for heavy drinking and mass atrocity, and primarily composed of hunters and convicted poachers, epitomized "anti-partisan activity on the Eastern front that emerged from the image of the hunt and the animalization of the enemy."[89] Even after the war such rhetoric continued to find expression in exculpatory and revisionist literature, such as *Der große Rausch* (The great intoxication), by a former Waffen-SS member,

Erich Kernmayr, who depicted Soviet troops in the language of prey as "hunted and cornered animal[s]."[90]

Indeed, several of the perpetrators at the time adopted the language of hunting to describe their acts of killing. In one example, SS guards under the influence of a "bloodlust" (*Blutrausch*, literally "the intoxication of blood") used the phrase "rabbit hunt" in referring to the mass shooting of twenty-one prisoners in Dachau as retribution for a failed assassination attempt against Hitler in November 1939.[91] Similarly, the SS man Josef Blösche rode through the Warsaw ghetto at times on a rickshaw powered by a Jewish prisoner, on which occasions he would use the vehicle as a platform to test his marksmanship and shoot Jews either on the street or those standing at their windows. During a postwar interrogation by the East German State Police, he described these trips as the "hunt of Ghetto inhabitants."[92] A Jewish witness, Sol Liber, stated that Blösche "hunted Jews like others hunted animals."[93] Another SS killer, Hans Baumgartner, also described his unit's participation in a ghetto-clearing operation in Liepāja in July 1941 in the language of the hunt. Baumgartner recalled, "It was like one said at the time; the hunting of the Jews."[94] Members of the SS even used the hunting term *Fangschuss*, or "kill shot," to describe the coup de grâce given to wounded animals—in this case in their murder of wounded victims.[95]

It should be noted that during World War II the language of the hunt and instances of the "trophy taking" of body parts also occurred in the Pacific in a "war without mercy" in which racial prejudice on both sides led to atrocities.[96] In this theater, Harrison argued, "Many [US] servicemen, whether hunters themselves or not, must have shared this image of hunting, rich with associations of male camaraderie, coming-of-age, patriotism and white racial identity and brought it with them into combat with an enemy which many of them viewed as subhuman."[97] In a similar way, Japanese newspapers updated expectant readers on the tallies of a "friendly contest" between two Japanese officers as to which man "would be the first to cut down 150 Chinese with his samurai sword."[98] On the eastern front, the perversion of the hunt into an activity in which racial beliefs justified indiscriminate killing was demonstrated in the postwar testimony of SS general Otto Rasch, the head of *Einsatzgruppe* C, a man responsible for the murder of hundreds of thousands. At his trial, Rasch stated that he learned the lessons of becoming a hunter from his father, and he remarked without a trace of irony that he understood as a boy that one does not shoot animals out of season, nor does one shoot "the mother as long as her young ones need her."[99] Obviously, for Rasch and his killing squads, such prohibitions did not apply to Jews.

The performative nature of stalking and shooting one's prey is striking and is clearly overlaid with issues of masculinity. With respect to Nazi Germany, several instances demonstrate the incorporation of alcohol, celebration, and stalking into the killing process. In the first example, German police officials organized a hunting expedition during an inspection tour in the area of Radun in Belorussia. Disappointed by their failure to find sufficient game in the forest, these men enjoyed a "drunken lunch" and then rounded up over forty Jews from the town's ghetto. Leo Kahn recalled, "These unfortunates were trucked about a mile and a half from the town, unloaded and told to scatter." He continued, "They did as they were told, and the Germans, using the trucks to fire from as if they were on an African safari, gunned them all down."[100] In Ukraine, German perpetrators also combined the elements of a traditional picnic, including alcohol consumption, with the activity of a hunt in which the Jews became the intended prey. A Jewish survivor recalled being tasked to flush rabbits for a senior German official, his staff, and their wives and girlfriends: "They were all drunk, lying around their seats in the carriage hugging and shouting, their peals of laughter echoing in the distance. . . . One of the drunken officers aimed his hunting rifle and started shooting at Jews to the raucous pleasure of his staff. The bullets struck some marchers who collapsed in pools of blood."[101] In this example, the shooters were not only performing for their male comrades, but also for the females in the group, whom they sought to impress with both their marksmanship and their power over the victims.

Whether such killings were organized events or ad hoc, it is striking how often witnesses used the term "hunt" to describe them. A Polish woman in the city of Buczacz testified about one such police action: "The Jews were hunted on the streets like rabbits. Fleeing Jews were shot on the spot."[102] In the labor camp of Zaslaw in occupied Poland, an SS sergeant chose Sundays to arrange "hunts on Jews in the streets of the camp."[103] Patrick Desbois, in his study of the murder procedures of the *Einsatzgruppen*, concluded, "It's not a rounding up of the Jews but a veritable hunt."[104] The targeting of individuals in these "hunts" reflected in a very concrete sense the success of Nazi ideology in characterizing the victims, both Jews and Slavs, as subhuman animals. Likewise, these hunts reflected a desire and a pride on the part of the killers in tracking and taking down a "trophy." In these cases, alcohol was not a necessary ingredient to such acts, but it could and did facilitate such killings, as seen in the drunken lunches that led to mirth and murder among the perpetrators.

The fact that some perpetrators used killing as demonstrations of performative masculinity among their colleagues, wives, and lovers is also revelatory of their mind-set and pride in these acts. In this sense, the scene in Steven Spielberg's *Schindler's List* depicting Amon Göth shooting from his balcony into the Płaszów camp and his girlfriend's angry reaction can be contrasted with the documented reality of SS lieutenant Gustav Willhaus, the commandant of the Janowska camp in Lwów, who created a "sport and type of amusement for his wife and daughter" that involved shooting prisoners from the balcony of his office, another case of an SS man engaging in murder as a manifestation of performative masculinity.[105] In another example, Kazimierz Sakowicz recalled how some killers escorted two "ladies" into the Ponary Forest in August 1941 "on a day excursion to see the executions." He continued, "After the shootings they returned; I did not see sadness on their faces."[106] Once again, mass murder became the backdrop for a bizarre courting ritual in which a summer stroll over an execution site proclaimed the masculinity and authority of the perpetrators to the female objects of their desire.

Keeping Count

For many SS and policemen, keeping score of the number of their victims provided another manifestation of performative masculinity in a practice that mirrored the trophy-taking rituals of the hunt. The practice of keeping count of one's total extended from the highest to the lowest levels of the SS and police complex, a key indicator of the importance attached to such numbers at both an institutional and individual level. In the case of the former, the heads of the *Einsatzgruppen* and the higher SS and police leaders in the East not only kept track of their murder totals, but competed against one another for the highest body count.[107] For their part, Nazi district leaders in the East vied for the "honor" of being the first to report their areas as "free of Jews."[108] At the lower level, one former SS guard at Mauthausen described how his SS colleagues "seemingly only had interest in killing as many prisoners as possible, something they often stated."[109] For his part, SS lieutenant Max Täubner, a "fanatical Jew hater," entered the Soviet Union in June 1941 as part of a Waffen-SS supply unit with the self-proclaimed object of killing twenty thousand Jews, a goal he openly shared with his unit.[110]

The practice of keeping score was not unusual among SS and policemen. A former policeman with PB 9 revealed, "I also know that several [men] kept exact count of the number of people they had shot. They also bragged among themselves about the numbers."[111] One gendarme combined the act of killing as a "sport" with the objective of achieving one thousand kills, a goal that he kept track of with hundreds of notches carved into his locker.[112] In each of these cases, body counts served as a direct reflection of the toughness of the individual and as a method for ranking oneself against his colleagues.

The performative masculinity associated with tracking scores also led to public competitions among the perpetrators. During guard duty in the Warsaw ghetto, officers and senior enlisted men of PB 61 promoted "shooting contests" to encourage the murder of Jews.[113] For these policemen, the barroom became a site for celebrating and comparing their "scores" with their colleagues during "drinking orgies."[114] In a similar example, a uniformed policeman on duty in the Tomaszów Mazowiecki ghetto bragged about his 160 kills and proclaimed his intent to "catch up" with a colleague who had 190. In Riga, two policemen, Damskopf and Tuchel, made a "bet" as to who could kill the most Jews, with the former tallying seventy victims and the latter "only" sixty.[115] For such men, their score of victims clearly served as a personal marker of masculinity and established their standing among their peers.[116] Similarly, two Austrian policemen who had participated in the liquidation of the Jewish ghetto of Borysław in February 1943 gathered to drink schnapps in the wake of the killings of some six hundred men, women, and children. As they downed their shots, they began to argue over who had killed more Jews.[117] For PB 61, the unit's glorification of the act of mass murder found its expression in the five hundred or so notches carved in groups of five on the bar's door, as well as in the drunken celebrations that occurred inside after these killings.[118] Once again, competitions and body counts not only reflected the killers' proficiency with their weapons, but also served as a manifestation of masculinity and an act to be shared with their comrades at the killing site and at the bar.

For some policemen, the bar or barracks became sites for drinking while sharing stories involving participation in acts of atrocity and murder. The men of *Einsatzkommando* 3 gathered in the SS canteen after massacres to drink and carouse while bragging about their deeds.[119] Albert Emmerich, a uniformed policeman, remembered hearing such stories of atrocity from a colleague upon his arrival in Ukraine in 1943. In response to the question of when he first heard about mass murders, he observed, "We were in our lodgings and we were drunk. In the morning when we got up, we immediately received schnapps. So we were all drunk." He recalled how a colleague had taken him to a nearby gravel pit to show him a series of mass graves and told him each contained "three hundred Jews."[120] In this example, drinking with his comrades, touring an execution site, and discussing mass murder served as a type of initiation ritual for the newly arrived Emmerich, and the barracks functioned as a locus for his socialization into genocide. This process also became a method for establishing the expectations of behavior and a direct measure of one's masculine virtue.

While the act of counting was one way in which perpetrators kept score of their so-called accomplishments, bars, canteens, and barracks became locations for boasting and celebrating such achievements, as in the case of policemen who competed in "shooting contests" for the highest murder totals. Likewise, SS canteens within the concentration camps and killing centers became sites of "long booze-filled parties" during which the perpetrators would cement the bonds of comradeship and celebrate their brutal acts over free beer and schnapps and plates of schnitzel with fried potatoes.[121] Reinhold Meyer, a former prisoner in Sachsenhausen, recalled how SS guards gathered at the camp canteen to drink and to "boast" about their "heroic deeds."[122] Boasting or bragging about one's prowess at murder, whether at the canteen, on the selection ramp at Auschwitz, or in the killing fields, became a ubiquitous practice among the killers.[123]

An exceptional exhibition of male bravado extended to ritual celebrations of "whole numbers" of victims killed. One German official recalled witnessing an intoxicated Gestapo agent in 1942 leaving a bar after a "drinking-bout," with a beer coaster pinned to his uniform blouse with

"1,000" inscribed in red ink. The Gestapo man drunkenly exalted, "Man, today I'm celebrating my thousandth killing [*Genickschuß*]."[124] Another perpetrator boasted about having killed two thousand people, and, when told that this was a "reason to celebrate," he "beamed with joy" and responded, "That's what we did!"[125] As the historian Saul Friedlander observed, these men who kept count of their victims were experiencing a twofold sense of "intoxication"—the psychological "elation stemming from repetition, from the ever-larger numbers of the killed other," combined with the physical act of celebratory drinking rituals.[126] The public celebration among colleagues of such achievements not only normalized mass murder, but created benchmarks for mass murder.

For SS men assigned to the T4 or euthanasia program, camaraderie and masculine rituals were instrumental aspects of group identity, especially for those assigned to the killing centers in the East. As Sara Berger notes, "Toughness, the justification of might makes right, and the elimination of empathy belonged to the[ir] most prominent masculine values."[127] These SS men competed against each other in boxing matches and with acts of brutality against prisoners, and they socialized newcomers through "rites of initiation" to set them on the "course of the camp." Regular fellowship evenings with "large amounts of vodka and beer" played a key part in this process of socialization and development of camaraderie. During these evening celebrations, the perpetrators sang and played musical instruments in a ritual that echoed the parties conducted during the initial days of the euthanasia program in Germany proper.[128]

The act of boasting and staging killing contests also extended to SS doctors and SS men working within the euthanasia program. At Auschwitz, SS doctors competed against one another for most persons killed using phenol injections into the heart of the victim and then bragged about their murder rates. After the war, one witness testified, "The executioners used to boast about their records. 'Three in a minute.'"[129] In fact, some doctors were so eager to increase their rate of killing that the victims were thrown onto a pile of corpses before they died. These contests and the satisfaction of keeping track of one's total served to normalize the killing process, a fact that can be seen in a diary entry of Johann Kremer, an SS doctor at Auschwitz-Birkenau. Kremer began a one-paragraph diary entry of November 8, 1942, with a description of his participation in his twelfth and thirteenth *Sonderaktionen* (i.e., mass gassings) and ended it with a remark about a "cosy evening company" that included "Bulgarian red wine and Croatian plum brandy."[130]

In the case of nonmedical T4 personnel, SS sergeant major Josef Oberhauser "proudly announced having burned 20,000 corpses" and celebrated this milestone with his T4 colleagues at Grafeneck in a drinking bout.[131] In a similar manner, the camp administration at Treblinka hosted a special celebration, including additional schnapps rations at the SS canteen, to commemorate reaching the milestone of one hundred thousand victims.[132] Once again, alcohol proved to be the reward for a day's work in support of the Third Reich's murderous agenda and served as a social lubricant for boasting and celebrating among one's fellow genocidaires.

4

Alcohol and Sexual Violence

The issue of sexual violence offers one of the clearest expressions of the ways in which geography, war, and the colonial mentality of the perpetrators allowed for transgression of Nazi racial strictures in the East. Research on sexual violence against women, especially Jewish women, has revealed the widespread sexual predation by German forces in the occupied eastern territories.[1] Acts of sexual violence by SS and police forces were commonplace in spite of the Nazi regime's own prohibition against racial defilement (*Rassenschande*), an act punishable by death or imprisonment, as witnessed in numerous cases within Germany proper.[2] In the East, far away from Berlin and senior SS and police leaders, these prohibitions were widely ignored, and the abuse of alcohol often proved to be a key contributing factor.[3] Likewise, acts of rape were not limited to the SS and police murder squads but included numerous examples of drunken SS personnel and local auxiliaries operating in the concentration camps, the ghettos of the East, and the killing fields who sexually brutalized women, both Jews and Slavs, on a large scale.[4] In a dispatch in February 1942,

Ilya Ehrenburg highlighted the atrocious behavior of the German occupiers: "In our towns, they are violating women and hanging men; they are guzzling [alcohol] and sleeping off their orgies like swine."[5] For its part, Soviet propaganda leaflets in the fall of 1942 continued to focus on the nexus between bestial behavior, drinking, and sexual assault by German forces: "The Fascists have abused our women and girls like animals and driven them into public houses where they were helplessly exposed to SS men and [German] soldiers."[6]

These bestial acts of sexual violence included "genital beatings; sexual torture; anal, oral, and vaginal rape with objects, fingers, or other body parts; penile rape, gang rape; sexual enslavement; enforced prostitution; genital mutilation; sterilization; and experiments with reproductive organs."[7] In contrast, acts of "sexualized violence" included forced labor or beatings of naked or partially clothed victims, sexual voyeurism, mockery, and obscene or lascivious comments.[8] The distinction between acts of sexual violence and sexualized violence may seem merely an academic artifice to some; however, the distinction is important in highlighting the limits of individual transgression in specific cases. For example, just as some policemen drew the line by declining to murder women or children in the killing fields, some maintained other specific boundaries, no matter how horrific, in their treatment of women. Similarly, as in the killing of women and children, some perpetrators used alcohol as a means for overcoming inhibitions related to sexual violence.[9] Intoxication often served as a "facilitator" that promoted sexual and sexualized violence as part of a ritual of abuse in the East.[10] In fact, alcohol consumption was a recreational act, and "heavy drinking ma[de] men feel more powerful, stronger, and assertive," feelings that facilitated acts of sexual violence.[11] Regardless of the role of alcohol, it is apparent that sexual violence served as a "demonstration of [male] power and dominance through the humiliation and degradation of the other."[12]

The intersection between alcohol consumption, aggression, and male bravado found repeated expression in crimes of sexual violence in the East. In describing the actions of SS men in a Polish labor camp, Felicja Karay, a survivor and historian, described "orgies of drunkenness and gang rapes of Jewish girls" as the manner in which the SS demonstrated their "rites of manhood."[13] The counting of victims and the competitive nature of killing that arose among some of the perpetrators was itself an expression of hypermasculinity and the "arrogance [that] was typical of many SS men" who "not only flaunted their power over the inmates, but also tried to outdo or trump each other as well."[14] Not surprisingly, such competitions extended to the ultimate expression of performative masculinity, sexual relations and acts of sexual violence, in which the perpetrators "reaffirm[ed] their masculinity and sexual potency" by keeping count of the number of their sexual victims.[15] In the case of the liquidation of the Slonim ghetto in September 1942, policemen "bragged about the number of women they had abused in this manner and tried to outdo one another."[16] Much like keeping score of one's body count, the numbers of rapes served individual perpetrators as a personal record of their own virility and masculinity, and as a means of group bonding.

Hypermasculinity, Group Identity, and Misogyny

In her analysis of the German army, the historian Ute Frevert identified the method by which "sexuality became a communal experience, with 'immoral' language, laughter and applause as the ties binding the diverse individuals" within military units.[17] Barracks humor involving boasts of sexual prowess and sexual "conquests" was certainly not unique to the German military. The barracks and the pub were both key sites for the expressions of male bravado, misogyny, and group bonding, while group drinking rituals loosened tongues, lowered inhibitions, and inflated male swaggering and tales of sexual exploits. Braggadocio and shared lewd language, like the act of communal drinking, was an element for building group identity and camaraderie among soldiers and for emphasizing one's virility.

Military units are one example of a "primary group," a concept in which the individual's identification with the unit and the idea of group cohesion are seen as paramount, and community is associated with the "separation by members from other commitments and relationships."[18] The creation of the primary group begins with the basic training and the drill and disciplinary processes associated with learning the elements of martial life. Similarly, the group's social interactions and activities, including communal recreational activities involving the consumption of alcohol in bars, dance halls, or brothels, provide another venue for reinforcing group expectations and establishing group norms related to masculine behaviors, whether for combat, drinking, or sex. In the case of the last, the use of crude or salacious language among one's peers in descriptions of sexual exploits acted as a marker of one's masculinity, but also as a means for creating a male community in which these "conquests" became shared group experiences.[19] For example, one Wehrmacht soldier's diary entry reveals that he and a buddy had met two Russian girls and "finish[ed] them off," which was not a euphemism for murder, but rather a synonym for sexual conquest expressed in the language of annihilation.[20]

The prevalence of primary groups in which women were seen as sexual objects, combined with an ideology in which "foreign" women, whether Jew or Slav, were by definition denied their humanity, created an environment in the East in which sexual violence had free rein. With respect to masculinity and rape, one study found that "standards of masculinity that emphasize dominance, assertiveness, aggressiveness, independence, self-sufficiency, and willingness to take risks, and that reject characteristics such as compassion, understanding and sensitivity have been found to be correlated with rape propensity."[21] Not surprisingly, attitudes associated with the concept of hypermasculinity also have been "correlated with rape and rape proclivity" in military units.[22] In this sense, the ideal of hypermasculinity established within Nazi paramilitary organizations and the Wehrmacht, combined with the colonial mentality of the conqueror, created a situation in which sexual transgressions became a fact of life in the East.

The Sexualized Semantics of Alcohol Use

The words SS and policemen used to describe their drinking during occupation duties offer important insights into some of the ways in which alcohol consumption was framed and intended. Viktor Klemperer's oft-cited *LTI-Lingua Tertii Imperii* examines the National Socialist perversion of the German language in a process by which "Nazism permeated the flesh and blood of the people through single words, idioms and sentence structures."[23] In fact, the use of words such as *Zechgelage, Trinkgelage,*

Sauftage, and *Sauforgien* offer revealing insights into the conceptualization of drinking, the ritualistic use of alcohol, and the ultimate meaning and importance of the process of drinking itself. For example, the German verbs *saufen* and *zechen* both are linguistically tied to *excessive* drinking, with the former often being used to describe animal drinking behavior. These two terms also have sexualized connotations of carousing or orgy. Likewise, the use of the word *Gelage* connotes acts of carousal, revelry, and drinking bouts.[24] The sexualized nature of such activities is most apparent in the term *Sauforgien* (literally, drinking orgies), a word that explicitly combines the act of extreme alcohol consumption with the concept of unrestrained sexual activity. The perpetrators' use of these terms to refer to their drinking behaviors intersected with their views of masculinity at two levels. First, it highlighted their ability to consume large quantities of alcohol in an almost animalistic sense, and, second, the act of drinking was explicitly tied to an expression of virility and sexual prowess. Indeed, such linguistic constructions perfectly reflected drinking rituals to celebrate rape, gang rapes, and murder in the East.[25] Furthermore, for some of the perpetrators their "lust for conquest" (*Eroberungslust*) found one expression in acts of sexual violence against Slavic and Jewish women in subjugated colonial spaces.[26]

Alcohol, (Sexual) Power, and Violence

It is critical to note that in the East, drinking was a communal activity in which participation was expected among members of Nazi paramilitary organizations as well as soldiers, a norm especially true for the men of the *Einsatzgruppen*.[27] Refusal to participate in drinking rituals not only labeled the individual as having rejected the group and its actions, but also signified weakness or feminized behavior. In his 2007 study focusing on the relationship of drinking and expressions of masculinity, Robert Peralta argues that alcohol use provides a way masculinity can be affirmed by the amount consumed and one's tolerance to its effects. Those incapable of "holding their liquor" are characterized as weak or feminine. Peralta contends that "men use alcohol to express their presumed superiority over women and marginalized men," with heavy drinking representing male power and strength.[28] In this regard, it is not surprising that one expression of this power includes sexual violence. For example, one male participant explicitly linked alcohol consumption with sexual assault: "Men drink. They get violent, rape." Likewise, a female participant expressed her fear of becoming a victim of alcohol-related violence, both physical and sexual, by noting, "I think especially with guys . . . when they are drunk their drinking gives them this power."[29]

For those serving in the Nazi East, the sense of power was in fact twofold, with the effects of alcohol use multiplied by the control they enjoyed over subject male and female populations in a colonial space, where physical inebriation intersected with the metaphorical high of imperial authority. However, feelings of power over women were intrinsic to the Nazi hypermasculine ideal in general and can be seen as linking crimes of physical and sexual violence by "Aryan" men against German women as well. For example, drunken German men enjoying state-sponsored holiday cruises engaged in "egregious . . . assaults against the [German] women and girls on board."[30] Likewise, in her study of gender and power in the Third Reich, Vandana Joshi argues, "[German men] become visible as oppressive sexual beings." She asserts that women were denied legal protections since the police "considered cases of violent outbursts by men in a drunken state, arguments between couples resulting in physical abuse and so on as 'private matters' not worthy of consideration."[31] In this view, the effects of alcohol consumption, combined with conceptions of "Aryan" masculinity, found legitimate outlets in acts of physical or sexual domination over women even within the borders of the "old Reich."

The relationship of alcohol and physical or sexual violence perpetrated against women offers an important perspective for evaluating the actions of the male occupiers. Investigations have found that "men anticipate feeling more powerful, sexual and aggressive after drinking alcohol."[32] Occupiers experienced the "empowering effect of sexual violence," while their transgressions, like mass murder, combined "violent male bonding— with the acceptance of a man's comrades."[33] The fact that one-third of all sexual assaults in the East were gang rapes provides an indication of such "violent male bonding" in communal violence.[34] The historian Regina Mühlhäuser, in her pathbreaking study of sexual violence by German soldiers serving in the East, identified acts of individual and group rape as a "proof of masculinity" among the perpetrators.[35]

Again, feelings of power or dominance, whether physical or sexual in nature, characterized the male ideal in general in Nazi Germany. In her study on the influence of culture on sexual violence, Peggy Sanday argued that in "rape prone societies, social relations were marked by interpersonal violence in conjunction with an ideology of male dominance enforced through the control and subordination of women."[36] While not a focus of her study, the hypermasculine ideal glorified under National Socialism appears to constitute the paradigm for Sanday's definition of a rape-prone society. In fact, the demise of the regime in 1945 led one postwar German male observer to lament, "The dominance of the man, which was so strongly emphasized in the Third Reich, has collapsed."[37] The National Socialist preoccupation with procreation was one area in which the concept of hypermasculinity found its most visible expression, and the manifestation of hypersexual activity, both consensual and transgressive, should therefore not be surprising, especially in conjunction with alcohol consumption, which served to disinhibit and facilitate acts of physical and sexual aggression among the perpetrators.[38]

Colonization and the Conquest of the Body

Based on the clear relationship between masculinity, alcohol, sexual aggression, and violence, it is not surprising that drinking played a role in acts ranging from voyeurism, sexual humiliation, and rape in a regime that glorified a hypermasculine ideal. In some cases, SS and policemen selected attractive young girls during the killing operations and forced them into sexual bondage in exchange for a temporary reprieve. These types of arrangements might last as little as a day or as long as several weeks, at the discretion of the perpetrators. During a postwar interrogation, one German soldier remembered entering the rooms of three different SS men and finding each with a young Jewish woman. In the third room he saw a "very pretty young woman" in bed with an SS man. He heard the girl ask, "You're not going to shoot me, right my little Franz?" Later the soldier asked the SS man if the girl would be killed, to which the latter remarked, "All the Jews would be shot, there were no exceptions," even if it meant killing one's own concubine. In his 1965 testimony, the soldier recalled his feelings of shock and concluded, "First these beautiful girls were the playthings of the SS and then they were murdered."[39] Like this soldier, one Ukrainian woman also remembered how the Germans had spared a number of beautiful Jewish girls for sexual bondage, but "when the girls got pregnant, they were killed."[40]

Not surprisingly, such manifestations of dominance and humiliation extended to Polish Gentiles under German control. The identity of the conquerors was based in part on a hypermasculine and colonial character in which they exercised the power of life and death over all the conquered, Gentiles as well as Jews. The Szmalcówka camp in Toruń, as one example, served as a site of ethnic cleansing and a gathering point for Poles resettled out of the territory being annexed to Germany. In February 1941, the camp was overseen by a detachment of forty policemen under the command of SS lieutenant Richard Reddig, a man known as "the boxer," based on his style of beating prisoners. Reddig's nickname was well earned, as he and the men under his command used beatings as part of an "official ritual" for dealing with the camp's prisoners.[41]

At the Szmalcówka camp, alcohol consumption by the perpetrators played a conspicuous role in beatings, acts of humiliation, and sexual assaults. The ubiquity of the beatings stands out, as does the integration of the abuse into an "official ritual." Likewise, the perpetrators' routine use of weekend "holidays" to administer mass beatings points to the sportlike or festive nature of these events. The frequent mention of alcohol use by the perpetrators also reinforces the celebratory aspect of the abuse.[42]

Tekla Chmielewska worked in the camp's kitchen and recalled frequent systematic beatings by "drunk and amused SS men" as she returned to her barrack. Intoxicated SS and policemen often chose weekends to engage in organized beatings using canes, billiard cues, and whips. One survivor noted, "Drunken SS men often fell into the crowd of prisoners gathered in the courtyard and tortured them as much as they could by beating and kicking them." Another prisoner testified that the "Gestapo" men, who were "mostly drunk," would come to the barracks and call out women and girls, who were then raped.[43]

Sexual assaults also occurred in Auschwitz-Birkenau, as noted by Ruth Elias, who recalled repeated nighttime incidents of drunken SS men bursting into Block 6, the barrack that housed the camp orchestra and "mostly young women." Elias remembered, "First of all they [the SS men] woke up the orchestra and *the music had to play* . . . and then they started to climb up and look for nice women and take them out, and the girls had to sleep with them. . . . The girls were screaming, and that was terrible, terrible."[44] For these intoxicated SS men, the incorporation of music apparently provided an important festive accompaniment to their communal acts of rape. In another example, Laura Varon testified about being raped along with several other women in their barrack at Auschwitz by three SS men who "smelled like beer."[45] In all these cases, alcohol consumption served to facilitate acts of sexual abuse against girls and women who were seen as disposable if not dehumanized objects in the eyes of their tormentors.

At the Szmalcówka camp, Reddig's reputation as "the boxer" and his practice of punching his victims reflected once again a recognized trope of hypermasculinity and male dominance within Nazi Germany.[46] Similar brutality, fueled by alcohol, also can be seen in the actions of the German policeman Georg Barg, who was stationed in the city of Buczacz in modern Ukraine. Barg, a heavy drinker and a cruel man, was in charge of supervising the city's Jewish workforce. In postwar testimony a fellow policeman asserted, "That swine Barg drank the whole time. . . . He would force the Jews coming to do military gymnastics and then make them stand at attention. He pounced on the Jews and did not desist from boxing their ears."[47] Like many other perpetrators, Barg regularly made use of a dog whip during these "workout" sessions. In his case, drinking was not a prerequisite for such actions but seemed rather to be a natural accompaniment to actions he enjoyed.

As can be seen from the examples above, the dynamic between sexual aggression and power was prevalent in the occupied East among soldiers, policemen, and members of the SS. The historian Annette Timm contends that under National Socialism, "sexual gratification" was equated "with masculine power to a degree unprecedented in Germany." She also notes, "Masculine vitality was thus viewed as highly dependent on sexual gratification . . . [with] the purpose of achieving the racial state."[48] While Timm focuses on prostitution and the soldiers' use of brothels, the power dynamic of sexual domination she describes reflects a generalizable mentality among members of the SS and police complex in the Third Reich, especially in the occupied territories. SS men on duty in the East routinely employed sexual violence as a means for the "total exploitation of power and the demand for total subjugation [of the victims]."[49]

The prevalence of the practice proves as shocking as the number of men who avoided punishment for such acts. One SS judicial investigation of cases of rape and gang rape by SS men estimated that "at least 50 percent of all members of the SS and the police violated the 'ban on undesirable intercourse with ethnically alien women.'"[50] When SS authorities chose to prosecute cases related to sexual assault in the East, judicial officers received instructions to consider the "lack of opportunity for sexual intercourse as well as excessive alcohol consumption" as extenuating factors in sentencing, a view that propagated the Nazi concept of masculinity and legitimized sexual violence, "especially if it was committed against women from an 'inferior race.'"[51] In comparison, in cases of consensual or nonconsensual homosexual behavior among SS men, excessive alcohol consumption was raised as a mitigating factor, but Himmler and SS and police courts did not view drunkenness as exonerating this behavior, and punishment could and did include the death sentence.[52] In this sense, the SS and police maintained a gendered distinction in which rape and acts of sexual violence against women were simply one aspect "of a continuum of violence that resulted from genocide" and a natural expression of the perpetrator's "power and dominance through the humiliation and degradation of the other."[53]

Subjugation and the Intoxication of Sexual Violence

While alcohol was neither a necessary nor sufficient cause of sexual violence, it was linked to the intoxication of male power over the victims and played an important role in individual and, more significantly, group acts of sexual assault. The reports of sexual violence involving alcohol consumption by soldiers, policemen, and SS are striking both for their scale and frequency. During the opening weeks of the campaign into Russia, "drunken" German soldiers carried away and raped all the women between the ages of sixteen and thirty in the village of Beresowka in the district of Smolensk. In the city of Lemberg (Lvov), intoxicated SS men forced women into a city park, where they were brutalized and raped. In this case, a local priest attempted to intervene but was beaten, had his beard set on fire, and was then stabbed to death. In a final example, German soldiers, after capturing seventy-five women in the vicinity of the Belorussian town of Borrissow, raped and murdered thirty-six of them.[54] In each of these cases, the conquest of territory was accompanied by the sexual subjugation of the women in these areas as an expression of racial domination, a practice largely absent from the German invasion and control of areas in the West, such as France.[55]

Sexual violence by German troops also included mass rapes of Jewish girls and women in shtetls, as in the case of Yedintsy in Moldava and Telshyay in Lithuania.[56] These abuses extended into the ghettos and labor camps under German control. In the case of the former, Raisa Dudnik fled the Rakovka ghetto in Uman in the fall of 1941, but she could not forget how "every night, drunken bandits [i.e., Germans] burst into our little homes. They raped girls. They beat up old women and took their last belongings."[57] In the case of the latter, SS personnel at the Skarżysko labor camp routinely engaged in drunken orgies in which they victimized Jewish prisoners. In but one example, during a roll call in October 1942, SS guards selected six recently arrived Jewish female prisoners who "were ordered to serve diners in the nude, and at the end of the meal were raped" before being executed the following day.[58]

The significance of the widespread nature of these transgressions and the fact that they began from the earliest days of the invasion cannot be overstated. Indeed, the accompaniment of the physical conquest of the East with acts of sexual humiliation and subjugation established a precedent and a regular practice that would last throughout the German occupation. In comparison, while acts of sexual violence certainly occurred in the occupied western territories under German military control, they did not approach the scale and frequency of such behavior in the East.[59] In a secretly recorded conversation of a group of senior German prisoners of war, SS brigadier general Kurt Meyer mentioned that he had a German noncommissioned officer executed for raping a French girl in Caen. He stated that the soldier, who was drunk at the time of the assault, was shot the day following the attack, with the village mayor and other city officials present as witnesses. During this discussion, General Heinrich Eberbach remarked, "But I believe that the FÜHRER [*sic*] issued an order for the East that the raping of women and girls should not be [considered] . . . as a criminal offence, but only as a disciplinary [offense]—as terror was part of the rules of war." Eberbach then commented, "That order wasn't issued for the West, merely for the East."[60]

Eberbach's contention is interesting in several respects. First, although there was no specific order from Hitler allowing German forces to sexually assault women in the East, the Wehrmacht High Command at Hitler's instruction had issued a decree in May 1941 prior to the invasion of the Soviet Union that limited the jurisdiction of the courts over "enemy civilians" and established "no obligation to prosecute a member of the Wehrmacht for crimes committed against civilians, even if such crimes constituted offenses against military law."[61] In other words, individual commanders had the discretion to punish troops for criminal offenses committed against civilians, including sexual assaults and murder. Second, this decree, along with a series of other "criminal orders," established an environment in which German forces "literally became judge, jury, and executioner."[62] Finally, such decrees provide another manifestation of the way in which the geography of the East became a zone of exception in which acts of brutality and atrocity were normalized by statute and in practice. The May 1941 decree demonstrates the way in which the Nazi concept of hypermasculinity, with its emphasis on conceptions of extreme militarized masculinity and a rigid racial hierarchy, exerted its most profound influence in a colonial space populated by "inferior" men and women.

The "Soft West" and the "Wild East"

Geography and space also played an important role in the incidence of sexual violence during World War II.[63] In his study of Wehrmacht operations in the East, the historian Waitman Beorn makes a key point: "At the local level, sexuality in the East seems to have operated under a moral code different from that observed in Western Europe."[64] In fact, senior SS, police, and Wehrmacht leaders were clearly aware of the crimes committed by German forces in the East. SS general Kurt Daluege, the chief of the Order Police, sent an order on December 13, 1939, to all Higher SS and Police Leaders (HSSPF) in Germany directing them to remind returning police units that they were "no longer in enemy territory" and were expected to observe the "laws of the homeland." The HSSPFs also were instructed to reiterate secrecy obligations concerning the "special tasks" (i.e., executions) the men performed in the East.[65] In the case of the army, the commander in chief of the German army, General Walther von Brauchitsch, worried in October 1939 about the "lack of a firm inner bearing" among army officers in the wake of the defeat of Poland, based in part on widespread reports concerning acts of indiscipline including "drunkenness, insubordination, and rape."[66] In fact, the demonstrated misbehavior of troops in occupied Poland led military leaders to "tighten their control over the troops' conduct" during the May 1940 invasion of France "particularly as regards alcohol."[67]

This existence of a double standard concerning acceptable behavior for troops in the East and the West was primarily a manifestation of Nazi racial ideology and reached into the highest ranks of the German army.[68] Such ideas also filtered down to the unit level, where bonds of male camaraderie took precedence over official prohibitions on having sex with local women, as one former policeman admitted after the war: "It is true that in the circle of one's comrades such incidents were not relayed [up the chain of command]."[69] In the East, physical conquest of territory, racial and gender-based concepts of superiority, and perceptions of male camaraderie combined with excessive alcohol consumption to create a mind-set among the perpetrators in which the prohibition of acts of sexual aggression existed as "reality only on paper."[70]

In contrast, one study of the reaction of French women to the German invasion in 1940 found two dominant attitudes toward the German army. The first was that the "German army appeared more organized and disciplined than the French," and the second was that "the Germans, seemed polite or, as the French say, 'correct.'"[71] A seventeen-year-old French Jewish girl, Jackie De Col, remembered the soldiers offering candy to children and remarked, "They obeyed orders. Plenty of them were not Nazis. There were plenty who were not zealots."[72] To be sure, German forces, especially SS and police units, stationed in France could and did participate in acts of reprisal and atrocity during anti-partisan and anti-resistance operations; however, the choice of means and methods revealed a "large difference between [Western Europe and] the East and Southeast Europe."[73]

In contrast to the state of affairs in Western Europe, a survey of Nazi occupation policies in the East emphasized that "violence against women and girls was part and parcel of the system of persecution established by the occupiers and their helpers."[74] In fact, one Security Police report in May 1943 for the Polish district of Galicia emphasized that "it is not a minority [of Germans] who stand outside of the written as well as the unwritten laws," as exemplified by an "addiction to pleasure, plans for enrichment, and undignified conduct."[75] The report discussed an array of misbehavior, including a district official who "almost only celebrated parties and went hunting" and another police official who "normally in a drunken state regularly had Jewesses in his apartment" and who had tried to force his Polish secretary to spend the night with him, ostensibly to read "bible verses" to her.[76] The colonial attitudes of such officials and their proclivity for dissolute behavior not surprisingly promoted numerous acts of sexual coercion and sexual violence.

Pola Ajzensztajn recalled how numbers of SS and SD men from Chełm regularly visited the Polish town of Krasnystaw on Mondays, Thursdays, and Saturdays in 1939 and "organized 'little games.'"[77] In fact, SS and police fellowship evenings often combined "gang rapes, torture, and drink" in both the occupied East and within the concentration camps.[78] SS guards and auxiliaries at Treblinka routinely committed gang rapes and held "regular orgies" involving newly arrived transports of Jews.[79] Again, in cases of communal sexual violence, such as gang rape, perpetrators sought to demonstrate their virility and dominance, while these acts also solidified a sense of fraternity and "male bonding" in which the perpetrators declared their allegiance to the social group.[80]

Sexual/Sexualized Violence, Masculinity, and Rituals of Humiliation

The historian Dagmar Herzog argued, "Sexuality in the Third Reich was after all, also about the invasion and control and destruction of human beings."[81] These acts of sexual aggression not only demonstrated one's dominance, but "abusing women in the occupied areas was the ultimate performative masculinity, that is, an assertion of the sovereignty of the male bond."[82] Additionally, such acts symbolically castrated and feminized one's opponent by emphasizing the inability of the conquered male to protect "his" women.[83] For the perpetrators of sexual violence, these acts also played a role in defining group belonging, as "sexual gratification . . . was secondary to the celebration of fraternity bonding and group pride."[84] The prevalence of sexual humiliation offers another perspective for examining demonstrations of power and performative masculinity by the perpetrators.

The Use of Mockery and Lewd Humor

Sexual humiliation was a part of German conquest from the earliest days of the war. In September 1939, German forces took Jewish women from their homes in the Polish town of Ostrów Mazowiecka and ordered them to do naked "gymnastics."[85] Similarly, a Gestapo official in Tarnopol routinely engaged in "orgies" of violence by making Jewish men and women undress and do "gymnastic exercises" as he beat them with his whip.[86] Mockery and vulgar comments about the physical attributes of Jewish women also extended to the killing sites as SS and policemen exchanged "dirty comments" while their naked victims waited for their deaths.[87] In February 1943, an SS man and his comrade selected "thirteen young, beautiful women" from the Minsk ghetto for execution. A witness recalled, "The animals stripped the women naked and mocked them," and one of the killers took the bra of a murdered woman as a keepsake and exclaimed, "To remember a beautiful Jewess."[88] This was one of many cases in which the ritual sexual humiliation of women was accompanied by "trophy taking" of underwear or the taking of souvenir photographs of partially clad or naked women.[89]

The combination of sexual humiliation and violence can be found in a number of examples involving SS guards and auxiliaries in the camps. Acts of sexual humiliation might embrace psychological or physical violence, but in either case they served as expressions of male physical and sexual domination over the victims. In the case of the former, Chil Rajchman, a survivor, recalled German SS men and SS auxiliaries at Treblinka watching naked women and girls being led to the gas chamber. During the process, the men amused themselves by making "jokes" about the women and "laughing," incidents that continued throughout the winter.[90] Such acts were a frequent occurrence and should be seen as a form of vocal violence in which "verbal humiliation and vulgar insults" could easily cross over into "beatings and intimate touching."[91] For example, Eva Schloss recalled the circumstances of her arrival at Auschwitz as a fifteen-year-old girl; as she and her fellow female prisoners entered the showers, "from time to time SS officers came in, walked around the room, and jeered at the sight of our naked bodies." She continued, "It amused them to pinch the buttocks of the women who were young and pretty. . . . I felt really humiliated."[92] Similarly, SS sergeant Adolf Taube accompanied the camp's SS doctor on a "health inspection" of a group of Jewish women. Charlotte Delbo recalled, "Taube who is not a physician, examines us also, makes us turn round and round—can you imagine us, naked, with thermometers up our asses, whirling like tops—and [he] feels us."[93]

Sexual Humiliation through the Lens of the Camera

In the ghetto at Rawa Ruska, SS sergeant first class Helmut Späth was notorious for his brutality and heavy drinking. One female survivor, Ida Scheiner, described Späth as a man who "personally killed hundreds, raped women, and mistreated the Jewish population."[94] Wanda Kirschenbaum detailed one of Späth's special rituals of sexual humiliation, which involved the construction of a fenced podium in the ghetto where he would force Jewish women to undress, assume pornographic poses, and make them "smile" while he photographed them. After these "photo shoots," he led the women to his private apartment, where he "forced them to drink alcohol" and raped them before allowing the victims to return to the ghetto.[95] In one case, Späth began beating a woman who refused to participate in a photo session. Despite the abuse, she still refused to pose, at which point he shot her.[96] Späth's behavior illustrates the ways in which initial acts of humiliation could lead to sexual assault and in some cases murder, and it also highlights the way in which male perpetrators dealt with female resistance as a threat to their control.

The Feminization of Humiliation

As noted previously, the "gendering of humiliation as feminine is intimately connected to vulgar views of the sexual act."[97] The political scientist Sanjay Palshikar argues that the use of humiliation in wartime is "predicated upon already existing notions of manhood and glory."[98] In this sense, such crimes are an overt expression of masculinity and male power, and these traits are perhaps most clearly seen in acts of sexual humiliation involving physical violence against the victims, both male and female. In the summer of 1943, four SS men found a group of Jews hiding in a bunker in Warsaw. According to one witness, they ordered the men and women to undress: "SS men were lifting women's breasts, looking inside their mouths, they inspected their sexual organs. They were putting their fingers into their colons groping them like good housewives at the market searching for a fatty goose for lard." The witness continued, "Everybody, women, children and men were subjected to these unheard of inspections. . . . The SS-men jeered and enjoyed the sight of the inhuman suffering of their victims."[99] Similar scenes were repeated at Auschwitz during the first Slovakian deportation as SS men conducted "gynecological exams" under the pretext of searching for valuables before engaging in mass rapes.[100] For many, body cavity searches of women and men were a routine occurrence that accompanied the entire process of deportation, from leaving the ghetto, boarding the trains, and arriving at the killing centers. The ghettos, the camps, and the killing fields, all under the absolute control of the SS, provided a singularly unrestricted environment for a multitude of acts of humiliation and sadism that preceded the murder of the victims.

The combination of sexualized violence, humiliation, and murder can be found in a number of examples that accompanied German rule in the East. One Polish witness detailed the cruel mistreatment of Jewish women by noting, "On a freezing January day, they [the Germans] forced them to wash floors with their own underwear and then made them put these dirty, wet garments on their naked bodies and walk this way in the streets."[101] In another example, SS guards at Treblinka incorporated "sadistic humour" as part of a ritual of humiliation and violence for menstruating prisoners. While the conditions of camp life led to a halt in menstruation for many women, those who continued to have menses lacked any type of sanitary napkins and were forced to resort to using leaves. Not only was this a risk to the health of the women from a hygienic perspective, but "blood showing on a dress meant death" at the hands of SS executioners.[102]

Sexual Enslavement

In addition to acts of humiliation, there are numerous examples of sexual coercion in camps and at the killing sites. In the case of the former, SS men at Auschwitz employed "beautiful young Jewish girls" as maids, and one guard recalled the men's need for "some recreation" after a "heavy night's work."[103] According to one witness, such "recreation" also involved "forced orgies" by SS officers who sent SS guards into Birkenau with their "special wishes."[104] At Treblinka, the SS guard Otto Horn had a reputation among his colleagues of "always larking about with the [Jewish] girls in the laundry."[105] Sara Ritterband testified that the SS at Belzec selected "only young and especially beautiful women" for work in the camp's kitchen and laundry.[106] She also recalled how the SS for their enjoyment made these women dance at night to music played by the prisoner orchestra before presumably raping them. At the Janowska camp, Leon Wells noted the arrival in August 1943 of twenty-four girls expressly chosen for the purpose of sexual enslavement by the SS personnel. After the ordeal of the first night in the camp, several of the women attempted to flee, but they were captured and then shot by their SS tormentors.[107]

The practice of sexual coercion also extended to the civilian and SS staffs of smaller labor camps. Felicja Karay commented, "The various German managers and commanders chose for themselves the prettiest girls to clean their rooms and the precise nature of their relationship was never openly displayed." She continued, "In all three werks [camp work sections] there were rumors of affairs of this sort, the overwhelming majority of which ended with the men murdering their Jewish lovers [sic], particularly if they should become pregnant."[108] Similarly, SS men at Majdanek, after impregnating female prisoners, sent them to the crematorium.[109] The murder of women who were impregnated by their tormentors reflected the perpetrators' view of the victims as disposable objects of desire in which sexual violence was merely an intermediary step to murder.

The conjunction of sexual violence and murder could not have been more apparent at some killing sites. Perpetrators employed sexual coercion at these locations. SS and policemen assured mothers that their children would be spared if they consented to sex, often leading to gang rapes before the murder of the victim and her child.[110] In the summer of 1941, Jews forced into the Warsaw ghetto from towns throughout occupied Poland told "tales of rape and mass executions."[111] A policeman from PB 45 discussed his unit's actions in a mass killing in Ukraine during postwar testimony by describing how the men "enjoyed themselves" by forcing "the young and the beautiful girls" to undress next to the grave.

In this case, the policemen ordered the naked girls to clamber back and forth across the bodies of the dead. He then revealed, "Before being shot, many of these young girls and women were raped by the soldiers and officers of our regiment."[112] In September 1941 in the Latvian town of Olaine, SS and policemen gang raped a group of women and young girls in front of their friends and relatives before burying them alive.[113] In the same month, witnesses recalled how a group of SS men from *Einsatzkommando 9* executed the entire ghetto of the Belorussian town of Yanavichy, including 1,025 men, women, and children. Tellingly, for the first round of executions, the SS men chose a group of young girls, whom they raped before killing.[114] In other words, these men chose to begin their day of murder by demonstrating their virility and power in gang rape, a communal activity that conjoined sexual subjugation and killing. In this case, the perpetrators chose to establish male community through both gang rape and mass murder.

In a final example, a former policeman testified about a young Jewish woman who ran to the leader of the police unit at a killing site, begged for her life, and reportedly agreed to voluntarily entering a "brothel" for German forces. The leader of the unit ordered the woman to strip and then to turn in a circle in front of him, after which he pulled out his pistol and shot her.[115] This incident perfectly illustrates the humiliation inflicted on the victim and the loss of power over her own sexuality. It also shows the titillation experienced by the perpetrator and the conjoining of sexualized violence with the act of mass murder. Further, the comment about the willingness of the woman to enter a brothel may simply reflect the fantasy of the policeman observing the events, but it may also demonstrate what Lawrence Langer describes as a "choiceless choice" faced by this victim, since rumors of such brothels were exchanged by Jewish girls in the East.[116] While this policeman did not mention the presence of alcohol at the execution site, other examples demonstrate the integration of drinking and sexualized violence into the ritual of killing.

Intoxication, Arousal, and Mass Murder

The combination of alcohol, sexual predation, and murder found expression in a broad range of sexualized and sexual violence. For example, the widespread act of making women undress before executions was not merely associated with the plundering of their clothes and a search for valuables, but also served the purpose of humiliating the victims and sexually arousing the perpetrators, as demonstrated by a mass execution of Jews in Odessa. A participant in this massacre remarked that the SD men involved were "so drunk that they could barely conduct their duties." He continued by describing the operation: "Finally the victims at the orders of the SD [security service] had to undress. This was demanded above all from the women. . . . The victims then had to pass through a gauntlet of SD men whereby primarily the women were beaten with dog whips."[117] In a similar incident, intoxicated security policemen in German-occupied West Galicia forced two Jewish girls to pull down their pants in order to expose their buttocks before shooting them.[118] Likewise, an inebriated SA man and two of his "drinking buddies" forced their way into a prison in October 1939 in the Polish territories annexed to the Third Reich where they proceeded to murder fifty-six inmates, but not before coercing some of the victims to engage in sex acts.[119]

The need to preface the killing of the victims with acts of physical abuse and sexual humiliation mirrored similar actions taken against Jewish men such as the targeting of male genitalia. In both cases, attacks aimed at the individual's sexuality were intended to strip away the victim's humanity and to reinforce the emasculation of Jewish men in terms of their ability to protect themselves and their women. Through these acts, the perpetrators also sought to establish their superior masculinity, a practice in which rituals of abuse and humiliation easily could progress to rape.

During the Warsaw Uprising in August 1944, "time and again women were assaulted, dragged out and violated by the drunken soldiers," both German forces and their foreign auxiliaries. During the operation to crush Polish resistance, there were multiple incidents of gang rapes followed by the murder of the victims.[120] One witness to the mass executions, a pregnant mother who saw her children killed and who miraculously survived a gunshot to the head, remarked, "During these dreadful doings they [the killers] sang and drank vodka."[121] Another witness to the crushing of the rebellion described a group of SS officers: "They looked attentively at the passers-by, took from our ranks three pretty young girls, the two sisters R. and an unknown girl, and drove off. The girls cried and tried to escape from their caresses."[122]

A Man's "Weapon"

The metaphorical equation of a penis with a weapon had its origins in the SS basic training practice of the "penis inspection" (*Schwanzappell*), during which a noncommissioned officer conducted regular hygiene examinations of each recruit's genitalia in a procedure evocative of a rifle check.[123] Similarly, it appears that some SS camp guards used their firearms as both symbols of their potency and as symbolic extensions of their own sexuality. In the Warsaw ghetto, a group of German policemen raided a late-night meeting of a Jewish house committee in order to rob the participants. After confiscating money from the men, they ordered the women to undress and "kept [them] naked for more than two hours while the Nazis put their revolvers to their breasts and private parts and threatened to shoot them."[124] Friedrich Heinen, an SS guard at a forced labor camp in Lemberg, "made advances" toward two Jewish prisoners but was rejected by both women. As a result, Heinen forced the women "to undress, lie on the floor, and spread their legs. He then shot into the genitalia of the first girl and killed her with a shot in the mouth" before repeating the process on the second victim.[125] In a related example, after being rebuffed in his sexual advances, a Gestapo man shot "a Russian, pretty as a picture . . . and then screwed her when she was dead."[126] In this case the invasion and control over the victim's body was exercised after her murder in the act of necrophilia.

The description of victims as "beautiful" women or "very pretty" girls appears in a number of testimonies and appears to have been used by the perpetrators as a further testament to their own masculine qualities and as a reflection of their ability to exert domination over the most desirable of women. The men of *Einsatzkommando* 11b imprisoned some fifteen "good looking" Jewish women in a building near their barracks; the men would force these women to undress and to take a bath in a nearby lake.[127] In an examination of a group of Jewish fighters who were under German guard at the *Umschlagplatz* (deportation site) during the Warsaw ghetto uprising in 1943, SS general Jürgen Stroop "picked out" a young, attractive Jewish woman and began asking her questions. Stroop then ordered the woman to undress in front of him before having her shot at the site.[128] Karl Schultz, a gendarme in Belorussia, "expressly reserved the right to shoot four 'ravishing teenage girls'" and waited to do so until the end of a massacre of some forty men, women, and children.[129]

Similarly, Auschwitz survivors testified on the actions of SS guard Otto Moll at the cremation pits. Mel Mermelstein, a prisoner, recalled how Moll selected twenty "beautiful" women from a newly arrived transport. He remarked, "He had them undress and stand naked facing him in a single row. He then shot all of them, one by one, in full view of witnesses."[130] In fact, Moll routinely engaged in a ritual of the sexual humiliation of his victims before he killed them. Filip Müller, a member of the *Sonderkommando*, also noted, "Moll had a morbid partiality for obscene and salacious tortures. Thus it was his wont to turn up in the crematorium when the victims were taking off their clothes." He continued, "Like a meat inspector he would stride about the changing room, selecting a couple of naked young women and hustling them to one of the pits. . . . In the end he shot them from behind so that they fell forward in the burning pit."[131] For Schultz and Moll, sexual titillation and murder were conjoined in an act where the sexual humiliation of the victim became a key element of the ritual of destruction.

Müller's description of Moll as "sexually excited" by the nakedness of his victims can also be found in the accounts of sexual aggression against males. At Dachau, SS men used eighteen-inch-long dried ox penises (pizzles) to flog prisoners, a device that at one and the same time symbolized the virility and hypermasculinity of the perpetrator and reinforced the submissiveness or femininity of the victims.[132] Heinz Heger, a concentration camp survivor, "witnessed innumerable ritual floggings" of male prisoners in several camps. Heger remembered, "The victim was tied to the notorious 'whipping post' in such a way as to make his buttocks arch upward above the rest of his body." Heger then described the reaction of the camp commandant supervising the flogging. "His eyes lit up with every stroke; after the first few his whole face was already red with lascivious excitement."[133] The ritualistic form of violence in this case was not only sexualized in nature but also embraced elements of male dominance. In fact, Heger identifies these floggings as "celebrations of torture," and he contends that he witnessed SS concentration camp commanders who masturbated on "more than thirty occasions" as male prisoners were being beaten on their bare buttocks.[134]

Sexual Torture

The targeting of male and female genitalia by the perpetrators appears to have been a routine practice at sites under SS control. In Płaszów, the SS man Franz Grün was notorious for his practice of kicking male prisoners in the groin, while at Auschwitz Oswald Kaduk waited for prisoners to exit the showers in order to stick his baton between their legs and strike their genitalia.[135] During the massacre at Kamenets-Podolskiy at the end of August 1941 in which over twenty-three thousand Jewish men, women, and children were murdered, one witness observed, "The butchers tried to hit the most sensitive places of their [the victims'] bodies."[136] In some cases, the perpetrators used objects such as sticks or truncheons to rape their victims.[137]

Another expression of a ritual of public humiliation by Germans and their auxiliaries involved forcing male and female prisoners to engage in intercourse for the amusement of the perpetrators. For example, male and female prisoners were taken to the guards' dining area and beaten with clubs during forced acts of copulation and then killed, with their bodies tossed out of a window to be collected the following day.[138] Another case highlights the perverse ideal of masculinity among some SS guards. Anton Streitwieser, described by one former prisoner as "often drunk" and "happy to kill," led a male prisoner incarcerated for homosexual activities to the camp bordello, where he forced the man to engage in sexual intercourse with a woman as Streitwieser beat him.[139] Public acts of sexual assault performed in front of prisoners as well as crimes of sexual violence, whether beatings of male or female genitalia or sexual mutilations involving cutting off female breasts, demonstrated not only the prisoner's lack of power but more importantly the perpetrators' sexual control and dominance over their victims.[140]

Sexual Violence as Public Spectacle

Among the perpetrators, rituals of humiliation and mass murder often occurred in broad daylight and in public spaces that allowed spectators to view or vicariously participate. Not surprisingly, alcohol consumption "generally played an important role in the abuse."[141] Acts of public humiliation and sexual violence extended to both women and men. Boris Glushkin, a Jew, was taken by SS men from his house in Krasny on August 8, 1941. The SS men beat him on the street and then threw him into a cellar. The next day, he was stripped naked and "tied to the tail of a horse and dragged off" to a public site for execution. At two o'clock the following morning, the SS men returned for his wife, whom they dragged out of her house before gang raping her in the front yard.[142] Sofia Ozerskaya, a teacher, recalled the ubiquity of such violence in the city of Minsk: "The drunken Nazi troops could open fire at random on the street without any rhyme or reason. . . . Day and night, fascist youths would burst into the apartments of the people of Minsk and rob, rape, and murder."[143]

Ozerskaya's testimony reflects the particularly horrendous fate that awaited many Jewish women in the Minsk ghetto. Lilya Gleizer, another witness to German atrocities in the city, remembered the events of a pogrom in July 1942. Gleizer stated, "Before the eyes of mothers who either fainted or went insane, the drunken Germans and [local] policemen raped young girls without a trace of shame either in front of each other or in front of onlookers." Not content with rape alone, "They took their knives and cut out sex organs, forced bodies, both dead and alive, into the most disgusting poses, and cut off noses, breasts, and ears."[144]

The use of public sites in Minsk for sexual violence, mutilation, and murder offers several important if appalling insights into the nature of such crimes. First, intoxication among the perpetrators points to preparatory drinking ritual in advance of the planned rapes. Second, the conduct of the assaults in public spaces and in front of family members, neighbors, and onlookers symbolized the perpetrators' domination over the victims, but also made the acts a violation of the individual and the community as a whole. Furthermore, the violation of daughters in front of their mothers and fathers, like the killing of children in front of their parents at execution sites, was intended to cause the maximum amount of mental and psychological trauma for the victims by attempting to destroy the fundamental ties of familial support and protection. Finally, the torture and mutilation of the victims not only demonstrated the essential dehumanization of the victims by the perpetrators, but also reflected the desire on the part of the killers to take grotesque trophies symbolizing their conquests.

Orgies of Celebration

Stanisław Szmajzner, a survivor of Sobibor, testified, "In the yard reserved for the Germans, a casino [club] was built for the officers. From now on they would eat and drink there, as well as entertain themselves. . . . Many a time they held real orgies there to celebrate the victories won by the German armies in the war. On these occasions they sang and drank until the early hours of the morning, and made terrible noise."[145] In a similar manner, the camp canteen at Ravensbrück became the site of "wild drinking evenings" (*wüste Saufabende*) involving "indecencies" against the female prisoner staff, and the scene of profligate sexual encounters between male and female SS personnel, including by one prisoner's account a female guard who lay on a table to copulate with a male counterpart during a drunken celebration.[146] Such alcohol-fueled orgies occurred among SS men at Auschwitz and Chełmno as well.[147] In the case of the latter, a teacher whose school was next to the SS commandant's quarters recalled how the SS men "engaged themselves in orgies with German girls and women on [a] daily basis." In the early mornings the SS men would "throw them out of the quarters . . . [where] they lay on the ground, drunk and naked."[148] The image of SS men preparing for another day of atrocity by throwing out their sexual conquests of the night before provides a perfect example of a hypermasculine mind-set in which women were simply disposable objects to be used and discarded in preparation for the next night's festivities. Indeed, such orgiastic excess was part of a celebratory ritual involving banquets or drunken revelry, a process that combined aspects of "alcohol, cruelty, rage, and possession."[149]

In some cases, alcohol served a celebratory function among the murderers either in the wake of mass killings or as part of a surreal sexualized courting ritual. Participation in mass killing as a means of seeking female approval or sexual gratification offers another insight into the method by which murder became an overt symbol of masculine prowess. One German policeman, after returning from a killing action, sought to impress a German secretary by showing her his bloodstained boots and uniform. These acts of performative masculinity also intersected with acts of sexual violence as exemplified by SS men who "often returned drunk from the *Aktion* and went to the [German] women's dormitory. . . . They dragged women from their rooms and, as another secretary put it delicately, 'sought our company.'"[150] In this last instance, the intoxication of power experienced by the killers over the victims, amplified by drinking, led to the desire to forcefully take the bodies of these female auxiliaries as a further affirmation of their toughness and masculinity.

Without doubt, alcohol consumption often played a prominent role in acts of subjugation committed by groups of men. In August 1941, Genia Demianova, a Russian schoolteacher, was interrogated by a German soldier who tortured, whipped, and brutally raped her. She remembered:

> There is a roar of cheering, the clinking of many glasses. The sergeant is standing in the open doorway: "The wild cat is tamed," he is saying. "Boys, she was a virgin. What do you say to that?"
>
> Another burst of cheering. . . . The others came in. Ten, a hundred, a thousand, one after another. The[y] flung themselves upon me, digging into my wounds while they defiled me.[151]

After the attacks ended, she lay naked and battered on the floor and heard "the sound of a sentimental Schumann song. . . . The sounds came from the next room where my executioners were singing."[152]

Again, Genia Demianova's terrible ordeal raises two important points. First, the German perpetrators not only engaged in rape to demonstrate their virility and power over a woman and a "racial inferior" but also used the act of rape as a mechanism for fraternal and male bonding in which they demonstrated their allegiance to the group.[153] Second, the act of toasting the initial rape, followed by the additional rapes, points to the use of alcohol in a celebratory fashion and was reflected in the conduct of "orgies" involving heavy drinking and unrestrained sexual activity on the part of the perpetrators.

In the East, physical conquest of territory, racial and gender-based concepts of superiority, and perceptions of male dominance combined with excessive alcohol consumption to create a mind-set among the perpetrators in which sexual aggression was either ignored or even encouraged as the right of the victor. These crimes were perpetrated by men who "frequently abused alcohol to excess and participated in depraved sexual acts outside the pale of acceptability in the West." For the political soldiers of the Third Reich, the military campaigns in the East offered the ultimate arena for displaying "masculine virtues like will, determination, and action" as part of an "active and aggressive concept of masculinity" in which geography itself was represented in the gendered space of the "manly battlefront" and the "womanly home front" (*weibliche Heimat*).[154] In this environment, physical and sexual violence against women and girls emerged as a fact of daily life in which male fellowship and self-conceptions of masculinity found expression in "gang rapes, torture, and drink" that often preceded the murder of the victims.[155]

5

CELEBRATING MURDER

For some perpetrators, killing in the East seemed to function in many cases as a "kind of entertainment" accompanied by a "carnivalesque atmosphere."[1] During the invasion of Poland, SS colonel Ludolf von Alvensleben expressed exactly this sentiment as he commanded ethnic German paramilitaries involved in the mass murder of Poles. In a report to Himmler on September 17, 1939, Alvensleben gushed, "As you can imagine, *Reichsführer*, the work is a huge joy."[2] The pleasure taken by some of the killers in their "work" also was apparent to Poles who witnessed the behavior of German forces during the invasion. Mieczysław Imala, a thirteen-year-old boy at the time of the German invasion, detailed how the SS brought groups of Poles "every several days" between nine and ten in the morning to a forest near Zakrzewo in 1939.[3] He could hear shooting and see the trucks piled with the victims' clothing and possessions leave the killing site in the afternoon. After the massacres, the trucks headed to a local restaurant, where the SS, SA, and policemen divided the plundered goods and engaged in drinking parties. Imala remembered "feasting Germans" enjoying vast quantities of schnapps, beer, and cigarettes as they celebrated their day's work. He then noted, "Every one of them was under the influence and a wedding atmosphere reigned" among the participants.[4]

These celebratory rituals continued into the invasion of the Soviet Union. Boris Grushevsky, a Belorussian, who witnessed a mass killing in Mir by German policemen and Belorussian auxiliaries in November 1941, also remarked that the killers "behaved as if they were at a wedding party."[5] The festive environment surrounding Nazi murder actions and the use of a "wedding metaphor" even entered into the Yiddish lexicon of *khurbn-shprakh* (destruction language), as "in the usage of *bal* (ball, festivity) as a synonym for *aktsye* [i.e., killing action], which specifically refers to the heavy intoxication of the perpetrators with alcohol."[6] The importance of the description of these killings by local inhabitants and Jews in terms of marriage celebrations cannot be overstated, as such celebrations would constitute perhaps the single most joyous event experienced in the daily lives of farmers and laborers from these small communities, replete with music and song and enormous quantities of food and drink. In this respect, their testimony vividly evokes the immense enjoyment taken by the perpetrators and the festive atmosphere that accompanied the murders.

The celebrations of mass murder at Zakrzewo and Mir were not isolated occurrences. Such festivities became a regular part of the German occupation in the East. In the spring of 1942, SS men ordered Leon Wells, a Jewish prisoner, to bury the victims of a just-completed massacre. On his arrival at the site, he observed, "A group of SS men were there, entertaining themselves with schnapps and music. Round about them lay a countless number of corpses."[7] In another example, SS and Ukrainian auxiliaries celebrated the murder of twelve hundred men, women, and children from the Zbaraż ghetto in April 1943 with "a whole-night orgy," a post-killing party subsidized by forced contributions from the ghetto's Jewish council.[8]

Whether at the killing site, the unit canteen, or in a local restaurant or bar, members of SS and the police gathered to drink and boast in the wake of their murderous exploits. One participant described these alcohol-fueled gatherings: "They [the killers] were then always very loud and described that they had once again executed Jews."[9] Wells depicted the SS as being "intoxicated" with the act of killing, while Auguste Drzonsgalla, a female prisoner in the "Gypsy" camp at Auschwitz, referred to such men as being "addicted" to violence.[10]

Violence, Alcohol, and SS Masculinity in the Concentration Camps

The incorporation of victory celebrations, especially in the wake of violence directed against putative political, social, or racial enemies, was a hallmark of SA and SS forces that predated the Nazi regime, as witnessed in killings of communists by drunken SA men celebrating the New Year in their Berlin SA pub in 1931.[11] Later, triumphant and violent rituals accompanied Nazi Party "holidays" from the start of the concentration camp system, whether during commemorations of the failed Beer Hall Putsch of November 9, 1923, or of Hitler's birthday on April 20. In the case of the latter, the SS promotions were scheduled to coincide with the führer's birthday, leading to a situation in which promotion parties associated with heavy drinking led to violence by SS men against prisoners, as was the case in Sachsenhausen on April 20, 1941, or for two drunken SS men who entered the Slonim ghetto the following year to terrorize the inhabitants.[12] Within the ranks of the SS and the police, celebratory rituals involving high levels of alcohol consumption facilitated brutal acts of humiliation, physical abuse, and murder throughout the Reich and the occupied territories.[13]

Like their erstwhile allies in the SA, early members of the SS, especially those serving in the concentration camps, exhibited the negative characteristics associated with drinking rituals and violence. With the creation of Dachau in March 1933, abusive behavior, ranging from the notorious "welcome beatings" inflicted on prominent newcomers, summary executions of those "shot while trying to escape," and on to quotidian acts of brutality, set the tone of the camp despite its ostensible rehabilitative function. Upon their assumption of control over the camp, the historian Timothy Ryback remarks, "the SS men exercised their newfound authority that evening with drink and gunfire," a jubilant ritual that linked alcohol and the specter of lethal violence.[14] The atrocious behavior of individual SS guards within the camp, such as Johann Unterhuber and Karl

Ehmann, was clearly in part due to their consumption of alcohol but also was consistent with a customary "violent SS ritual" for inflicting major bodily injury on the prisoners.[15] Harry Quindel, a former prisoner at the Fuhlsbüttel penitentiary in Hamburg, detailed the "kicks and punches" and the "especially popular blow to the neck" used by the SS guards during an hours-long torture session on his arrival in September 1933. Quindel also noted the literal and metaphorical intoxication of the guards who made nocturnal visits to his cell. He asserted, "Often the responsible SS men were totally drunk. . . . I had the feeling they experienced a [sense of] blood lust" as they abused their victims.[16] One army officer described an SS director of music "in a mad lust for blood" evidenced by the number of Jews he had killed, while another SS killer remarked, "If I would not see blood every day, I would be thirsty for it."[17] In these latter cases, the perpetrators appeared to have become intoxicated with the act of murder itself.

The violence inflicted on the prisoners, especially by new SS guards in the camps, was part of a rite of initiation and a public manifestation of one's toughness and masculinity in front of one's SS comrades. While alcohol consumption was not a prerequisite for such abuse, drinking by the guards often prepared for, accompanied, and facilitated these acts. In the case of Unterhuber, his imbibing resulted in "set-piece beatings and drunken night-time chicanery." For his part, Ehmann became "notorious in the city for binge-drinking and wife-beating." Ehmann's brutality within the camp was an extension of his earlier violent behavior, including a failed drunken assassination attempt against a local Communist Party functionary in August 1932.[18] Likewise, his wife-beating was only one extreme manifestation of the underlying misogyny associated with the Nazi hypermasculine ideal and an extension of the movement's "contempt for women."[19]

Without doubt, readiness for physical violence and a willingness to engage in brutality characterized these men and their behavior within the camps. SS guards strove to maintain "[Theodor] Eicke's tradition of handling prisoners," competing to "outdo one another" as an expression of masculinity in a community based on a "shared practice of abuse."[20] The failure to engage in such behavior left one open to derision and the feminized epithets of being a "weakling," "sissy," or the revelatory sobriquet of "limp dick"—terms serving as a ready foil for the SS masculine ideal.[21]

Importantly, SS and policemen who refused to murder or attempted to avoid shooting during the war couched their opposition in terms of their own weakness rather than on moral grounds.[22] In this sense, killing became a direct reflection of male toughness and masculinity. These expectations help explain the attitude of one SS guard at the Janowska camp who allowed prisoners certain freedoms when alone with them but warned, "If the *Untersturmführer* [SS lieutenant] was here, you can bet your life that I would have struck you down on the spot!"[23] In this case, he chose to adapt his behavior to group norms when among his peers, just one reflection of the powerful influence of organizational expectations on individual behavior within the SS.

Modeling Masculine Behavior

The pressure to appear tough was not confined simply to the lower ranks. In fact, the officers and senior enlisted members of these units felt compelled to model desired behaviors and to demonstrate their own mettle. One Gestapo agent in the Polish city of Tarnów used mass killings as a type of manhood ritual for his own son by bringing the seventeen-year-old along in order to "teach him how to shoot the Jewish captives."[24] The head of *Sonderkommando* 11b, Bruno Müller, a "brutal man and a heavy drinker . . . insisted on giving the NCOs [higher-ranking enlisted men] an example of what the leadership expected" by executing an infant and then the mother, an act of performative masculinity and extreme cruelty that demonstrated the perpetrator's absolute power and inflicted the maximum trauma on the female victim.[25] In a similar horrific expression of the Black Corps' standard of toughness, one SS man exclaimed, "[One] must be capable of slitting the throat of a 4-year old child without batting an eyelid. . . . When he can't do that, he's not an SS man."[26] Others recalled the need for "tough but necessary measures in an ideological battle" and the "nerves of steel" needed to carry out this kind of "dirty work."[27] Such views represented the ideal for SS men in the field and at the camps, whether alone or in a group, as one who took pride in his "hardness" and ability to stand in the front ranks of the Nazi genocidal project.

For the victims of SS brutality, hardness and toughness were the expectation and compassion a virtue absent in their captors. Leon Wells lamented, "Their [the SS men's] pleasure in inflicting suffering on us was inexhaustible."[28] Similarly, Eugen Kogon, a former political prisoner at

Buchenwald, described SS block leaders, men ranging in rank from corporal to technical sergeant, as "hardened bullies and brutes." He also remarked on their habit of conducting "nocturnal invasions" when drunk, involving visits to the barracks that resulted in the "merciless punishment" of prisoners for infractions of camp rules, such as beatings for wearing underwear or socks to bed.[29] These drunken nighttime punitive forays were rituals of recreational violence that continued during the war, a clear example of the way in which training received in Eicke's "Dachau school" spread across the camps into the occupied East.[30]

SS Comradeship and Celebratory Ritual in the Camps

Within the camps, fellowship evenings, featuring alcohol, song, and performative acts of male dominance, constituted a customary celebratory ritual for the perpetrators. One survivor of Buchenwald remarked on the introduction of these events at the camp: "A special chapter was the social evenings of the SS, which started at Buchenwald with a magnificent open-air celebration in 1938." He recalled, "They were eating and drinking sprees that almost invariably ended in wild orgies."[31] As previously noted, the SS camp canteen became a site of revelry and camaraderie, especially for single men; alcohol was available every day at lunch and until late at night. In Sachsenhausen, fellowship evenings constituted an important ritual for washing away "grisly experiences" in a flood of free beer and schnapps, along with fried schnitzel and potatoes.[32] Camp canteens at the killing centers at Belzec, Sobibor, and Treblinka also were sites of bacchanalian excess involving alcohol, music, and sexual coercion. At Belzec, "crates of wine and schnapps were delivered daily," and fellowship evenings there devolved into "drunken parties" as a regular feature of SS life. Rudolf Reder, a prisoner, recalled that every Sunday evening the SS ordered the camp orchestra to play for their entertainment as the guards "gorged themselves" and "threw scraps of leftovers to the musicians."[33] In this case, Sunday, a traditional day of rest and religious ceremony, experienced a transformation into a ritualistic SS celebration of the previous week's killings and a preparation for the next.

The inclusion of the prisoner musicians and the public nature of such rituals within or near the camp complex offer clear examples of the way in which the perpetrators remade these spaces into festive sites. Such activities also demonstrate the manner in which alcohol was incorporated into orgiastic excess, whether of a sexual or murderous nature. Additionally, the culinary and sexualized extravagance of such celebrations, especially within sight of the prisoners, served as a further symbol of the ritualistic dehumanization and emasculation of the camp's inmates. In this sense, the throwing of scraps of food to the musicians, as one might do with a pet, exemplified the dehumanization of the prisoners by their SS "masters."

One celebration in Auschwitz dramatized the SS appropriation of the camps' killing spaces. Filip Müller, a Jewish member of the *Sonderkommando* tasked with the cremation of those killed in the gas chambers, recalled the SS promotion party of Johann Gorges to the rank of sergeant. The party itself was less significant than its location. The event was held in the senior SS guard's office, a room separated from the cremation chamber by a single door. Furthermore, while the festivities were in "full swing," hundreds of bodies awaiting cremation lay literally within feet of the drunken revelers.[34] Müller described an office table spread with "delicacies from all over the world" and ample amounts of Polish vodka and cigarettes for the celebrants. He recalled, "They [the SS men] sat round the table eating and drinking. One of them had brought his accordion and was playing folk and pop songs with the others joining in."[35] The party ended around midnight as the drunken guests left the building. In this case, drinking ritual and celebration in a location of mass murder served to normalize the killing space, to cement male camaraderie, and to bind the perpetrators in a shared sense of purpose at the site of extreme transgressive violence. Selections on the ramp at Auschwitz offer another example involving the combination of alcohol, mass murder, and celebratory ritual. One SS doctor recalled, "[The drinking] was during the selection. . . . A certain number of bottles were provided for each selection and everybody drank and toasted the others." He also noted of the drinking and toasting, "One could not stay out of it."[36] Once again, the requirement for *everyone* to participate in the celebratory act of toasting mass murder publicly bound the perpetrators together in the process of genocide.

Heavy drinking also occurred at gatherings marking the winter solstice or *Julfest*, an SS celebration with a detailed and standardized liturgy, including poems, readings, and ceremonial activities.[37] At Auschwitz in 1941, the SS commandant invited civilians from the I. G. Farben company to

Members of Police Battalion 101 celebrating Christmas in Łódź, Poland, in 1940. This picture conveys the sense of group camaraderie that was incorporated into fellowship evenings throughout the SS and police forces in the East.

Two members of Police Battalion 101 in Łódź, Poland, who appear to be involved in a drinking game. Drinking games and the ability to hold one's liquor without showing visible effects of impairment constituted one key marker of masculinity within the SS and police complex.

Member of Police Battalion 101 being lifted up by a comrade. The incorporation of drinking into celebratory rituals to commemorate unit activities was a key element in establishing shared group identity and consensus for their actions among the perpetrators.

Group photo of members of Police Battalion 101 in which some appear to be singing as one policeman plays a violin. Music and singing became important elements in celebratory ritual for SS and police forces in the East. While such celebrations were largely male-only affairs, a woman has been allowed to join the group and is standing in the middle of the last row.

Members of Police Battalion 101 integrated a skit depicting a policeman dressed as a Jewish smuggler during their 1940 Christmas celebration in Łódź, Poland. At the time of the party, the policemen had spent a month guarding the city's Jewish ghetto, duty that included the shooting of Jews who were involved in smuggling or who came too close to the wire surrounding the ghetto. This picture epitomizes an act of ritual humiliation and the amusement taken by the perpetrators as they celebrated their duties involving the persecution and killing of Polish Jews.

participate in the event. In a company report, these representatives described the "party" with the SS men as "very festive" and "alcoholically gay."[38] Indeed, the acquisition and distribution of massive amounts of alcohol among SS and policemen at these celebrations appear incredible, based on the growing scarcity of such luxury products within the Reich proper.[39] As late as December 1944, the quartermaster for the Higher SS and Police Leader (West) procured sixty-five hundred bottles of wine and three hundred thousand cigarettes for SS and police celebrations of the winter solstice in his area alone.[40] At Wewelsburg castle, Himmler sought to re-create his version of an Arthurian roundtable for the highest ranks of the SS with meetings, rituals, and celebrations and a cellar stocked with forty thousand bottles of liquor, wine, and champagne.[41] It is important to note that such celebrations emphasized the masculine ideals of "camaraderie and martial comradeship" and bound these men in a fraternity with a shared racial mission.[42] Indeed, one of the purposes of senior SS officers drinking with their subordinates was the creation of a "comradely tone between them," an attitude not possible between the senior and lower ranks during normal duty hours.[43]

In January 1942, Himmler discussed the "hard duty" of men tasked with the "elimination in its most drastic form of the enemies of the German people." He noted that men facing such duties were at risk of "damaging their character" and becoming "brutalized." His solution to this threat called for maintaining "strict discipline" within the ranks and conducting "comradely gatherings" with food, music, and alcohol on the evenings following mass-killing actions. He warned, however, that such gatherings must "never end with alcohol abuse" among the participants.[44] In the East, however, fellowship evenings often involved heavy drinking and raucous revelry. In fact, one Nazi district leader complained about the "binge drinking" and "dancing" at these functions.[45] As events in the camps, the ghettos, and the killing fields demonstrate, Himmler's repeated exhortations on the moderate use of alcohol, whether meant as a general admonition or a strict injunction, repeatedly fell on deaf ears throughout his black and green legions.

Holiday Celebrations and Murder

One of the most revealing aspects of SS behavior with respect to the role of alcohol, celebration, and murder was evident in the actions of these units on holidays, both secular and religious. In the case of the former, Sofia

Ozerskaya testified about a mass execution of Jews conducted by German SS and policemen in Minsk on November 7, 1941, the anniversary of the Russian Revolution. She remembered that days prior to the killings, the Germans had used dynamite to create a number of long trenches at the cemetery. On the day of the massacre, she and a number of other spectators followed German trucks filled with Jews from the city's ghetto "right up to the place of slaughter."[46] Once again, the timing and location of the executions offered a public spectacle demonstrating German control and emphasizing the loss of Soviet authority. Reflecting on the style of German rule in Minsk, Ozerskaya stated, "At any moment, the drunken Nazi troops could open fire at random on the street without rhyme or reason, killing anyone at hand, without regard to sex, age, or nationality."[47] In this sense, the behavior of the killers reflected the metaphorical and literal intoxication experienced by the conquerors in their rule of the occupied territories.

Jewish holidays and "Jewish feasts" also became opportunities for the SS to demonstrate their sadistic humor with "tasteless jokes" and mass killings.[48] At Dachau, during Yom Kippur in 1937, "friendly" SS guards promised "reconciliation" with the camp's Jewish prisoners before herding them off to hard labor in a cold, driving rain. During the work shift, an SS guard sought to disorient one prisoner by ordering him to dance and twirl as he waited to shoot him if he crossed the boundary line, a situation the guard hoped to instigate by demanding that the prisoner spin faster.[49] But it was not simply Jews who were brutalized on holidays. On Sundays, during the open-air Catholic service within the camp, SS guards at Dachau regularly held their own celebration that included abusing prisoners near the Mass site, with the screams of the victims intended to disturb the liturgy. One prisoner bitterly recalled, "The Death's Head, or SS, named by many as Satan's sons, normally young men between 18 and 25, celebrated once more a beautiful, victorious Sunday."[50]

SS and police personnel also undertook holiday killings outside the camps, as was the case for the members of *Einsatzgruppe* D who murdered some ten thousand Jews in a "Christmas massacre" at Simferopol in 1941. Despite a long day of murder, these men still celebrated the holiday with food and drink and listened to the "pastoral" message of their commander, SS general Otto Ohlendorf.[51] Likewise, a group of policemen from PB 101 stationed in Łódź and charged with guarding the city's ghetto partied on drunkenly through the night of December 31, 1940, and then decided to ring in the New Year by killing a Pole. Whether owing to their state of intoxication or simply by mistake, the men shot and killed an ethnic German instead, and then "covered it up by switching the victim's identity card."[52] Similarly, SS guards at the Pawiak prison in Warsaw "gaily" welcomed in the New Year in 1943; as Mary Berg recalled, "I heard the sound of shots, followed again by laughter and . . . roaring drunken voices."[53] As these examples demonstrate, celebratory ritual could serve as either a culmination or a prelude to murder.

Celebrations that led to additional killing not only demonstrate the role of alcohol as a facilitator of atrocity but also provide an important insight into the mentality of the perpetrators. The existence of a dynamic in which group revelry catalyzed additional killing highlights the communal pride expressed in murder. For example, a Jewish survivor of the Międzyrzec ghetto recalled how drunken Gestapo men came into the ghetto on New Year's Eve 1942: "They invaded the ghetto and embarked upon a so-called 'killing spree.' They went from house to house shooting people as they lay in their beds. These Gestapo men killed lots of people 'as a sport.'"[54] Significantly, these acts of murder facilitated by drinking bouts continued until the last days of the war. In April 1945, Franz Ziereis, the commandant of the Mauthausen camp, spent a booze-filled night with the Nazi district leader, August Eigruber, before the two men went into the camp at 4:00 a.m. to execute twelve prisoners, including five Poles, two Britons, two Germans, one Belgian, one Czech, and one Russian.[55]

"Doing Shots" at the Grave

The common practice of consuming alcohol at the killing sites offers one of the best-known examples of the integration of drinking into the ritual of murder. For example, alcohol rations were distributed to SS men in *Einsatzkommando 2* on the night prior to planned executions in the form of a bottle of vodka, which could be consumed at the discretion of the perpetrator, before, during, or after the killings.[56] While some of the killers drank to the point of intoxication, there are also numerous examples in which alcohol was used in an almost clinical fashion. In 1941, a young Ukrainian girl and her sister watched as trucks carrying groups of fifty

Jews began arriving at a murder site near the village of Senkivishka. The Jews, mostly women and children, were beaten and marched to a large ditch and then forced to undress. At the ditch, a lone German policeman "advanced, upright . . . pistol in hand, and murdered each Jew, one after the other with a bullet in the back of the neck." Dressed in a white smock, the policeman took breaks at regular intervals, during which he drank "a small glass of liquor" before returning to the ditch to kill another group. Over the course of an entire day, this policeman single-handedly murdered the town's entire Jewish population.[57] In another case, Leah Bodkier witnessed a daylong massacre in the Sosenki Forest near Rovno in November 1941 and detailed how a German killer "would walk up to a table, drink a class [sic] of vodka, snack on a sandwich with sausage, and then continue his vile work anew."[58]

The deliberate and measured use of alcohol in these cases is in fact not remarkable and is apparent in the actions of Felix Landau, a member of the Security Police, who joined an *Einsatzkommando* at the start of the campaign into Russia. In his diary, Landau provides another example of a seemingly stone-cold sober killer. Despite his clear faith in National Socialism, Landau mocked some of his unit's young officers as "megalomaniacs" based on their careerist ambitions and overt enthusiasm for murder. For his part, he recorded that he had "little desire to shoot unarmed people—even if they are only Jews."[59] Despite these reservations, Landau was prepared to join in cold-blooded murder if ordered. In fact, the source of his greatest psychological torment did not result from his duties, but rather from the unrequited affection for his "little Trudy," a torment that left his "soul broken."[60]

As his unit moved eastward, Landau and his SS comrades enjoyed a fellowship evening the night before a planned "special mission" in the Polish town of Drohobycz on July 7, 1941, with some of the men drinking and celebrating until 6:30 a.m. the next day. Over the course of the next week, Landau split his time between acting as a "General of the Jews" by supervising Jewish work details, participating in killing actions, and attending fellowship evenings while anxiously awaiting word from his "little Trudy." He spent the evening of July 9 with his comrades downing ten liters of beer, several glasses of schnapps, and a liter of red wine in an effort to "forget his [relationship] worries for a moment," a failed effort that left him with a terrific hangover the following day.[61]

On July 11, Landau had to "work" through the night shooting Jews and Ukrainians. Nevertheless, he and a colleague still managed to find time between the killings to grab a snack of sour milk and new potatoes, while his "thoughts remained" with his Trudy.[62] Early the following morning, he was back at work executing twenty-three men and women. Subsequently, Landau recorded, "Strange, *I am completely unmoved. No pity, nothing.*" Moreover, he took time to reflect on the technical aspects of the killings. "The shots were fired and the brains whizzed through the air. Two in the head is too much. They almost tear the head off."[63] Throughout his diary, he describes mass murder as his "work," including a one-sentence entry for July 17: "Nothing much happened. I messed around with the Jews some more and that's my work."[64] While several of his colleagues spent their free time hunting for game instead of humans, Landau's duties as the "General of the Jews" kept him busy, a task that included the approval of his request to have twenty Jewish workers executed for refusing to work. Likewise, he found time to record a joke about a "little [case of] special handling" (*kleine Sonderbehandlung*) in which he fractured the skull of a Ukrainian, causing the victim's blood to spray throughout his barrack's room.[65]

Landau's diary offers a number of insights into the killing ritual from the perspective of a lower-level SS functionary. First, the entries provide a view of the normalization of murder and the daily routine of the killers in the first weeks of the invasion of the Soviet Union, a routine that included acts of killing and rituals of communal drinking and celebration. Second, Landau's words offer a frank assessment of his state of mind and, more importantly, his attitude concerning the killing process, characterized by stoic compliance, an absence of pity, and a dark sense of humor. Finally, and perhaps most interestingly, mass murder was simply a form of "work" in which reflections on the technical efficiency of murder could be combined with a comment on taking a hurried dinner of sour milk and potatoes in the midst of an all-night killing operation.

Eating among the Dead

One of the most striking aspects of the ritual of mass murder by SS and policemen in the East involves the presence of tables laden with food and alcohol at the killing sites. Indeed, the very act of eating at a murder scene in which one has witnessed the horrific and grisly deaths of men, women, and children seems incomprehensible. In postwar testimony, one former policeman described his own astonishment at hearing about a colleague who took a break during a massacre by sitting on the naked corpse of a Jewish woman in order to eat a sandwich.[66]

In some respects, the incorporation of eating, even more so than drinking, demonstrates the normalization of the killing process among the killers, a point underlined by the normal reaction of one civilian witness who was forced to visit an execution site and could not eat for two days after. When asked by his sister why he was not eating, he replied, "If you would see it [the execution site], you would not eat for the whole month."[67] In contrast, a policeman charged with cordon duty during the killing of eighteen thousand prisoners in Majdanek on November 3, 1941, recalled taking a lunch break to eat his rations.[68] A female prisoner at Ravensbrück described the "preparations" of one SS execution squad as "especially horrible" based on the men's consumption of a "huge schnitzel, wine, schnapps, and cigarettes" prior to the murder of a group of Polish female prisoners.[69] In another example, Marija Todorović, a cook for a group of Gestapo men in the Yugoslavian town of Niš, detailed the abundant use of alcohol by the killers. In particular, she recalled the Gestapo officer Albert Freisdorf as a regular participant in executions. She stated, "There were many other small and large shootings . . . I remeber [*sic*], on many occasions after supper and heavy drinking his [Freisdorf] saying 'Now we are going for a little stabbing.'"[70] If eating prior to murder was a common practice for some killers and a normal routine for the men of the *Einsatzgruppen*, even the latter occasionally drew a line. In a letter to his wife and children, Karl Kretschmer revealed, "One can get used to seeing blood, only blood sausage is not popular among us."[71]

A Ukrainian boy, Andreï from Rokytne, remembered one SS man by his simple act of taking refreshment at the killing site. During the liquidation of the village's Jewish ghetto in 1942, Andreï recalled how an SS man shot more than seven hundred Jews over the course of the day from a distance of about a meter away, "just far enough to avoid the blood splatter." With magazines of bullets in his pocket, the killer methodically murdered groups of Jews as he moved alongside the ditch. Midway through the shootings, he took a break due to a "sore trigger finger" in order to drink some buttermilk purchased from a farmer in a nearby house. Andreï explained, "He was thirsty because he'd been shooting so long without a break." He continued, "He drank a whole bottle in one gulp and then he took two deutsche marks from his pocket to pay the villager." After this break, the killer returned to his task and executed the remaining Jews "before he climbed into the truck and went back to Kovel."[72] For Andreï, the end of the killings left him with the job of filling in the mass grave, a scene he described as "a bloodbath, the smell was unbearable. . . . The odor was nauseating so the German came to give me a cigarette."[73]

Andreï's description with all its horrific implications offers a key but often unremarked detail related to the killings. "Murder has a particular smell," and its "nauseating odor" is an important and often overlooked part in the massacres.[74] In the 2012 critically acclaimed film *The Act of Killing*, one of the perpetrators of mass murder in Indonesia after the country's military coup in 1965 described the process of killing groups of suspected communists. While demonstrating the procedure to the film team on a rooftop patio, the site of the murders, he boasted about his improvement to the process, since the initial killing method created so much blood that "it smelled awful."[75] Similarly, Josef Blösche, an SS man, admitted during postwar testimony that "the sweat and blood smell" at mass execution sites was so overpowering that he reached for the bottle to deal with it.[76] In a related example, a group of Waffen-SS men justified their heavy drinking in the suppression of the Warsaw ghetto uprising based on "the nerve-wracking conditions and the constant stench of the corpses."[77] Likewise, a Polish railway worker living near Treblinka remarked on the "awful odour" emanating from the camp and the "stench [that] made eating impossible" for those living in the vicinity.[78] The odor of blood and death, especially at the shooting sites, while underappreciated, highlights a physiological obstacle that the perpetrators needed to overcome before consuming food at these locations. It also provides an added perspective for evaluating the perpetrators' mind-set and for thinking about their practice of bringing food to, and eating at, the murder sites.

Murder Feasts

The integration of alcohol, food, and in some cases music at the killing sites evokes a festive atmosphere that seems unimaginable; nevertheless, there are numerous examples of the refashioning of the killing grounds as sites of entertainment. Izaak Izrael, a horse cart driver from Tarnów, described a mass killing of Jews classified as unfit for work. From his house near the cemetery, he listened as shots rang out throughout the day. The number of Jews was so great that electric lights were set up in the cemetery to allow the killing to continue after dark. In order to see what was happening, Izaak crept into the attic and removed several roof tiles. He later testified, "They worked in the cemetery throughout the night. . . . They transported vodka, kielbasa [sausages], cigarettes, from the *Judenrat* to the cemetery all night long and the Schupo [uniformed policemen] ate and drank while they were shooting and burying [their victims]." He also remarked on the actions of one "drunk SS-man" who entertained himself by making Jews perform exercises and ordering them to climb on gravestones and up trees before he shot them.[79] Another witness described a similar scene with a killing site "brightly lit up with bonfires" and "sumptuously set tables" replete with food and alcohol.[80]

The historian Alon Confino depicted a similar mass killing in the town of Stanisławów in southern Galicia on October 12, 1941, in which "murder mixed with drinking and eating in a tableau dominated by mockery."[81] Led by the local commander of the Security Police, Hans Krüger, SS and policemen murdered between ten and twelve thousand Jews in the town's cemetery. As in Tarnów, food and alcoholic refreshments were set up at the killing site, and Krüger circulated among the men throughout the day, offering salami sandwiches and schnapps to the killers. The presence of food, like the inclusion of acts of humiliation at the murder sites, provides unmistakable insight into how the perpetrators orchestrated and normalized participation in mass murder. It is in this sense that a remark by the police sergeant Helmuth Schmidt, the "Terror of Lemberg," that he "could shoot a Jew in the head while eating a sandwich" seems explicable.[82] This process also explains the ability of Felix Landau to take a break with a comrade from a mass shooting in order to grab a serving of sour milk and new potatoes.[83] If eating and snacking were possible during the killing, then it should come as little surprise that a group of German gendarmes who traveled to the Polish village of Gniewczyna, after some villagers had captured a group of sixteen Jewish men, women, and children, prefaced their killings with a meal. Upon their arrival at the village, these gendarmes first "were given a good meal [presumably with alcohol]. Then they took the Jews into the courtyard and ordered them one by one to lie face down on the ground. All of them, beginning with the small children, were shot dead."[84] In this case, a hearty lunch and jovial conversation provided a normal preamble to the murder of children, women, and men.

In truth, mass murder was by its very nature a communal event. Whether conducting selections, escorting Jews to the killing sites, guarding the cordon line, or pulling the trigger, SS and policemen participated as a group in the conduct of genocide. It is therefore not surprising that individuals who failed to participate in these celebratory events, including the refusal to drink with their comrades, found themselves subject to verbal ridicule or threatened with physical abuse and social ostracism.[85] In fact, voluntary absence was viewed as "antisocial and above all as separation" from one's comrades and the unit's mission.[86] In this respect, graveside gatherings to eat and drink during the executions or post-killing banquets acted to normalize these acts and to serve as a ritual for binding men in common cause. Similarly, the celebratory nature of such rites with alcohol, music, singing, and laughter, along with the boasting of the perpetrators, reflected the men's "toughness" and symbolized their own conception of masculinity.

The Laughter of the Killers

A number of witnesses reference the "laughter" of the perpetrators during acts of physical abuse and murder. A prisoner at Auschwitz recalled how a group of Jewish boys were taken to be gassed on the Jewish New Year in 1944. He remembered how the boys called out for their mothers as they were loaded onto a truck and how the SS men laughed in response to their cries.[87] In some trophy photos, one can see the perpetrators' faces frozen in mirth as they engage in acts of humiliation and brutality. The presence of laughter serves as another trenchant indicator of the mind-set of those involved in the killing. Leah Bodkier, a witness to the killings in the Sosenki Forest on November 7, 1941, described the cooperation of SS and police auxiliaries in the preparation for mass murder, including the marching of the "stark naked" Jews to the execution pits. Bodkier observed, "Every [executioner] practiced his own special type of murder: some lined their victims up along the edge of the pit facing forward. . . . Others stood their victims on their knees in front of the pit, while others forced their victims to run toward the pit and shot them as they approached the edge, and so on." She continued, "Some threw young children alive into the pits, while others hurled them into the air and shot them in flight." "All of this was accompanied by deathly groans and screams of the dying, and by the laughter of the executioners," she concluded.[88] During a postwar interrogation by Soviet authorities, Boris Drachenfels, a former member of Police Battalion 320, testified about the same massacre in the Sosenki Forest. "Adults were forced to lie down in the ditches and were shot, while children were torn away from their mothers and shot. Most of the shooters were drunk. . . . People begged for mercy, mothers begged us to spare their children."[89]

Taken together, the testimonies on the same event by Bodkier and Drachenfels offer a number of important observations and insights into the ritual of mass murder. First, Drachenfels noted the widespread use of alcohol among the killers at the site, a point not mentioned by Bodkier. Second, Bodkier's testimony demonstrates the degree of individual choice among the perpetrators concerning the exact method of killing, as well as the "creativity" displayed by some. Both recalled the murder of the children, with some of the perpetrators creating a "shooting game" by using children as flying targets, a practice mentioned in numerous survivor testimonies. Third, the behavior of some policemen in literally tearing children from their mothers' arms offers an indication of their malice and the intent to torment the parents. Finally, Bodkier recalled the laughter of the executioners as they set about their task, and Drachenfels remembered the "begging" and "pleas" of the mothers to spare their children. In this regard, it is reasonable to assume that some of the killers chose to laugh at the abasement of these naked women and as a means of further demeaning their victims before pulling their triggers.

Calel Perechodnik, a member of the Jewish police (*Ordnungsdienst*) at the labor camp in the Polish town of Legionów, documented the killing of approximately eighty Jews, mostly women and children, conducted by German policemen. In his journal, he described the entire killing ritual that began with the arrival of ten policemen who were "so drunk they could hardly stand on their feet." At first, the Germans ordered ten prisoners to take shovels and dig a grave, an operation supervised by the Jewish police. The victims were then brought to the execution site, forced to undress, and ordered to lie down. Perechodnik recalled, "The Germans begin the executions. Too drunk to shoot the rifles in rounds, they use pistols." He continued, "Often the victims are wounded, but they don't kill them right away. As the gendarmes *laugh*, they also kill the worker busy throwing the corpses into the pit, another one is shot with a bullet in the buttocks. Finally, they order the pit to be filled."[90] After the pit was filled, the policemen gathered the possessions of the murdered Jews and left, apparently to continue their drunken revelry in the barracks. While the German policemen celebrated their acts with laughter and alcohol, the Jewish policemen attempted to forget their role in the murders with vodka.[91]

"Prussian Humor"?

Rudolf Vrba, a survivor of Auschwitz, described the presence of a twisted sense of humor among the SS, something he labeled "Prussian humor." One example involved SS men stationed on the selection ramp who during a "slow" day greeted arrivals by saying "how nice that you arrived. We are so sorry that it wasn't too convenient, but now things will be different," before leading them to the gas chambers.[92] The Russian military journalist Vasily Grossman also referred to "unsubtle German humor" by noting "hardly anyone on this planet could have imagined what the SS humour in Treblinka was like, what the SS amused themselves with, and what jokes were made."[93] Similarly, the Russian propagandist Ilya Ehrenburg wrote about the sadistic amusements of the SS guards at Sobibor, including an SS man who gave candy to naked children before they entered the gas chamber with the cynical remark, "'Eat it and grow bigger'" as he "roared with laughter."[94] In a similar example, a group of drunken killers, after murdering children, stood along the edge of an open grave and "laughed" as they threw candy into the pit while the parents were forced to look on.[95] The staging of executions as a type of cruel joke offers an insight not only into the mind-set of the killers, but also as to how they attempted to amuse and impress one another. This dark humor was evident in the jokes SS men made among themselves. At Chełmno, the German gendarmes responsible for guarding the murder site routinely joked, "One day, one thousand" in reference to the daily number of victims. Likewise, the Nazi Party county leader (*Kreisleiter*) for the area, upon passing the Chełmno cremation site, quipped to the local forestry administrator, "Soon your trees will grow better. . . . Jews make good fertilizer."[96]

In addition to verbal jesting and mockery, the perpetrators incorporated physical abuse into acts of cruel humor. For example, an SS detachment from the German town of Heydekrug crossed into the Lithuanian town of Sveksna on June 27, 1941, in the wake of the invasion of the Soviet Union. The SS men amused themselves by shaving off half the beards or cutting off one earlock of Jewish men and later that night staging a mock execution of the town's rabbi.[97] In another case, an SS killer approached a girl in a group of Jewish women awaiting execution in the Ponary Forest by asking, "Look the moon is beautiful, and you, you are young and beautiful. Don't you want to live?" The SS man, the commander of the local Gestapo, then told her to simply walk away, but not to look back. As the girl slowly moved away, the Gestapo man pulled out his revolver and shot her in the back as "the Lithuanians [i.e., auxiliaries] burst out laughing."[98] One uniformed policeman testified to the "sadistic joy" displayed by a senior enlisted policeman during prisoner interrogations. The policeman would have prisoners' arms bent backward before firing a pistol at the victim's elbow that resulted in a bullet traveling along the upper arm to the shoulder of the victim.[99] In Rawa Ruska, Ida Steiner recalled how SS sergeant Helmut Späth, a man notorious for his daily killings, would "laugh" and tell the prisoners that "he felt no guilt since the Jews came to him themselves," or he would quip, "Give me a cat or a Jew today."[100] One Jewish prisoner recalled a German official's visit to the grave site at Chełmno: "He [the official] examined the corpses, talked to SS-officers and laughed."[101]

In at least one case, two German youths adopted the malicious behaviors modeled by their elders. Jan Karski, a member of the Polish underground, secretly entered the Warsaw ghetto in late 1942 and witnessed the deprivation and brutality faced by the Jewish population. He also observed two young boys from the Hitler Youth walking down a deserted street in the ghetto as they "chattered, laughed, pushed each other in spasms of merriment." The boys' purpose for being there soon became apparent as one pulled a revolver from his pocket. Karski commented, "He was looking for a target with the casual, gay absorption of a boy at a carnival."[102] Karski watched as the boy took aim at a window and fired a shot, followed by "the terrible cry of a man in agony." The boys "shouted with joy" and then "linked their arms and walked off grace-fully toward the exit of the ghetto, chatting cheerfully as if they were returning from a sporting event."[103]

The perpetrators' sense of amusement in the act of killing continued into the last days of the Third Reich. Michael Kraus, a survivor of a death march from Auschwitz, remembered how an SS guard ordered one prisoner to "run ahead only so that he could shoot him from the back." He then remarked, "Our 'supervisors' amused themselves with these and similar occupations!"[104] Likewise, Alfons Heck, a senior Hitler Youth leader, recalled a SS man using "shot while trying to escape" as the punch line for a joke involving the killing of a prisoner who lay sprawled in a ditch during a death march as the German western front collapsed.[105] The use of dark humor and the incorporation of murderous amusements into the act of killing, especially late in the war, once again point to the degree to which brutality and murder had been normalized among the perpetrators.

Post-murder Banquets

Celebratory banquets also took place in the wake of large-scale killing actions such as the notorious massacre at Babi Yar near Kiev in Sep-tember 1941 and after a liquidation in the Slonim ghetto in November 1941. At Babi Yar, SS and policemen murdered almost thirty-four thou-sand Jews in a two-day killing operation. The members of PB 303 not only received extra alcohol rations for their participation, but these po-licemen also attended a banquet hosted by SS general Friedrich Jeckeln, who gave a speech in which he emphasized the "necessity of the execu-tion of the Jews."[106] Alfred Metzner participated in the mass execution of Jews from the Slonim ghetto.[107] He recalled that "the troops were well supplied with schnapps and cigarettes to ensure an orderly conduct of the task."[108] After the conclusion of the day's massacre, the district com-missar, Gerhard Erren, held a debriefing with the killers during which he "praised many men and reprimanded the *weak* who were told to do better in the future. . . . After the debriefing, they drank and celebrated. The total dead for the day was between four and eight thousand Jews, including men, women, and children."[109] Over the course of the next seven months, these men continued their murderous rampage with "lots of schnapps" to "stimulate their work zeal."[110]

In his postwar testimony, Metzner detailed the "final solution to the Jewish problem" in Slonim, including the liquidation of the ghetto and the murder of as many as ten thousand men, women, and children. The ordeal for the ghetto inhabitants began on the night before the planned massacre, as German and auxiliary policemen entered the ghetto and sexually assaulted Jewish women, with some of the men "boasting" of the number of women they had "used in this way trying to outdo" their colleagues.[111] The major killing began at four the following morning as the policemen drove Jews out of their houses or shot them inside. Tellingly, some of the perpetrators chose to use tracer ammunition to kill their victims, a round that inflicted especially large wounds and could set fires to wooden structures. According to Metzner, the continuous distribution of schnapps sustained the "murderous courage" (*Angriffsmut*) of the killers, who finished the massacre at 10 p.m., completing an eighteen-hour murder orgy. Despite being "fully covered in blood," the men gathered for the usual post-massacre debriefing, and Metzner stated, "At the same time, the annihilation [of the ghetto] was celebrated with schnapps and I was praised [by the district administrator]."[112]

Metzner's testimony is revealing in several respects. First, it highlights the prevalent belief among the killers that those who proved unable to kill or performed poorly were "weak," men who lacked the "toughness" and "hardness" espoused by the Aryan masculine ideal—but even these men might still be able to reclaim their masculinity with a better performance at the next opportunity. Second, the inclusion of boasting—whether related to the number of kills or rapes—demonstrates the men's efforts to proclaim their virility and feats of performative masculinity in order to establish their ranking within the group. Finally, the description of the killers as they "celebrated" after the massacres offers another clear indication of the way in which murder conjoined with festive ritual. In the example of the liquidation of the Mir ghetto mentioned above, the killing operation conducted by German gendarmes and Belorussian auxiliary policemen was followed by a banquet that included "excellent food, vodka, and a variety of wines." This celebration "led to a more relaxed mood and lively conversations" among the participants, including that of a German policeman who "became very talkative, very gay."[113]

In another example, Baruch Engler remembered a mass killing of almost twenty-one hundred of the town's Jews in October 1941 at the hands of SS security policemen and Ukrainian auxiliaries under the command of SS lieutenant Erwin Gay.[114] The massacre began at six o'clock on the morning of October 16 with cries of "Jews out [of your houses]!" with men, women, and children herded toward a group of waiting trucks. The trucks ferried the victims to a nearby hill, thereafter known as "Jew hill," where they had to undress and stand near freshly excavated pits. Nearby, the SS men gathered around tables laden with alcohol, where they enjoyed breaks from the murders. At dusk, the policemen halted the killings and accepted an invitation from the Viennese-born wife of a local Ukrainian doctor to attend a "dance party," where the perpetrators "drank and danced and conducted various orgies."[115] In fact, there were allegations that the doctor's wife, Mrs. Stefurak, participated in the day's shootings. The next morning, after partying through the night, these same men returned to their work of killing and ended the second day again with a party at the Stefurak residence.[116]

In some cases, celebrations occurred at or near the sites of the killings as the perpetrators tried to erase the evidence of their deeds. In one surreal example, a police official supervised the burning of some eight hundred Jewish corpses while tapping a keg of beer. This policeman, based on his leading role in the murders, was given the "honor" of setting fire to the bodies; and when the fire department arrived to investigate the blaze, he sent them away by stating, "It's only the Jews burning."[117] In a similar manner, Hubert Gomerski and Kurt Bolender, SS guards at Sobibor, had a small cabin built near the camp's cremation site. At this spot, they not only oversaw the burning of the victims' bodies, but also amused themselves by "roasting potatoes over the fire" and drinking heavily. In a clear attempt to emphasize his own masculinity and toughness, Gomerski bragged about his ability to consume "a litre of vodka a day, as well as a lot of beer."[118]

The Role of Song and Music in Celebratory Ritual

The integration of music and song during and after acts of mass murder is striking and offers another insight concerning celebratory ritual among the killers. During the Third Reich, song played a key role in promoting the creation of "imagined communities" within the Nazi paramilitary arms, a fact manifested in the party's adoption of the martial and apocalyptic "Horst Wessel Lied" as its anthem, a song that assumed a key ritualistic element in Hitler Youth ceremonies. In fact, during all official events within the Hitler Youth, the act of singing became a key ceremonial ritual for emotionally binding boys and girls to National Socialism in this "dictatorship of song" (*Singediktatur*).[119] In his memoir of the Third Reich, Alfons Heck claimed that "no political organization in the history of the world sang as much as the Hitler Youth; it was a tool to bind us together in the common cause of Germany." He continued, "When we roared . . . 'Today Germany belongs to us and tomorrow the world,' . . . it was a cry of utter conviction."[120] Visual images also promoted song as a unifying communal ritual; one SS recruiting poster featured a blond boy "holding an equally blond girl in his arms . . . singing in front of a campfire."[121] It is important to note that under National Socialism, song was an "ideologized propaganda tool," especially within the party's paramilitary organizations.[122] Under fascism, song and music were critical for "expressing an ideology suffused with anger, hatred, and violence." Songs with aggressive lyrics served to "prime aggressive thoughts, perceptions, and behavior," particularly when combined with alcohol consumption.[123]

Song also was a means for expressing ideological belief and personal commitment. In his memoir, Rudolf Höss remarked on the bellowing of "old battle songs of defiance" after he and some of his *Freikorps* comrades were convicted of a political murder in 1924, and SS general Karl Wolff recalled "barroom brawls" in 1932 as his SS cohort belted out the verse "Beat the Red Front [i.e., communists] to a pulp!"[124] Song signified protest and aggression; but within the SS and police complex, singing and music also became an element of celebratory ritual, especially in the wake of mass killings. In postwar testimony, former prisoners at the Sachsenhausen camp described massacres there in the fall of 1941 as "SS murder orgies . . . [that] grew into real parties [*Feste*]. . . . Schnapps poured in rivers and loudspeakers played music over the screams of the victims."[125] In another gruesome example, a Jewish woman recalled the aftermath of a killing operation at Przemyśl: "I smelled the odor of burning bodies and saw a group of Gestapo men who sat by the fire, singing and drinking."[126] For these Gestapo men, "victory celebrations" proved to be the order of the day, and these festive rituals followed every "liberation from the Jews [i.e., killing action]."[127] On the morning after the execution of his father and a group of elderly men, Jacob Biber learned that "when the Germans were done, they jumped into their truck, singing a song of victory."[128] In a similar example, SS colonel Walter Blume, the commander of *Sonderkommando* 7a, took his men on recreational outings after mass killings, where, according to Blume, "in the evenings I had songs sung at the campfire," presumably with a bottle in hand.[129]

As Gestapo men sang around campfires at killing sites or near a bonfire of burning corpses, one wonders what lyrics were used to commemorate the occasion, but it seems plausible that these men, like many of their colleagues, might have chosen a song from the Nazi antisemitic repertoire, as in the case of an SA favorite, "When Jewish blood drips from the knife then things go twice as well."[130] In his analysis of the Third Reich, the historian George Mosse identified the methods by which both poetry and song became instruments of German nationalists during the interwar period to promote concepts of camaraderie, sacrifice, and "the ideal of manliness as symbolic of personal and national regeneration."[131] Not only the lyrics, but also the volume and intensity of the song signified camaraderie, aggression, and belligerent masculinity. Furthermore, music and song in the Third Reich reinforced the regime's martial goals and gender roles by promoting soldierly values among young men and domesticity and childbearing among young women.[132]

For the paramilitary formations of the Nazi Party, heavy drinking combined with song served as "an inspiration for political battle" and as an important ritual emphasizing male camaraderie and advertising the group's readiness to use terror against its enemies.[133] In Cologne on March 13, 1927, the day of local Jewish community elections, a group of forty Nazi Party members marched past the synagogue in the Roonstraße, bellowing "provocative anti-Semitic songs." Individual marchers then began to "bump into" Jews leaving the synagogue, leading to a brawl in which three Jews received knife wounds.[134] In another example, an SA unit marched through a Berlin suburb singing the refrain, "We are the Nazi guys from the murderer unit of Charlottenburg."[135]

Song also became an expression of community, camaraderie, and shared values in the wake of mass murder. A unit of SS cavalrymen returning from a mass killing in the city of Mozyr´ "marched back into town singing, like a group of recruits back from a field exercise."[136] In a second example, a group of Gestapo men, Wehrmacht soldiers, and civil servants singing the Horst Wessel anthem paraded in ranks to the Gestapo headquarters in Nowy Sącz after executing some three hundred Jews.[137] In both cases, the use of song, like the close military formations used by the perpetrators, were not only an expression of shared camaraderie and male bonding, but also a demonstration of political belief and an affirmation of mass murder. Likewise, men who sang in communal spaces arrayed in ranks laid physical and verbal claim to these sites, a public assertion of their acts combining military and celebratory ritual in one. Some SS and police auxiliaries also adopted this practice, and one survivor recalled "the voices of men [police auxiliaries] singing a Ukrainian song of victory" in the wake of a massacre of Jews.[138]

Striking Up the Band

Other types of music besides song played a role in the ritual of mass murder. In Ukraine near the village of Cutnow in September 1941, members of PB 303 conducted an execution of some three to four hundred Jewish men, women, and children at a site near the unit's accommodations. One member described the presence of a "band" (*Musikkapelle*) that was playing as the Jews were led away to their deaths. He stated, "It was loud just like a carnival [*Volksfest*]."[139] In postwar testimony, one policeman explained the presence of the band as a way to mask the sounds of the execution. At first glance, such statements may appear reasonable. However, they neglect the fact that by the end of September 1941, such massacres had become routine for police battalions in the East and open knowledge among the inhabitants of communities throughout these areas. Furthermore, as anyone who has ever visited a military firing range knows, rifles and automatic weapons have a distinct sound that under the right conditions is audible for miles. In contrast, the association of the band with a "carnival" atmosphere offers an entirely different context for the events and provides another possible interpretation concerning the policeman's own unconscious association of the killings with a real act of celebration. In support of this interpretation, another uniformed policeman testified to hearing his drunken colleagues on several occasions exclaim, "It is really nice to shoot to the accompaniment of marching music."[140]

At a killing site in the Ukrainian village of Gerasimovka, inebriated German policemen murdered groups of civilians and Soviet prisoners of war to the accompaniment of accordion music played by a unit member. Likewise, SS lieutenant Max Täubner, the man with the self-proclaimed goal of killing twenty thousand Jews, played the accordion for his men at various massacre sites during breaks between killings.[141] At the Janowska forced-labor camp near Lwów, the German staff created a special orchestra to accompany "tortures, atrocities, and shootings" perpetrated by the SS in the camp.[142] At Majdanek on November 3, 1943, specially selected SS and police personnel murdered eight thousand Jewish men, women, and children as part of operation "Harvest Festival." The victims were forced to undress and herded into prepared ditches, where they were shot as "Vienna waltzes, tangos, and marches" blared over the camp's loudspeakers. At the conclusion of the massacre, "Several volunteers from the Camp SS who had participated in the shootings returned to their quarters and held a wild party, drinking much of the vodka they had received as a special reward; some did not even bother to wash off the blood from their boots before they reached for the bottle."[143] That some SS men chose to celebrate with the remains of their victims still adhering to their uniforms was not a result of neglect or laziness but instead served as a visible sign to their comrades of individual toughness and hardness. The availability of extra alcohol rations at fellowship evenings no doubt provided a welcome addition to the post-killing festivities.[144]

This discussion on the role of music illustrates three key points. First, Nazi Party organizations emphasized music and song as expressions of political, martial, and ideological identity in addition to entertainment. Second, music and song played an important role in the ritual and ceremony of the Third Reich, ranging from military fanfares to the antisemitic lyrics bellowed by SA men in taverns, and, after the outbreak of war, even as part of mass murder. Finally, music proved an effective means for defining gender roles and promoting a range of "masculine" virtues, including camaraderie, toughness, and martial identity.

Again, singing and drinking were both ritual acts of celebration and served as mechanisms for promoting male bonding and identification with the task of murder. Indeed, the use of songs to express aggression and celebrate violence was a key element of male bonding. This applied to those assembled in a bar, or, as in the case of members of the *Einsatzgruppen*, to those who gathered in the countryside after executions for "diversion and recreation" and to sing around evening campfires.[145] It also applied to the actions of an SS unit in Poland that arrived at a local hospital and "immediately executed all the Polish wounded, and attacked the nurses, who were soon stripped and raped." A German witness testified, "When we could come back that night . . . there was tumult on the execution grounds. Soldiers from all the units, SS, Ukrainians, were playing flutes and singing, and there I saw something so frightening and horrible I can hardly describe it, fifty years later."[146] On this night and at this hospital, killing, sexual violence, alcohol consumption, and song each symbolized the individual's toughness and masculinity, but also reflected the creation of a fraternity of rapists and mass murderers.

Barroom Celebrations

As the historian Omer Bartov aptly observed, for perpetrators operating in "small, isolated German communities, joint complicity in mass murder nourished a grotesquely merry intimacy."[147] In this sense, bars, unit canteens, barracks, and restaurants in the East served as important sites for accentuating one's masculinity and for celebrating violence. Additionally, there is a correlation between alcohol consumption and violent behavior and the environment in which this behavior occurs, specifically bars or public drinking establishments. One study found that "the barroom provides an environment in which masculinity and power displays are paramount and where young men compete for potential sexual partners and the approval of peers, facilitating hypermasculine behaviors, which, in turn, promote violence."[148]

The unit bar created by the men of PB 61 outside the Warsaw ghetto perfectly illustrates the use of a ritual space to celebrate murder and to catalyze additional killing. Among a number of police battalions involved in the murder of Jews and other putative enemies of the Third Reich, three companies of PB 61 were transferred to the Warsaw ghetto in January 1942 to serve as guards. The creation of the "Krochmalna" bar near the ghetto not only provided a place for off-duty policemen to engage in "drinking orgies," but the bar itself became a site of commemoration and male competition with respect to murder. It also became a place for these men to boast about their accomplishments.[149]

During a postwar investigation of the unit's activities in Warsaw, a West German prosecutor commented that "victory celebrations" were a customary part of the unit's ritual after mass executions.[150] For the men of PB 61, the Krochmalna bar, which was "decorated" with a light fixture shaped like a Star of David and walls covered with antisemitic murals, became the site for celebrating killing and engaging in ritual drinking, song, and male boasting. Indeed, the bar's murals celebrated the policemen's dominance over their victims, One mural showed a Jew bending to retrieve some food while a policeman levels his rifle and fires.[151] In this case, "art" reflected reality. The unit's members routinely shot Jews involved in trade along the ghetto boundaries and within the ghetto itself. The image of a policeman using his weapon graphically illustrated the ideal of masculinity propagated among SS and policemen and aptly demonstrated a lethal and dominant act over one's victim. The willingness and capability of such men to use their weapons was one aspect that defined their masculinity in the eyes of the regime's leadership.[152] In fact, the ninth of the ten "commandments" (*Grundsätze*) of the police under National Socialism made this point explicit: "As a bearer of a weapon, you share in the greatest honor of a *German man*, always remember this."[153] In this sense, a weapon and the authorization to carry and use it symbolized "an essential element" in the "construction of masculine fraternity."[154]

In a telling contrast to their male peers, female SS concentration guards within the old Reich, despite their authority to inflict brutal punishments, were not allowed to have firearms, as these weapons were reserved exclusively for men.[155] As the historian Elissa Mailänder notes, the restriction on the use of firearms by female guards was part of a "gendered taboo" in which "women lacked the physical and mental capacity necessary to handle a pistol."[156] However, in one reflection of the wider boundaries enjoyed by SS personnel in the East, this prohibition did not apply at Majdanek and Auschwitz, where female guards were permitted firearms. Interestingly, these women used their firearms primarily as clubs to pistol whip the prisoners, a practice seemingly influenced by the expectations of the SS organization and their male peers.[157]

In the case of pubs, acts of excessive drinking combined with the celebrations of mass killing point to the importance of the barroom as a site for commemorating murder and for recognizing the perceived accomplishments of the perpetrators. The importance of the bar as a site of male contestation can be seen in the testimony of a former policeman who noted that the locale was dominated by a "certain clique" of individuals "who had especially distinguished themselves in the Jewish ghetto."[158] Similarly, Oscar Dirlewanger, commander of a notorious SS anti-partisan unit, used heavy drinking sessions as "an occasion for festivity, bringing his men and officers together in a certain fraternity."[159] In such cases, both the act of killing Jews and the ability to hold one's liquor served as demonstrations of one's masculinity and belonging to a closed male community of violence. Not only did such men go to the bar to commemorate and to celebrate murder, but their participation in drinking rituals, including song, often inspired some to leave on drunken patrols of the ghetto in a hunt for more victims.[160]

The incorporation of send-off parties for SS and police units after their involvement in mass murder provides a final example of the way in which senior SS leaders incorporated festive ritual into the process of genocide. Prior to a unit's transfer for duty with EK 8, the commander of EK 9, SS lieutenant colonel Alfred Filbert, held a "small party" for uniformed policemen from the third platoon, second company of PB 9 during which he thanked the men for their efforts in the mass murder of the Jews.[161] Filbert, a Nazi true believer and an utterly ruthless man, was not easily impressed. In fact, he fully embraced the SS standards of masculine hardness and expected the same from his subordinates. When one of his subordinates broke down and had a "screaming fit" the evening after the unit had killed forty Jewish children, he remarked, "And something like that wants to be an SS officer?"[162] For Filbert, toughness and body count were what mattered. Indeed, EK 9 was one of several killing units involved in a "race for the highest numbers [killed]," a competition Filbert sought to win by instituting "Jew hunts" using small squads of killers sent out on "search and destroy missions."[163] In another festive send-off, Arthur Greiser, the Nazi Party district leader of the Wartheland, invited the SS and police detachment responsible for the murder of Jews at Chełmno to a celebratory party in the spring of 1943 as the unit prepared to close down operations at the camp after having killed almost 150,000 men, women, and children at the site.[164]

Shared Community, Masculinity, and Murder

In one respect, the act of *sharing* a drink and song with one's comrades before, during, or after a killing action served an important function related to group identity and group solidarity, and such activities were merely a continuation of prewar rituals conducted in the SA and SS. The act of communal drinking was in a sense also an act of shared communal responsibility. Refusal to take part in this ritual could be interpreted as both a rejection of the group and criticism of the group's actions. After a day's work in the killing fields, Karl Kretschmer told his wife, one was expected to take part in drinking or card play, and he stated "one cannot set oneself apart [from the group]."[165] Similarly, Otto Horn, an SS enlisted man, reported being "threatened" by an SS colleague because he refused to drink alcohol with the group. Importantly, Horn was seen as an "outsider" in part because he was not considered "as brutal as his colleagues."[166] One's level of brutality determined status and reflected masculine toughness among one's peers, while refusal to participate in murder marked the nonconformist as a "coward," "shithead," or "weakling."[167]

Again, the excessive drinking, boasting, and song in bars, taverns, and in many cases makeshift unit canteens served to emphasize Nazi masculine ideals of hardness and camaraderie and to prepare men for their roles in violence against those deemed outside of this closed community. Hans Baumgartner, a member of *Einsatzkommando* 2 stationed in the Latvian city of Liepāja, participated in numerous mass executions during his time in the East. In a series of postwar interrogations by the East German state police, Baumgartner noted that executions took place in an area dominated by sand dunes along the coast of the Baltic Sea, and the killings normally began at first light. Notification of upcoming executions occurred at "group dinners" the night before the killings, accompanied by the distribution of bottles of vodka to the participants. Importantly, Baumgartner emphasized that "despite his drinking on execution days, I was always capable of duty [*einsatzfähig*]."[168] In other words, he remained in control of his faculties and was not made weak by his drinking as he prepared for and participated in mass murder.

It is important to stress that group meals provided key occasions for binding SS and policemen to their unit and their collective mission; like unit bars, these meals were in private spaces enjoyed by the perpetrators as a communal body.[169] In the case of EK 2, Baumgartner stated that for "smaller" executions, groups of fewer than twenty, the execution squad would conduct the killings at first light in the dunes and then return for breakfast.[170] For these men, drinking before, during, or after killings, even at breakfast, was a normal part of their routine, a practice shared by other

SS and police units in the East.[171] Similarly, a member of *Einsatzkommando* 3, a unit that ate and drank together in the canteen and shared evenings over alcohol and conversation, recalled how the men gathered after the killings. "Normally they had been drinking. They were then very loud and described that they had executed Jews again."[172] A female secretary noted how the killers returned and traded details on the murders and critiqued each man's participation.[173] These group meetings over breakfast and dinner or at the bar not only allowed for the exchange of information, the ranking of one's colleagues, and the formation of group identity among the individual perpetrators, but they also provided the opportunity for senior leaders to emphasize the necessity and importance of their actions in the context of Nazi war aims, and even to discuss the "beauty of work"—that is, murder.[174]

Baumgartner's testimony offers several trenchant insights into the ritual of mass murder in the East by SS perpetrators. First, shared settings were used to prepare the killers for their coming duties. In this sense, pre-execution evening group meals with the distribution of alcohol served as a communal site for announcing the operation and priming the killers for their role in mass murder. Second, post-execution group breakfasts not only highlight the importance of maintaining unit solidarity after the executions, but the incorporation of food and alcohol once again points to the normalization of such activities. Finally, Baumgartner's insistence that he was not incapacitated by alcohol during the killings reflects the way in which drinking was viewed by the perpetrators, even if they themselves refused to admit its effects on their performance. One cannot help but imagine that conversations at post-killing breakfasts and dinners must have revolved around these events, whether in assessment of the procedures or discussion of the reactions of the victims and the loot gathered by the killers.

The post-killing actions of some SS units in occupied Poland offer a particularly revealing view of these communal celebrations. In the town of Wejherowo, SS men would return to a local bar after each massacre. One witness overheard these men "who had obviously just come from a shooting" bragging and joking about how "the damned brains [of the victims] just squirted everywhere."[175] Similarly, Marianna Kazmierczak, a seventeen-year-old Polish girl working at a restaurant in Zakrzewo, testified that SS men routinely gathered there to drink beer and schnapps and to celebrate after mass killings in the fall of 1939. She remarked, "Finally, they were half drunk, and the mood was very merry, as if they were intoxicated. They sang and danced." She also noted, "Such drinking bouts were repeated after every mass shooting . . . sometimes several times a week. The drinking bouts went on into the late hours."[176]

Kazmierczak's recollections are instructive in three respects. First, she not only highlights the celebratory nature of these events, with plentiful supplies of alcohol and group singing, but her testimony clearly notes this was an established ritual that followed killing actions, with such celebrations occurring in some cases several times a week. Second, she notes the importance of song and merriment in these drinking bouts, with its vocalization of male camaraderie and shared beliefs. These celebratory rituals were not limited, however, to German forces alone. Police auxiliaries in the East adopted the same behaviors to commemorate their own role in genocide.

6

ALCOHOL, AUXILIARIES, AND
MASS MURDER

While the SS and police are the focus of this study, they were joined by other perpetrators, including Wehrmacht soldiers, non-German auxiliaries, and local policemen who engaged in acts of brutality and mass murder often in very similar ways. Foreign auxiliaries, whether serving in German Security or Order Police units, in the labor and death camps in Poland, or with armed formations of the Waffen-SS and the Wehrmacht, proved a key adjunct to overstretched German forces and critical instruments for mass murder in the East.[1] As the historian Peter Black correctly asserted, "The Nazis could not have implemented their 'Final Solution of the Jewish Question' without assistance from ethnic German and non-German auxiliaries."[2] For the auxiliaries, the consumption of alcohol was a common practice, and in many instances alcohol was provided by the German occupiers as both an incentive and facilitator for security operations and acts of mass murder.[3] Official Soviet descriptions of the actions of both Germans and their auxiliaries incorporated the trope of intoxicated murderers and emphasized the brutality of these men by describing them as "drunk" or as "drunken bands" who "tortured people worse than cattle. . . . For them murdering a person is like an amusement and a bestial pleasure."[4] Despite the propagandistic aim of this description, it is clear from witness accounts in the camps, ghettos, and killing fields that auxiliaries and local policemen drank heavily and engaged in widespread atrocity during the German occupation.[5]

Drinking Patterns in Eastern Europe

In the Soviet Union under Stalin, the pattern of prodigious consumption of alcohol by Soviet citizens served as both a mechanism for social control and a critical source of state funding.[6] One historian asserted that "brewing vodka was easier than making bread," while one in four peasant households distilled their own vodka. Local officials described heavy drinking as a general phenomenon that crossed age and gender lines, as "even girls learned to drink." By the 1940s, "brewing and conspicuous alcohol consumption," especially among farmers and peasants in the Soviet Union and Poland, resulted in alcoholism reaching a "spectacular scale."[7]

In the East, a "culture of vodka" existed that became a key component of both masculine and military identity. In this sense, the consumption of alcohol influenced the actions of not only those serving in the Red Army, but auxiliaries and local policemen under German command as well.[8] Already in the nineteenth century, vodka was the national drink of Poland and Lithuania across all social classes, and the clear liquor "was celebrated in Polish drinking songs and exalted in Polish poetry."[9] Predictably, the heavy consumption of vodka within taverns led to acts of physical and sexual violence by drunken patrons.[10] With respect to ethnic and religious violence, it was no coincidence that excessive consumption of vodka catalyzed pogroms aimed at entire Jewish communities, attacks that often occurred at Easter and Christmas during the "high tides of drunkenness" associated with the celebration of both Christian holidays.[11]

The example of Poland also demonstrates the process by which antisemitic stereotypes were integrated into social custom in a country in which many of the tavern owners were Jewish. Using circular reasoning, some locals blamed Jews for public drunkenness and alcoholism and used the prevalence of Jewish-owned taverns as a justification for "anti-Semitic rhetoric." In the words of one observer, "You go into the tavern for tobacco and the Jew . . . begins to praise his liquor and make fun of sobriety. . . . Before you know it, you've had one drink then another." According to this account, the Jewish tavern owner, not content with having cleaned out his patron's wallet, "puts his hands in his pockets, jingles his money, laughs and makes fun of the drunk."[12]

While alcohol served a number of functions, in the rural communities of Eastern Europe "bouts of hard drinking" among men was an established and important social ritual and an important manifestation of masculinity among the participants.[13] For some, the act of heavy alcohol consumption at village taverns intertwined perceptions of masculinity and antisemitism. For example, some Polish Gentiles "mocked" Jews for drinking in moderation, employing the phrase to "drink Jewishly" as both a criticism and a feminization of such behavior.[14] The widespread cultural practice of heavy drinking among Slavic men not only facilitated acts of aggression but also was associated with increased interpersonal violence throughout Eastern Europe.[15] In this sense, drinking ritual, perceptions of masculinity, antisemitism, and acts of violence became intertwined and existed prior to the war. With the German occupation, the nature and aims of Nazi policy magnified the brutal behavior of local policemen and auxiliaries, who provided a critical adjunct to German SS and police forces between 1939 and 1945.

Organizing the Police Auxiliaries

On July 17, 1941, Hitler transferred authority for the security of the newly occupied eastern territories to Himmler. Hitler ordered Himmler to work with local Nazi Party leaders in the East to establish a police structure designed for the expropriation of these conquered areas and their subsequent Germanization.[16] For his part, Himmler quickly realized that the vast conquered territories could not be secured solely with the limited SS and police forces available for duty in the East, and he subsequently notified the Higher SS and Police Leaders (HSSPF) that the planned "tasks" associated with the occupation of these areas required support from the indigenous populations. In a letter dated July 25, 1941, he stated his intention to create auxiliary formations (*Schutzformationen*) from "suitable" ethnic groups from Ukraine, the Baltic states, and Belorussia to support German uniformed and security police forces. Himmler also explicitly referred to the prior use of such auxiliaries by the *Einsatzgruppen*.[17]

The fact that Himmler, in the conception and creation of auxiliary police formations, referenced the role of these units in the mass murder of the Jews cannot be overemphasized. Indeed, the conceptualization of these forces as adjuncts to Nazi plans for the exploitation and mass murder of indigenous populations, starting from the first weeks of German occupation, clearly demonstrates the method by which the radical demographic restructuring of these lands was to take place and set the precedent for the use of auxiliary police forces as a major instrument of draconian German occupation policies.[18]

It is important to note that these units were to be commanded by Germans, specifically by SS and police officers or experienced senior enlisted personnel from the police.[19] In fact, German control of the auxiliaries was a paramount consideration, with the lowest-ranking German policemen exercising authority over the most senior non-German auxiliary.[20] The issue of command authority was emphasized repeatedly as the auxiliary units, whether organized into small posts or precincts or in larger company and battalion-size formations, were seen as adjuncts to German police forces. In an order on November 6, 1941, Himmler stressed that auxiliary forces could operate only under German command. Further, he noted that individual and small groups of auxiliary policemen within cities, towns, and throughout the countryside were primarily tasked with general police duties and intended to mirror the existing German police organization in these areas. He ordered the establishment of auxiliary police battalions and companies, with these units subordinated to the HSSPF in the army rear areas.[21] Led by German officers and senior enlisted personnel, these battalions consisted of three companies of approximately 140 men each.[22] It was these auxiliary police battalions, like their German counterparts in the uniformed police and the *Einsatzgruppen*, that emerged as paramilitarized, purpose-built instruments for imposing Nazi control over the occupied territories and critical adjuncts for the prosecution of racial policy and mass murder.[23]

Alcohol and Local Auxiliaries

These companies and battalions of auxiliary police, along with small detachments for duty in the countryside and towns, drew their members primarily from former members of the police and the military.[24] At the end of 1941, the total number of auxiliaries serving under German command in the East was forty-five thousand, but a year later the number had ballooned to almost three hundred thousand, including one hundred thousand Ukrainians alone, an increase that not coincidentally corresponded with a massive wave of killing of Jews, as well as the growing partisan threat faced by German forces in the East.[25] While these men may not have been "natural born killers," they did come from social backgrounds in which antisemitism was not uncommon, an attribute that German forces attempted to leverage to their advantage through ideological instruction and the promise of material benefits, including alcohol.[26]

Although the auxiliaries were known for their drinking binges, it is true that excessive consumption of alcohol and high rates of alcoholism, as noted above, reflected a broader trend in Russia, Ukraine, and eastern Poland that predated the German invasion. Nevertheless, with the German occupation, Poland experienced "a plague of wartime banditry and alcoholism," and, in a diary entry of January 10, 1941, the Polish doctor Zygmunt Klukowski noted, "Drunkenness is growing. More and more people are drinking, and naturally there are more drunken fights."[27] Likewise, "heavy drinking" among Belorussian auxiliary policemen was customary and viewed as "natural, something they had always done, like eating and sleeping."[28] In fact, the tradition of high alcohol consumption among the police auxiliaries led to German complaints by late 1942. German officials bemoaned the "very poor work ethic" of Ukrainians and the steep rise in alcoholism, but apparently accepted such behavior as the price for gaining the cooperation of these men in genocide.[29] As noted previously, the connection between excessive alcohol consumption and violence against the region's Jewish population had historical roots. In fact, a study of pogroms conducted in eastern Poland and central Ukraine between 1917 and 1920 emphasized the similarity of these events to those in 1941, including the "unlimited licentiousness and drinking" that preceded the mass killings.[30]

In any case, after the German invasion, the widespread abuse of alcohol clearly played a variety of roles among the auxiliaries in the murder of the Jews. For example, the killing of Jews provided these men with opportunities to steal goods from their victims;[31] auxiliaries were known to trade these goods, including the clothing of the victims, with local inhabitants for alcohol.[32] Indeed, the plundering of Jewish goods was an important part of the killing and celebratory ritual among the auxiliaries. A German SS trainer of Ukrainian auxiliaries remarked not only on the men's heavy drinking, but on the fact that they always had plenty of money. He noted that the auxiliaries "thronged" to participate in the killing actions, a motivation tied in part to the availability of alcohol, but more so to the opportunity to acquire the valuables of the victims. The division of the property of the murdered Jews was a key element in post-celebratory ritual, as even those men not chosen to participate waited anxiously for their chance to take part in the spoils during the "general exchange" of plundered items that took place after the killings.[33]

In one especially grisly example, a Ukrainian SS auxiliary from Sobibor arrived to purchase vodka from a local Pole, Jan Piwonski. Instead of offering money for the alcohol, the guard placed gold dental crowns, with pieces of flesh still attached, on the counter as payment.[34] The use of looted items to purchase alcohol was not limited to the auxiliaries, as one German policeman testified to his platoon's practice of buying beer with money taken from the victims.[35] From Berlin's perspective, the proceeds of the victims' wealth were intended for the Reich, and in an order of March 18, 1942, distributed to the SS and police, Himmler warned of severe consequences for the "withholding of even the smallest amount."[36] In fact, during his speech to SS and police leaders in Posen in October 1943, Himmler threatened death sentences for those within the SS found guilty of keeping "even one Mark." Then, referring to a Jewish stereotype and mass murder in the same sentence, he remarked, "We don't want in the end, as we exterminate a bacillus, to become sick and to perish from that same bacillus."[37] Despite Himmler's draconian threats, his efforts to stop the plunder of Jewish victims by the SS, the police, and local auxiliaries proved largely futile, and theft was widespread among all three groups.

While the plunder of the victims' wealth provided one means of obtaining alcohol for the killers, German-supplied liquor was routinely available at the killing sites for the murderers' consumption, and stories of intoxicated shooters are commonplace.[38] In fact, the consumption of vodka was part of the induction ritual into some auxiliary units and even extended to a young boy, Alex Kurzem, serving as a "mascot" for a Latvian police unit. After being fed "capfuls" of vodka upon his entry into the unit, the boy woke with a hangover the next morning. Kurzem recalled being admonished by the unit's commander that "I'd have to learn to hold my

liquor if I was going to be a soldier."[39] Similarly, as in the case of German
SS and police units, the refusal to drink with one's fellow perpetrators
could lead to physical violence, including the use of firearms, against those
who rebuffed offers to participate.[40] Interestingly, this behavior extended
to partisan units battling against the German occupiers, where one's ability or inability to consume a "tankard" of home-brewed moonshine elic-
ited either "everyone's respect," or "contempt" in the case of those who
failed.[41] In fact, Tuviah Bielski, a member of the famed Bielski partisans,
attributed his success in dealing with Russian partisan bands in part to his
ability to "out-drink them."[42]

While one study of auxiliary forces in Belorussia argued against the
stereotype of auxiliaries as "alcoholic policemen in shabby clothes with
missing or obsolete weapons," these men clearly engaged in prolific drinking bouts and widespread acts of atrocity.[43] In the case of Ukrainian auxiliaries, an SS trainer described them in the lexicon of the Third Reich as
"a wild race [*Volk*] without self-restraint, especially when they drank,"
while another complained, "The Ukrainians were uncouth and unreliable, especially under the influence of alcohol. . . . They felt all-powerful,
and, after all, an NCO cannot run after 150 wild animals."[44] Zygmunt
Klukowski shared his perception of SS Ukrainian auxiliaries in a diary
entry, describing them as "known for their cruelty."[45] Another witness recalled the actions of a group of Lithuanian auxiliaries during the wartime
murder of the Jewish population in the town of Kuršėnai. The killings
lasted half the day, as Jews were shuttled to the execution site in groups
of approximately 150 and then shot six at a time. The witness, a local
Lithuanian Christian, recalled, "They [the shooters] ate and drank after
the shooting," and he continued, "They had a party in the city [after the
murders]." He also remembered one of the killers exclaiming, "We got rid
of those bastards!"[46]

Regardless of the auxiliaries' national origins, traditional antisemitism
was certainly a factor, especially among those men who "in the first weeks
and months of the Nazi invasion played an active role in the persecution
of Jews," a trend witnessed throughout the Baltic states and their eastern neighbors.[47] Similarly, the consumption of alcohol, normally vodka,
before, during, or after the killings was common. Witness memories of
the ritual of mass murder at the execution sites often included "the wild
shouts of drunks who have sung and raped and shot off rounds near

blistering bonfires the night through."[48] These were the same drunken men who would engage in senseless acts of cruelty and humiliation before the killings and then sit down to "parties" with a banquet feast among the piles of looted goods after their gruesome work was concluded.[49]

During the killing actions, the auxiliaries performed a number of roles, including rounding up the Jewish population, transporting the victims to the execution sites, creating cordons, pulling the trigger, and supervising the burial of the victims. Again, the consumption of alcohol was a frequent part of this process, as "many . . . were intoxicated during the executions . . . [and their behavior] aroused loathing even among the Germans."[50] The widespread availability and consumption of "large quantities of alcohol," as elsewhere in the East, was a routine part of executions conducted by Lithuanian and Latvian auxiliaries under SS command.[51] One witness remembered a "whole barrel of vodka" and a ladle used by the shooters at an execution site in the Poligon Forest in October 1941.[52] Communal drinking from a shared ladle once again underlined shared camaraderie in mass murder. During a massacre in the Riga ghetto in November 1941, Gertrude Schneider detailed the brutality of "drunken Latvian policemen" operating under German command as they tossed infants from apartment windows and "shot randomly," killing and wounding numerous Jews.[53] In a similar manner, Ukrainian auxiliaries often drank before, during, and after deportations and mass executions, and their state of intoxication led to wild shooting that at times threatened victims and their German superiors alike.[54]

In the case of the SS-trained Trawniki guards, auxiliaries from various Eastern European occupied countries posted to the killing centers, most were born prior to 1910, came from rural backgrounds, and were soldiers recruited from the ranks of former Soviet prisoners of war.[55] A study of Ukrainian auxiliaries found three socio-psychological types among these men. The first group consisted of "political activists" whose "ideological antisemitism provided the motivation for participation in anti-Jewish actions." The second group were "enterprising conformists" who lacked any moral convictions and simply adapted to the political realities of German rule. Finally, "ordinary task performers" were men from lower-class and rural backgrounds who saw service as "a means for upward social movement."[56] While there were some regional variations in spontaneous acts of local violence against Jews in the East, the majority of the perpetrators incorporated drinking rituals in the abuse and murder of their victims, their actions once again demonstrating the importance of alcohol as both a reward for and facilitator of murder.

Continuing the practice established at the start of the invasion, pogroms aimed at the Jews in the East often were perpetrated by auxiliaries but instigated by German Security Police forces. The Germans then sought to place the blame for these "spontaneous" actions at the feet of the local populace.[57] Not all these men necessarily embraced Nazi ideology concerning the Jews, but again, many of them came from a social background where antisemitism was common, and their training did include political education involving virulently antisemitic material.[58] This social background, combined with German ideological education, proved a two-edged sword, as some German officials worried about maintaining discipline within the ranks of men who "had lost all moral restraints" during their participation in the "liquidation of the Jewish population."[59] In addition to ideological affinity, "material expectations provided from early on a major incentive for locals to join the ranks of auxiliary police units."[60] The promise of plunder gained from the murdered Jews or the chance to receive additional rations or alcohol provided practical incentives for the participation of some auxiliaries in genocide.[61]

Militarizing the Police

In the face of a Soviet winter counteroffensive and spiraling Wehrmacht losses, Hitler approved the formation of auxiliary police battalions at the end of January 1942, and SS and police leaders launched a major recruitment campaign the following month.[62] In a speech to senior police leaders in February 1942, the chief of the German Order Police Kurt Daluege remarked that manpower shortages within the police by the end of 1941 required the creation of "auxiliary forces from the occupied territories . . . organized, trained, and equipped for the fulfillment of police tasks." In the Reich Commissariat Ostland, auxiliary police forces drawn from among ethnic Latvians, Lithuanians, Estonians, and Belorussians numbered 31,652 men, almost ten times the size of German police forces in the region. Similarly, the Reich Commissariat Ukraine mobilized 14,452 police auxiliaries drawn from among ethnic Germans and Ukrainians in support of the area's 3,880 German uniformed policemen. Daluege praised the auxiliaries assigned to these companies and battalions for their efforts in the economic exploitation of the conquered territories and especially their performance in the "never-ending battle against partisans, [Soviet] paratroopers, and communist criminals."[63]

Daluege's comments offer several insights into the role and importance of the auxiliaries in the eastern campaign. First, German control over the occupied territories could hardly have been possible without the assistance of these forces. Indeed, auxiliaries formed the vast preponderance of total police forces in these areas. Second, Daluege's emphasis on the military organization of these forces, and especially their employment in anti-partisan operations, is a critical point. Already at the end of September 1941, a three-day conference on anti-partisan warfare, including representatives from the Wehrmacht, the SS, and the police, had been held at Mogilev in Belorussia. Guidelines prepared as part of the conference dictated that "the enemy must be completely annihilated" and further argued, "The constant decision between life and death for partisans and suspicious persons is difficult even for the hardest soldier. . . . He acts correctly who fights ruthlessly and mercilessly with complete disregard for any personal surge of emotion."[64] Not only did this conference establish annihilation as the standard for combating partisans, but it also introduced the equivalency of partisans with Bolsheviks and Jews. Indeed, Hitler equated Jews with partisans in a meeting with Himmler on December 18, 1941, that resulted in the latter's telegraphic notation, "Jewish question. [To be] exterminated as partisans."[65] In other words, as Daluege delivered his speech in February 1942, the terms "partisans" and "communist criminals" had already linked the mission of the police formations to the annihilation of the Jews.

Like their uniformed police counterparts, German Security Police units faced their own personnel crisis by early 1942 as they prosecuted a campaign of racial cleansing.[66] As a result, the Reich Security Main Office issued orders on January 19, 1942, calling for the creation of auxiliary police battalions of the Security Police based on the existing model of the Order Police. These Security Police auxiliaries, like their uniformed police counterparts, were tasked primarily with "anti-partisan combat" and "security duties" and most tellingly were assigned for duties with each of the four *Einsatzgruppen*. Each *Einsatzgruppe* received authorization to establish ten battalions of auxiliary security policemen.[67] Testifying after the war, a former member of *Einsatzgruppe* A indicated that "these [auxiliary] units were primarily intended to do the 'dirty work' [*Sauarbeit*]."[68] The timing of the augmentation of the *Einsatzgruppen* with these auxiliaries once again offers a vital clue related to their mission. These newly organized auxiliary police formations would provide critical assistance in the conduct of mass murder.[69]

Instruments for Mass Murder

By the fall of 1941, the use of auxiliary police formations for the mass murder of Jews was a common practice in the occupied territories. For example, a company of Lithuanian auxiliaries under German command, after torturing many of the victims, executed 864 Jewish men, 2,019 Jewish women, and 817 Jewish children in the Ponary Forest on September 2, 1941, as part of an operation aimed at clearing the Vilna ghetto.[70] Likewise, a Lithuanian auxiliary battalion conducted "the first act of mass murder of Reich Jews" near Kovno (Kaunas) at the end of November 1941 by murdering 4,934 Jews deported from Germany.[71] The auxiliary formations were not limited to the Baltic nationalities, as Ukrainians and even Crimean Tatars were recruited to serve under German police command.[72] In the case of the former, Ukrainian auxiliaries assisted *Einsatzkommando* 4a in the murder of Jewish men in the town of Sokal in the first week of the invasion. By the fall of 1941, Ukrainian auxiliaries emerged as an important adjunct assisting both the *Einsatzgruppen* and Order Police battalions in mass executions of Jews at numerous killing sites, including, in Ukraine itself, Kamenetz-Podolsk, Dnepropetrovsk, and Babi Yar near Kiev. These killing actions claimed the lives of approximately 23,600, 11,000, and 34,000 victims, respectively.[73]

The importance of ethnic police auxiliaries in the annihilation of Jews in the East increased with the clearing of the Jewish ghettos in 1942, the "killing year" of the Holocaust during which some three million Jews perished, as these forces assisted Order Police and Security Police units in a murderous campaign stretching from Poland into Russia.[74] In the prosecution of genocide, the auxiliary police battalions played a variety of roles, including the surrounding of ghettos and killing sites to prevent escapes and as execution squads for mass shootings.[75] As auxiliaries forayed into Jewish ghettos, they often plundered apartments in their search for valuables and alcohol.[76]

In the case of deportations, one historian noted, "There is barely a story from a survivor that does not reference how Ukrainian auxiliary policemen herded Jews together, shot the old and the sick on the spot or beat them to death, and then delivered the remaining [Jews] to German authorities for execution."[77] Mendel Balberyszski described the festive atmosphere present during the clearing of the Vilna ghetto in September 1943 and how the police "kept taking bottles of drinks, expensive wine and candied fruit . . . [and] holding an all-night party."[78] Another indication of the ubiquity of drinking during these operations appears in the testimony of men from PB 101 who described the participation of Ukrainian auxiliaries in a mass deportation of Jews from the town of Parczew to Treblinka in August 1942. These policemen described the event as involving "little shooting" and largely free from "their [i.e., the auxiliaries'] *usual* drunkenness and brutality."[79] This situation proved short-lived, however, as later that month, in another ghetto-clearing operation, an intoxicated security policeman supervised a group of drunken Ukrainian auxiliaries who "shot so often and so wildly that the [German] policemen frequently had to take cover to avoid being hit." Still, the drunken state of the auxiliaries did not prevent them from murdering almost a thousand of the town's Jews on the way to the train station or completing the deportation of the remaining ten thousand victims to Treblinka.[80] Witness comments on the intoxication of the killers are prevalent and are not limited to Ukrainian auxiliaries. Neonila Grigorjeva, as a young girl, witnessed "drunk and irritated" Latvian policemen escorting Jews to a killing site.[81]

Violence, Alcohol, and Ritual Humiliation in the Killing Centers

As in the case of their German masters, auxiliaries often engaged in acts of humiliation as an initial step in the killing ritual, frequently under the influence of alcohol. Ukrainian guards at Treblinka, who were described as "always drunk," physically abused Jewish prisoners upon their arrival and supported their own drinking habit by exchanging the property of murdered Jews for alcohol.[82] Franz Stangl, upon his arrival to take command of the Treblinka camp, described the Ukrainians as "weaving drunk, dancing, singing, [and] playing music," while another SS guard testified how a Ukrainian boasted about killing a Jewish mother and her child "with one shot."[83] In a further example, Yakov Zak described the reactions of Lithuanian auxiliaries to the murder of Jews at a special camp in the town of Kelmė, where several of the Jewish women had fallen to their knees and begged for their lives. Some of the drunken auxiliaries "tried to mimic the women while the other murderers had to hold their stomachs from laughing so hard."[84] Another witness shared his memories of Lithuanian auxiliaries "hacking off beards while German soldiers jeered [and] snapped trophy photos," and "[Jewish] elders [were] commanded to strip and then dance, perhaps on a Torah or clumsily on the body of someone they went to shul with."[85] When guarding convoys of Jewish prisoners, these men, often drunk, "engage[d] in their 'games' with trapped and suffering prisoners." In these cases, the auxiliaries accepted bribes from the prisoners to allow them to escape; however, after receiving their reward, the guards would shoot the prisoners "when they tried to run away."[86]

In the examples noted above, it is clear that the behavior of the auxiliaries mirrored in many respects the drinking rituals, acts of mockery and humiliation, sadistic games, and homicidal behavior of their German superiors. In this sense, it appears that these auxiliaries were merely taking advantage of the expanded boundaries of accepted behavior created under the German occupation for SS and police forces in general. Likewise, they engaged in their own competitions and acts of performative masculinity among their peers.

It was not only the perpetrators who reveled in the fate of their Jewish neighbors. Thomas Blatt escaped an initial deportation from his town of Izbica by hiding. As he returned to his childhood home, he "heard drunken voices singing a popular song with the new class of unscrupulous, war-enriched Poles." He continued, "They were celebrating [and singing] Drink, drink, drink, brother drink, And the war should longer thunder."[87] Nachum Alpert also asserted the close relationship between the Germans and the local police in Slonim: "There now arose between them a mutual understanding, a brotherhood of murderers who got drunk together and 'sang together' on the basis of anti-Semitism and anti-Communism."[88]

Once again the community of perpetrators bonded through murder and celebrated their acts with vodka and song.

Similarly, some Polish youth forced into German service as members of the construction service became accomplices in atrocity. While some refused to participate in acts of brutality and murder against their Jewish neighbors, others "decided to 'chop off the heads of Jews'" or "killed them with blunt instruments." Archbishop Stefan Sapieha, in a letter to the governor-general of Poland, Han Frank, protested the use of members of the construction service to "liquidate the Jews" and cited the German provision of alcohol prior to the killings as a key facilitator in the killings.[89] In fact, some Christian Poles rationalized the participation of Polish killers as a function of the influence of drugs or alcohol.[90] While alcohol certainly played a role in promoting the disinhibition that allowed some individuals to conduct such acts, it is clear that others refused to participate. And the repeated mention of song, sadistic amusements, and celebrations by the killers places their actions in a different context, from grudging acquiescence into the realm of enthusiastic participation.

Holiday Celebrations and Murder

In their memoirs and testimonies, numerous survivors comment on the timing of acts of humiliation and mass murder to correspond with traditional Jewish or Soviet holidays.[91] Avraham Tory, a survivor of the Kovno ghetto, confided in a diary entry on September 30, 1943, "Holy days keep bringing unpleasant surprises down on our heads."[92] These actions continued an existing historical precedent in Eastern Europe in which Christian holidays, especially Holy Week and Easter, often witnessed outbreaks of antisemitic violence and pogroms.[93] As noted previously, the use of Jewish holidays and the Sabbath for acts of violence against the Jews served the primary function of persecution of the Jewish population, but, at a broader level, the ridicule and humiliation that accompanied the murders also represented a cynical desacralization of Jewish tradition and Judaism itself. For the inhabitants of the Vilna ghetto, the Jewish New Year (Rosh Hashanah) in 1943 signaled the start of the "final liquidation" of the ghetto, and continued a pattern of killing by the Germans and Lithuanian police auxiliaries in which "executions were purposefully carried out on

Jewish holidays, like Yom Kippur or Passover."[94] Similarly, in the Kovno ghetto, the holiday began with prayers and the blowing of the shofar intermingled with "the sounds of murder and destruction."[95] The numerous examples of such abuse offer insight into the mentality of the perpetrators and their use of violence as both a physical and a spiritual weapon.

In the case of the Lithuania community of Eisysky, Zvi Michalowsky recalled how "drunken" Lithuanian auxiliaries crowded the local population into the shtetl's synagogues on the eve of the Jewish New Year in September 1941. As a joke, the intoxicated auxiliaries included some sixty "lunatics" from a local asylum and appointed them as "supervisors." In the following days, the auxiliaries marched the town's entire Jewish community to the local cemetery and murdered some four thousand men, women, and children. Michalowsky survived by falling into the execution ditch just before being shot. Later that evening after the conclusion of the shootings, he made his way out of the mass of bodies and could hear the auxiliaries "singing and drinking, celebrating their great accomplishment," a massacre that ended eight hundred years of Jewish life in the village.[96]

The mass murder of Jews also extended to the populations of larger cities from the very first days of the occupation, and such actions were often primarily the work of SS and police auxiliaries. In Kovno, the German entry into the city had included widespread acts of physical and sexual abuse by Lithuanian auxiliaries against their former neighbors. William Mishell recalled numerous executions, involving the murder of men, women, and children by auxiliaries, taking place in the city and the surrounding countryside, and he repeatedly noted the intoxication of the killers.[97] He also stated, "Quite often they were committed in broad daylight with sightseers watching the gruesome procedure. When possible, these murders were carried out on a Saturday, the Jewish Sabbath, to 'reward' the Jews on their holy day."[98]

Mishell's testimony raises several important points related to the role of the auxiliaries. First, they were integral to German control of the region, and their participation in mass murder was a key part of the process of genocide. Second, they chose to incorporate, on their own or following the lead of the Germans, many of the ritual elements of mass killing involving alcohol consumption and acts of humiliation and abuse. Likewise, the presence of sightseers at the killing sites once again highlights the nature of such events as spectacular violence conducted during the day and in public spaces open to the local non-Jewish population. Finally, as Mishell went on to note, celebratory dinners and drinking bouts, with song and music, routinely followed the mass executions.

In his memoir, Mishell also noted that many of the executions continued into Sunday morning, with some of the killers moving from the mass graves to participate in Christian religious services. He observed, "After the executions, which lasted to the early hours on Sunday, the partisans [i.e., police auxiliaries] would join the villagers in church for early mass."[99] In this case, the ritual of mass murder was followed and celebrated in a religious rite during which the participants approached the altar to receive the body and blood of Christ in the form of a wafer and a chalice of wine. Whether from a chalice or a bottle in the hand, at least for these men, alcohol proved a key element in the ritual profession of faith and in mass murder.

According to another witness, a group of Lithuanian auxiliary policemen chose Christmas Day 1941 to liquidate the remaining Jews in the ghetto at Telšiai in Lithuania, a massacre in which some four hundred Jewish women perished at the hands of these policemen.[100] Similarly, a witness from a cooperative farm near Berezovka in Transnistria detailed weekly massacres by ethnic Germans. Gregory, a fourteen-year-old boy during these events, recalled, "During all this time [January–March 1942], on Sundays, the men from the village of Kartakai, a German colony, went around to the villages . . . and every Sunday, they shot a group of Jews in one of the villages. Every Sunday, they shot around two or three hundred people."[101] In preparation for these killings, the perpetrators brought along a jug of eau de vie (fruit brandy) and incorporated drinking ritual into the process of mass murder. Gregory noted, "They took drinking breaks between shooting. . . . They would go up to the cart and take turns drinking their alcohol from a tumbler."[102] Here again recreational drinking among the killers found its place in the midst of massacre.

Jew Hunts and the Killing Fields

Within the Baltic states, the large-scale killings of Jews that began with the German invasion often involved auxiliary policemen whom witnesses described as drunk. For example, Liuba Klor detailed the murder of Jewish men, women, and children in Šaukėnai by "drunken" Lithuanian auxiliaries on July 30, 1941.[103] Another witness of mass killings in the Ponary Forest recorded the daylong murder of more than four thousand persons in a diary entry of September 2, 1941: "Eighty Shaulists [i.e., Lithuanian auxiliaries] did the shooting. . . . They shot while they were drunk. Before shooting they tortured men and women horribly."[104] In this case, the killers continued their drunken revelry into the next day. The testimony also demonstrated that the drunken murderers often engaged in acts of physical and sexual abuse of their victims during the movement to the killing sites. Once again, the integration of sexual abuse, combined with the festive nature of the killings, provides an important insight for evaluating the mind-set of the perpetrators as they conjoined rape with mass murder, both involving public acts among their male colleagues.

Latvian auxiliaries also routinely drank during mass executions. Alex Kurzem, the young boy who served as one auxiliary unit's "mascot," outfitted with a customized uniform and military gear, described the course of events during the mass execution of Jews in the Belorussian town of Koidanov on October 21, 1941. Kurzem recalled the shooting of the adults, but noted, "They didn't waste their bullets on babies or children; they simply used the bayonet." He outlined the killing process: "A new group was shot and shoved into the pit. Like clockwork. Even though you could see that many of the soldiers were drunk, they were efficient."[105] For these auxiliary policemen, alcohol consumption was evidently a normal precursor to the killing of the Jews. Kurzem also discussed the unit's involvement in the killing of a group of *"partizani"* being held in a large building. As the auxiliaries approached the building, the men passed around flasks of *samogonka* (home-brewed vodka) as they "swaggered along."[106] The so-called partisans were quickly revealed to be a group of hundreds of Jewish women, children, and the aged. The auxiliaries barred the windows on the ground floor with pieces of wood and then set the building on fire.

As in the case of German mass murderers, there were auxiliaries who took delight in keeping track of the number of their victims and boasting about these totals among their peers. One Belorussian witness reflected on a mass execution by auxiliary policemen: "I remember that some of them, like Sklimovski and Logoch, who had participated in the shooting of the Jews, took great pleasure in counting by the dozens the Jews they had personally shot."[107] In this instance, upon finishing the executions, the policemen sat near the grave, drinking and smoking. In some cases, the physical possessions of the victims became a "tally board" for establishing one's superiority over his colleagues. Some Ukrainian auxiliary policemen wore a number of watches on each arm, prizes taken from the victims that symbolized their "scores." Nahum Kohn, a survivor, remembered seeing these auxiliaries with "watches lined up on their arms" who engaged in "vicious boasting about deeds against innocent Jews, and those deeds were so cruel as [to] make my hair stand on end." He continued, "Death is one thing, but sadistic torture is another matter, and those Ukrainian policemen boasted about the slow, painful and gruesome deaths they had especially devised for 'their' Jews."[108]

This braggadocio in the wake of mass murder mirrored the actions of the German killers discussed earlier and strongly reflected the individual's attempt to establish his masculine dominance or rank within the group. Not surprisingly, this masculine swaggering also embraced individual sexual performance, both consensual and transgressive. For example, Ukrainian auxiliaries in the Reichshof labor camp would boast of body counts as part of their courting ritual of female Polish workers. These auxiliaries openly bragged about their role in mass killings and "tried to outdo each other with stories of Jewish men they had humiliated and the thousands of naked Jewish women they had seen."[109]

As the behavior of these auxiliaries demonstrates, bragging or boasting, whether related to physical and athletic prowess or sexual exploits, is an important constituent of performative masculinity, since it demonstrates the individual's desire to valorize his own acts and to establish his superior masculine prowess in comparison to other men. The boasting among perpetrators about numbers killed constituted a need to demonstrate one's superior masculinity and achievements versus one's colleague who was also at the same time one's competitor. Similarly, sexual violence by auxiliaries against Jewish women provided a means for asserting one's domination over the victims as a manifestation of male power not only with respect to the women, but also with respect to the Jewish males who had been unable to "protect" them.

Alcohol, Auxiliaries, and Sexual Violence

Like their German overseers, SS and police auxiliaries often pressed young Jewish women and girls into domestic service prior to assaulting them.

In one example, a number of Lithuanian auxiliaries who became drunk as they "partied and danced" proceeded to sexually assault four Jewish girls who worked in the unit's kitchen. After the assaults, the girls were taken to a nearby Jewish cemetery and shot.[110] The integration of sexual assaults with the subsequent murder of the victims is a recurring theme of witness testimonies. In the forts surrounding the city of Kovno, SS auxiliaries would enter the prison basement and order Jewish women to strip and dance for them. One witness noted, "When they [the auxiliaries] got sufficiently excited they picked out the more beautiful ones and took them out by force and raped them." Women who resisted the sexual attacks were "raped and then shot."[111] Acts of sexual violence extended into the Kovno ghetto as well. In a December 1942 diary entry, Avraham Tory referred to the trauma of Jewish women who came to report the attacks at meetings of the Jewish council: "I heard the weeping of the women who were raped in public and humiliated despicably . . . devoid of any purpose or hope—lives which were nothing else but protracted physical and mental torture." He ended this entry with the words, "Eternal shame on the Nazis and their collaborators—the Lithuanians, the Ukrainians, and the others!"[112]

The establishment of ghettos in the occupied East created numerous opportunities for the physical and sexual abuse of the inhabitants by both Germans and their auxiliaries. In a number of cases, the auxiliaries bragged about their acts of abuse and murder within the ghettos. The historian Leonid Rein detailed the drunken boasting of a police commander who described how he personally threw Jews from balconies during a massacre of the Jews of Baranovichi in June 1943. Rein observed, "The perpetrators themselves often spoke openly about 'ghetto cleansings' and were not ashamed to describe in detail all the atrocities they committed during the *Aktionen*."[113] Indeed, the act of boasting was itself a manifestation of the perpetrators' pride in their deeds and by extension a public affirmation of their acts.

There are numerous examples of the integration of drinking, sexual torture or rape, and murder by SS and police auxiliaries. In a situation report of April 30, 1942, one German commander of an auxiliary police battalion noted that the men's drinking "had already repeatedly led to numerous unpleasant incidents."[114] An example of such an "unpleasant incident" involved a young Jewish woman from the Ukrainian village of Nove-Selo who was captured by Ukrainian auxiliaries and taken to the center of the village. The auxiliaries "tore off her clothes and then tied her hands and feet to a tree in such a way that she could be easily raped. After being raped by most of the men of the village through the night, she passed out and then bled to death."[115] At Treblinka, drunken auxiliaries selected Jewish women upon arrival at the camp and sexually assaulted them before forcing them into the gas chambers.[116] Similarly, SS auxiliaries in Belorussia traded plundered goods for homemade schnapps, which then initiated "a new wave of violence," including sexual assaults by the perpetrators. As one historian noted, "In general, schnapps played an important role in the abuse . . . [and] rapes were not uncommon."[117] While these incidents reaffirm the linkage between alcohol consumption and sexual violence, they also highlight the intoxication of power enjoyed by the perpetrators over their victims and their expression of virility and camaraderie through rape.

The linkage between sexual violence and killing also extended to the process of preparing for murder when auxiliary policemen surrounded ghettos on the night before planned executions. One participant, Alfred Metzner, testified, "At 4:00 a.m. the ghetto was surrounded by local policemen. Any Jews who tried to escape were immediately shot. . . . The night before, women had been raped by the police and then shot as well." He continued, "The police bragged about the number of women they had abused in this manner and tried to outdo one another."[118] Once again, the perpetrators conjoined conceptions of masculine prowess with acts of sexual and physical abuse to measure themselves among their comrades.

The participation of Lithuanian auxiliaries in acts of sexual and sexualized violence also is well documented. In Žasliai, auxiliaries gathered the town's entire Jewish population of one thousand on July 15, 1941, locked the women and children in the synagogue, and confined the men to the market square. As some of the auxiliaries searched for valuables, a witness recalled, others "stripped the women completely naked . . . while mocking them and behaving sadistically."[119] While forcing women to undress was a regular part of the killing process, one of the ways in which Lithuanian auxiliaries behaved "sadistically" involved the perpetrators' conduct of body cavity searches prior to the executions. One survivor recalled the drunken singing of the auxiliaries at an execution site in the Poligon Forest in September 1941, while another remembered the laughter of the guards as they probed inside their victims' bodies in search of valuables.[120] In this sense, the men's visible enjoyment and amusement in these acts provide a clear indication of the celebratory aspect of sexual violence among the perpetrators.

Murder Banquets

As in the case of their German superiors, the conduct of killing banquets by SS and police auxiliaries offers some of the most compelling evidence of the ways in which the perpetrators integrated celebratory ritual into their acts of murder. Simon Wiesenthal recalled his arrest by local Ukrainian policemen on July 6, 1941, and his transport to the Brygidki Prison in Lwów. At the prison, he watched as Ukrainian auxiliaries under German command murdered groups of Jews in the courtyard. At the center of the courtyard, there was "a table covered with bottles of vodka, sausages, plates of hors d'oeuvres, and bullets. . . . They [the Jews] were shot one by one in the neck by a Ukrainian executioner. After killing three or four men, he would go over to the table and help himself to a drink and some food while another Ukrainian reloaded the weapon."[121] Upon hearing the bells from a local Catholic church, the killers interrupted the murders to attend Mass. Wiesenthal observed that the perpetrators "took real pleasure in killing us," and these men returned to the courtyard after Mass to finish "their food and drink by candlelight while celebrating their day's accomplishments."[122]

In some cases, the perpetrators incorporated celebratory banquets into pre- and post-killing ritual. In the case of the former, upon the decision to liquidate the majority of the Jewish inhabitants of the Ukrainian labor camp at Gerulyay, a group of Ukrainian auxiliaries under Commandant B. Platakis "feasted throughout the night" before the murders. Early the next morning, after having extorted the camp's inhabitants of their last remaining hidden valuables, the auxiliaries began separating the prisoners into two groups: on one side young women and girls capable of work, and on the other those too old or too young to work. The group selected for execution numbered approximately four thousand women and children, and they were taken in groups of twenty to an execution site, ordered to undress, and then shot. In the case of the children, however, the killers simply "took them by the legs and smashed their little heads against trees."[123]

In one case of post-killing banquets, Lithuanian auxiliaries during a mass execution in September 1941 took breaks to eat and drink. These auxiliaries left the execution site and arrived at lunch "bloody and hungry and sometimes drunk before going back for the rest of their day's work."[124] A further indication of the perpetrators' mind-set was captured in the statement of a witness who recalled the killers returning from their day's efforts "singing songs in high spirits."[125] Similarly, Leo Kahn observed a group of Lithuanian auxiliaries reveling after the killing of the Jewish population of Eisiskes, including the murder of most of his family. It was near midnight as the young boy came out of his hiding place and heard "the sounds of carousing going on all over the town." He saw a neighbor's house "where a huge drunken party was in progress accompanied by wild laughter, rifle shots, and breaking bottles," a gathering by the perpetrators in "celebration of the annihilation of the Jews."[126]

Zenon Tumalovič witnessed the mass murder of Jews by Lithuanian auxiliaries in a forest in 1941. In a journal entry he described the aftermath:

> When they [the auxiliaries] were over with shooting all the shooters went to Švenčionys and they were singing Lithuanian songs . . . they were very joyful. They were drunk beforehand. In Švenčionys there was a big long table in the open air with food, like a holiday. The mood was supported by the orchestra. They got drunker. They took from the orchestra two men with beards, old believers, Russians. They took them away, and they were found killed as well. . . . It was a duty for them to shoot.

Tumalovič also noted the post-killing auction of the victims' belongings, items that filled two synagogues. "It was like euphoria. I saw it. People were very excited. It was after the killings, so everyone knew."[127] Once again, the perpetrators' intoxication or "euphoria" with the act of genocide was evident, as was their willingness to incorporate additional acts of killing into their drunken celebratory rituals.

Song, Music, and Celebratory Ritual

As Tumalovič's testimony shows, auxiliary policemen, like their German counterparts, also included song and music into the ritual of mass murder.

In many of these cases, mass executions featured alcohol and feasting as well. In one instance, a local priest witnessed the return of a group of Lithuanian auxiliaries from a mass execution at the Merkinė ghetto. He commented on how the perpetrators "returned from the cemetery with their sleeves rolled up, their hands covered with blood and their clothing and boots spattered with blood and marrow." More significantly, he remarked, "Their faces glowing, they sang happily and loudly the Lithuanian national anthem and other national songs."[128] The night following the executions, these men held an "elaborate ball" in the home of one of the victims, during which they "got very drunk and danced" as their wives and children "came to the ball dressed in the clothes of the murdered Jewish women and children."[129]

The incidents that Zenon Tumalovič and the priest described both highlight the incorporation of several practices within the overall killing process. First, the use of phrases such as "like a holiday" and an "elaborate ball" by the witnesses demonstrate the viewers' perception of the festive and celebratory atmosphere surrounding the killings. Similarly, the incorporation of singing and dancing offers another clear manifestation of the perpetrators' pride and enjoyment in these crimes. At times, the perpetrators even forced their victims to join in the singing as a method of public humiliation. After beating a group of Jewish women and children with rifle butts and wooden boards, Lithuanian auxiliaries sipped liquor from flasks and forced the victims to join them in their singing as they escorted the condemned to an execution site near the town of Kybartai on September 12, 1941.[130] In one sense, the use of "nationalist" songs by the killers reflected the symbolic denaturalization of the victims by the killers and their exclusion from the national community, a practice designed to legitimate the murders. Finally, these events underscore the incorporation of alcohol as an integral element in celebratory ritual, rather than as an instrument of disinhibition or coping by the killers.

The Role of the Polish "Blue" Police

During the German occupation of Poland, the Polish "blue" police, so named for their dark blue uniforms, emerged as an important adjunct for German security operations in the German zone of occupation. In the first months of the occupation, SS and police authorities envisioned the responsibilities of the blue police as restricted to traditional police duties related to the maintenance of public order and the enforcement of legal and economic regulations; however, this charter later expanded to include anti-partisan and anti-Jewish operations.[131] Initially, German assessments of the performance of the blue police were generally favorable, with a report of January 28, 1940, stating that "the employed Polish police officials have shown themselves to be very adept, willing and zealous during search actions [and] especially as scouts during combat against the bandits."[132] By May of that year, however, one German police official indicated growing concern with their performance: "While a part of the Polish police satisfactorily discharges its duty . . . another group of officials is lazy and neglectful in the discharge of duty in a manner that apparently borders on sabotage."[133] This complaint led to several arrests and a "cleansing action" within the blue police.[134]

While the actions of the Polish police reveal the complexity of the relationships between the occupied and the occupier, as well as the fraught relationship between Jews and Polish Gentiles, it is clear that some of these men, whether motivated by fear, hopes for material advantage, antisemitism, or a combination of all these factors, engaged in acts of murder and abuse. One study of the Polish blue police remarked on their increasing persecution of Jews and Sinti and Roma over the course of the German occupation and concluded, "Although not all Polish officers, but rather small groups of Polish policemen took part in such actions, they assumed horrific proportions, particularly in the large cities." The authors explained, "Most of the perpetrators from the ranks . . . [were] motivated by self-serving expectations and a sense of impunity—to abuse, extort or even murder others."[135]

As with the German forces, drinking ritual often became part of the killing process. In his examination of the blue police, Jan Grabowski stated that, when facing execution duties, some Polish policemen "liked to fortify themselves with vodka" and would "raise a glass, or two." More tellingly, he found that among policemen in the Tarnów area, "Another drinking session usually followed the executions, indicating a ritual, or pattern of behavior" for the policemen from this area.[136] In another study, the historians Jan and Irena Gross discussed the actions of the blue police as having "a large element of freedom and independence from superior

German authority" and concluded that the "direct motive to commit the majority of murders and denunciations of Jews hiding in the countryside was the desire to plunder them, to take over their belongings, which were imagined to be considerable."[137] In their analysis of more than a dozen of these cases, they identified a characteristic ritual among the perpetrators in which "after having finished [the killings], peasants gathered in the apartment of one of the participants to drink vodka, as if to celebrate with a meal their joint deed, to divide the spoils, and probably also to decompress."[138]

In his wartime diary, Zygmunt Klukowski repeatedly refers to acts of violence by intoxicated German and Polish policemen. As to the latter, he recorded an incident in April 1942 concerning a Polish policeman who "being completely drunk, began shooting out the windows in Jewish homes." He added, "The Jews were terrorized."[139] In another case, German gendarmes and Polish police arrived at the scene of a fire at a sugar refinery. Described as "totally drunk," the policemen apparently mistook the local fire brigade for partisans and opened fire, wounding one of the firemen before recognizing their error.[140] This incident clearly resulted from the intoxication of the policemen and reflected the common practice of both gendarmes and Polish policemen of drinking on duty. Furthermore, it not only highlights the alcohol consumption among these men, but also shows the adverse effects of such behaviors for the local Jewish and Gentile population.[141]

The Need for "Helping Hands"

In the final analysis, it is not surprising that SS and police auxiliaries engaged in the full range of activities pursued by their German masters. Indeed, the German administration created these units for the express purpose of enforcing Nazi legal measures and racial policy, and, based on the limited number of German policemen, the successful subjugation of the eastern territories depended on these adjuncts. It also is apparent that their motivations ranged from opportunism, nationalism, antisemitism, and anticommunism, to a dynamic confluence of all these factors, based on changing local conditions and the course of the war.[142] Nevertheless, it is clear from the evidence that ethnic auxiliaries and local policemen integrated alcohol consumption into their daily routine, whether that involved the control of the population or mass murder. Drinking ritual not only provided a means for disinhibition and facilitation of mass murder among these men, but it incorporated cultural perceptions of masculinity and found expression in acts of physical and sexual brutality in which song, feasting, and laughter served as overt expressions of celebration. Similarly, soldiers of the Wehrmacht who marched into the East as conquerors also experienced their own sense of metaphorical and literal intoxication in these colonial spaces.

ALCOHOL AND THE GERMAN ARMY

Writing in his journal during the campaign in Russia, the infantryman Willy Peter Reese expressed the attraction of devastation in the language of drinking: "Now we humans could survive in inhumanity and love the intoxication [*Rausch*] and beauty of destruction, praise the shards of our own destinies, adore carrion, and give it our yes." He added, "Our comradeship was made from mutual dependence, from living together in next to no space. Our humor was born out of sadism, gallows humor, satire, obscenity, spite, rage, and pranks with corpses, squirted brains, lice, pus and shit, the spiritual zero."[1] In this sentence, Reese encapsulated the idea of a comradeship that was established by sharing in intoxicating acts of obliteration that encompassed the most atrocious manifestations of human behavior, deeds that became not only commonplace but also a perverse source of amusement among the perpetrators. To be sure, the linkage between intoxication, fury, and destruction existed in the German army prior to the rise of National Socialism. In his diary of the Great War, Ernst Jünger reflected on combat by exclaiming, "The turmoil of

our feeling was called forth by rage, alcohol, and the thirst for blood. . . .
I was boiling over with a fury that gripped me—it gripped us all. . . . The
overpowering desire to kill gave us wings."[2] While combat itself was imbued with the intoxication of destruction and killing, the Third Reich
would exalt violence and warfare and make them defining characteristics
of a hypermasculine identity, a process that would find its apotheosis on
the eastern front.

Alcohol, Race, and Atrocity

The maelstrom of violence inflicted on the peoples of the occupied East
occurred in the context of an apocalyptic ideological contest in which perceptions of racial superiority and a colonial mentality created the framework for acts of brutality. From his perspective, Ilya Ehrenburg described
the German invaders as "drunk with schnapps and blood."[3] In fact, for
Reese and his fellow soldiers, drinking and the abuse of the local population often went hand in hand. Zygmunt Klukowski's diary repeatedly detailed the violence committed by intoxicated Luftwaffe (air force) men
on visits into town from the surrounding airfields. In an entry for August
6, 1941, he noted, "Especially at night they [the airmen] begin drinking,
making lots of noise, and beating Jews."[4] Such visits could be lethal, as
in the case of a "German flyer [who] shot a young twenty-two-year-old
woman to death" a month earlier.[5] As the historian Wendy Jo Gertjejanssen aptly observed, "Alcohol played a large role in the behavior of soldiers on the eastern front, and it helped fuel people's animosity already
present in war-torn eastern Europe."[6] With respect to the SS and police,
atrocities committed by these men emerged from an "organizational culture and the ideology that underpinned it . . . that created an environment
in which persecution, exploitation, and murder became both acceptable
and desirable attributes."[7] The Wehrmacht, like its SS and police counterparts, also had a distinct organizational culture, and this culture was defined by specific beliefs, norms, and rituals, including hard drinking, that
reinforced group identity and established expectations of its members.
In her study of the Imperial German Army, the historian Isabel Hull identified a "military culture" that "propelled the army to ever greater, and in
the end, dysfunctional extremes of violence." In Hull's view, this military

culture "bequeathed practices, habits of action, and ways of behaving" that established a "cult of violence" and created a trajectory for the armies of the Third Reich leading to genocide in World War II.[8]

Whether one accepts the argument concerning the transmission of a cult of violence between the *Kaiserreich* and Hitler's Reich, the creation of culture within an organization is nevertheless a powerful force. With respect to the Wehrmacht, the historian David Stahel argued that "the culture of violence sustained and propagated within the German army goes a long way to understanding how so many 'ordinary men' became complicit in so much violence."[9] While the "culture of violence" reflected in the SS and police was not the same as that of the German army, these organizations incorporated many of the same ritualistic devices into their everyday operations on the eastern front. Likewise, the celebration of a martial military ethos and a sense of being part of a racially superior masculine community were shared beliefs.[10] All these organizations incorporated alcohol consumption into their "'manly' rituals, all of them violating or transgressing domestic and civilian norms," in which excessive drinking became one means for facilitating and celebrating deeds of physical and sexual violence, acts that were "practiced, reported, or applauded—*together.*"[11] Wehrmacht fellowship evenings replete with large quantities of alcohol served for some as proof of the "strong, unshakeable belief in the German Reich."[12]

If SS and policemen, along with their auxiliaries, reached for the bottle as they conducted and celebrated their duties in the East, their counterparts in the Wehrmacht also used alcohol in massive amounts during the conquest and subjugation of these areas. Already in the Polish campaign, the senior leadership of the German army recognized the "temptations of alcohol misuse" and the role played by drunkenness in acts of brutality and indiscipline.[13] Vasily Grossman, a Red Army correspondent, reported on drunkenness among German troops and the widespread presence of alcohol within their ranks from the first days of the invasion of the Soviet Union in June 1941. In an interview that summer, one Red Army battalion commander told Grossman that "the Germans attacking him were completely drunk. Those they captured stank of alcohol, and their eyes were bloodshot." Based on his own inspection of German positions, Grossman published the following account in the military newspaper *Krasnaya Zvezda* (Red star): "German trenches, strongpoints, officers' and soldiers' bunkers . . . There are French wines and brandy; Greek olives; yellow, carelessly squeezed lemons . . . a big oval tin of fish preserve. . . . And fragments of a Soviet shell are lying amid this fascist feast."[14] As the British newspaper correspondent Alexander Werth visited captured German fighting positions in September 1941, he also noted "biscuit cartons and empty vodka bottles" scattered among recent copies of "German illustrated newspapers."[15] Tellingly, the soldiers on the opposing sides tied the brutal behavior of their adversaries in part to the consumption of alcohol. While Soviet soldiers and correspondents cited atrocities committed by drunken Germans, Karl Fuchs, a member of a tank crew, used the same language to describe the Red Army in a diary entry on August 4, 1941. He remarked, "The pitiful hordes on the other side are nothing but felons who are driven by alcohol and the threat of pistols pointed at their heads."[16]

By December 1941, supplying the *Ostheer* (Eastern army) with its "fascist feast" became increasingly difficult, as evidenced by *wagonloads* of French red wine shipped to the front that had frozen, bursting the bottles and leaving only "chunks of red ice and glass splinters."[17] The shipment to the East of massive quantities of French wines, cognac, and even champagne, as well as schnapps, reflected in one sense the regime's attempt to keep the combat front supplied with luxury items such as alcohol and tobacco. The consumption of alcohol, however, above all, became an important rite for creating the closed martial and masculine communities of the combat soldier.

Drinking among the "Band of Brothers"

Based on the diaries and memoirs of German soldiers, it is clear that drinking rituals were prevalent within the Wehrmacht, especially in the East. Such practices were in part merely a continuation of traditions established within the Imperial army where "over-indulgence in brandy" led to "excesses" including "damage to property and, occasionally, even, physical assault."[18] Likewise, barracks life among one's comrades, including heavy drinking, bellowing "obscene songs," and visits to brothels, created "the image of a soldier that embodied a masculine ideal of a man who is strong and smart, yet gruff and ready to use force."[19] Although group drinking rituals, misogyny, song, and readiness for violence among soldiers were not an invention of the Third Reich, these rituals found even more radical expression in the German army under a regime in which racial identity and hypermasculinity would be translated into acts of domination, whether on the battlefield or in the bedroom.

Like their counterparts in the SS and the police, soldiers used alcohol for a variety of reasons, including for disinhibition, facilitation of violence, celebration, and coping, while some used alcohol as a remedy against the cold of the Russian winters.[20] They also integrated drinking, music, and song into celebratory activities of male camaraderie. Reese recalled "being wired" after battle and using "brandy and card games" to come down from the adrenaline-induced high of combat. At such times, he also noted the importance of camaraderie among his fellow soldiers as they "sang songs . . . and got drunk every night. . . . We sang and walked, buzzy and optimistic on rum and champagne, and accepted the adventures ahead with an alcoholic equanimity."[21] Reese's description of routine drinking bouts as a method for male bonding is confirmed in the memoir of Lieutenant Gottlob Bidermann, who described his platoon's consumption of homemade schnapps in Russia: "As we passed the bottle, we felt an instinctive bond that only the survivors [of battle] could know. Together we had known wind and heat, life and death."[22] Indeed, shared bottles provided a visible demonstration of comradeship that linked individuals with the unit's actions, whether in the wake of battle or atrocity.

In the first months of the invasion of Russia, the physical act of drinking for many soldiers was related to the psychological intoxication of combat and conquest in the East, as individual men experienced their own feelings of *Ostrausch*. Erich Hager, a soldier with a tank division, listened with his comrades to a speech by Hitler on October 3, 1941, in which the führer proclaimed, "This opponent [the Red Army] has already broken down and will never rise again!" In his diary, Hager reflected on the effects of the broadcast: "All sorts were really enthused. Many were drunk."[23] For these men the psychological intoxication of impending victory prophesied by their führer found expression and release in drunken revelry with their comrades in arms. It did not take much for such revelry to cross over into acts of physical abuse and murder, as was the case with two German officers from the Twentieth Armored Division who after getting drunk shot the family they were quartered with.[24]

As the dreams of rapid victory evaporated and the campaign in Russia stretched into its second year, the bottle became both a source of coping and courage for many *Landser* (infantrymen) stationed in the East. Guy Sajer, after surviving a combat engagement in Ukraine in the spring of 1944 that resulted in the deaths of seventy of his comrades, recalled, "We drank everything we could get hold of, trying to blot out the memory of a hideous day."[25] Another soldier, Harry Mielert, after enduring an intense Russian artillery barrage, noted, "Cattle cried, soldiers searched through all the buildings, barrels of red wine were taken away in small *panje* wagons [horse carts], here and there men were drinking and singing, in the meantime explosions again and new roaring fires."[26]

At the front lines, alcohol, described by soldiers as *Wutmilch* (literally, rage milk), also served to steel one's nerves in the face of impending battle. In a conversation with a comrade, one soldier exclaimed, "'There's as much vodka, schnapps and Terek liquor on the front as there are Paks [antitank guns].'" This soldier then asserted that alcohol consumption was "'the easiest way to make heroes. Vodka purges the brain and expands the strength. I've been doing nothing but drinking for two days now. It's the best way to forget that I've got seven pieces of metal in my gut.'"[27] For this soldier, alcohol was both an intoxicant and a pain reliever that allowed him not only to deal with his physical and psychological wounds but also to express male bravado and his own toughness in dealing with *seven* pieces of shrapnel embedded in his body. Still, he was not alone among his army comrades who "stoked" their courage "with quantities of schnapps."[28]

The "Intoxication of Destruction"

In the occupied eastern territories, alcohol consumption within the Wehrmacht was frequently associated with acts of indiscipline, especially cases of physical and sexual violence. In November 1941, a drunken soldier assaulting a Russian woman was interrupted by her husband, who was then shot by the soldier. The intoxicated soldier then entered another house and killed a second man.[29] Sometimes, acts of armed violence by inebriated soldiers also extended to fellow Germans, as was the case when a tipsy Wehrmacht officer, Egon Wilke, sought to oppose his late-night arrest by a police patrol by firing five shots from his sidearm. Fortunately for Wilke, his aim, obviously influenced by his intoxicated state, was off, resulting in no injuries to the policemen, but did lead to his arrest for five days on the charge of "disturbing the peace."[30]

As might be expected, acts of indiscipline, especially sexual assaults, were often associated with heavy consumption of alcohol, a trend that existed in both the occupied territories of the East and the West.[31] The Wehrmacht High Command was clearly aware of the relationship between heavy drinking and violence among the troops. In a report from a conference of German military doctors held in Berlin in 1942, alcohol abuse figured as one of four main reasons for "criminal acts" by soldiers. The report noted, "Higher attraction to alcohol through the influence of comrades or increased alcohol availability, especially in the occupied territories, lead a considerable proportion of soldiers of high quality and good character to come into conflict with the law."[32] The report's findings are unsurprising, given the historical connection between alcohol and armies and resulting acts of indiscipline, abuse, or atrocity. However, this does not explain the role of alcohol in cases in which atrocious behavior itself had been normalized, including the killing of Jews, Sinti and Roma, or Slavs. In fact, Nazi racial ideology, criminal orders issued to the Wehrmacht, and the imperial and colonial framework of occupation combined with alcohol consumption to facilitate atrocious behavior far beyond the boundaries of traditional warfare.

One particular incident offers an insight into the way in which some soldiers consumed alcohol and its connection to atrocity. In a conversation secretly recorded by British intelligence, two senior German POWs, General Wilhelm Ritter von Thoma and General Heinrich Eberbach, traded stories on their wartime experiences, including an incident involving soldiers under Thoma's command in Russia. Thoma mentioned court-martial proceedings against an army captain, a lieutenant, and several enlisted men based on an incident that occurred as the men drank their wine ration along with half a field cup of schnapps. The men, quartered in a peasant's hut with a Russian family, obviously were enjoying themselves. As they drank, the army captain, at some point, "pulled out his revolver and shot down the peasant [male head of the family]," who was sitting at the table across from him. The captain then ordered the body be removed. The dead man's wife began to scream, gathered her three children, including a two-month-old infant, and retreated to the sleeping platform above the oven across the room. Disturbed by the woman's screaming and the children's weeping, the captain turned to the lieutenant and commanded, "'I want peace, clear them out from up there!' And he drew his revolver and shot down the woman."[33]

The story did not end with the second killing, however. After the mother's body had been taken outside, one of the men began to play the accordion, and the men continued to drink. Sometime later the captain ordered that the girl and the boy be shot, and, finally, the infant was "knocked" off the stove and "picked up by its foot" before being thrown out into the snow to die. When the news of these killings reached Thoma's headquarters, a military judge interviewed the killers, who "completely denied that they were in the least bit drunk and said they were absolutely sober." In justification of their actions, the accused stated, "'They [the Russians] weren't human beings, they only count as animals, nothing at all can happen to us.'"[34] In the end, the perpetrators were proved right, as Hitler overturned their initial prison convictions and Thoma's recommendation for the death penalty for the two officers. According to Thoma, he received notification that "'the FÜHRER confirms that it is absolutely in order for the men to be punished. But he refuses to authorize the death sentence, because according to his standards, the Russians are not human beings.' . . . They [the soldiers] were sent to a sort of penal 'Kompanie.'"[35]

In addition to the apparent connection of alcohol to the murders, this incident once again demonstrates the combination of drinking ritual, music, and male camaraderie that helped to create the atmosphere for the killings. Interestingly, the only reason the men faced charges in the first place was that a senior officer elected to put them on trial instead of choosing to ignore their actions, as was his discretionary prerogative. Also, the killer's description of the Russian family as not "human beings," including a two-month-old infant, perfectly demonstrates the way in which atrocity became justified and normalized throughout the occupied eastern territories.

The incident involving the murder of the Russian family is also indicative of what one historian described as "the extremist culture, indeed fanaticism, of the German Wehrmacht, especially in the east."[36] The historian Ben Shepherd aptly observed that the invasion of the Soviet Union "stoked [Wehrmacht] officers' anti-Bolshevik attitudes and steeled them to be more ruthless in the cause of smooth-running occupation."[37] For his part, General Gotthard Heinrici, a senior German army commander in the East, expressed these thoughts in letters home to his family in which he described a "revolting countryside" under the yoke of a "loathsome animal" (i.e., Bolshevism).[38] These perceptions and this type of rhetoric "helped the Wehrmacht and the SS to murder, rape, take control of villages, or run the camps. . . . Not only were the soldiers and officers able to commit atrocities more easily, but in all likelihood, they would have been more willing to break rules to be sexual or to rape."[39]

The experience of Lieutenant Richard Wagner, a supply officer, stationed in the East in December 1941, offers another illustration of the influence of the anti-Slavic prejudice that accompanied German officers into the East. In a letter dated December 6, 1941, to his former SA colleagues, Wagner recounted his experiences in Russia. He emphasized, if not embellished, his combat experience on the front lines during the invasion and described his unit's position "now as always the farthest in the East." He described the Russians as a "rabble" but admitted a grudging respect for the Russian air force. He noted that several former SA comrades had crossed his path and that these meetings provided a ready opportunity to "have a snifter" (*einen zu verlöten*), normally "raw vodka" but "on occasion a bottle of French cognac or even champagne" as well. He then returned to a portrayal of the local villages, a description that includes the words "dirty," "filthy," and "putrid." He ended his letter by promising to share "all sorts of interesting news" upon his return home.[40] In fact, Wagner was in charge of maintaining the unit's war diary, a position that gave him access to a great amount of information related to his division's combat and "security" activities, certainly one of the reasons he was able to make such a promise to his colleagues at home.

While Wagner's letter refers obliquely to acts of atrocity in its closing sentences, it does raise important points. First, Wagner, like many of his SA colleagues, ended up in the German armed forces during the war, and they continued to identify with the SA and their compatriots after entering the army. Second, drinking rituals remained an essential part of reaffirming their camaraderie when these men met in the occupied territories. Third, the portrayal of Russians and Russia as "dirty," "filthy," and "putrid" offers an explicit insight into the mentality of Wagner and his fellow occupiers and perfectly reflects the portrait painted by National Socialist propaganda of the East and its peoples in general. Fourth, his boast of always being nearest to the front lines, whether true or not, was intended as an expression of male military bravado, distinguishing him from his less masculine comrades farther to the rear.

East versus West

The experience of German military occupation in France also indicates that heavy alcohol consumption, combined with song and celebratory ritual, threatened to, and often did, cross over into acts of violence between soldiers and local civilians. In her study of Wehrmacht sex crimes, the historian Birgit Beck not only identified the consumption of alcohol as a prelude to acts of sexual aggression by soldiers, but also noted the differences in the ways military authorities prosecuted such crimes in the occupied territories of Western and Northern Europe as opposed to those committed in the East.[41] Drinking resulted not only in acts of sexual aggression, but also in acts of general aggression between males. In one example, a bar in Paris was closed by order of a senior German officer "when drunken members of the military administration sang Nazi songs . . . and physical violence threatened to break out."[42] The experience of this Parisian bar was echoed in drinking establishments throughout the Loire region as "drunken brawls were widespread," a pattern attributed by one French policeman to "the mingling of males and females and above all because of the abuse of alcohol."[43] And while intoxication and aggression, including incidents of sexual violence, certainly were not unknown in France, military authorities "ruthlessly punished" public drunkenness and frequently executed soldiers for rape, as the German occupiers "drew on gendered metaphors to style themselves not as dominators, but as chivalrous, 'fatherly protectors[s]' of a feminised and infantilised French nation."[44]

After the Allied landings at Normandy in June 1944, France became the front line for German soldiers attempting to repel the Allied onslaught. Under these circumstances, Wehrmacht soldiers in France increasingly reached for the bottle to deal with the stress of combat. Infantryman Helmut Hörner was no exception, as he started his day on July 2, 1944, in a bunker by filling his canteen with calvados (apple brandy). Facing American lines, Hörner wrote in his diary, "I don't want anything to do with food. My friend the good French Calvados tastes much better and I still have two canisters in the bunker. . . . When the mail arrives I am no longer in any condition to read the letters from far-away Germany."[45] The following day, July 3, he again began his day by sharing brandy while under attack and reflected, "I believe we will all become drunkards who will have to be treated in hospitals after the war."[46]

Like their counterparts in the West, Wehrmacht soldiers in the East huddled to drink in bunkers (or in requisitioned peasant huts) while their staff and garrison counterparts gathered in Wehrmacht canteens with bottles of beer, wine, cognac, or schnapps. A policeman, Josef Reiter*, testified after the war about the mass murder of the Jews of Vilna in late 1941, a killing action that lasted several days with participation by the police and Wehrmacht forces. Reiter recalled the sounds of the daylong firing of machine guns, machine pistols, and rifles. At the end of one such day, he joined a group of soldiers in the army canteen, and during a discussion of the killings, the soldiers stated, "The police were the worst of all during the executions of the Jews."[47] Without a doubt, SS and police units conducted the vast majority of the killings; however, German army units engaged in their own massacres, especially related to reprisal and "anti-partisan" operations. While some soldiers sought to avoid participation in the killings, others stood over the dead bodies of the victims "cracking jokes" about the corpses, and participants got "copiously drunk" in the wake of massacres, even if there was "*no universal appetite* for celebration."[48]

While their reasons for drinking may have varied, German soldiers in the field gathered regularly at fellowship evenings to celebrate promotions, the award of combat medals, or to deal with the stresses of combat by having a "good booze up."[49] In a letter home from Russia, dated October 6, 1943, Corporal Gustav Gerhardts wrote, "Yesterday there was a whole bunch of schnapps again from all possible types as well as Underberg, Steinhagen, rum, etc. We can't get away from the booze!"[50] Another soldier, in a letter to his father, described one such drinking bout in which seven soldiers finished four bottles of wine, a bottle of brandy, a bottle of cognac, a bottle of rum, and a bottle of gin, all during one evening.[51] These drinking bouts often resulted in sexual encounters, both consensual and coerced, either with local women or with German women from among the myriad of Wehrmacht, police, and party auxiliaries, largely in clerical or administrative positions, sent east to support the conquest.[52]

Sexual Assault and the German Army

Soldiers garrisoned in or near cities could visit soldier's homes or German cultural houses to drink, dance, and to seek the companionship of female auxiliaries. Under wartime circumstances, short-term romantic liaisons emerged that abruptly ended with the departure of either partner.[53] In addition to such consensual relationships, the invasion of the Soviet Union opened the door to acts of physical and sexual abuse on a broad scale, not only based on the size of the invasion force, some three million men, but perhaps more importantly based on the way in which Hitler and the Wehrmacht High Command had framed the campaign. In many cases, "consensual" relationships in fact involved sexual coercion, as the victims had little choice but to submit to the demands of the occupier. For example, Sergeant Erich Aichinger took at least two Jewish "girlfriends" during his time in Slonim. The girls lived with him in his room, and at least one of them routinely served alcohol at gatherings of local Nazi officials. Despite his relationship with the women, Aichinger watched as one of his "girlfriends" and her mother were killed during the liquidation of the local ghetto. In order to be able to watch the execution, Aichinger allegedly drank so much at the massacre site that he was warned to stop.[54]

In a war of annihilation underpinned with racial prejudice, sexual violence by members of the Wehrmacht emerged as a distinct part of the process of conquest. The criminal orders that preceded the invasion, the Third Reich's glorification of violence and aggression, and the apocalyptic framework in which the attack was launched all served to radicalize the behavior of individual soldiers as they marched east in a self-styled racial Armageddon against "Judeo-Bolshevism."[55] Even apart from the virulently racist and hypermasculine standards that Wehrmacht formations marched under as they moved into the East, war by its very nature has forever been tied to acts of sexual aggression by soldiers against subject populations.

Indeed, throughout twentieth-century European history, as Dagmar Herzog observed, "sexual violence accompanied warfare at almost every point . . . in quite distinct, historically and geographically specific, ways. . . . Instances of sexual violence ranged from gang rape and genital mutilation of both women and men to forced impregnation and sexual slavery and coerced marriage for women . . . to terrifying systematic and inventive sadisms within the concentration camps."[56] The eastern front and occupied zones certainly fit this description. From the opening days of the invasion, "rape, gang rape, and sexual torture were forms of violence that accompanied the brutal German war in Eastern Europe."[57] Soviet witness testimonies detailed mass rapes of specific groups such as nurses and hospital workers, as well as specific acts of sexual violence, including genital mutilations and the cutting off of women's breasts.[58] In contrast to the occupied western territories, the East was a "space without law" in which traditional legal norms lost their meaning and their power to deter acts of physical and sexual abuse by Wehrmacht soldiers.[59]

Soldiers, Alcohol, and Sexual Violence

In his study of one German army division in Russia, Waitman Beorn concluded, "German civil authorities (as well as military men) frequently abused alcohol to excess and participated in depraved sexual acts outside the pale of acceptability in the West [e.g., France, Belgium, Holland], where "fraternization" with racially equal and more familiar partners was easier and more widespread."[60] These acts of violence, often linked, as we have seen, with heavy drinking and celebratory occasions, accompanied the German occupation from the start. For example, a group of officers from a grenadier regiment "celebrated" the successful occupation of Riga in July 1941 by creating a "drinking den" and forcing "several dozens of Jewish girls . . . to strip naked, dance, and sing songs" before they raped and shot them.[61] Later that year, three soldiers from the 253rd Veterinary Company celebrated Christmas Eve in a Russian village by leaving the unit party, breaking into a house, and gang raping a local woman. In this case, the men were brought up on charges, but a court of appeals vacated the original fifteen-month prison sentences based on the men's long period of enforced abstinence as a result of the war and the "lack of sustained injury or psychological damage" to the raped woman.[62] In another instance, a group of soldiers, after partying, decided to "pick up a young Russian woman for the evening." Unsuccessful in their approach, the men broke into a house and abused and raped a young mother in the presence of her three children. In defense of their actions, the men justified the assault by arguing that the woman had not resisted, a defense that ultimately led to a nominal three-month sentence for the assailants in a penal unit.[63] Another group of German soldiers attempted to rape a Russian woman in her home as she prepared dinner for them. The woman, however, was able to escape and hide outside with her daughter. When the two reentered the house the next morning after the soldiers' departure, they found the child's grandmother naked and tied to the bed with ropes, a victim of gang rape.[64]

In his study of Wehrmacht trials of soldiers charged with sex crimes, David Snyder addressed cases in which drinking played a role. He declared, "Despite the alcohol-fueled asocial antics, the focal point in such cases remained the defendants' degree of intoxication, not the degree of danger a defendant's asocial behavior posed to the Volksgemeinschaft [people's community]. . . . Toxicology rather than ideology dominated the process."[65] In a sample of some eighty cases involving alcohol consumption and acts of homosexuality or rape, Snyder found that only nineteen of the defendants, or about 24 percent, were judged to have diminished capacity as a result of "complete inebriation" (*Volltrunkenheit*). Interestingly, he also notes that military courts were more inclined to punish officers and senior enlisted men for intoxication "as a grievous violation of command responsibility."[66] Some courts do appear to have treated junior enlisted men involved in alcohol-related sex crimes more leniently. In one case, a drunken army corporal who had plundered a home and raped a Jewish girl in occupied Poland in 1942 was found guilty only of the offense of "intoxication," despite the fact that the crimes of sexual assault and race defilement appeared in the court's judgment.[67]

In addition to the inclusion of mitigating or even exculpatory factors by Wehrmacht judges concerning degree of intoxication or the length of a soldier's forced abstinence, these courts acted as mediators of "female honor" by applying standards of acceptable and respectable behavior for women who came forward to accuse their assailants of sexual violence. In this sense, the courts became arbiters of the accepted standards of masculinity as well. The racial background of the victim, of course, was a factor in the court's considerations, often to the detriment of the accuser, as the court greeted female victims in the occupied East with "a certain mistrust" under the assumption that Russian civilians exhibited a "tendency to exaggeration and false descriptions."[68]

Sexual Boasting and Sexual Torture

Boasting about sexual conquests is one of the clearest manifestations of performative masculinity and male bravado, and such bragging often occurs among groups of men as a means of establishing one's superior virility or as a means to seek admiration and approval from colleagues. Under the Third Reich, stories of "alcohol excesses and stories of sexual exploits" reached from the front lines all the way to the home front.[69] The boasts of one German lieutenant perfectly illustrate the nature of sexual violence and aggression present on the eastern front, as well as his pride in these crimes. In a secretly recorded conversation, a German POW recounted how he and six other POWs had listened as a Wehrmacht lieutenant described his exploits in Russia. The lieutenant told the group, "We got hold of a female spy who was running around in the area. We hit her on the noggin with a stick and then flayed her behind with an unsheathed bayonet. Then we fucked her, threw her out on her back, lobbed grenades, . . . In the end, she died, and we threw her body away." As shocking as this story was to hear, the listener was more outraged by the reaction of the other POWs—all officers—who were "all laughing their heads off."[70]

The lieutenant's account of the torture, rape, and murder of the woman is illustrative in several respects. First, the narrator and participant in these horrific events clearly expected the approval of his fellow officers, an affirmation that he achieved in the case of all but one of the listeners. As this example shows, the language used by the perpetrators in cases of sexual abuse embodied martial and male performance. As Ute Frevert notes, "Crude imagery, often violent, induced an almost cathartic effect: apparently reassuring each other that one could 'use' women sexually, and one could 'supply' it reinforced male self-esteem." Such behaviors "enhanced and upgraded the male primary group."[71] Second, the sexual nature of the initial torture with a bayonet and the "flaying" of the woman's buttocks clearly was used as a preliminary ritual to gang rape. Third, the description of throwing the woman out "on her back" was not an inconsequential detail, and one can surmise that the tossing of the grenades was part of a "game" of hitting the target, in this case the woman's genitalia. Finally, the perpetrator's pride in his role in the abuse and murder of the woman is apparent, as was his success in illustrating not only his sexual prowess, but his readiness to murder—both manifestations of the hypermasculine standards of performative masculinity under the Nazi regime.

The incorporation of torture and killing into sexual assaults by soldiers offers further insights into the ways in which group solidarity and acts of communal performative masculinity bound the perpetrators together. In early 1944, a group of German soldiers who were preparing to withdraw from their headquarters in a Ukrainian village near the Cherkassy Pocket "were drinking there, they were having fun." The soldiers' "fun" included shooting at the religious icons hanging on the wall of a local house and the sexual assault of a young woman living there. In this case, the woman was crucified on the wall of the home, her breasts were sliced, and an empty alcohol bottle was inserted into her vagina. Upon his arrival at the house, a Soviet officer witnessed the scene, including the food and alcohol still on the table, and heard the story of how the Germans had been drinking and shooting in the house before their retreat.[72]

The terrible fate of this woman and the details of her abuse and murder once again highlight the ways in which acts of atrocity became conjoined with drinking ritual, group camaraderie, and manifestations of male power. First, the sexual assault and the killing took place within the context of a group celebration involving eating, drinking, and a shooting competition in which the participants demonstrated their skill by using the religious icons in the house as targets. Second, the abuse of the woman was orchestrated with clear intent and included acts of sexual torture, along with posing her Christ-like on the wall previously occupied by the icons. Third, as noted by another Ukrainian survivor, acts of rape and violence became especially prevalent during German evacuations, as the soldiers "became cruel, even more cruel, you know, with their power and killing, and everything, and rape."[73] Finally, the treatment of Soviet women in the face of their liberation by the Red Army also can be seen as a concluding manifestation of the German male's control over these "foreign" bodies and a final ritual of humiliation aimed at the Soviet men who were charged with protecting them, but arrived too late.

Rituals of Humiliation and Trophy Photos

Like their counterparts in the SS and police, soldiers engaged in rituals of humiliation of the conquered populations in the East, and they took and exchanged photos of their activities. In a familiar pattern, soldiers during the Polish campaign also forced Jews to scrub streets and cut off their beards. One soldier noted, "It was a Saturday, and they presented themselves in front of us with kaftans and little round hats. Many of them had shaggy beards. But it was their bad luck, for a schoolhouse in which we were quartered needed cleaning."[74] Already in 1939, many soldiers used their position as conquerors as "an opportunity to humiliate them [the Jews] by cutting their beards and administering beatings."[75] In letters home to friends and family, soldiers described acts of humiliation and degradation that they had seen or participated in. One German soldier shared his experience during the conquest of Poland in a letter home in September 1939. Failing in his attempt to extort a Jewish man of a radio, the soldier was surprised when the man revealed a cache of 130 bottles and seven barrels of wine. Fearing the wine was "poisoned," soldiers made the man drink from several bottles with the cynical remark, "Now wench, cheers!" He wrote, "It's better for the pistol to sound, before I believe [a Jew], because we have plenty of ammunition."[76] In this instance, the act of drinking was turned into a ritual of humiliation for the Jewish man by making him guzzle from several bottles while he was linguistically emasculated by being called a "wench." Another soldier, Harry Kupke, took "delight" in the physical emasculation of his victims by "tieing [*sic*] hand grenades to the genitals of male victims and forcing them to run till the grenade exploded." According to one witness, Kupke frequently recounted these events, and "he would laugh and boast about it."[77]

Reflecting on the vast number of cameras carried eastward by German forces and their penchant for using them, Ilya Ehrenburg wrote, "The Germans like to take photographs of their exploits. I have seen photographs of gallows for Serbians and of murdered Greek women. I have seen photographs taken by Germans in Russia: an old Russian peasant being shot, a naked girl in the square of a Ukrainian town."[78] In addition to the images, captions on the backs of photos captured the perpetrator's mind-set and intent. For example, one photograph shows a German soldier cutting the hair of a kneeling Jew, explained by the cynical comment, "The locks fall. Jewish rascals at the mobile barber shop."[79] Wehrmacht troops in Yugoslavia also indulged in acts of "cruel humor" by throwing food to prisoners in a camp in order to "take photographs of the starving men running and fighting for a mouthful of food."[80]

One Jewish witness, Lev Rozhetsky, recalled his family's deportation along with the Jews of Odessa in January 1942 and the suffering they endured due to the bitter cold and German brutality. As children and the elderly fell dead or dying to the ground in a "howling blizzard," Rozhetsky observed, "the Germans laughed and took pictures of us with their cameras."[81] Similarly, Jakob Lewi, a Polish witness, testified about mass killings in Lwów during which German officers and military policemen snapped photos of the murder of "children, women, and the elderly."[82] In another gruesome example, a member of a Luftwaffe antiaircraft unit sent his parents a letter in May 1942 from Poland along with a photo. In his letter, he remarked that he hoped the snapshot wouldn't "make them sick." He also noted that it displayed Jews and told his parents not to share the photo with "too many people" and to "keep it safe," since he no longer had the negative. The photo in question was of an open ditch filled with the naked bodies of Jewish men, women, and children.[83]

The taking of trophy photos, especially involving the humiliation of Jews, was commonplace during the German conquest of Poland in the fall of 1939. For example, Corporal Paul Kluge "got there early" at an execution site in Schwetz in order to be able to stand close to the grave while his comrades "took rolls of photographs" of the killings.[84] In his detailed study of the campaign, the historian Alexander Rossino noted, "The tremendous number of photographs showing the public humiliation of Jewish men suggests that the cutting of hair and beards, signifying emasculation and disdain for the 'dirty Jew,' was common practice among Germans who encountered Jews in Poland and elsewhere in the 'East.'"[85] Both the film industry and the regime's propaganda organs promoted this effort, including through the creation of mass-produced photo albums designed especially for soldiers, with front covers displaying a relief of an Iron Cross and a superimposed swastika or a Wehrmacht eagle grasping a swastika. Articles in popular magazines also offered tips for soldiers on the best ways to format and arrange their photos.[86] Such appeals evidently found millions of ready participants, and the exchange of photos became a popular pastime among soldiers. In one example, the father of a fallen soldier contacted his son's commander concerning some seventeen hundred copies of photographs reproduced by his son related to the unit's actions in Serbia, a particularly brutal campaign by Wehrmacht forces with large-scale atrocities and reprisal killings that in many respects set the tone for the later invasion of the

Soviet Union.[87] The photos had been requested by members of the unit, and the father wanted to make sure that they received them in fulfilling his son's final wish.[88] In many cases, soldiers' photographs reflected the regime's fixation with race and its own propagandistic impulse, whether in the widespread exchange of snapshots of French black African troops in the campaign in France in 1940 or in the multitude of photographs framing "inferior" Jews and Slavs in the East.[89] In some cases, the soldiers included denigrating drawings, such as bedbugs, lice, or cockroaches, alongside the photographs of Polish and Soviet Jews.[90]

Not only racial prejudices, but gender norms found expression in the trophy photographs of soldiers in the East. For example, snapshots of female Red Army soldiers, the pejoratively named *Flintenweiber* (rifle wenches), were another frequent photographic artifact, reflecting in one sense the men's reaction to a perceived perversion of gender norms, but also a traditional German army paranoia with respect to unconventional warfare.[91] German soldiers demonstrated a "downright hatred" toward female Red Army soldiers, and Field Marshal Günther von Kluge, the commander of the Fourth Army, ordered their suppression "with immense brutality" and their immediate execution.[92] One German soldier described how these women "fought like wild beasts" and laconically noted how they were shot when captured.[93] While it is not clear how many female soldiers became victims of sexual violence, the authorization for summary execution, combined with the men's pathological revulsion toward these women, almost certainly found expression in acts of both physical and sexual brutality.

Killing Games in the Wehrmacht

The creation of "killing games" provides one of the clearest insights into the way in which acts of murder and atrocity became normalized within some Wehrmacht units. In one example, Luftwaffe pilots at an airfield in the Soviet Union devised a nighttime killing game involving drinking and marksmanship. As a group especially renowned for male bravado, including "terrific drinking bouts" and sexual exploits, these pilots created a competition involving the stalking and murder of Jewish prisoners.[94] Yehuda Lerner was part of a group of forced laborers constructing buildings at the airfield. He remarked, "At night they'd [the pilots] get drunk and amuse themselves by shooting Jews, usually in the head." He continued, "Their game was to arrive from behind, press the barrel to your temple and try to blow your eyes out."[95] Air force pilots, who routinely celebrated aerial kills with double shots of brandy, not only chose to compete with one another for the number of shoot-downs during the day as a marker of their performative masculinity, but also extended their competition to the ritual murder of Jewish forced laborers during nocturnal drinking bouts in a game in which not only the killing of the victim mattered, but the "marksmanship" of the perpetrator as well.[96] In another example, the role of alcohol remained unclear, as in the case of a group of Luftwaffe airmen who took advantage of an "invitation" from their SS colleagues "to go out and shoot Jews. All the troops went along with rifles . . . and shot them up. Each man could pick the one he wanted."[97]

In some instances of joint Wehrmacht, SS, and police killing operations, the presence of alcohol, especially at the execution sites, appears to have functioned in a variety of roles. Alcohol served as a facilitator and as a means of disinhibition for the killers, as well as a coping mechanism. For example, a mass execution of more than eight thousand Jewish men, women, and children at Slonim on November 14, 1941, was led by SS and auxiliary forces but also included a number of volunteers from a nearby infantry unit. A former soldier described the killings, during which his peers drank heavily and "held up Jewish infants in the air and shot them with pistols." Another soldier remembered the murders as a "real massacre," and he observed, "The shooting was somewhat haphazard [and] the shooting commandos were very drunk."[98] In this case, the consumption of alcohol during a daylong massacre appears to have played multiple roles for the soldiers involved. In another massacre, a group of soldiers volunteered to assist *Einsatzkommando* 10b in an execution and then celebrated their participation that evening with a "drinking binge."[99] With respect to examples of cooperative killing between the SS and the armed forces, the willingness of airmen or soldiers to volunteer for such duties provides one insight into the mentality of these individuals. Likewise, the integration of drinking into the ritual of murder and post-killing celebration offers further evidence concerning the perpetrators' mind-set and the varied uses of alcohol among these men.

Alcohol and Armies in the East

The Wehrmacht certainly was not the only military that viewed entry into the ranks as a rite of manhood. For Russian males, induction into the Red Army constituted a "route to manhood," and many of these young men arrived at basic training in a drunken state, a "tradition" dating to the tsarist era.[100] Isaak Kobylyanskiy, an artillery officer, noted the importance of one's "ability to drink more liquor without getting demonstrably drunk" as a way to demonstrate masculine prowess in the Red Army.[101] Likewise, alcohol was a part of daily life for Soviet troops at the front. The introduction of a hundred-gram (3.53 ounce) daily vodka ration at Stalin's order during the war reflected the importance of alcohol within the military culture of the Red Army and served to boost morale among the combat troops.[102] For its part, German military intelligence attempted to monitor alcohol distribution at the Soviet lines as an indicator of an imminent Red Army attack.[103] As in the case of the Wehrmacht, alcohol served as a symbol of masculinity, and drinking was an expression of camaraderie. Similarly, drunkenness in the Red Army resulted in firearms indiscipline, and intoxication played a major role in acts of plunder, sexual violence, and mass rapes as Soviet forces moved west.[104] Soviet troops, fueled by "hate and the desire for revenge," including "a widespread atavistic view . . . that the spoils of war go to the winner," whether in the form of plunder, alcohol, or women, engaged in their own acts of brutality as they marched to Berlin.[105]

In his study of alcohol and drug abuse in the Wehrmacht, Peter Steinkamp argues that the Wehrmacht was successful in quickly removing "officers with deviant alcohol consumption" from the ranks.[106] However, this contention appears largely to have applied to older officers on duty *within Germany* during the war whose alcohol-related conduct damaged the image of the military among the German public or led to cases of fraternization or indiscipline within the ranks. In contrast, officers with experience at the front appear to have been treated more leniently with respect to alcohol-related offenses.[107] This distinction once again highlights the different standards of acceptable behavior between the home front and the battlefront, especially with respect to the war in the East. In any event, by the last half of 1944, as the Allies' grip on Germany tightened, officers and men from the ranks appear to have taken increasing solace from the bottle in both the East and the West. In France, one officer confided, "alcohol is the only thing which can comfort anyone in our position," while a Wehrmacht counterpart in Russia observed how his fellow soldiers increasingly "lost themselves in alcohol."[108]

At the end of 1944, a German sergeant stationed in the East penned a letter in which he clearly anticipated the end of the "Thousand Year Reich." He conceded that the treatment of Jews and Poles had been not only a "fatal political mistake, but also a crime against humanity." He explained these crimes as originating from "a satanic seduction and a devilish system of mass intoxication."[109] For this soldier and for most Germans, the psychological intoxication of conquest and subjugation had faded away by the end of 1944; nevertheless, the process of murder would continue until the final hours of the regime. In the end, the hangover of collapsing fronts and the sobering thought of a German defeat did not result in the end of the killing. While drinking offered a temporary release for some soldiers, alcohol consumption among the SS and police continued to play a role in mass murder and atrocity even as the Third Reich crumbled around them.

CONCLUSION

Even in its final weeks, as the Third Reich crumbled into ruins, the men of the SA and the SS continued to murder their racial and political enemies and even their own colleagues.

On the eve of Palm Sunday, March 24, 1945, Nazi administrators and female guests gathered for a party in the town of Rechnitz. Franz Podezin, the local Nazi Party leader, received a phone call in the evening concerning the execution of some two hundred Jews confined at the town's railway station.[1] Taking a break from the party, a group of ten Nazi administrators and a female teacher left the festivities and participated in the murder of the Jews, after which they returned to continue their revelry. After the war, a German press story detailed the murders using the catchphrase "massacre as a party game."[2] Whether interpreted as a "party game" or business as usual, mass murder continued within the Third Reich until the bitter end, as evidenced by the actions of Gestapo men in Dortmund who murdered some three hundred men and women in ten separate mass shootings in March and April 1945. These killings followed a familiar pattern and were "to the smallest details . . . small-scale reproductions of the crimes of the Einsatzgruppen," and according to one historian reflected the "ritualistic scheme of events" perfected in the East, including the distribution of tobacco and alcohol rations among the killers after they completed their "work."[3]

Men who had become addicted to violence and intoxicated by murder apparently found it hard to break the habit. As Soviet forces approached the town of Stein an der Donau during the first week of April 1945, SS and SA men massacred some five hundred political inmates from a local prison and began a forced march with over eight hundred additional prisoners toward Bavaria on April 8. Franz Fuchs, a prisoner, recalled the atrocious conditions and the brutality of the guards, a combination of SS, SA, and *Volkssturm* (people's militia): "A part of the guards were already drunk at the beginning of the journey and during the journey got more drunk as almost every guard had taken lots of wine or schnapps." He continued, "The treatment was overall very brutal, really Nazi-like."[4] Fuchs stated that the "anger of the Nazis raged" through the guards' acts of "appalling murder."[5] At the Neuengamme concentration camp, as overcrowding, lack of food and water, and disease led to the decimation of the prisoner population, the SS guards drank heavily, partying "day and night" as they sang "martial and SS songs" and engaged in "orgies" with German female auxiliaries.[6] A group of SS guards murdered forty-five men and thirteen women over the course of two nights on April 23 and April 24, 1945. The victims included the German actress Hanne Mertens, imprisoned for an anti-Nazi joke, who was bludgeoned to death as she knelt and begged for her life. In the wake of these murders, the SS guards gathered in the camp's bathhouse to wash off the blood of the victims as they "boasted" about their exploits before finishing the evening with a schnapps party.[7] The continuation of murders into the final hours of the Nazi regime and the way in which the perpetrators committed them once again demonstrated the celebratory atmosphere of such acts, in which bragging of one's deeds while naked in a tub of water among one's comrades, followed by a night of drinking, had become the order of the day.

By the end of the war, the Nazi revolution began to devour not only its enemies but also its own. On April 30, 1945, Manfred Klein, a Waffen-SS officer, detailed the court-martial and hanging of a fellow SS soldier for desertion. The execution squad hung a sign on the deserter's neck stating,

"I am a traitor. I received the punishment I deserved." Klein then noted the reactions of some of the unit's members. "During the night I observed a few officers who had become drunk from the inn. They walked up to the gallows, one of them struck the hanged man from the side with his stock [*sic*], whereupon the man turned on his own axis. This was a great source of amusement to the drunken men, who yelled with laughter."[8] Apparently for such men, pranks with corpses after a night of drinking had become a natural activity, especially if it included the body of someone who had failed in his role as a comrade.

As the fighting fronts collapsed in the spring of 1945, SS and policemen now reached for the bottle in order to escape the reality of the impending German defeat. At Ravensbrück, the families of SS men had been evacuated, and "many SS men were permanently drunk and talking openly of the need to head towards the relative safety of American lines, or better still, to vanish."[9] At Auschwitz, the Hungarian prisoner Dr. Miklos Nyiszli detailed the last days of the camp: "More and more often our SS guards sought refuge in drunkenness. It was rare that they had their wits about them for more than a few minutes a day."[10] Even then, however, such drunkenness did not signal the end of brutality and killing, as intoxicated SS sergeant major Erich Mussfeldt warned the prisoners, "Good evening, children, soon you're going to die, but afterwards our turn will come."[11] Michael Kraus, a survivor of a death march from Auschwitz, remembered how an SS guard ordered one prisoner to "run ahead only so that he could shoot him from the back." He then remarked, "Our 'supervisors' amused themselves with these and similar occupations!"[12] At the same time that drunken SS men played with corpses and murdered in the camps and on the death marches, German generals and Nazi officials in Hitler's bunker engaged in a "final dead drunk party" replete with singing, a celebration that continued even after the news of Hitler's suicide and that of his bride, Eva Braun.[13]

Alcohol as Alibi

During the trial of the major war criminals at Nuremberg, Hjalmar Schacht responded to a question concerning internal opposition to Hitler's policies by asserting, "I would like to say that within the [Nazi] Party, of course,

the decent elements were by far in majority." He then attempted to exonerate these "decent" perpetrators by asserting that those who participated in the regime's crimes only had done so by resorting to alcohol and
drugs. Schacht asserted, "I observed that even many Party members who
had fallen into this net of Hitler and who occupied more or less leading
positions, gradually became afraid because of the consequences of the in-
justices and the evil deeds to which they were instigated by the regime.
I had the definite feeling that these people resorted to alcohol and various narcotics in order to flee from their own conscience, and that it was
only this flight from their own conscience that permitted them to act the
way they did."[14]

In his testimony, Schacht attempted to absolve the German people of
genocide by placing the blame on intoxicated Nazis or those good Germans who had submerged their moral qualms in floods of alcohol. In
contrast, one of the defendants at the Nuremberg SS-*Einsatzgruppen*
trial (1947–1948), SS captain Felix Rühl, "indignantly denied" that his
commander had ever been too drunk to perform his duties and testified
that the SS general and commander of *Einsatzgruppe* D "Herr Ohlendorf
wouldn't have stood for this."[15] Despite Rühl's denial of drunkenness, we
know that many of these men drank heavily in spite of the guidelines issued to these units prior to the invasion of the Soviet Union, which stated
that "excessive drinking is strictly prohibited."[16] In his death-row memoir,
Rudolf Höss discussed the "many suicides" among the men of the *Einsatzgruppen* and those "who could no longer mentally endure wading in
the bloodbath . . . [and] went mad." He continued, "Most of the members
of the Special Action Squads [i.e., *Einsatzgruppen*] drank a great deal to
help get through this horrible work."[17] Likewise, SS colonel Paul Blobel,
the commander of *Sonderkommando* 4a, who enjoyed his reputation as
"'an efficient killer of Jews' as well as a 'drunk and a monster,'" still attempted to place himself in the role of the victim by citing the "psychological trauma" of his experience, in which alcohol became a means for
dealing with his participation in genocide.[18]

Based on these statements, how is the historian to understand and to
explain the use of alcohol by the perpetrators? First, it is important to state
that while drinking did provide disinhibition for murder in some cases, as
seen in some of the perpetrators' reactions to killing women or children,
the consumption of alcohol during the killings did not ipso facto mean

that the killers needed it to do their jobs, as demonstrated by numerous examples given throughout this book.[19] Second, it is imperative to take into account when and where statements by the perpetrators were made concerning their use of alcohol in the process of mass murder. Indeed, heavy drinking as a psychological defense mechanism and excuse for their actions became a prevalent alibi in postwar statements and testimony by those involved in genocide. After the war, a thread running through testimony in trials of the perpetrators was the excuse that the only way to participate in such actions was through heavy drinking. In her interview with Claude Lanzmann during the filming of *Shoah*, Martha Michelson, the wife of a German schoolteacher in Chełmno and "one of the most unpleasant characters in the film," elided questions about her knowledge of the murder of hundreds of thousands of Jews at the killing center.[20] Paradoxically, she sought to exonerate the SS camp commandant, Hans Bothmann, of his actions by asserting that he once told her he could not do the "work" with a "clear head"—that is, sober—but only by being drunk.[21] In a similar manner, Franz Suchomel, a guard at Treblinka, confided to Lanzmann that drinking was the only way he could perform his duties in the camp.[22] When questioned by Lanzmann concerning Bothmann's and his SS subordinates' regular drinking parties and nighttime orgies with German female auxiliaries after the killings, Michelson apparently found no contradiction in her friend's behavior in light of his supposed mental anguish, just as Suchomel proved oblivious of his own expression of pride in his service at Treblinka as he unashamedly belted out a rendition of the camp song.[23]

Postwar interrogation protocols are also replete with both hearsay and accounts from perpetrators who state that heavy drinking was the only way they could take part in murder or deal with their participation after the fact. The military city commandant of Kolomea, a seventy-eight-year-old retired lawyer at the time of his questioning by West German authorities, asserted that the SS men who committed mass murder in his town were "broken men." He then admitted that he did not know this from firsthand knowledge but rather had heard from others that the killers "were under the influence of alcohol all day, completely drunk, because they couldn't forget the images [they had seen]."[24] The postwar affidavit of Alfred Metzner offers another example of the way in which perpetrators reframed alcohol use in their later testimony. While admitting his participation in a number of massacres, Metzner's affidavit, entered into evidence during the International Military Tribunal at Nuremberg, provides a number of important details on the course and conduct of mass killing in the East, including the incorporation of alcohol and celebratory ritual. Importantly, he states that he and his fellow perpetrators needed to "drink a great deal of schnapps to stimulate our work ethic." At another point, he compared his unit's need for alcohol in order to kill with the motivation of the SS, who did not require schnapps to murder but who instead relied on their "ideology" (*Idealismus*).[25]

Despite Metzner's attempt to create a narrative of murder based on alcohol rather than belief, witnesses described his behavior as that of a true believer, beginning with his participation in the massacre at Slonim in July 1941. Nachum Alpert not only described one German killer at the massacre who made the Jews dance for his pleasure as "drunk on whisky and Jewish blood," but also specifically referred to Metzner as "one of those Nazis who loved to get drunk on Jewish blood."[26] Likewise, a West German legal investigation of the killings found that the Jews were "free game" and that Metzner, far from being the unassuming translator depicted in his own testimony, was in fact feared by Jews throughout the Slonim ghetto for his consistent brutal behavior.[27]

Men like Metzner, Bothmann, and Suchomel experienced their intoxication in both a physical and psychological sense. Likewise, the thirty-six-year-old Viennese police official Walter Manner shared the truth of his voluntary participation in a massacre in two letters to his wife in October 1941. In the first, dated October 2, Manner wrote that he had been given twenty-eight bullets for his pistol but did not expect that that would be enough, and he promised, "By the time I get home, I will have some pretty things to tell you."[28] In a letter three days later, Manner admitted that his hands "shook" as the first group of victims was brought to the execution site, but he noted that by the time the tenth group arrived, "I calmly and surely shot at the many women, children, and infants." He then admitted that he also participated in a contest involving shooting infants launched into the air over the grave, and he revealed, "Now I understand the meaning of the word bloodlust [*Blutrausch*]."[29] In his letters, Manner made no mention of alcohol consumption either by himself or his fellow perpetrators, and, as is clear from the text, he did not need to drink in order to kill children and infants. As Michael

Burleigh and Wolfgang Wippermann noted almost three decades ago, "passionate hatreds" and "group intoxication with violence" prepared the perpetrators for genocide.[30] In this sense, killing became the natural manifestation of the metaphorical and literal high enjoyed by the conquerors. For these men, alcohol was a luxury item, and its excessive consumption was not only a perquisite of the occupiers but also a form of refreshment, whether in the barroom or on the killing fields. Likewise, it is not surprising that men who regularly drank large quantities of alcohol on and off the "job" should become alcoholics or suffer adverse side effects to their health in the form of stomach ailments and difficulty sleeping.[31] In this case, their alcoholism, with its associated symptoms, was not caused by their need to drown their sorrows but rather was the *effect* of their profligate drinking behavior and the physiological effects that accompanied their actions.

Coping with Murder

While some may have cited alcohol use as simply an alibi to excuse their behavior, it is also apparent that some of the perpetrators indeed reached for the bottle in order to deal with their actions. In a diary entry during a tour of the Russian front in the fall of 1941, Major General Erwin von Lahousen mentioned a discussion with a German intelligence officer concerning the execution of seven thousand Jews from Borrisow. Lahousen noted the intelligence officer's comment, "Even many of the SD [men] can't keep it up and maintain themselves only by heavy drinking."[32] While Lahousen's testimony is widely cited by scholars, it should be emphasized that it is once again hearsay and perhaps even a third-hand account. It may in fact reflect Lahousen's or his subordinate's natural response to hearing about the cold-blooded killing of men, women, and children and the resulting rationalization for such acts based on intoxication alone. As Raul Hilberg contended, "It is hard to say what happened to these men as a result of the shootings. For many, undoubtedly, the task became just another job. . . . However, every once in a while a man did have a nervous breakdown, and in several units the use of alcohol became routine."[33] Undeniably, there were men who "broke" under the strain of continuous killing, and these actions had a psychological effect on some who reached their limit. After the war, in response to a question on the "psychological burden" of the murders, Karl Kretschmer, a member of the *Einsatzgruppe*n whose wartime letters to his family detailed his role in mass murder, provided a revealing if brief answer. While he accepted the premise that killing defenseless persons was not easy, he added an important caveat, stating, "Well for . . . for a new guy let's say."[34] In other words, it was normal for newcomers to need some time to acclimate themselves to killing, a period that might be as brief as the time taken between the arrival of the first and the tenth group of victims, as noted in Manner's letters to his wife.

Still, as Hilberg observed, "Clearly, alcohol, speeches, and gas vans did not eliminate the psychological problems generated by the killings. Yet there was no breakdown in the operations as a whole."[35] While some of the perpetrators sought solace in the bottle as a method for coping with their participation in mass murder, it also must be noted that such coping did not in itself indicate a fundamental disagreement with the acts of the killers. Nor can coping be used to explain or excuse the manifold examples of the use of alcohol in cases of "nonlethal" brutality and acts of humiliation by the perpetrators. Bernhard Daenekas, a longtime criminal investigator of the crimes committed by Germans in the East, remarked, "Often the men were not ashamed of their acts. After completing 'work,' there was normally an alcohol ration and during the resulting fellowship evenings one unit wanted [to assert] to have killed more persons than the other."[36] In a similar manner, one might join a competition that highlighted one's marksmanship and toughness by demonstrating the ability to shoot infants launched into the air over an execution site. In both cases, such acts of performative masculinity were linked to a corrupt, racialized, hypermasculine ideal that propagated cruelty as hardness and brutality as toughness.

Alcohol, Policy, and the SS: The Extraordinary to the Mundane

The preceding chapters have established the ubiquitous consumption of alcohol by the perpetrators of mass murder, as well as the keen interest taken by senior SS and police leaders concerning drinking among the ranks. Policies on alcohol ranged from Himmler's warnings against drunkenness to the practice of Higher SS and Police Leaders in the East who rewarded "successful" service in "hunting detachments" with eight days of leave that included nightly fellowship evenings with beer and wine and the showing of German films.[37] The proof of the prominent role of alcohol within the SS and police complex ranges from the extraordinary to the mundane. Himmler's appointment calendar itself provides evidence concerning the importance of this topic for the Reich leader of the SS. In a meeting on October 9, 1941, with SS general Oswald Pohl, the head of the SS Economic and Administration Main Office (WVHA), Himmler noted two agenda items, including the notation "Schnapps f[or] the troops."[38] Significantly, the provisioning of alcohol to SS and policemen in the East proved a topic worthy of discussion between the two men, and Pohl, in his capacity as head of the WVHA, was most certainly given responsibility for ensuring delivery to the troops as the German offensive in the East began to stall in late 1941. On a more routine level, an inventory of items sent to the battalion staff of an SS infantry unit stationed in Lublin in September 1943 lists authorization for the issuing of ten items, including ten sets of utensils, ten plates, five bowls, ten coffee cups with saucers, one coffee-pot, as well as five beer glasses *and twenty schnapps glasses.*[39] It is striking that schnapps glasses proved to be the single item issued at double the standard allotment for the unit, a banal but telling indication of the conspicuous role of alcohol consumption among these men.

Rhetoric and Reality: Alcohol in the Third Reich

The Reich minister of health and the head of the Reich Office against Alcohol and Tobacco Dangers, Leonard Conti, issued a proclamation in 1939 declaring, "Next to the service duty of the soldiers of our Wehrmacht stands the civil service duty of every German. . . . Every German man and woman has to live healthfully and avoid anything that can endanger or damage health." He continued, "The struggle against alcohol and tobacco dangers is thereby not only an urgent task of health leadership and administration; it also serves the acquisition and the strengthening of German defense power."[40] While Conti's sentiments may have been sincere, one wonders how SS and policemen and German soldiers would have responded to this proclamation later in the war or to the aphorism of another racial hygienist, Max von Gruber, that "alcohol harms too many, but kills too few."[41] Perhaps one of the ultimate tragic ironies of a National Socialist regime riven with paradoxes was the Nazi belief concerning the "intrinsic connection between alcohol, crime, and racial inferiority," a belief that stigmatized the habitual drunk and threatened her or him with public shaming, incarceration, and forced sterilization.[42] Ultimately, however, it was not this kind of habitual drunk who most clearly exemplified the convergence between alcohol, crime, and degeneracy, but rather the "racial elite" of the SS and police who became drunk on the act of killing itself.

Alcohol, Celebration, and Genocide

The correlation between alcohol, celebratory ritual, and acts of mass killing or sexual assault was not simply a Nazi phenomenon. The conflict in the Balkans in the 1990s dramatically exposed the connection between drinking, systematic rape, and mass executions.[43] Similarly, the Rwandan genocide offers a number of troubling parallels to the events described in the destruction of the European Jews. The widespread use of alcohol, normally in the form of beer and banana beer (*urwagwa*), among the Hutu perpetrators of genocide in Rwanda is well documented.[44] Likewise, one killer described the "hunt" for the victims: "The genocide was like a festival. At day's end, or any time there was an occasion, we took a cow from the Tutsis, and slaughtered it and grilled it and drank beer." He continued, "There were no limits anymore. It was a festival. We celebrated."[45] Another perpetrator remembered, "They [the killers] went around together. You saw that they shared and shared alike with field work and drink at the *cabaret*. During the genocide I know that gang went out cutting from the first day to the last."[46] One Canadian doctor, an eyewitness to the genocide, described the *interahamwe* (Hutu paramilitaries) as "terrifying, bloodthirsty, drunk—they did a lot of dancing at roadblocks."[47] Similarly, Immaculée Ilibagiza, a female Tutsi survivor, repeatedly referenced these intoxicated paramilitaries as they hunted for new victims and engaged in mass rapes.[48] Furthermore, the Hutu killers incorporated drinking, song, and celebratory ritual resembling a "carnival romp" into the process of mass murder.[49] In this sense, the genocide in Rwanda offers an additional manifestation of celebratory murder and a subject worthy of study in its own right.

A Story Too Horrible to Tell?

Vera Inber, a witness to German atrocities in Odessa, exclaimed, "The pen and paper do not exist that could describe the inhuman suffering endured by us the Soviet people."[50] Among those who made an attempt was the Soviet writer and journalist Vasily Grossman, who compiled overwhelming evidence concerning German crimes in the Soviet Union. After detailing the mass murder at the Treblinka killing center, he remarked, "It is infinitely hard even to read this. The reader must believe me, it is as hard to write it. Someone might ask: 'Why write about this, why remember all that?'" In response to his own question, Grossman answered, "It is the writer's duty to tell this terrible truth, and it is the civilian duty of the reader to learn it. Everyone who would turn away, who would shut his eyes and walk past would insult the memory of the dead." He continued, "Everyone who does not know the truth about this would never be able to understand with what sort of enemy, with what sort of monster, our Red Army started on its own mortal combat."[51] In the study of Nazi Germany, it is perhaps a blessing and a curse that today's reader may find much of what is discussed in this book too hard to read or too difficult to believe. Nevertheless, we owe it to the victims to document these "lonely voices reaching from the abyss" if we are to truly appreciate the horror faced by Jews and the other racial enemies of the Nazi regime during the Third Reich.[52]

In his study of the German occupation of Buczacz and the mass killings that accompanied it, Omer Bartov observed, "This normalization of murder, the removal of the Jews as part of a day's work, as entertainment, as background noise to drinking bouts or amorous relationships . . . were part and parcel of the German experience of genocide, rarely reflected in postwar representations and ruminations, let alone historiography."[53] This study, in part, is intended to correct this lacuna in the historiography of the Holocaust by examining the ways in which drinking and celebratory ritual came to play a heretofore underappreciated role in mass murder. In an earlier work on police perpetrators, I argued that the success of SS and police leaders in creating an organizational culture based on antisemitism and anti-Bolshevism "broadened the boundaries of acceptable and desired behavior" within the police corps.[54] Likewise, in researching this book, it became apparent to me that alcohol was not the cause of the atrocious behaviors of the perpetrators, but merely a pleasurable accessory for inducing disinhibition, for facilitating, celebrating, and in some cases coping with the expanded boundaries of permissible behavior and the power over life and death enjoyed by the killers.

Such was the case for the SS men at Auschwitz who celebrated the camp's first successful gassing at Block 11 with a "big party," as well as for their colleagues, who after an hour of drinking and singing entered a prisoner barrack and began torturing a group of twelve naked Soviet prisoners of war by kicking them in the groin, a physical beating that only three survived.[55] Similarly, Ruth Elias's comment that "the music had to play" before drunken SS guards began their rapes of young women in Block 6 is a chilling and telling indictment of the premeditation and enjoyment taken by these men as they forged bonds of male community through acts of physical and sexual abuse.[56] Finally, SS and policemen who kept score of their "body counts" and celebrated milestones of one thousand and two thousand victims in drunken parties undoubtedly were intoxicated with the act of murder, as was the heavy-drinking SS sergeant Martin Weiss, a brutal and prolific killer. Weiss once commented, "If I would not see blood every day, I would be thirsty for it."[57] For such men, alcohol consumption may not have been a prerequisite for murder, but in the colonial spaces of the East, it is clear that many of the perpetrators, whether holding a bottle or a pistol in their hand, were intoxicated with their control over life and death and ultimately drunk on genocide.

NOTES

Introduction

1. Jochen von Lang, *Das Eichmann-Protokoll: Tonbandaufzeichnungen der israelischen Verhöre* (Munich: Severin und Siedler, 1982), 83–86. For an excellent analysis of the Wannsee Conference see Mark Roseman, *The Wannsee Conference and the Final Solution: A Reconsideration* (London: Folio Society, 2012).

2. State of Israel, Ministry of Justice, *The Trial of Adolf Eichmann: Recordings of Proceedings in the District Court of Jerusalem*, vol. 3 (Jerusalem: Trust for the Publication of the Proceedings of the Eichmann Trial, in cooperation with the Israel State Archives and Yad Vashem, 1993), 1367.

3. Martin Broszat, *The Hitler State: The Foundation and Development of the Internal Structure of the Third Reich*, trans. John W. Hiden (London: Longman, 1981), xi.

4. Adolf Eichmann, *Götzen: Die Autobiographie von Adolf Eichmann*, ed. Raphael Ben Nescher (Berlin: Metropol, 2016), 223. Emphasis added. Eichmann used the phrase "freudiger Zustimmung," a clear linguistic expression of the celebratory atmosphere that framed the meeting.

5. State of Israel, Ministry of Justice, *Trial of Adolf Eichmann*, vol. 4, 1423.

6. State of Israel, Ministry of Justice, *Trial of Adolf Eichmann*, vol. 3, 1367.

7. Robert Gerwarth, *Hitler's Hangman: The Life of Heydrich* (New Haven, CT: Yale University Press, 2011), 74.

8. The "Jäger Report," RG 14.101M, reel 8, folder 14120, p. 58, USHMMA.

9. Wolfram Wette, *Karl Jäger: Mörder der litauischen Juden* (Frankfurt am Main: Fischer Taschenbuch Verlag, 2011), 112.

10. Gitta Sereny, *Into That Darkness: An Examination of Conscience* (New York: Vintage Books, 1983), 200. In his interview with Sereny, Stangl asserted that the only way he could deal with his duties was to drink, a claim belied by numerous eyewitness accounts of his behavior and a justification that came to typify the "cliché" of the drunken Nazi used by many SS and police during postwar investigations of their activities. See Bettina Stangneth, *Eichmann vor Jerusalem: Das unbehelligte Leben eines Massenmörders* (Zurich: Arche Verlag, 2011), 502.

11. Melita Maschmann, *Account Rendered: A Dossier on My Former Self*, trans. Geoffrey Strachan (London: Abelard-Schuman, 1964), 106.

12. Elissa Mailänder, "Making Sense of a Rape Photograph: Sexual Violence as Social Performance on the Eastern Front, 1939–1944," *Journal of the History of Sexuality* 26, no. 3 (2017): 500–501, 503.

13. Stangneth, *Eichmann vor Jerusalem*, 225–26.

14. Testimony of Dr. Stefan Janeczek, February 3, 1964, RG 14.101M, reel 322, folder 2441, frame 384, USHMMA.

15. Thomas Kühne, *Belonging and Genocide: Hitler's Community, 1918–1945* (New Haven, CT: Yale University Press, 2013), 167–68.

16. Victor Klemperer, *I Will Bear Witness: A Diary of the Nazi Years*, trans. Martin Chalmers (New York: Modern Library, 2001), 66. Emphasis added.

17. Ilya Ehrenburg, *Russia at War* (London: Hamish Hamilton, 1943), 131.

18. Hans Bernd Gisevius, *To the Bitter End*, trans. Richard and Clara Winston (Boston: Houghton Mifflin, 1947), 95, 293.

19. Gisevius, 103.

20. Quoted in Detlev Peukert, *The Weimar Republic: The Crisis of Classical Modernity*, trans. Richard Deveson (New York: Hill & Wang, 1989), 105, and Theodore Abel, *Why Hitler Came into Power* (New York: Prentice-Hall, 1938; reprint, Cambridge, MA: Harvard University Press, 1986), 100.

21. Saul Friedländer, *Memory, History, and the Extermination of the Jews of Europe* (Bloomington: Indiana University Press, 1993), 110.

22. Walter Tausk, *Breslauer Tagebuch, 1933–1940* (Berlin: Siedler Verlag, 1988), 57, 230.

23. Friedrich Kellner, *My Opposition: The Diary of Friedrich Kellner—a German against the Third Reich*, trans. and ed. Robert Scott Kellner (Cambridge: Cambridge University Press, 2018), 33, 76.

24. Kellner, 155. For entries on intoxication see 88, 94, 124, 127, 132, 228, and 313, and for entries on mass murder and atrocity see 133–34, 143, 145, 155, and 201.

25. Heinz Guderian, *Panzer Leader*, trans. Constantine Fitzgibbon (Boston: Da Capo, 1996), 235.

26. Photo from a Fasching parade in Nuremberg in 1938. Designation#4.559, WS#94675, USHMMA photo archives.

27. Heidi Rosenbaum, *"Und trotzdem war's eine schöne Zeit": Kinderalltag im Nationalsozialismus* (Frankfurt am Main: Campus Verlag, 2014), 171.

28. Bella Fromm, *Blood and Banquets: A Berlin Social Diary* (New York: Harper and Brothers, 1942), 180.

29. Pierre Ayçoberry, *The Social History of the Third Reich, 1933–1945*, trans. Janet Lloyd (New York: New Press, 1999), 25, and Abel, *Why Hitler*, 108–12.

30. Wendy Lower, *Hitler's Furies: German Women in the Nazi Killing Fields* (Boston: Houghton Mifflin Harcourt, 2013), 165.

31. Franka Maubach, *Die Stellung halten: Kriegserfahrungen und Lebensgeschichten von Wehrmachtshelferinnen* (Göttingen: Vandenhoek und Ruprecht, 2009), 130.

32. Willy Peter Reese, *"Mir selber seltsam fremd": Die Unmenschlichkeit des Krieges, Russland, 1941–44*, ed. Stefan Schmitz (Munich: Claassen Verlag, 2003), 197.

33. Klaus-Michael Mallmann, Jochen Böhler, and Jürgen Matthäus, *Einsatzgruppen in Polen: Darstellung und Dokumentation* (Darmstadt: Wissenschaftliche Buchgesellschaft, 2008), 171.

34. Włodzimierz Borodziej, *Terror und Politik: Die Deutsche Polizei und die polnische Widerstandsbewegung im Generalgouvernement, 1939–1944* (Mainz: Verlag Philipp von Zabern, 1999), 55.

35. Timothy Snyder, *Bloodlands: Europe between Hitler and Stalin* (New York: Basic Books, 2010), xviii.

36. Donald Bloxham, *The Final Solution: A Genocide* (Oxford: Oxford University Press, 2009), 282.

37. Frank Werner, "'Hart müssen wir hier draussen sein': Soldatische Männlichkeit im Vernichtungskrieg, 1941–1944," *Geschichte und Gesellschaft* 34, no. 1 (2008): 16, 20.

38. Stephan Lehnstaedt, "The Minsk Experience: German Occupiers and Everyday Life in the Capital of Belarus," in *Nazi Policy on the Eastern Front, 1941: Total War, Genocide, and Radicalization*, ed. Alex J. Kay, Jeff Rutherford, and David Stahel (Rochester, NY: University of Rochester Press, 2012), 255.

39. Sven Oliver Müller, *Deutsche Soldaten und ihre Feinde: Nationalismus an Front und Heimatfront im Zweiten Weltkrieg* (Frankfurt am Main: S. Fischer, 2007), 154.

40. "Der SS- und Polizeiführer Lettland, Kommandeur der Ordnungspolizei, Tagesbefehl 1 [January 21, 1943]," RG 18.002M, reel 9, fond R-82, opis 1, folder 21, USHMMA, and "Der SS- und Polizeistandortführer Libau, Standortbefehl [February 4, 1943]," RG 18.002M, reel 30, fond R-83, opis 1, folder 6, USHMMA. Emphasis added.

41. Norbert Frei, Thomas Grotum, Jan Parcer, Sybille Steinacher, and Bernd Wagner, eds., *Standort- und Kommandanturbefehle des Konzentrationslagers Auschwitz, 1940–1945* (Munich: K. G. Saur, 2000), 18, 198, 399–400, and Daily Order Number 4E, item 7 "Drunken Offenses," March 24, 1943, RG 18.002M, reel 9, fond R82, opis 1, folder 2, USHMMA.

42. Peter Longerich, *Heinrich Himmler*, trans. Jeremy Noakes and Lesley Sharpe (Oxford: Oxford University Press, 2011), 114, 323. With reference to drunken behavior by members of Hitler's personal security detail and disciplinary consequences see Peter Hoffmann, *Hitler's Personal Security: Protecting the Führer, 1921–1945* (New York: Da Capo, 2000), 52–54.

43. Stefan Klemp, *Freispruch für das "Mord Bataillon": Die NS-Ordnungspolizei und die Nachkriegsjustiz* (Münster: Lit Verlag, 1998), 24.

44. Testimony of Ludwig F. concerning Karl Chmielewski, RG 14.101M, reel 554, folder 4756, p. 7, USHMMA.

45. Waitman Wade Beorn, *Marching into Darkness: The Wehrmacht and the Holocaust in Belarus* (Cambridge, MA: Harvard University Press, 2014), 140.

46. United Nations War Crimes Commission, Polish Charges against German War Criminals, Charge No. 3, RG 67.041M, reel 14, USHMMA.

47. Nechama Tec, *In the Lion's Den: The Life of Oswald Rufeisen* (Oxford: Oxford University Press, 1990), 80.

48. Tec, 103.

49. Robert J. Lifton, *The Nazi Doctors: Medical Killing and the Psychology of Genocide* (New York: Basic Books, 1986), 443–44.

50. Stephan Lehnstaedt, *Occupation in the East: The Daily Lives of German Occupiers in Warsaw and Minsk, 1939–1944*, trans. dbmedia (New York: Berghahn, 2016), 144.

51. Christopher R. Browning, *Remembering Survival: Inside a Nazi Slave Labor Camp* (New York: W. W. Norton, 2010), 287, and Lifton, *Nazi Doctors*, 159.

52. Michael Musmanno, *The Eichmann Kommandos* (Philadelphia: Macrae Smith, 1961), 234–35.

53. Quoted in Jürgen Matthäus with Emil Kerenji, eds., *Jewish Responses to Persecution, 1933–1946: A Source Reader* (New York: Rowman & Littlefield, 2017), 153.

54. Richard Breitman, *The Architect of Genocide: Himmler and the Final Solution* (New York: Alfred A. Knopf, 1991), 173–74.

55. Lifton, *Nazi Doctors*, 443–44.

56. Norman Ohler, *Blitzed: Drugs in the Third Reich*, trans. Shaun Whitside (New York: Mariner Books, 2016), 39.

57. Richard J. Evans, "A Crass and Dangerously Inaccurate Account," review of *Blitzed: Drugs in the Third Reich*, by Norman Ohler, *Guardian*, November 16, 2016.

58. Dagmar Herzog, "Hitler's Little Helper: A History of Rampant Drug Use under the Nazis," review of *Blitzed: Drugs in the Third Reich*, by Norman Ohler, *New York Times*, March 27, 2017.

59. Herbet Fingarette, *Heavy Drinking: The Myth of Alcoholism as a Disease* (Berkeley: University of California Press, 1988), 100, 110.

60. Dominic J. Parrott and Amos Zeichner, "Effects of Alcohol and Trait Anger on Physical Aggression in Men," *Journal of Studies on Alcohol* 63, no. 2 (2002): 196, 202.

61. Geoffrey P. Hunt and Karen Joe Laidler, "Alcohol and Violence in the Lives of Gang Members," *Alcohol Research and Health* 25, no. 1 (2001): 66.

62. Müller, *Deutsche Soldaten*, 159, and Abel, *Why Hitler*, 100.

63. Tausk, *Breslauer Tagebuch*, 33–34, 37–39, and 62.

64. Sven Reichardt, *Faschistische Kampfbünde: Gewalt und Gemeinschaft im italienischen Squadrismus und in der deutschen SA* (Cologne: Böhlau Verlag, 2002), 462. See also Anna Pawełczyńska, *Values and Violence in Auschwitz: A Sociological Study*, trans. Catherine S. Leach (Berkeley: University of California Press, 1979), 8.

65. R. Barri Flowers, *Murder, at the End of the Day and Night: A Study of Criminal Homicide Offenders, Victims, and Circumstances* (Springfield, IL: Charles C. Thomas, 2002), 25–26.

66. Jonas Landberg and Thor Norstrom, "Alcohol and Homicide in Russia and the United States: A Comparative Analysis," *Journal of Studies on Alcohol and Drugs* 72, no. 5 (2011): 723.

67. Valeriy Chervyakov et al., "The Changing Nature of Murder in Russia," *Social Science and Medicine* 55, no. 10 (2002): 1716–17, 1721.

68. Susanna Barrows and Robin Room, eds., *Drinking: Behavior and Belief in Modern History* (Berkeley: University of California Press, 1991), 7.

69. Brendan Simms, *Hitler: A Global Biography* (New York: Basic Books, 2019), 92, and Robert N. Proctor, *The Nazi War on Cancer* (Princeton, NJ: Princeton University Press, 1999), 147.

70. Proctor, *War on Cancer*, 153.

71. Richard Grunberger, *The 12-Year Reich: A Social History of Nazi Germany* (New York: Holt, Rinehart and Winston, 1971), 30.

72. Geoffrey Giles, "Student Drinking in the Third Reich: Academic Tradition and the Nazi Revolution," in *Drinking: Behavior and Belief in Modern History*, ed. Susanna Barrows and Robin Room (Berkeley: University of California Press, 1991), 142. Giles provides these quantities in hectoliters, which I have converted to US gallons.

73. Jonathan Lewy, "A Sober Reich? Alcohol and Tobacco Use in Nazi Germany," *Substance Use and Misuse* 41, no. 8 (2006): 1182–83.

74. Grunberger, *12-Year Reich*, 228.

75. Michael Burleigh, *The Third Reich: A New History* (New York: Hill & Wang, 2000), 354.

76. Hermann Fahrenkrug, "Alcohol and the State in Nazi Germany, 1933–1945," in *Drinking: Behavior and Belief in Modern History*, ed. Susanna Barrows and Robin Room (Berkeley: University of California Press, 1991), 322.

77. Nikolaus Wachsmann, *Hitler's Prisons: Legal Terror in Nazi Germany* (New Haven, CT: Yale University Press, 2004), 155.

78. Fahrenkrug, "Alcohol and the State in Nazi Germany," 322–23. Fahrenkrug asserts that this was the fourth leading factor associated with sterilizations, following diagnoses of "mental deficiency, schizophrenia, and epilepsy." He also notes that the second version of the law in 1937 was expanded to include "all socially undesirable alcohol-deviant population segments," including those who did not "manifest the symptoms of chronic alcoholism."

79. Peter Padfield, *Himmler: Reichsführer-SS* (New York: Henry Holt, 1990), 40.

80. Quoted in Longerich, *Heinrich Himmler*, 323.

81. Stephen R. Haynes, "Ordinary Masculinity: Gender Analysis and Holocaust Scholarship," in *Genocide and Gender in the Twentieth Century: A Comparative Survey*, ed. Amy E. Randall (London: Bloomsbury, 2015), 170.

82. "Der Chef des Rasse- und Siedlungshauptamtes-SS, RuS Befehl Nr. 4/42, Mißbrauch der Schußwaffe [November 17, 1942]," RG-68.035M, reel 1, USHMMA.

83. Norbert Frei et al., *Standort- und Kommandanturbefehle*, 510. This incident occurred in the fall of 1944.

84. Bradley F. Smith and Agnes F. Peterson, eds., *Heinrich Himmler Geheimreden 1933 bis 1945 und andere Ansprachen* (Frankfurt am Main: Propyläen Verlag, 1974), 173.

85. Breitman, *Architect of Genocide*, 173–74.

86. "Der Reichsführer-SS, Tgb. Nr. 35/44/41 [February 22, 1941]," RG 68.035M, reel 3, USHMMA.

87. Quoted in Longerich, *Heinrich Himmler*, 321.

88. Longerich, 301, 323–24.

89. Christopher Dillon, *Dachau and the SS: A Schooling in Violence* (Oxford: Oxford University Press, 2015), 71–73, 88, 144, 227. For an eyewitness account of SS drunken abuse in Dachau see Hugo Burkhard, *Tanz mal Jude! Von Dachau bis Shanghai* (Nuremberg: Verlag Richard Reichenbach, 1967), 28, 58.

90. Peter Leßmann, *Die preußische Schutzpolizei in der Weimarer Republik: Streifendienst und Straßenkampf* (Düsseldorf: Droste Verlag, 1989), 290.

91. Smith and Peterson, *Heinrich Himmler Geheimreden*, 89.

92. Quoted in Dillon, *Dachau and the SS*, 75.

93. Dillon, 75.

94. Hoffmann, *Hitler's Personal Security*, 53.

95. Giles, "Student Drinking in the Third Reich," 136.

96. Jutta Mühlenberg, *Das SS-Helferinnenkorps: Ausbildung, Einsatz und Entnazifizierung der weiblichen Angehörigen der Waffen-SS 1942–1949* (Hamburg: Hamburger Edition, 2010), 14–15.

97. Kimberly Allar, "From Recruitment to Genocide: An Examination of the Recruitment of Auxiliary Guards in National Socialist Concentration Camps," in *Orte und Akteure im System der NS-Zwangslager*, ed. Michael Becker, Dennis Bock, and Henrike Illig (Berlin: Metropol Verlag, 2015), 177. Allar estimates that by the end of the war, women auxiliaries made up 10 percent of the total guard force.

98. Mühlenberg, *Das SS-Helferinnenkorps*, 302–7.

99. Florian Dierl, "The 'Internal Wehrmacht': German Order Police and the Transformation of State Power, 1936–1945" (PhD diss., Royal Holloway College, 2007), 125.

100. "Tagesbefehl 10 [July 18, 1942]," RG 53.002M, reel 3, fond 389, folder 1, USHMMA.

101. "I. Gend-Btl (mot), Batl.-Befehl Nr. 7, [March 16, 1943]," RG 15.011M, reel 22, file 286, USHMMA.

102. Borodziej, *Terror und Politik*, 55.

103. Lewy, "Sober Reich," 1187.

104. Smith and Peterson, *Heinrich Himmler Geheimreden*, 138.

105. International Military Tribunal, *Trials of the Major War Criminals before the International Military Tribunal*, vol. 29 (Nuremberg: Secretariat of the Military Tribunal, 1948), 165.

106. Borodziej, *Terror und Politik*, 55.

107. Longerich, *Heinrich Himmler*, 325.

108. Quoted in Longerich, 324.

109. Battalion order for the First Gendarmerie Battalion, March 31, 1943, RG 15.011M, roll 22, file 286, USHMMA, Karl Schneider, *"Auswärts eingesetzt": Bremer Polizeibataillone und der Holocaust* (Essen: Klartext, 2011), 176, and Norbert Frei et al., *Standort- und Kommandanturbefehle*, 519. Methyl alcohol or wood alcohol is toxic for humans and can lead to blindness or death.

110. Jules Schelvis, *Sobibor: A History of a Nazi Death Camp*, trans. Karin Dixon (Oxford: Berg, 2007), 112, 256.

111. Karl Schneider, *"Auswärts eingesetzt,"* 254.

112. "Der Chef des Rasse- und Siedlungshauptamtes-SS, RuS Befehl Nr. 4/42, Mißbrauch der Schußwaffe [November 17, 1942]," RG 68.035M, reel 1, USHMMA.

1. Alcohol and the Masculine Ideal

1. *International Military Tribunals*, vol. 12, 462. In an elaboration of this point, the historian Geoffrey Giles stated, "Within the Nazi party heavy drinking does not seem to have been a particular issue before Hitler's accession to the Chancellorship in January 1933. . . . After the seizure of power, however, the Nazi rank and file insisted on the spoils of victory and went on what amounted to an eighteen-month binge." See Giles, "Student Drinking in the Third Reich," 134.

2. Ian Kershaw, *Hitler: 1889–1936 Hubris* (New York: W. W. Norton, 1998), 261–62.

3. David Clay Large, *Where Ghosts Walked: Munich's Road to the Third Reich* (New York: W. W. Norton, 1997), 210.

4. Bruno Manz, *A Mind in Prison: The Memoir of a Son and a Soldier of the Third Reich* (Washington, DC: Brassey's, 2000), 60.

5. Hasso Spode, *Die Macht der Trunkenheit: Kultur- und Sozialgeschichte des Alkohols in Deutschland* (Opladen: Leske and Budrich, 1993), 265.

6. Alfred Rosenberg, "Volksgesundheit und Männlichkeitsideal," *Der Schulungsbrief* 6, no. 2 (1939): 43. In an article dedicated in part to highlighting the harmful effects of excessive alcohol consumption, Rosenberg argued for a model based on moderation and one emphasizing physical fitness. I would like to thank Yves Müller for providing me with this document.

7. Alfons Heck, *A Child of Hitler: Germany in the Days When God Wore a Swastika* (Phoenix: Renaissance House, 1985), 128.

8. Russell Lemle and Marc E. Mishkind, "Alcohol and Masculinity," *Journal of Substance Abuse Treatment* 6, no. 4 (1989): 214. Lemle and Mishkind cite a study of Finnish men

published in 1959 as one example of the broader generalizability of their findings. For a discussion of the relationship of alcohol, aggression, and masculinity see Kenneth Polk, "Males and Honor Contest Violence," *Homicide Studies* 3, no. 1 (1999): 6–29.

9. Catherine Gilbert Murdock, *Domesticating Drink: Women, Men, and Alcohol in America* (Baltimore: Johns Hopkins University Press, 1998), 4.

10. William B. Taylor, *Drinking, Homicide, and Rebellion in Colonial Mexican Villages* (Stanford, CA: Stanford University Press, 1979), 32–33, 41.

11. Pete Hamill, *A Drinking Life: A Memoir* (Boston: Little, Brown, 1994), 16–17, 42, 57, 62, 87. Hamill notes that women were not allowed to drink at the bar with the men but had to do so in a back room.

12. Kenneth Mullen et al., "Young Men, Masculinity and Alcohol," *Drugs: Education, Prevention and Policy* 14, no. 2 (2007): 153.

13. Lemle and Mishkind, "Alcohol and Masculinity," 215.

14. Robert L. Peralta, Lori A. Tuttle, and Jennifer L. Steele, "At the Intersection of Interpersonal Violence, Masculinity, and Alcohol Use: The Experiences of Heterosexual Male Perpetrators of Intimate Partner Violence," *Violence against Women* 16, no. 4 (2010): 390, 401.

15. Susan Jeffords, "Performative Masculinities, or, 'After a Few Times You Won't Be Afraid of Rape at All,'" *Discourse* 13, no. 2 (Spring–Summer 1991): 102–18.

16. Berno Bahro, *Der SS-Sport: Organisation-Funktion-Bedeutung* (Paderborn: Ferdinand Schöningh, 2013), 36, 38, 72–73, and Abel, *Why Hitler*, 108–9.

17. *Das Schwarze Korps*, March 20, 1935, LM0343, reel 1, USHMMA.

18. Quoted in George L. Mosse, *Nazi Culture: Intellectual, Cultural and Social Life in the Third Reich* (New York: Grosset & Dunlap, 1966), 30.

19. Large, *Where Ghosts Walked*, xiii.

20. Gisevius, *To the Bitter End*, 66.

21. Transcript of the *Shoah* interview with Franz Schalling, RG 60.5034, p. 30, USHMMA.

22. Thomas Kühne, *The Rise and Fall of Comradeship: Hitler's Soldiers, Male Bonding and Mass Violence in the Twentieth Century* (Cambridge: Cambridge University Press, 2017), 293.

23. Lifton, *Nazi Doctors*, 443–44.

24. Peralta, Tuttle, and Steele, "Intersection of Interpersonal Violence," 396, and Abel, *Why Hitler*, 142, 259.

25. Gerhard Weinberg, ed., *Hitler's Second Book: The Unpublished Sequel to Mein Kampf by Adolf Hitler*, trans. Krista Smith (New York: Enigma, 2003), 30.

26. Ute Frevert, *A Nation in Barracks: Modern Germany, Military Conscription and Civil Society*, trans. Andrew Boreham and Daniel Brückenhaus (Oxford: Berg, 2004), 171–72.

27. Mark Jones, *Founding Weimar: Violence and the German Revolution, 1918–1919* (Cambridge: Cambridge University Press, 2017), 4.

28. Peukert, *Weimar Republic*, 106.

29. Quoted in Nigel H. Jones, *A Brief History of the Birth of the Nazis: How the Freikorps Blazed a Trail for Hitler* (New York: Carroll and Graf, 2004), 135.

30. Ernst von Salomon, *The Outlaws*, trans. Ian F. D. Morrow (London: Arktos, 2013), 95, 191.

31. Catherine Collomp and Bruno Groppo, eds., *An American in Hitler's Berlin: Abraham Plotkin's Diary, 1932–33* (Urbana: University of Illinois Press, 2009), 169, and Johannes Schwarze, *Die Bayerische Polizei, 1919–1933* (Munich: Kommissionsbuchhandlung R. Wöfle, 1977), 237. Schwarze discusses the public singing of prohibited songs by members of the Communist Party in Bavaria in a confrontation with the police.

32. Quoted in Timothy W. Ryback, *Hitler's First Victims: The Quest for Justice* (New York: Alfred A. Knopf, 2014), 102–3. See also Emil Gumbel, *Vier Jahre politischer Mord* (Berlin: Verlag der neuen Gesellschaft, 1922), 27–42.

33. Emil Büge, *1470 KZ-Geheimnisse: Heimliche Aufzeichnungen aus der Politischen Abteilung des KZ Sachsenhausen* (Berlin: Metropol Verlag, 2010), 139.

34. Yves Müller, "Männlichkeit und Gewalt in der SA am Beispiel der 'Köpenicker Blutwoche,'" in *SA-Terror als Herrschaftssicherung*, ed. Stefan Hördler (Berlin: Metropol Verlag, 2013), 130; Victor Klemperer, *The Language of the Third Reich: LTI-Lingua Tertii Imperii*, trans. Martin Brady (London: Athlone, 2000), 3. Klemperer uses the expression "heroes of bar-room brawls" in his description of the SA.

35. Quoted in Mosse, *Nazi Culture*, 25.

36. Quoted in Large, *Where Ghosts Walked*, 164.

37. Quoted in Jeremy Noakes and Geoffrey Pridham, eds., *Nazism 1919–1945*, vol. 1, *The Rise to Power, 1919–1934* (Exeter: Exeter University Press, 1998), 94–95. See also Bahro, *Der SS-Sport*, 72–73.

38. Claudia Koonz, *Mothers in the Fatherland: Women, the Family and Nazi Politics* (New York: St. Martin's, 1987), 53.

39. Quoted in Mosse, *Nazi Culture*, 102–3.

40. Peukert, *Weimar Republic*, 95. Emphasis added.

41. Ayçoberry, *Social History of the Third Reich*, 20.

42. William L. Shirer, *Berlin Diary: The Journal of a Foreign Correspondent, 1934–1941* (New York: Alfred A. Knopf, 1941), 270. Shirer attributes this belief to a quote by Dr. Robert Ley, a senior Nazi Party figure. See also Christina Wieland, *The Fascist State of Mind and the Manufacturing of Masculinity: A Psychoanalytic Approach* (London: Routledge, 2015), 26.

43. Geoffrey Cocks, *The State of Health: Illness in Nazi Germany* (Oxford: Oxford University Press, 2012), 105.

44. Amy Carney, *Marriage and Fatherhood in the Nazi SS* (Toronto: University of Toronto Press, 2018), 49–53, 100–103. Unfortunately for Himmler, the rank and file of the SS did not respond to his call for large families.

45. *Das Schwarze Korps*, June 26, 1941, LM0343, reel 7, USHMMA.

46. Jane Caplan, "Gender and the Concentration Camps," in *Concentration Camps in Nazi Germany: The New Histories*, ed. Jane Caplan and Nikolaus Wachsmann (New York: Routledge, 2012), 86.

47. For a discussion of militarized masculinity see Björn Krondorfer and Edward Westermann, "Soldiering: Men," in *Gender: War*, ed. Andrea Petö (New York: Macmillan, 2017), 19–35.

48. Haynes, "Ordinary Masculinity," 169.

49. Letter from Karl Kretschmer, October 7(?), 1942, RG 14.101M, reel 434, folder 3517, p. 12, USHMMA.

50. Michael Wildt, *An Uncompromising Generation: The Nazi Leadership of the Reich Security Main Office*, trans. Tom Lampert (Madison: University of Wisconsin Press, 2010); Edward B. Westermann, *Hitler's Police Battalions: Enforcing Racial Policy in the East* (Lawrence: University Press of Kansas, 2005); and Klaus-Michael Mallmann, Volker Riess, and Wolfram Pyta, eds., *Deutscher Osten 1939–1945: Der Weltanschauungskrieg in Photos and Texten* (Darmstadt: Wissenschaftliche Buchgesellschaft, 2003), 137.

51. For an excellent review of this research see R. W. Connell and James W. Messerschmidt, "Hegemonic Masculinity: Rethinking the Concept," *Gender and Society* 19, no. 6 (2005): 829–59. The term "hypermasculinity" can be seen as a specific manifestation of militarized masculinity or a type of hegemonic masculinity and also has been used to refer to Protestant paramilitary groups, the B Specials, in Northern Ireland, groups engaged in

extensive acts of political violence. See Fidelma Ashe, "Gendering War and Peace: Militarized Masculinities in Northern Ireland," *Men and Masculinities* 15, no. 3 (2012): 237.

52. Koonz, *Mothers in the Fatherland*, 6, and Jacqueline M. Moore, *Cow Boys and Cattle Men: Class and Masculinities on the Texas Frontier, 1865–1900* (New York: NYU Press, 2010), 9. While Moore's claim in this case pertains to the nineteenth-century Texas frontier, it is equally applicable to the Nazi case.

53. Michael Stewart, "The Soldier's Life: Early Byzantine Masculinity and the Manliness of War," *Byzantina Symmeikta* 26, no. 1 (2016): 11, 37.

54. Müller, *Deutsche Soldaten*, 164.

55. George L. Mosse, *Fallen Soldiers: Reshaping the Memory of the World Wars* (Oxford: Oxford University Press, 1990), 162, 165, and Abel, *Why Hitler*, 253.

56. Hermann Rauschning, *The Voice of Destruction* (New York: G. P. Putnam's Sons, 1940), 6–7.

57. N. Gangulee, *The Mind and Face of Nazi Germany* (London: Butler & Tanner, 1942), 128–29. Banse was the author of *Wehrwissenschaft: Einführung in eine neue nationale Wissenschaft* (Leipzig: Armanenverlag, 1933).

58. Ernst Jünger, *In Stahlgewittern* (E. S. Mittler und Sohn, 1920).

59. Frank Werner, "'Hart müssen wir hier draussen sein': Soldatische Männlichkeit im Vernichtungskrieg, 1941–1944," *Geschichte und Gesellschaft* 34, no. 1 (2008): 15.

60. Lemle and Mishkind, "Alcohol and Masculinity," 214.

61. Spode, *Die Macht der Trunkenheit*, 261.

62. Spode, 262.

63. James Roberts, *Drink, Temperance and the Working Class in Nineteenth-Century Germany* (Boston: George Allen & Unwin, 1984), 47, 129.

64. Richard J. Evans, ed., *Kneipengespräche im Kaiserreich: Die Stimmungsberichte der Hamburger Politischen Polizei, 1892–1914* (Hamburg: Rowohlt, 1989), 20–33. Evans notes that by the turn of the century, beer halls took on an increasing role as sites for political activity and mobilization.

65. Peter Miller et al., "Alcohol, Masculinity, Honour and Male Barroom Aggression in an Australian Sample," *Drug and Alcohol Review* 33, no. 2 (2014), 136.

66. James S. Roberts, "The Tavern and Politics in the German Labor Movement, c. 1870–1914," in *Drinking: Behavior and Belief in Modern History*, ed. Susanna Barrows and Robin Room (Berkeley: University of California Press, 1991), 100–1.

67. Quoted in Roberts, "Tavern and Politics," 103.

68. Roberts, 107.

69. Herbert Freudenthal, *Vereine in Hamburg: Ein Beitrag zur Geschichte und Volkskunde der Geselligkeit* (Hamburg: Museum für Hamburgische Geschichte, 1968), 334–37.

70. Peter Longerich, *Die braunen Bataillone: Geschichte der SA* (Munich: C. H. Beck, 1989), 119–20.

71. Klemperer, *LTI*, 3. Klemperer states that Nazis received head wounds "inflicted by beer mugs or chair legs," while communists could be identified by "a stiletto wound in the lung."

72. Mosse, *Nazi Culture*, 32.

73. Alan E. Steinweis, *Kristallnacht: 1938* (Cambridge, MA: Harvard University Press, 2009), 59.

74. Thomas Kühne, "The Pleasure of Terror," in *Pleasure and Power in Nazi Germany*, ed. Pamela Swett, Corey Ross, and Fabrice d'Almeida (New York: Palgrave Macmillan, 2011), 239. See also Longerich, *Die braunen Bataillone*, 22–23.

75. Richard Bessel, "Violence as Propaganda: The Role of the Storm Troopers in the Rise of National Socialism," in *The Formation of the Nazi Constituency, 1919–1933*, ed. Thomas Childers (Totowa, NJ: Barnes & Noble Books, 1986), 144 (emphasis in the original).

76. Mosse, *Nazi Culture*, 17, and Daniel Siemens, *Stormtroopers: A New History of Hitler's Brownshirts* (New Haven, CT: Yale University Press, 2017), 188, 191.

77. Collomp and Groppo, *American in Hitler's Berlin*, 69.

78. Howard K. Smith, *Last Train from Berlin* (New York: Alfred A. Knopf, 1942), 11.

79. Maschmann, *Account Rendered*, 11.

80. Willy Cohn, *Kein Recht, nirgends: Tagebuch vom Untergang des Breslauer Judentums, 1939–1941*, vol. 1 (Cologne: Böhlau Verlag, 2007), 49.

81. Quoted in Eric Johnson and the Karl-Heinz Reuband, eds., *What We Knew: Terror, Mass Murder, and Everyday Life in Nazi Germany* (Cambridge, MA: Basic Books, 2005), 35.

82. Fromm, *Blood and Banquets*, 101.

83. Thomas Klein, ed., *Die Lageberichte der Geheimen Staatspolizei über die Provinz Hessen-Nassau, 1933–1936*, vol. 1 (Cologne: Böhlau Verlag, 1986), 190–91. These lyrics are included in a Gestapo report for November 1934 mentioning concerns about what effect these songs might have on business visitors with regard to foreign investment.

84. Henning Borggräffe, *"Schützenvereine im Nationalsozialismus" Pfllege der "Volksgemeinschaft" und Vorbereitung auf den Krieg, 1933–1945* (Münster: Ardey-Verlag, 2010), 1, 25–30.

85. Borggräfe, 59–67, 97–98.

86. Dirk Walter, *Antisemitische Kriminalität und Gewalt: Judenfeindschaft in der Weimarer Republik* (Bonn: J. H. W. Dietz Nachfolger, 1999), 214. For a contemporary popular culture depiction of this process see Walter Schönstedt, *Auf der Flucht erschossen: Ein SA Roman 1933* (Paris: Éditions du Carrefour, 1934), 11–32. This popular novel, although written by a German communist exile in Paris with an anti-Nazi moral, still captures the atmosphere of the *Sturmlokal* as a site of male camaraderie, ritual, and political violence.

87. Reichardt, *Faschistische Kampfbünde*, 449, and Abel, *Why Hitler*, 108–9.

88. Albert Krebs, *The Infancy of Nazism: The Memoirs of Ex-Gauleiter Albert Krebs, 1923–1933*, ed. and trans. William Sheridan Allen (New York: New Viewpoints, 1976), 57–58.

89. Longerich, *Die braunen Bataillone*, 142.

90. Malose Langa and Gillian Eagle, "The Intractability of Militarised Masculinity: A Case Study of Former Self-Defence Unit Members in the Kathorus Area, South Africa," *South African Journal of Psychology* 38, no. 1 (2008): 155.

91. Bahro, *Der SS-Sport*, 34.

92. *International Military Tribunal*, vol. 12, 452.

93. Reichardt, *Faschistische Kampfbünde*, 469, 471.

94. Dillon, *Dachau and the SS*, 183.

95. Kühne, "Pleasure of Terror," 239.

96. Reichardt, *Faschistische Kampfbünde*, 458.

97. Freudenthal, *Vereine in Hamburg*, 337.

98. Jürgen Matthäus et al., *Ausbildungsziel Judenmord? "Weltanschauliche Erziehung" von SS, Polizei, Waffen-SS im Rahmen der Endlösung* (Frankfurt am Main: Fischer Taschenbuch, 2003), 61–64.

99. Westermann, *Hitler's Police Battalions*, 118–20.

100. Andrew Wackerfuss, *Stormtrooper Families: Homosexuality and Community in the Early Nazi Movement* (New York: Harrington Park, 2015), 200.

101. Longerich, *Die braunen Bataillone*, 127.

102. Wackerfuss, *Stormtrooper Families*, 201.

103. Collomp and Groppo, *American in Hitler's Berlin*, 58.

104. Quoted in Shlomo Aronson, *Reinhard Heydrich und die Frühgeschichte von Gestapo und SD* (Stuttgart: Deutsche Verlags-Anstalt, 1971), 32. This portrayal comes from

Heydrich's former commander in the navy, Capitan Heinrich Beucke, describing his former subordinate's character and ambition prior to joining the SS.

105. Catherine Epstein, *Model Nazi: Arthur Greiser and the Occupation of Western Poland* (Oxford: Oxford University Press, 2010), 27.

106. Longerich, *Die braunen Bataillone*, 141.

107. Longerich, 127, and Koonz, *Mothers in the Fatherland*, 196. Beer was the primary beverage for such occasions, and SA men who demonstrated an inability to drink and maintain control were served low-alcohol-content bier (*Malzbier*) instead, a humiliating experience for the concerned individual.

108. Guido Fackler, "Cultural Behavior and the Invention of Traditions: Music and Musical Practices in the Early Concentration Camps, 1933–6/7," *Journal of Contemporary History* 45, no. 3 (July 2010): 615.

109. Friedrich Grupe, *Jahrgang 1916: Die Fahne war mehr als der Tod* (Munich: Universitas Verlag, 1989), 181, 299.

110. Mosse, *Nazi Culture*, 24, 123.

111. Heinz Boberach, ed., *Meldungen aus dem Reich, 1938–1945*, vol. 3 (Herrsching: Pawlak Verlag, 1984), 799; "Der Reichskommissar für das Ostland, Betrifft: Ehrembezeugung [*sic*] beim Spielen der Volkshymnen [October 29, 1943]," RG 18.002M, reel 2, fond R-69, opis 1A, folder 6, USHMMA; Order from the RFSS and Chief of the German Police, "Unerwünschte Musik in der uniformierten Ordnungspolizei," dated June 28, 1939, T-175, reel 227, frame 2766052, NARA; and Klein, *Die Lageberichte der Geheimen Staatspolizei*, 96.

112. "Heavy Drinking Rewires Brain, Increasing Susceptibility to Anxiety Problems," *Science News*, September 2, 2012, https://www.sciencedaily.com/releases/2012/09/12090 2143143.htm.

113. Sven Reichardt, "Violence and Community: A Micro-study on Nazi Storm Troopers," *Central European History* 46, no. 2 (2013): 276.

114. Reichardt, "Vergemeinschaft durch Gewalt," 113–14.

115. Letter from Willy Lenz to the Central Office for the Prosecution of National Socialist Crimes, October 8, 1959, RG 14.101M, reel 562, folder 4850, pp. 3–4, USHMMA. Lenz wrote this letter in reference to the alleged beatings of himself and over 120 Socialist Party members by SA men using wooden rods on the buttocks of the victims in March 1933. These beatings took place in the "*Sturmlokal* Schelsky" (SA club Schelsky).

116. Müller, "Männlichkeit und Gewalt in der SA," 135–36.

117. Siemens, *Stormtroopers*, 191–92.

118. Ayçoberry, *Social History of the Third Reich*, 23, and Westermann, *Hitler's Police Battalions*, 37–38.

119. Siemens, *Stormtroopers*, 336–37.

120. Steinweis, *Kristallnacht*, 4.

121. Burleigh, *Third Reich*, 325, and Uta Gerhardt and Thomas Karlauf, eds., *The Night of Broken Glass: Eyewitness Accounts of Kristallnacht*, trans. Robert Simmons and Nick Somers (Cambridge: Polity, 2012), 21.

122. Willy Cohn, *Kein Recht, nirgends: Tagebuch vom Untergang des Breslauer Judentums, 1939–1941*, vol. 2 (Cologne: Böhlau Verlag, 2007), 535.

123. Steinweis, *Kristallnacht*, 59. See also Wolf Gruner, "'Worse Than Vandals': The Mass Destruction of Jewish Homes and Jewish Responses during the 1938 Pogrom," in *New Perspectives on Kristallnacht: After 80 Years, The Nazi Pogrom in Global Comparison*, ed. Wolf Gruner (West Lafayette, IN: Purdue University Press, 2019), 25–49.

124. Longerich, *Die braunen Bataillone*, 230, and Siemens, *Stormtroopers*, 190.

125. Siemens, *Stormtroopers*, 191.

126. Steinweis, *Kristallnacht*, 75, 77–78.

127. Smith, *Last Train from Berlin*, 188–89.

128. Quoted in Siemens, *Stormtroopers*, 196.

129. Quoted in Johnson and Reuband, *What We Knew*, 112.

130. Gerhardt and Karlauf, *Night of Broken Glass*, 19, 22.

131. Investigation of Fritz Johan Rueckl* for accessory to murder, Case 117 AR-Z 351–9, RG 14.101M, reel 50, folder 14703, pp. 373–74, USHMMA. The symbol "*" indicates the use of a pseudonym. By November 1938, there were only sixty-one Jews living in Neidenburg (today Nidzica, Poland). See Esther Sarah Evans, "Neidenburg," Destroyed German Synagogues and Communities, http://germansynagogues.com/index.php/synagogues-and-communities.

132. Investigation of Fritz Johan Rueckl* for accessory to murder, Case 117 AR-Z 351–9, RG 14.101M, reel 50, folder 14703, p. 375, USHMMA.

133. Investigation of Fritz Johan Rueckl* for accessory to murder, Case 117 AR-Z 351–9, RG 14.101M, reel 50, folder 14703, p. 376, USHMMA.

134. Investigation of Fritz Johan Rueckl* for accessory to murder, Case 117 AR-Z 351–9, RG 14.101M, reel 50, folder 14703, p. 378, USHMMA.

135. Investigation of Fritz Johan Rueckl* for accessory to murder, Case 117 AR-Z 351–9, RG 14.101M, reel 50, folder 14703, pp. 378–80, USHMMA. Unfortunately for these SA men, the first man who had been stabbed was an "Aryan" German, Duscha, who along with his wife had been visiting Naftali. Duscha, however, survived the attack.

136. Steinweis, *Kristallnacht*, 75.

137. William Ian Miller, *Humiliation: And Other Essays on Honor, Social Discomfort, and Violence* (Ithaca, NY: Cornell University Press, 1993), 169. For descriptions of acts of sexual humiliation and sexual assault during the pogrom see Gruner, "'Worse Than Vandals,'" 31–32, and Gerhardt and Karlauf, *Night of Broken Glass*, 60.

138. Steinweis, *Kristallnacht*, 77.

139. Müller, "Männlichkeit und Gewalt in der SA," 146, and Reichardt, *Faschistische Kampfbünde*, 696.

140. Longerich, *Die braunen Bataillone*, 237.

141. Reichardt, *Faschistische Kampfbünde*, 469, 471.

142. Sara Berger, *Experten der Vernichtung: Das T4-Reinhardt-Netzwerk in den Lagern Belzec, Sobibor und Treblinka* (Hamburg: Verlag des Hamburger Instituts für Sozialforschung, 2013), 336. In her study, Berger also provides an excellent discussion of the use of alcohol and the concept of comradeship among the camps' SS guards.

143. Siemens, *Stormtroopers*, 237. For a discussion of this practice within the Order Police see Westermann, *Hitler's Police Battalions*, 62–66.

144. Detlev Peukert, *Inside Nazi Germany: Conformity, Opposition, and Racism in Everyday Life*, trans. Richard Deveson (New Haven, CT: Yale University Press, 1987), 205.

145. Haynes, "Ordinary Masculinity," 170.

146. Jürgen Matthäus, Jochen Böhler, and Klaus-Michael Mallmann, *War, Pacification, and Mass Murder, 1939: The Einsatzgruppen in Poland* (Lanham, MD: Rowman & Littlefield, 2014), 59.

147. Angelika Benz, *Handlanger der SS: Die Rolle der Trawniki-Männer im Holocaust* (Berlin: Metropol, 2015), 212.

2. Rituals of Humiliation

1. David Kertzer, *Ritual, Politics, and Power* (New Haven, CT: Yale University Press, 1988), 163–64.

2. J. David Knotterus, Jean Van Delinder, and Jennifer Edwards, "Strategic Ritualization of Power: Nazi Germany, the Orange Order, and Native Americans," in *Ritual as a Missing Link: Sociology, Structural Ritualization Theory and Research*, ed. J. David Knotterus (Boulder, CO: Paradigm, 2011), 74, 101.

3. Cohn, *Kein Recht, nirgends*, 57.

4. Gisevius, *To the Bitter End*, 96.

5. Tausk, *Breslauer Tagebuch*, 61.

6. Kühne, *Belonging and Genocide*, 78.

7. Ilya Ehrenburg and Vasily Grossman, eds., *The Black Book*, trans. John Glad and James S. Levine (New York: Holocaust Publications, 1981), 114.

8. Dillon, *Dachau and the SS*, 38–39, and Burkhard, *Tanz mal Jude!*, 22–23, 28.

9. Academy of Sciences of the Ukrainian SSR, Institute of Law, *Nazi Crimes in Ukraine, 1941–1944*, trans. V. I. Biley, S. I. Kaznady, A. E. Sologubenko (Kiev: Naukova Dumka, 1987), 209–10. After this event, the SS executed five of these individuals.

10. Radu Harald Dinu, "Honor, Shame, and Warrior Values: The Anthropology of Ustasha Violence," in *The Utopia of Terror: Life and Death in Wartime Croatia*, ed. Rory Yeomans (Rochester, NY: University of Rochester Press, 2015), 130–31.

11. Klemp, *Freispruch*, 36.

12. Jewish Black Book Committee, *The Black Book: The Nazi Crime against the Jewish People* (New York: Duell, Sloan and Pearce, 1946), 354, and Wolfgang Curilla, *Der Judenmord in Polen und die deutsche Ordnungspolizei, 1939–1945* (Paderborn: Ferdinand Schöningh, 2011).

13. Aba Gordin and M. Gelbart, eds., *Memorial (Yizkor) Book of the Jewish Community of Ostrowo Mazowiecka* (New York: JewishGen, 2013), 503, and transcript of the *Shoah* interview with Ada Lichtman, RG 60.5023, USHMMA.

14. Transcript of the *Shoah* interview with Paula Biren, RG 60.5001, pp. 4–5, USHMMA.

15. Testimony of Baruch Engler, RG 14.101M, reel 3052, folder 20186, p. 8, USHMMA.

16. Testimony of Ernst Bürger, RG 14.101M, reel 541, folder 4590, pp. 194–96, USHMMA.

17. Investigation of Josef Schwammberger, RG 14.101M, reel 50, folder 14702, pp. 54–56, USHMMA.

18. Investigation of Josef Schwammberger, RG 14.101M, reel 50, folder 14702, p. 181, USHMMA.

19. Investigation of Josef Schwammberger, RG 14.101M, reel 50, folder 14702, p. 175, USHMMA.

20. Joshua Rubenstein and Ilya Altman, *The Unknown Black Book: The Holocaust in the German-Occupied Soviet Territories*, trans. Christopher Morris and Joshua Rubenstein (Bloomington: Indiana University Press in association with the United States Holocaust Memorial Museum, 2008), 168.

21. Calel Perechodnik, *Am I a Murderer? Testament of a Jewish Ghetto Policeman*, ed. and trans. Frank Fox (Boulder, CO: Westview, 1996), 4.

22. Mary Berg, *Warsaw Ghetto: A Diary by Mary Berg*, ed. S. L. Shneiderman (New York: L. B. Fischer, 1945), 27.

23. Olga Lengyel, *Five Chimneys* (Chicago: Academy Chicago, 1995), 122.

24. Felicja Karay, *Death Comes in Yellow: Skarżysko-Kamienna Slave Labor Camp*, trans. Sara Kitai (Amsterdam: Harwood Academic, 1996), 80.

25. Elaine Scarry, *The Body in Pain: The Making and Unmaking of the World* (Oxford: Oxford University Press, 1985), 28.

26. Alon Confino, *A World without Jews: The Nazi Imagination from Persecution to Genocide* (New Haven, CT: Yale University Press, 2014), 186.

27. Jewish Black Book Committee, *Black Book*, 346.

28. Berg, *Warsaw Ghetto*, 45.

29. Lengyel, *Five Chimneys*, 129.

30. Nikolaus Wachsmann, *KL: A History of the Nazi Concentration Camps* (New York: Farrar, Straus and Giroux, 2015), 54–55, 114, and Colin Rushton, *Spectator in Hell: A British Soldier's Story of Imprisonment in Auschwitz* (Gretna, LA: Pelican, 2010), 63, 81.

31. Emilio Jani, *My Voice Saved Me: Auschwitz 180046* (Milan: Centauro Editrice, 1961), 89.

32. Quoted in Jewish Black Book Committee, *Black Book*, 376.

33. Miller, *Humiliation*, 168–69.

34. Curilla, *Der Judenmord in Polen*, 877.

35. Richard Plant, *The Pink Triangle: The Nazi War against Homosexuals* (New York: Henry Holt, 1986), 163.

36. Quoted in Wachsmann, *KL*, 128.

37. Investigation report of Hugo S., RG 14.101M, reel 5, folder 14071, pp. 11–12, USHMMA.

38. Burkhard, *Tanz mal Jude!*, 24, and Ryback, *Hitler's First Victims*, 150.

39. Ernst Klee, Willi Dressen, and Volker Riess, eds., *"The Good Old Days": The Holocaust as Seen by Its Perpetrators and Bystanders*, trans. Deborah Burnstone (New York: Free Press, 1991), 113.

40. Benz, *Handlanger*, 220.

41. Raul Hilberg, *The Destruction of the European Jews*, vol. 3, 3rd ed. (New Haven, CT: Yale University Press, 2003), 937.

42. Rubenstein and Altman, *Unknown Black Book*, 162.

43. Rubenstein and Altman, 265–66.

44. Jewish Black Book Committee, *Black Book*, 347–48.

45. Wieslaw Kielar, *Anus Mundi: 1500 Days in Auschwitz/Birkenau*, trans. Susanne Flatauer (New York: Times Books, 1980), 34, 146.

46. Thomas Toivi Blatt, *From the Ashes of Sobibor: A Story of Survival* (Evanston, IL: Northwestern University Press, 1997), 98.

47. Hanna Levy-Hass, *Inside Belsen*, trans. Ronald Taylor (Sussex, NJ: Harvester, 1982), 39.

48. Elissa Mailänder, *Female SS Guards and Workaday Violence: The Majdanek Concentration Camp, 1942–1944*, trans. Patricia Szobar (East Lansing: Michigan State University Press, 2015), 218–19.

49. Lengyel, *Five Chimneys*, 104. My emphasis added.

50. Yaffa Eliach, *Hasidic Tales of the Holocaust* (New York: Oxford University Press, 1982), 225.

51. Rubenstein and Altman, *Unknown Black Book*, 152.

52. Wachsmann, *KL*, 105.

53. Notarized witness statement of Franciszek Gondek, May 30, 1945, 1.2.7.10/82190855/ ITS Digital Archive, accessed March 13, 2019, at USHMMA; and United Nations War Crimes Commission, Yugoslav charges against German war criminals, Charge no. R/N/8, RG 67.041M, reel 24, p. 290, USHMMA.

54. In but one example, Olga Lengyel, a prisoner at Auschwitz-Birkenau, described the whip of an SS guard with its "leather thongs" and "iron wires." See Lengyel, *Five Chimneys*, 161.

55. Rebecca Anne Goetz, *The Baptism of Early Virginia: How Christianity Created Race* (Baltimore: Johns Hopkins University Press, 2012), 72.

56. Jennifer Hull Dorsey, *Hirelings: African American Workers and Free Labor in Early America* (Ithaca, NY: Cornell University Press, 2011), 87.

57. Wachsmann, *KL*, 39.

58. Lehnstaedt, *Occupation in the East*, 194, and Jan Grabowski, *Hunt for the Jews: Betrayal and Murder in German-Occupied Poland* (Bloomington: Indiana University Press, 2013), 39.

59. Paul M. Neurath, "Social Life in the German Concentration Camps Dachau and Buchenwald" (PhD diss., Columbia University, 1951), 128.

60. Dirk Riedel, "A 'Political Soldier' and 'Practitioner of Violence': The Concentration Camp Commandant Hans Loritz," *Journal of Contemporary History* 45, no. 3 (2010): 564–65.

61. Trial judgment against Rudolf Schelenz and Heinrich Frings, 1.1.47.0/82483790/ITS Digital Archive, accessed April 2, 2019, at USHMMA.

62. Burkhard, *Tanz mal Jude!*, 30.

63. Boria Sax, *Animals in the Third Reich: Pets, Scapegoats, and the Holocaust* (New York: Continuum, 2000). See text of the "Law on Animal Protection," 175–79.

64. Frei et al., *Standort- und Kommandanturbefehle*, 132–33, 163, 196, 310, 353.

65. Quoted in Markus Roth, *Herrenmenschen: Die deutschen Kreishauptleute im besetzten Polen-Karrierewege, Herrschaftspraxis und Nachgeschichte* (Göttingen: Wallstein Verlag, 2009), 233.

66. Quoted in Dierl, "'Internal Wehrmacht,'" 126.

67. Quoted in Klee, Dreßen, and Rieß, "*Good Old Days,*" 61.

68. Tuviah Friedman, ed., *Schupo-Kriegsverbrecher in Kolomea* (Vienna: Jewish Historical Documentation Center, 1990), 11, 18.

69. Dick de Mildt, *In the Name of the People: Perpetrators of Genocide in the Reflection of Their Post-war Prosecution in West Germany* (The Hague: Martinus Nijhoff, 1996), 283.

70. Rudolph Höss, *Death Dealer: The Memoirs of the SS Kommandant at Auschwitz*, ed. Steven Paskuly and trans. Andrew Pollinger (New York: Da Capo, 1996), 83.

71. Rushton, *Spectator in Hell*, 9–10.

72. Affidavit of Mosze Lifschütz, April 25, 1947, 1.2.7.7/82181115/ITS Digital Archive, accessed March 13, 2019, at USHMMA.

73. Blatt, *From the Ashes*, 98.

74. Quoted in Mailänder, *Female SS Guards*, 219.

75. Arne Brun Lie with Robby Robinson, *Night and Fog: A Survivor's Story* (New York: Berkley Books, 1992), 147–48.

76. Amy Louise Woods, *Lynching and Spectacle: Witnessing Racial Violence in America, 1890–1940* (Chapel Hill: University of North Carolina Press, 2009), 2. While Woods's study looks at spectacular violence in the US South, her conclusions are equally valid for the context of these practices under National Socialism.

77. Józef Marsałek, *Majdanek: The Concentration Camp in Lublin* (Warsaw: Interpress, 1986), 98.

78. Court judgment against Ernst August K., RG 14.101M, reel 50, folder 14700, p. 317, USHMMA.

79. Kazimierz Sakowicz, *Ponary Diary, 1941–1943: A Bystander's Account of a Mass Murder*, ed. Yitzhak Arad (New Haven, CT: Yale University Press, 2005), 49.

80. De Mildt, *In the Name of the People*, 282. See also Mailänder, *Female SS Guards*, 218. Mailänder quotes Germaine Tillion, a former prisoner at Ravensbrück, who stated, "When 50 lashes were administered all at once, the victim often died; 75 lashes meant certain death."

81. Quoted in Mailänder, *Female SS Guards*, 247.

82. Interrogation protocol of Erna Petri on September 19, 1961, RG 14.068, fiche 569, p. 197, USHMMA.

83. Statement of Ursula E, 5.1/82324001/ITS Digital Archive, accessed April 2, 2019, at USHMMA.

84. Burkhard, *Tanz mal Jude!*, 45.

85. Fackler, "Cultural Behavior and the Invention of Traditions," 617.

86. Hans Beimler, *Four Weeks in the Hands of Hitler's Hell-Hounds: The Nazi Murder Camp of Dachau* (London: Modern Books, 1935), 36. Dressel ultimately died of blood loss from injuries received during beatings and his attempt to commit suicide with a butter knife.

87. Beimler, 39.

88. Fackler, "Cultural Behavior and the Invention of Traditions," 607–8, 624. Fackler notes that prisoners also appropriated songs and music to establish "solidarity and fellowship" and as a "strategy of self-assertion" in the camps.

89. Klaus Theweleit, *Das Lachen der Täter: Breivik u.a Psychogramm der Tötungslust* (St. Pölten, Austria: Residenz Verlag, 2015), 48.

90. Mietek Pemper, *The Road to Rescue: The Untold Story of Schindler's List*, trans. David Dollenmayer (New York: Other Press, 2005), 44, 58, and Johannes Sachslehner, *Der Tod ist ein Meister aus Wien: Leben und Taten des Amon Leopold Göth* (Vienna: Styria, 2008), 163.

91. Sachslehner, *Der Tod*, 170–71.

92. Sereny, *Into That Darkness*, 160–61. One version of this story is that Eberl, a member of the T4 program, had Jewish women dance on tables for his entertainment. The T4 program was the so-called euthanasia program aimed at killing the mentally and physically disabled.

93. Jewish Black Book Committee, *Black Book*, 315.

94. Pawełczyńska, *Values and Violence*, 84–85.

95. George L. Salton with Anna Salton Eisen, *The 23rd Psalm: A Holocaust Memoir* (Madison: University of Wisconsin Press, 2002), 116.

96. Hermann Langbein, *People in Auschwitz* (Chapel Hill: University of North Carolina Press, 2004), 164. In this case, the kapo wore the black triangle associated with the category of "asocials" in the Nazi lexicon.

97. Wachsmann, *KL*, 114.

98. Pemper, *Road to Rescue*, 53.

99. David Bankier, *Expulsion and Extermination: Holocaust Testimonials from Provincial Lithuania* (Jerusalem: Yad Vashem, 2011), 163.

100. Rubenstein and Altman, *Black Book*, 303–4.

101. Karay, *Death Comes in Yellow*, 134–39; Charlotte Delbo, *Auschwitz and After*, trans. Rosette C. Lamont (New Haven, CT: Yale University Press, 1995), 132, 174; and transcript of the *Shoah* interview with Gertrude Schneider, RG 60.5015, pp. 37–45, USHMMA. Delbo remarks on French prisoners singing "La Marseillaise" in an act of political protest on at least two occasions. Likewise, Schneider discusses the use of song in the Vilna ghetto as a form of mutual support and resistance. For an academic study on music and song in Sachsenhausen see Juliane Brauer, *Musik im Konzentrationslager Sachsenhausen* (Berlin: Metropol Verlag, 2009).

102. Grabowski, *Hunt for the Jews*, 34. Hallel refers to Psalms 113–18 and is used as a prayer of praise and thanksgiving.

103. Omer Bartov, *Anatomy of a Genocide: The Life and Death of a Town Called Buczacz* (New York: Simon & Schuster, 2018), 211–12.

104. Jani, *My Voice Saved Me*, 72.

105. Confino, *World without Jews*, 186.

106. Rubenstein and Altman, *Black Book*, 102.

107. Testimony of former policeman Paul L. [June 28, 1962], 202 AR-Z 907/60, file 1, p. 121, Central Office for the Investigation of National Socialist Crimes (ZStl). Emphasis added.

108. Testimony of former policeman Paul L. [June 28, 1962], 202 AR-Z 907/60, file 1, p. 122, ZStl.

109. Testimony of policeman Franz J. [June 17, 1962], 202 AR-Z 907/60, file 1, p. 137, ZStl.

110. "Historical Film Footage, Einsatzgruppen (Mobile Killing Units)," Liepaja, Latvia, 1941, https://www.ushmm.org/wlc/en/media_fi.php?ModuleId=0&MediaId=183, USHMMA.

111. Stefan Klemp, *"Nicht ermittelt": Polizeibataillone und die Nachkriegsjustiz* (Essen: Klartext Verlag, 2011), 186.

112. For a discussion and photographic evidence of lynching in the United States see James Allen et al., *Without Sanctuary: Lynching Photography in America* (Santa Fe, NM: Twin Palms, 2000), and Amy Louise Woods, *Lynching and Spectacle: Witnessing Racial Violence in America, 1890–1940* (Chapel Hill: University of North Carolina Press, 2009).

3. Taking Trophies and Hunting Jews

1. Robert Strasser, ed., *The Landmark Thucydides: A Comprehensive Guide to the Peloponnesian War* (New York: Free Press, 1996), 357.

2. For a discussion of the dominance of the Comanche in this period see Brian DeLay, *War of a Thousand Deserts: Indian Raids and the US-Mexican War* (New Haven, CT: Yale University Press, 2008), and Pekka Hämäläinen, *The Comanche Empire* (New Haven, CT: Yale University Press, 2008).

3. For a discussion of these practices in the US West see Edward B. Westermann, *Hitler's Ostkrieg and the Indian Wars: Comparing Genocide and Conquest* (Norman: University of Oklahoma Press, 2016), 208–12.

4. David F. Crew, "Photography and Cinema," in *The Oxford Illustrated History of the Third Reich*, ed. Robert Gellately (Oxford: Oxford University Press, 2018), 172. The author would like to thank David Crew for sharing a prepublication version of this article.

5. Chaim A. Kaplan, *The Warsaw Diary of Chaim A. Kaplan*, ed. and trans. Abraham I. Katsh, rev. ed. (New York: Collier Books, 1973), 335–36. For an examination of the propaganda team's efforts in the Warsaw ghetto see *A Film Unfinished*, written and directed Yael Hersonski, Oscilloscope Laboratories, 2010, 88 min., DVD.

6. Maiken Umbach, "Selfhood, Place, and Ideology in German Photo Albums, 1933–1945," *Central European History* 48, no. 3 (2015): 337.

7. Christopher Browning, *Ordinary Men: Reserve Police Battalion 101 and the Final Solution in Poland*, rev. ed. (New York: Harper Perennial, 2017), 252.

8. Jan Tomasz Gross with Irena Grudzinska Gross, *Golden Harvest: Events at the Periphery of the Holocaust* (Oxford: Oxford University Press, 2012), 71.

9. Patrick Desbois, *In Broad Daylight: The Secret Procedures behind the Holocaust by Bullets*, trans. Hilary Reyl and Calvert Barksdale (New York: Arcade, 2015), 248.

10. Kathrin Hoffmann-Curtius, "Trophäen und Amulette: Die Fotografien von Wehrmachts- und SS-Verbrechen in den Brieftaschen der Soldaten," *Fotogeschichte* 20, no. 78 (2000): 71.

11. Hermann Wygoda, *In the Shadow of the Swastika*, ed. Mark Wygoda (Urbana: University of Illinois Press, 1998), 130–31; Bernd Boll, "Złoczów, July 1941: The Wehrmacht and the Beginning of the Holocaust in Galicia," in *Crimes of War: Guilt and Denial in the*

Twentieth Century, ed. Omer Bartov, Atina Grossmann, and Mary Nolan (New York: New Press, 2002), 82–90; and Felix Römer, *Comrades: The Wehrmacht from Within*, trans. Alex J. Kay (Oxford: Oxford University Press, 2019), 326.

12. Alan Levy, *The Wiesenthal File* (Grand Rapids, MI: William B. Eerdmans, 1993), 78.

13. Rubenstein and Altman, *Black Book*, 224.

14. Crew, "Photography and Cinema," 179, 182.

15. See *The Buchenwald Report*, trans. and ed. David A. Hackett (Boulder, CO: Westview, 1995), 41; for the "Auschwitz album" see http://www.yadvashem.org/yv/en/exhibitions/album_auschwitz/index.asp; De Mildt, *In the Name of the People*, 256; and Klee, Dressen, and Riess, *"Good Old Days."*

16. Unit diary entry for December 17, 1941, RG 14.101M, reel 344, folder 2635, p. 12, USHMMA.

17. Andreas Weigelt et al., eds., *Todesurteile sowjetischer Militärtribunale gegen Deutsche (1944–1947): Eine historisch-biographische Studie* (Göttingen: Vandenhoeck & Ruprecht, 2015), 147; Elissa Mailänder, "Making Sense of a Rape Photograph: Sexual Violence as Social Performance on the Eastern Front, 1939–1944," *Journal of the History of Sexuality* 26, no. 3 (2017): 495; and Willi Rose, *Shadows of War: A German Soldier's Lost Photographs of World War II*, ed. Thomas Eller and Petra Bopp (New York: Harry N. Abrams, 2004), 15.

18. Interrogation protocol of David F. Siwzon, November 24, 1969, RG-14.068, fiche 32, pp. 667, 670.

19. Witness statement of Nikolajewna Adler, November 21, 1969, RG-14.068, fiche 24, pp. 10–13, USHMMA.

20. Charge sheet for Erhard G. et al., January 18, 1968, RG 14.101M, reel 344, folder 2637, p. 24, USHMMA.

21. Witness statement of Richard Wiener, October 4, 1959, RG 14.101M, reel 342, folder 2621, p. 252a, USHMMA. In his statement Wiener says he doesn't know if Germans were involved in the killings and instead attributes these actions to Latvian auxiliaries. See also witness statement of Nikolajewna Adler, November 21, 1969, RG-14.068, fiche 24, pp. 10–13, USHMMA, and witness statement of Moshe Leib Tscharny, RG 14.101M, reel 344, folder 2632, p. 132, USHMMA. Adler found Baumgartner's photos in his wardrobe, while Tscharny found copies of the same photos in the desk of another SS staff sergeant, Carl Strott.

22. Westermann, *Hitler's Police Battalions*, 144–45.

23. Highest SS and Police Court Field Verdict against Max Täubner, May 24, 1943, RG 14.101M, reel 3115, folder 21020, pp. 10, 16, USHMMA. Täubner's case is in many respects unique and widely known among historians based on his conviction for the brutality used in the killings. In fact, absent the photographs and their distribution among German civilians, he likely never would have been charged or received a ten-year penitentiary sentence.

24. Römer, *Comrades*, 326.

25. See for example Schneider, *"Auswärts eingesetzt,"* 449, 470; Klemp, *"Nicht ermittelt,"* 132; and Christopher Browning, *Ordinary Men: Reserve Police Battalion 101 and the Final Solution in Poland*, rev. ed. (New York: Harper Perennial, 2017), 264, 267.

26. Quoted in Eugen Kogon, *Theory and Practice of Hell: The German Concentration Camps and the System behind Them*, rev. ed. (New York: Farrar, Straus and Giroux, 2006), 178.

27. Rubenstein and Altman, *Unknown Black Book*, 163.

28. Quoted in Levy, *Wiesenthal File*, 38.

29. Dieter Reifarth and Viktoria Schmidt-Linsenhoff, "Die Kamera der Henker: Fotografische Selbstzeugnisse des Naziterrors in Osteuropa," *Fotogeschichte* 3, no. 7 (1983): 57–71.

30. Mailänder, "Making Sense of a Rape Photograph," 489–520.

31. "Der Kommandeur der Gendarmerie, Shitomir, Kommandobefehl Nr. 18/42, June 6, 1942, RG 53.002M, fond 658, reel 5, file 2, USHMMA.

32. Desbois, *In Broad Daylight*, 249.

33. Pawełczyńska, *Values and Violence*, 78. Emphasis added.

34. Primo Levi, *The Complete Works of Primo Levi*, vol. 3, *The Drowned and the Saved*, trans. Michael Moore (New York: Liveright, 2015), 2515.

35. Karin Orth, "Egon Zill—ein typischer Vertreter der Konzentrationslager-SS," in *Karrieren der Gewalt: Nationalsozialistische Täterbiographien*, ed. Klaus-Michael Mallmann and Gerhard Paul (Darmstadt: Wissenschaftliche Buchgesellschaft, 2004), 267.

36. Delbo, *Auschwitz and After*, 19, 29, 69, 80–81.

37. Gordin and Gelbart, *Memorial (Yizkor) Book*, 499.

38. Polish Charges against German War Crimes, Case No. 273, RG 67.041M, reel 15, USHMMA. My emphasis added.

39. Johannes Lange, "The Proud Executioner: Pride and the Psychology of Genocide," in *Emotions and Mass Atrocity: Philosophical and Theoretical Explorations*, ed. Thomas Brudholm and Johannes Lange (Cambridge: Cambridge University Press, 2018), 80.

40. Gordin and Gelbart, *Memorial (Yizkor) Book*, 565–66.

41. Römer, *Comrades*, 349. In this case, the individual was describing a mass killing by Hungarian forces.

42. Polish Charges against German War Crimes, Case No. 212, RG 67.041M, reel 15, USHMMA.

43. Łucja Pawlicka-Nowak, ed., *Chełmno Witnesses Speak*, trans. Juliet Golden and Arkadiusz Kamiński (Łódź: Oficyna Bibliofilów, 2004), 126.

44. Testimony of Stanislaw Klauzinski, RG 14.101M, reel 2832, folder 9692, p. 407, USHMMA.

45. Court verdict in the case of Hugo S., September 27, 1957, RG 14.101M, reel 5, folder 14071, pp. 11, 31, USHMMA.

46. Benz, *Handlanger der SS*, 213–14.

47. Haynes, "Ordinary Masculinity," 170.

48. Testimony of Otto Welken, 5.1/82323937/ITS Digital Archive, accessed March 21, 2019, at USHMMA; and letter from Tuviah Friedman, dated December 27, 1959, RG 14.101M, reel 395, folder 3166, p. 23, USHMMA.

49. Transcript of the *Shoah* interview with Abraham Bomba, RG 60.5011, pp. 71–72, USHMMA.

50. Dov B. Schmorak, *Sieben sagen aus: Zeugen im Eichmann Prozess* (Berlin: Arani, 1962), 166.

51. Testimony of Michael J. Wind, 1.2.7.7/82183308/ITS Digital Archive, accessed April 11, 2019, at USHMMA.

52. Burkhard, *Tanz mal Jude!*, 78.

53. Quoted in Svetlana Alexievich, *Last Witnesses: An Oral History of the Children of World War II*, trans. Richard Pevear and Larissa Volokhonsky (New York: Random House, 2019), 227.

54. Kogon, *Theory and Practice of Hell*, 88.

55. Marsałek, *Majdanek*, 99.

56. Burkhard, *Tanz mal Jude!*, 53–54.

57. Jacob Biber, *Survivors* (New London, CT: Star, 1982), 44.

58. Wolfgang Curilla, *Die Deutsche Ordnungspolizei und der Holocaust im Baltikum und in Weißrussland, 1941–1944* (Paderborn: Ferdinand Schöningh, 2006), 262, 575, 825. See also Klemp, "*Nicht Ermittelt*," 283–84, 441.

59. "Der Kommandeur der Gendarmerie Shitomir, Kommandobefehl Nr. 27/43," April 12, 1943, RG 53.002M, fond 658, reel 5, folder 3, USHMMA.

60. Blatt, *From the Ashes*, 15.

61. Testimony of Mieczyslaw Garfinkel, 1.2.7.7/82181256/ITS Digital Archive, accessed June 14, 2019, at USHMMA.

62. Quoted in Jewish Black Book Committee, *Black Book*, 364–65.

63. Quoted in Sereny, *Into That Darkness*, 160.

64. Interrogation protocol of Josef Blösche, August 18, 1967, RG-14.068, fiche 64, p. 486, USHMMA.

65. Interrogation protocol of Josef Blösche, April 21, 1967, RG-14.068, fiche 65, p. 495, USHMMA.

66. Berg, *Warsaw Ghetto*, 157.

67. Jewish Black Book Committee, *Black Book*, 347.

68. *The Buchenwald Report*, trans. and ed. David Hackett (Boulder, CO: Westview, 1995), 33. This practice also was present throughout the camp system. For examples at Dachau and Natzweiler see Beimler, *Four Weeks*, 37; Burkhard, *Tanz mal Jude!*, 53; and Lie, *Night and Fog*, 179.

69. Kielar, *Anus Mundi*, 96–97.

70. Marsałek, *Majdanek*, 98.

71. Transcript of the *Shoah* interview with Franz Suchomel, RG 60.5046, p. 63, USHMMA.

72. Höss, *Death Dealer*, 125.

73. Felix Weinberg, *Boy 30529: A Memoir* (London: Verso, 2013), 72. The French historian Pierre Ayçoberry notes that SA "pulp fiction" integrated "countless brawls" in an attempt to mimic the westerns of Karl May. See Ayçoberry, *Social History of the Third Reich*, 21.

74. Bahro, *Der SS-Sport*, 27–28.

75. Benz, *Handlanger der SS*, 212.

76. Mailänder, "Making Sense of a Rape Photograph," 500.

77. Quoted in Mailänder, *Female SS Guards*, 246.

78. Klemp, *Freispruch*, 45.

79. Lucjan Dobroszycki, ed., *The Chronicle of the Łódź Ghetto, 1941–1944*, trans. Richard Lourie et al. (New Haven, CT: Yale University Press, 1984), 50.

80. Klemp, *Freispruch*, 45.

81. Avraham Tory, *Surviving the Holocaust: The Kovno Ghetto Diary*, trans. Jerzy Michalowicz (Cambridge, MA: Harvard University Press, 1990), 76.

82. For a discussion of the relationship of masculinity to hunting see J. A. Mangan and Callum McKenzie, *Militarism, Hunting, Imperialism: "Blooding" the Martial Male* (London: Routledge, 2010).

83. Transcript of the *Shoah* interviews with farmers near Chełmno, RG 60.5066, USHMMA.

84. Simon Harrison, *Dark Trophies: Hunting and the Enemy Body in Modern War* (New York: Berghahn, 2012), 7.

85. Schneider, *"Auswärts eingesetzt,"* 447.

86. Henry V. Dicks, *Licensed Mass Murder: A Socio-psychological Study of Some SS Killers* (New York: Basic Books, 1972), 118.

87. Hermann Langbein, *People in Auschwitz* (Chapel Hill: University of North Carolina Press, 2004), 573.

88. Edward B. Westermann, "'Ordinary Men' or 'Ideological Soldiers'? Police Battalion 310 in Russia, 1942," *German Studies Review* 21, no. 1 (February 1998): 49–50.

89. Christian Ingrao, *The SS Dirlewanger Brigade: The History of the Black Hunters*, trans. Phoebe Green (New York: Skyhorse, 2011), 4, 76–79, 116. The unit's commander Oskar Dirlewanger was well known for his heavy drinking.

90. Erich Kern, *Der große Rausch: Rußlandfeldzug 1941–1945* (Druffel and Vowinckel Verlag, 2008), 43. This book originally appeared in 1948 and went through a number of editions, including an English-language translation titled *The Dance of Death* published in 1951. The author's given name was Erich Knud Kernmayr.

91. Burkhard, *Tanz mal Jude!*, 128. These were reprisal killings for an attempt made by a lone assassin, Georg Elser, to kill Hitler with a bomb during the annual Nazi celebration of the failed "Beer Hall Putsch" of 1923. For an overview of the assassination attempt see Ian Kershaw, *Hitler: 1936–1945, Nemesis* (New York: W. W. Norton, 2000), 271–75.

92. Interrogation protocol of Josef Blösche, November 16, 1967, RG-14.068, fiche 65, pp. 511–12, USHMMA.

93. Interrogation protocol of Josef Blösche, April 13, 1967, RG-14.068, fiche 61, p. 248, USHMMA.

94. Interrogation protocol of Hans Baumgartner, March 13, 1970, RG-14.068, fiche 16, p. 192, USHMMA.

95. Andrej Angrick, "The Men of *Einsatzgruppe* D: An Inside View of a State-Sanctioned Killing Unit in the 'Third Reich,'" in *Ordinary People as Mass Murderers: Perpetrators in Comparative Perspectives*, ed. Olaf Jensen and Claus-Christian Szejnmann (New York: Palgrave Macmillan, 2008), 87.

96. John Dower, *War without Mercy: Race and Power in the Pacific War* (New York: Pantheon, 1986), 12–13, 33–73.

97. Harrison, *Dark Trophies*, 132.

98. Dower, *War without Mercy*, 42.

99. Quoted in Michael A. Musmanno, *The Eichmann Kommandos* (Philadelphia: Macrae Smith, 1961), 243.

100. Leo Kahn, *No Time to Mourn: A True Story of a Jewish Partisan Fighter* (Vancouver, Canada: Laurelton, 1978), 57.

101. Quoted in Lower, *Hitler's Furies*, 106.

102. Bartov, *Anatomy of a Genocide*, 229.

103. Polish Charges against German War Crimes, case no. 314, RG 67.041M, reel 15, USHMMA.

104. Desbois, *In Broad Daylight*, 234.

105. Academy of Sciences of the Ukrainian SSR, Institute of Law, *Nazi Crimes in Ukraine*, 211. Willhaus also reportedly allowed his wife to shoot on occasion and would shoot toddlers thrown into the air for the enjoyment of his nine-year-old daughter. For a detailed discussion of the Janowska camp and Willhaus's role see Waitman W. Beorn, "Last Stop in Lwów: Janowska as a Hybrid Camp," *Holocaust and Genocide Studies* 32, no. 3 (2018): 445–71.

106. Sakowicz, *Ponary Diary*, 17.

107. Hilary Earl, *Nuremberg SS-Einsatzgruppen Trial, 1945–1948* (Cambridge: Cambridge University Press, 2009), 145; Helmut Langerbein, *Hitler's Death Squads: The Logic of Mass Murder* (College Station: Texas A&M University Press), 2004, 58; and Richard Breitman, *Official Secrets: What the Nazis Planned, What the British and Americans Knew* (New York: Hill & Wang, 1998), 92.

108. Investigation report on Gerhard Erren, RG 14.101M, reel 39, folder 14527, p. 46, USHMMA.

109. Testimony of Andreas T., RG 14.101M, reel 540, folder 4588, USHMMA.

110. Highest SS and Police Court Field Verdict against Max Täubner, May 24, 1943, RG 14.101M, reel 3115, folder 21020, p. 8, USHMMA

111. Mallmann, Riess, and Pyta, *Deutscher Osten*, 132.

112. Curilla, *Der Judenmord in Polen*, 877.

113. Klemp, *"Nicht ermittelt,"* 407.

114. Klemp, *Freispruch*, 27, 48.

115. Witness testimony on German atrocities in Latvia, 1.2.7.4/82173567/ITS Digital Archive, accessed May 29, 2019, at USHMMA.

116. Curilla, *Der Judenmord in Polen*, 877.

117. Thomas Geldmacher, *"Wir Wiener waren ja bei der Bevölkerung beliebt": Österreichische Schutzpolizisten und die Judenvernichtung in Ostgalizien, 1941–1945* (Vienna: Mandelbaum Verlag, 2002), 117–19.

118. Klemp, *Freispruch*, 49.

119. Testimony of Richard W. Schweizer, RG 14.101M, reel 330, folder 2514, p. 6216, USHMMA.

120. Johnson and Reuband, *What We Knew*, 245, 249.

121. Judgment of the Hamburg Criminal Court against Paul Ellerhusen, 5.1/82322339/ITS Digital Archive, accessed May 14, 2019, at USHMMA; and Wachsmann, *KL*, 272.

122. Testimony protocol of Reinhold Meyer, 1.1.30.0/82134647-48/ITS Digital Archive, accessed April 25, 2019, at USHMMA.

123. Hermann Langbein, *Der Auschwitz-Prozeß: Eine Dokumentation*, vol. 1 (Frankfurt am Main: Verlag Neue Kritik, 1995), 271; and Michael J. Bazyler and Frank M. Tuerkheimer, *Forgotten Trials of the Holocaust* (New York: NYU Press, 2014), 175.

124. Mallmann, Riess, and Pyta, *Deutscher Osten*, 37.

125. Mallmann Riess, and Pyta, 47.

126. Friedländer, *Memory*, 110.

127. Berger, *Experten der Vernichtung*, 336.

128. Berger, 332–33, 335. Berger argues that the heavy consumption of alcohol in these celebrations served as "compensation and suppression of the daily atrocities, even if the men were not conscious of it," a contention that would benefit from additional explanation and support.

129. Quoted in Lifton, *Nazi Doctors*, 259.

130. Klee, Dressen, and Riess, *"Good Old Days,"* 267.

131. Quoted in de Mildt, *In the Name of the People*, 277.

132. Transcipt of the *Shoah* interview with Alfred Spiess, RG 60.5063, USHMMA.

4. Alcohol and Sexual Violence

1. See Birgit Beck, *Wehrmacht und sexuelle Gewalt: Sexualverbrechen vor deutschen Militärgerichten, 1939–1945* (Paderborn: Ferdinand Schöningh, 2004); Sonja M. Hedgepeth and Rochelle G. Saidel, eds., *Sexual Violence against Jewish Women during the Holocaust* (Hanover, NH: University Press of New England, 2010); Regina Mühlhäuser, *Eroberungen: Sexuelle Gewalttaten und intime Beziehungen deutscher Soldaten in der Sowjetunion, 1941–1945* (Hamburg: Hamburger Edition, 2010); Wendy Jo Gertjejanssen, "Victims, Heroes, Survivors: Sexual Survivors on the Eastern Front during World War II" (PhD diss., University of Minnesota, 2004); and Monika J. Flaschka, "Race, Rape, and Gender in Nazi-Occupied Territories" (PhD diss., Kent State University, 2009).

2. Richard Grunberger, *The 12-Year Reich: A Social History of Nazi Germany* (New York: Holt, Rinehart and Winston, 1971), 123.

3. Beorn, *Marching into Darkness*, 172, and Gertjejanssen, "Victims, Heroes, Survivors," 53–64.

4. Helene Sinnreich, "The Rape of Jewish Women during the Holocaust," in Hedgepeth and Saidel, *Sexual Violence against Jewish Women*, 112–15.

5. Ehrenburg, *Russia at War*, 113.

6. Report of the Wehrmacht Commander Ostland concerning "Enemy Propaganda," September 10, 1942, RG 18.002M, reel 4, fond 69, opis 1A, folder 25, USHMMA.

7. Regina Mühlhäuser, "Sexual Violence and the Holocaust," in *Gender: War*, ed. Andrea Petö (New York: Macmillan, 2017), 101. Mühlhäuser classifies "enforced disrobement" as an additional act of sexual violence, but I have chosen to refer to these acts as "sexualized violence."

8. For an additional discussion of sexual and sexualized violence see Waitman Beorn, "Bodily Conquest: Sexual Violence in the Nazi East," in *Mass Violence in Nazi Occupied Europe*, ed. Alex J. Kay and David Stahel (Bloomington: Indiana University Press, 2018), 195–218. The author would like to thank Waitman Beorn for sharing a prepublication version of this chapter.

9. Bazyler and Tuerkheimer, *Forgotten Trials of the Holocaust*, 182.

10. J. D. Vigil and J. M. Long, "Emic and Etic Perspectives on Gang Culture: The Chicano Case," in *Gangs in America*, ed. C. Ronald Huff (Newbury Park, CA: Sage, 1990), 47.

11. Mullen et al., "Young Men, Masculinity and Alcohol," 153.

12. Brigitte Halbmayr, "Sexualized Violence against Women during Nazi 'Racial' Persecution," in Hedgepeth and Saidel, *Sexual Violence against Women*, 30.

13. Karay, *Death Comes in Yellow*, 79.

14. Pemper, *Road to Rescue*, 112.

15. Regina Mühlhäuser, "Between 'Racial Awareness' and Fantasies of Potency: Nazi Sexual Politics in the Occupied Territories of the Soviet Union, 1942–1945," in *Brutality and Desire: War and Sexuality in Europe's Twentieth Century*, ed. Dagmar Herzog (New York: Palgrave Macmillan, 2009), 201.

16. Desbois, *In Broad Daylight*, 67–68.

17. Frevert, *Nation in Barracks*, 175.

18. Madeline Morris, "By Force of Arms: Rape, War, and Military Culture," *Duke Law Journal* 45, no. 4 (1996): 695.

19. Frevert, *Nation in Barracks*, 175.

20. Erich Hager, *The War Diaries of a Panzer Soldier*, ed. David Garden (Atglen, PA: Schiffer Military History, 2010), 57. Diary entry of November 13, 1941.

21. Morris, "By Force of Arms," 701.

22. Morris, 704.

23. Klemperer, *Language of the Third Reich*, 15.

24. *Cassell's New German Dictionary*, rev. ed. (1939), s.v. "Gelage," "saufen," and "zechen."

25. Mühlhäuser, "Between 'Racial Awareness' and Fantasies of Potency," 199–202.

26. Andrej Angrick, *Besatzungspolitik und Massenmord: Die Einsatzgruppe D in der südlichen Sowjetunion, 1941–1943* (Hamburg: Hamburger Edition, 2003), 450.

27. Letter by SS lieutenant Karl Kretschmer to his wife and children, dated October 15, 1942, RG 14.101M, reel 434, folder 3517, p. 16, USHMMA.

28. Robert L. Peralta, "College Alcohol Use and the Embodiment of Hegemonic Masculinity among European American Men," *Sex Roles* 56, nos. 11–12 (2007): 743.

29. Peralta, 747, 749.

30. Shelley Baranowski, *Strength through Joy: Consumerism and Mass Tourism in the Third Reich* (Cambridge: Cambridge University Press, 2004), 178.

31. Vandana Joshi, *Gender and Power in the Third Reich: Female Denouncers and the Gestapo, 1933–1945* (New York: Palgrave Macmillan, 2003), 189–90.

32. Antonia Abbey, "Alcohol-Related Sexual Assault: A Common Problem among College Students," *Journal of Studies on Alcohol Supplement* 63, no. 2 (2002): 118–28.

33. Mailänder, "Making Sense of a Rape Photograph," 497.

34. Ben H. Shepherd, *Hitler's Soldiers: The German Army in the Third Reich* (New Haven, CT: Yale University Press, 2016), 285.

35. Mühlhäuser, *Eroberungen*, 77.

36. Peggy Sanday, "Rape Free versus Rape Prone: How Culture Makes a Difference," in *Evolution, Gender, and Rape*, ed. Cheryl Brown Travis (Cambridge, MA: MIT Press, 2003), 337.

37. Quoted in Dagmar Herzog, *Sex after Fascism: Memory and Morality in Twentieth-Century Germany* (Princeton, NJ: Princeton University Press, 2005), 86.

38. Annette Timm, "Sex with a Purpose: Prostitution, Venereal Disease, and Militarized Masculinity in the Third Reich," in *Sexual and German Fascism*, ed. Dagmar Herzog (New York: Berghahn, 2005), 225–27, and Koonz, *Mothers in the Fatherland*, 56.

39. Mallmann, Rieß, and Pyta, *Deutscher Osten*, 155–56.

40. Patrick Desbois, *The Holocaust by Bullets: A Priest's Journey to Uncover the Truth behind the Murder of 1.5 Million Jews* (New York: Palgrave Macmillan, 2008), 126.

41. Tomasz Ceran, *The History of a Forgotten German Camp: Nazi Ideology and Genocide at Szmalcówka* (London: I. B. Tauris, 2015), 57, 113.

42. Bahro, *Der SS-Sport*, 27–28.

43. Ceran, *Forgotten German Camp*, 103, 115–17.

44. Transcript of the *Shoah* interview with Ruth Elias, RG 60.5003, pp. 33–34, USHMMA. My emphasis added.

45. Na'ama Shik, "Sexual Abuse of Jewish Women in Auschwitz-Birkenau," in *Brutality and Desire: War and Sexuality in Europe's Twentieth Century*, ed. Dagmar Herzog (Basingstoke, UK: Palgrave Macmillan, 2009), 232.

46. Bahro, *Der SS-Sport*, 27–28.

47. Quoted in Bartov, *Anatomy of a Genocide*, 205.

48. Timm, "Sex with a Purpose," 227.

49. Benz, *Handlanger der SS*, 213.

50. Mühlhäuser, "Between 'Racial Awareness' and Fantasies of Potency," 203.

51. Birgit Beck, "The Military Trials of Sexual Crimes Committed by Soldiers in the Wehrmacht, 1939–1944," in *Home/Front: The Military, War and Gender in Twentieth-Century Germany*, ed. Karen Hagemann and Stefanie Schüler-Springorum (Oxford: Berg, 2002), 266.

52. Geoffrey Giles, "The Denial of Homosexuality: Same-Sex Incidents in Himmler's SS and Police," *Journal of the History of Sexuality* 11, nos. 1–2 (2002): 271, 279, 286.

53. Halbmayr, "Sexualized Violence against Women," 30–31.

54. Mühlhäuser, *Eroberungen*, 74–75.

55. Ludger Tewes, *Frankreich in der Besatzungszeit 1940–1943: Die Sicht deutscher Augenzeugen* (Bonn: Bouvier Verlag, 1998), 207–8. In France, for example, soldiers found guilty of rape were shot as a deterrent to their fellow soldiers.

56. Rubenstein and Altman, *Unknown Black Book*, 157–58, 301–2.

57. Rubenstein and Altman, 198.

58. Karay, *Death Comes in Yellow*, 79.

59. Beorn, *Marching into Darkness*, 173.

60. Sönke Neitzel, ed., *Tapping Hitler's Generals: Transcripts of Secret Conversations, 1942–1945*, trans. Geoffrey Brooks (London: Frontline Books, 2007), 198–99.

61. Geoffrey P. Megargee, *War of Annihilation: Combat and Genocide on the Eastern Front, 1941* (Lanham, MD: Rowman & Littlefield, 2006), 37.

62. Westermann, *Hitler's Police Battalions*, 166–67.

63. Mühlhäuser, "Sexual Violence and the Holocaust," 109.

64. Beorn, *Marching into Darkness*, 172.

65. Wolf Kaiser, Thomas Köhler, and Elke Gryglewski, *"Nicht durch formale Schranken gehemmt": Die deutsche Polizei im Nationalsozialismus* (Bonn: Bundeszentrale für politische Bildung, 2012), 231. This work provides a facsimile copy of this order.

66. Omer Bartov, *Hitler's Army: Soldiers, Nazis, and War in the Third Reich* (Oxford: Oxford University Press, 1991), 62.

67. Bartov, 67.

68. Neitzel, *Tapping Hitler's Generals*, 199.

69. Interrogation protocol of Richard T. on May 24, 1965, 204 AR-Z 1251/65 Band 2 (René Rosenbauer), p. 407, ZStL.

70. Jeffrey Burds, "Sexual Violence in Europe in World War II, 1939–1945," *Politics and Society* 37, no. 1 (2009): 38.

71. Nicole Ann Dombrowski, "Surviving the German Invasion of France: Women's Stories of the Exodus of 1940," in *Women and War in the Twentieth Century: Enlisted with or without Consent*, ed. Nicole Ann Dombrowski (New York: Garland, 1999), 122.

72. Quoted in Dombrowski, "Surviving the German Invasion of France," 130–31.

73. Peter Lieb, *Konventioneller Krieg oder NS-Weltanschauungskrieg? Kriegführung und Partisanenbekämpfung in Frankreich 1943/44* (Munich: Oldenbourg Wissenschaftsverlag 2007), 506–7. For example, SS and police units committed nine of the ten largest massacres in the anti-partisan campaign in France. Likewise, units that had previous experience in the campaign in the East also tended to be harsher in their treatment of the French population than units that had not seen duty in the East.

74. Matthäus, Böhler, and Mallmann, *War, Pacification, and Mass Murder, 1939*, 77.

75. Report of the Commander of the Security Police and SD for the District of Galicia, May 14, 1943, 1.2.7.8/82187881/ITS Digital Archive, accessed March 14, 2019, at USHMMA.

76. Report of the Commander of the Security Police and SD for the District of Galicia, May 14, 1943, 1.2.7.8/82187891-92/ITS Digital Archive, accessed March 14, 2019, at USHMMA.

77. Mallmann, Böhler, and Matthäus, *Einsatzgruppen in Polen*, 154.

78. Ingrao, *SS Dirlewanger Brigade*, 85, and Sarah Helm, *Ravensbrück: Life and Death in Hitler's Concentration Camp for Women* (New York: Doubleday, 2014), 376–77.

79. Berger, *Experten der Vernichtung*, 344–45.

80. Peggy Sanday, *Fraternity Gang Rape: Sex, Brotherhood, and Privilege on Campus* (New York: NYU Press, 2007), 82.

81. Dagmar Herzog, "Hubris and Hypocrisy, Incitement and Disavowal: Sexuality and German Fascism," in *Sexuality and German Fascism*, ed. Dagmar Herzog (New York: Berghahn, 2005), 6.

82. Kühne, "Pleasure of Terror," 245.

83. Gerda Lerner, *The Creation of Patriarchy* (New York: Oxford University Press, 1986), 80, and Mühlhäuser, "Between 'Racial Awareness' and Fantasies of Potency," 200–201.

84. Sanday, "Rape Free versus Rape Prone," 343. Sanday's example is related to a case of gang rape by a group of men in a university fraternity; however, her argument also can be applied to the actions of the SS in the occupied East. Sanday's findings on the group-bonding motive for gang rape is supported in Dara Kay Cohen, *Rape during Civil War* (Ithaca, NY: Cornell University Press, 2016), 30.

85. Gordin and Gelbart, *Memorial (Yizkor) Book*, 516.

86. Testimony of Wladslaw Gostynski, October 1, 1947, 1.2.7.7/82181114/ITS Digital Archive, accessed March 14, 2019, at USHMMA.

87. Quoted in Theweleit, *Das Lachen der Täter*, 125.

88. Quoted in Ehrenburg and Grossman, *Black Book*, 173.

89. Mühlhäuser, *Eroberungen*, 137.

90. Benz, *Handlanger der SS*, 229.

91. Halbmayr, "Sexualized Violence against Women," 34.

92. Quoted in Shik, "Sexual Abuse of Jewish Women in Auschwitz-Birkenau," 230.

93. Delbo, *Auschwitz and After*, 175.

94. Testimony of Ida Scheiner, 1.2.7.8/82188272/ITS Digital Archive, accessed March 21, 2019, at USHMMA.

95. Testimony of Wanda Kirschenbaum, 1.2.7.8/82188262/ITS Digital Archive, accessed March 21, 2019, at USHMMA.

96. Testimony of Ida Scheiner, 1.2.7.8/82188272/ITS Digital Archive, accessed March 21, 2019, at USHMMA.

97. Miller, *Humiliation*, 169.

98. Sanjay Palshikar, "Understanding Humiliation," *Economic and Political Weekly* 40, no. 51 (December 17–23, 2005): 5430.

99. Gross, *Golden Harvest*, 91–92.

100. Nomi Levenkron, "'Prostitution,' Rape, and Sexual Slavery during World War II," in Hedgepeth and Saidel, *Sexual Violence against Jewish Women*, 18.

101. Perechodnik, *Am I a Murderer?*, 5.

102. Sereny, *Into That Darkness*, 237–38.

103. Dicks, *Licensed Mass Murder*, 121.

104. Testimony of Artur Mayer, 1.1.2.0/82347350/ITS Digital Archive, accessed June 19, 2019, at USHMMA.

105. Quoted in Sereny, *Into That Darkness*, 204.

106. Testimony of Sara Ritterband, RG 14.101M, reel 395, folder 3166, pp. 173–74, USHMMA. Sara Ritterband's testimony provides a clear example of a woman who for understandable reasons seeks to address the issue of sexual assault obliquely rather than directly in her testimony.

107. Dov B. Schmorak, ed., *Sieben sagen aus: Zeugen im Eichmann Prozess* (Berlin: Arani, 1962), 180–81.

108. Karay, *Death Comes in Yellow*, 95–96.

109. Testimony of Tadeusz Budzyn, 5.1/82323191/ITS Digital Archive, accessed March 15, 2019, at USHMMA.

110. Knut Stang, *Kollaboration und Massenmord: Die Litauische Hilfspolizei, das Rollkommando Hamann und die Ermordung der litauischen Juden* (Frankfurt am Main: P. Lang, 1996), 264.

111. Berg, *Warsaw Ghetto*, 69.

112. Interrogation protocol of Walter K., file no. 9294/35, Staatsanwaltschaft Regensburg, Amberg Staatsarchiv. I would like to thank Wendy Lower for providing me with a copy of her notes concerning this case.

113. Witness testimony on Nazi atrocities in Latvia, 1.2.7.4/82173565/ITS Digital Archive, accessed May 29, 2019, at USHMMA.

114. Alex J. Kay, *The Making of an SS Killer: The Life of Colonel Alfred Filbert, 1905–1990* (Cambridge: Cambridge University Press, 2016), 65.

115. Testimony of former policeman Josef R., July 17, 1962, 202 AR-Z 907/60, file 1, p. 142, ZStl.

116. Lawrence Langer, *Holocaust Testimonies: The Ruins of Memory* (New Haven, CT: Yale University Press, 1991), 26, and Judith Magyar Isaacson, *Seed of Sarah: Memoirs of a Survivor* (Champaign: University of Illinois Press, 1989), 36, 47, 53.

117. Mallmann, Rieß, and Pyta, *Deutscher Osten*, 153.

118. Klaus-Michael Mallmann, "'Mensch, ich feiere heut' den tausendsten Genickschuß': Die Sicherheitspolizei und die Shoah in Westgalizien," in *Die Täter der Shoah: Fanatische Nationalsozialisten oder ganz normale Deutsche?*, ed. Gerhard Paul (Göttingen: Wallstein Verlag, 2002), 119.

119. Epstein, *Model Nazi*, 132. In this case, the SS general and district leader Arthur Greiser urged leniency so as not to ruin "the life of a talented young daredevil" but was eventually overruled, and the perpetrator was sentenced to fifteen years in prison.

120. Central Commission for Investigation of German Crimes in Poland, *German Crimes in Poland* (New York: Howard Fertig, 1982), 189–90.

121. Central Commission, 203.

122. Central Commission, 214.

123. Mühlhäuser, *Eroberungen*, 210.

124. Berg, *Warsaw Ghetto*, 46.

125. Guenter Lewy, *Perpetrators: The World of the Holocaust Killers* (Oxford: Oxford University Press, 2017), 16.

126. Quoted in Sönke Neitzel and Harald Welzer, *Soldaten: On Fighting, Killing, and Dying*, trans. Jefferson Chase (New York: Alfred A. Knopf, 2012), 174.

127. Angrick, *Besatzungspolitik und Massenmord*, 187.

128. "Interrogation protocol of Josef Blösche, January 11, 1967, RG-14.068, fiche 58, pp. 29–30, USHMMA.

129. Quoted in Westermann, *Hitler's Police Battalions*, 211.

130. Mel Mermelstein, *By Bread Alone: The Story of A-4685* (Huntington Beach, CA: Auschwitz Study Foundation, 1979), 152.

131. Filip Müller, *Eyewitness Auschwitz: Three Years in the Gas Chamber*, trans. Susanne Flatauer (Chicago: Ivan R. Dee, 1999), 141.

132. Ryback, *Hitler's First Victims*, 150.

133. Quoted in Klaus Theweleit, *Male Fantasies: Psychoanalyzing the White Terror*, vol. 2, trans. Erica Carter and Chris Turner (Minneapolis: University of Minnesota Press, 1989), 300–301.

134. Theweleit, 2:301.

135. Sachslehner, *Der Tod*, 109, and testimony of Józef Seweryn, 5.1/82323899-900/ITS Digital Archive, accessed March 21, 2019, at USHMMA.

136. Academy of Sciences of the Ukrainian SSR, Institute of Law, *Nazi Crimes in Ukraine*, 159.

137. Burds, "Sexual Violence in Europe," 46.

138. Bernhard Chiari, *Alltag hinter der Front: Besatzung, Kollaboration und Widerstand in Weissrussland, 1941–1944* (Düsseldorf: Droste Verlag, 1998), 192. A similar incident took place in the Janowska camp: see Testimony of Michael J. Wind, 1.2.7.7/82183308/ITS Digital Archive, accessed April 2, 2019, at USHMMA.

139. Investigation file of Karl Schulz and Anton Streitwieser, RG 14.101M, reel 540, folder 4582, pp. 3470–71, USHMMA.

140. Mühlhäuser, *Eroberungen*, 98–99; Müller, "Männlichkeit und Gewalt," 136–37; and Burds, "Sexual Violence," 45–46.

141. Chiari, *Alltag hinter der Front*, 193.

142. Jewish Black Book Committee, *Black Book*, 342.

143. Rubenstein and Altman, *Unknown Black Book*, 253.

144. Quoted in Burds, "Sexual Violence in Europe," 45.

145. Stanislaw Szmajzner, *Hell in Sobibor: The Tragedy of a Jewish Teenager*, trans. Lucy de Lima Coimbra (N.p., 1979), 185.

146. "Berichte ehemaliger politischer Gefangener über das KZ Ravensbrück, 1946–8, 1963–5, 1971," NY 4178/52, pp. 80–81, Bundesarchiv, Berlin (BAB). I would like to thank Gabrielle Hauth for providing me with a copy of this document.

147. Dicks, *Licensed Mass Murder*, 122.

148. Pawlicka-Nowak, *Chełmno Witnesses Speak*, 201. The teacher subsequently protested to the German authorities by noting that the children were witnessing this behavior, whereupon the SS decided to close the school rather than stop the orgies. See also the transcript of the *Shoah* interview with Franz Schalling, RG 60.5034, p. 43, USHMMA.

149. Ingrao, *SS Dirlewanger Brigade*, 117.

150. Lower, *Hitler's Furies*, 110–11.

151. Genia Demianova, *Comrade Genia: The Story of a Victim of German Bestiality in Russia Told by Herself* (London: Nicholson & Watson, 1941), 58–59.

152. Demianova, 59.

153. Sanday, *Fraternity Gang Rape*, 82.

154. Werner, "'Hart müssen wir hier draußen sein,'" 12, 20.

155. Matthäus, Böhler, and Mallmann, *War, Pacification, and Mass Murder*, 77; Ingrao, *SS Dirlewanger Brigade*, 85; and Hedgepeth and Saidel, *Sexual Violence against Jewish Women*, 2.

5. Celebrating Murder

1. Quoted in Jacek Andrzej Młynarczyk et al., "Eastern Europe: Belarusian Auxiliaries, Ukrainian Waffen-SS Soldiers and the Special Case of the Polish 'Blue Police,'" in *The Waffen-SS: A European History*, ed. Jochen Böhler and Robert Gerwarth (Oxford: Oxford University Press, 2017), 188. Likewise, a Swedish member of the Waffen-SS told his parents an "amusing" story about the reprisal murder of three hundred Polish villagers. See Martin R. Gutmann, *Building a Nazi Europe: The SS's Germanic Volunteers* (Cambridge: Cambridge University Press, 2017), 173, and Confino, *World without Jews*, 186.

2. Quoted in Thomas Grasberger, "Der Totenwald," *Zeit Online*, January 20, 2011, https://www.zeit.de/2011/04/Nationalsozialismus-Massaker-Piasnica.

3. Testimony of Mieczyslaw Imala, RG 14.101M, reel 2832, folder 9691, pp. 213–14, USHMMA.

4. Testimony of Mieczyslaw Imala, RG 14.101M, reel 2832, folder 9691, p. 215, USHMMA.

5. Quoted in Martin Dean, *Collaboration in the Holocaust: Crimes of the Local Police in Belorussia and Ukraine, 1941–44* (New York: St. Martin's, 2000), 48.

6. For a fascinating analysis of Yiddish "destruction language" see Miriam Schulz, "'Gornisht oyser verter'?! *Khurbn-shprakh* as a Mirror of the Dynamics of Violence in German-Occupied Eastern Europe," in *The Holocaust in the Borderlands: Interethnic Relations and the Dynamics of Violence in Occupied Eastern Europe*, ed. Gaëlle Fisher and Caroline Mezger (Göttingen: Wallstein Verlag, 2019), 185–86. My thanks to Miriam Schulz for sharing a prepublication version of her paper.

7. Leon Weliczker Wells, *The Janowska Road* (New York: Macmillan, 1963), 81.

8. United Nations War Crimes Commission, Polish Charges against German War Criminals, 1.2.7.7/82180866/ITS Digital Archive, accessed April 2, 2019, at USHMMA, and *Encyclopedia of Camps and Ghettos, 1933–1945*, vol. 2, part A, 846–47.

9. Testimony of Aloys W., RG 14.101M, reel 329, folder 2509, p. 136, USHMMA.

10. Wells, *Janowska Road*, 84, and Testimony of Auguste Drzonsgalla, RG 14.101M, reel 50, folder 14700, p. 315, USHMMA.

11. Sven Reichardt, "Vergemeinschaft durch Gewalt: Der SA-'Mördersturm 33' in Berlin-Charlottenburg," in *SA-Terror als Herrschaftssicherung: "Köpenicker Blutwoche"*

und öffentliche Gewalt im Nationalsozialismus, ed. Stefan Hördler (Berlin: Metropol Verlag, 2013), 113, and Dillon, *Dachau and the SS*, 88.

12. Emil Büge, *1470 KZ-Geheimnisse: Heimliche Aufzeichnungen aus der Politischen Abteilung des KZ Sachsenhausen* (Berlin: Metropol Verlag, 2010), 126, and Nachum Alpert, *Destruction of the Slonim Jewry: The Story of the Jews of Slonim during the Holocaust*, trans. Max Rosenfeld (New York: Holocaust Library, 1989), 122.

13. Wachsmann, *KL*, 220.

14. Ryback, *Hitler's First Victims*, 89.

15. Wachsmann, *KL*, 114.

16. Testimony of Harry Quindel, February 11, 1948, 5.1/82322471-72/ITS Digital Archive, accessed April 30, 2019, at USHMMA.

17. Quoted in Neitzel, *Tapping Hitler's Generals*, 185, and Langerbein, *Hitler's Death Squads*, 68.

18. Dillon, *Dachau and the SS*, 39. In the case of Ehmann, his failed attempt to kill the communist leader by shooting into his home resulted in the severe wounding of the man's wife.

19. Joshi, *Gender and Power in the Third Reich*, 189, and Koonz, *Mothers in the Fatherland*, 59.

20. Höss, *Death Dealer*, 125, and Wachsmann, *KL*, 113.

21. Orth, "Egon Zill," 266–67, and Wachsmann, *KL*, 272.

22. Kühne, "Pleasure of Terror," 241, and Hans Buchheim, *Anatomie des SS-Staates*, vol. 1, *Die SS: Das Herrschaftsinstrument Befehl und Gehorsam* (Munich: Deutscher Taschenbuch Verlag, 1967), 255. The use of gendered insults to denote alleged weakness or femininity is not unique to Nazi Germany and can be found in the socialization process of many military organizations. See Frank J. Barrett, "The Organizational Construction of Hegemonic Masculinity: The Case of the US Navy," *Gender, Work, and Organizations* 3, no. 3 (July 1996): 133.

23. Wells, *Janowska Road*, 86.

24. Grabowski, *Hunt for the Jews*, 94.

25. Angrick, "Men of *Einsatzgruppe* D," 86–87.

26. Quoted in Römer, *Comrades*, 87.

27. Herbert Jäger, *Verbrechen unter totalitärer Herrschaft* (Franfurt am Main: Suhrkamp, 1982), 62, and Haynes, "Ordinary Masculinity," 173.

28. Wells, *Janowska Road*, 67.

29. Kogon, *Theory and Practice of Hell*, 51–52, 79–80. In periods of extremely cold weather, despite the prohibition allowing only the wearing of an undershirt, prisoners sought to stay warmer by adding layers to their clothing. See *Buchenwald Report*, 49, and Testimony of Hugo Stahl, RG 14.101M, reel 5, folder 14071, p. 11, USHMMA.

30. Wells, *Janowska Road*, 64.

31. Kogon, *Theory and Practice of Hell*, 118. See also *Buchenwald Report*, 44.

32. Wachsmann, *KL*, 272–73.

33. Testimony of Rudolf Reder, RG 14.101M, reel 395, p. 89, USHMMA.

34. Müller, *Eyewitness Auschwitz*, 93.

35. Müller, 94.

36. Quoted in Lifton, *Nazi Doctors*, 193. For SS drinking on the selection ramp see also Tadeusz Borowski, *This Way for the Gas, Ladies and Gentlemen*, trans. Barbara Vedder (New York: Penguin, 1967), 35.

37. Letter from Reichsführer-SS, November 16, 1937, and letter from the Reichsführer-SS and Chief of the SS Main Office, January 29, 1943, NS 19, folder 2240, fiche 1, pp. 9, 11–16, USHMMA.

38. Lifton, *Nazi Doctors*, 188.

39. Smith, *Last Train from Berlin*, 128–30, and Shirer, *Berlin Diary*, 264.

40. "Der Höhere SS- und Polizeiführer West, Fürsorgekommando, Bericht," December 2, 1944, T175, roll 224, frames 2762235–36, National Archives and Records Administration (NARA).

41. Jochen von Lang, *Top Nazi: SS General Karl Wolff, the Man between Hitler and Himmler*, trans. Mary Beth Friedrich (New York: Enigma, 2005), 49.

42. *Die Deutsche Polizei* 11, no. 2 (January 15, 1943): 23, holding of the BAB.

43. Quoted in Sereny, *Into That Darkness*, 104.

44. Daily Order Nr. 5, "Polizei-Einsatzstab Suedost, Ch. d. St.-, Veldes, Betr.: A) Bekanntgabe eines Befehls RFSSuChdDtPol," January 9, 1942, 503 AR-Z 9/1965, Band 1, Unbekannt, Tatort Veldes Jugoslawien, p. 280, ZStL.

45. Letter from the District Leader of Libau to the General Commissar in Riga, July 8, 1943, RG 18.002M, reel 2, fond R-69, opis 1A, folder 8, USHMMA.

46. Rubenstein and Altman, *Unknown Black Book*, 251.

47. Rubenstein and Altman, 253.

48. Transcript of the *Shoah* interview with Hersh Smolar, RG 60.5038, p. 19, USHMMA.

49. Burkhard, *Tanz mal Jude!*, 98–100. In this case, the prisoner was saved by his refusal to spin faster and thus lose his orientation and by the timely intercession of a senior SS guard.

50. Burkhard, *Tanz mal Jude!*, 41–42.

51. Musmanno, *Eichmann Kommandos*, 217–18, and Earl, *Nuremberg SS-Einsatzgruppen Trial*, 152.

52. Christopher R. Browning, *Ordinary Men: Reserve Police Battalion 101 and the Final Solution in Poland* (New York, HarperCollins, 1992), 41.

53. Berg, *Warsaw Ghetto*, 214.

54. Quoted in Mallmann, Rieß, and Pyta, *Deutscher Osten*, 110.

55. Testimony of Erich M., RG 14.101M, reel 540, folder 4588, USHMMA.

56. Interrogation Protocol of Hans Baumgartner, October 30, 1969, RG-14.068, fiche 15, p. 128, and February 11, 1970, RG-14.068, fiche 17, p. 237, USHMMA.

57. Desbois, *Holocaust by Bullets*, xviii–xix.

58. Quoted in Jeffrey Burds, *Holocaust in Rovno: A Massacre in Ukraine, November 1941* (New York: Palgrave Macmillan, 2013), 53.

59. Diary entries of Felix Landau, July 2–3, 1941, 1.2.7.8/82188057/ITS Digital Archive, accessed March 26, 2019, at USHMMA.

60. Diary entry of Felix Landau, July 5, 1941, 1.2.7.8/82188060/ITS Digital Archive, accessed March 26, 2019, at USHMMA.

61. Diary entries of Felix Landau, July 7–10, 1941, 1.2.7.8/82188061-64/ITS Digital Archive, accessed March 26, 2019, at USHMMA.

62. Diary entry of Felix Landau, July 11, 1941, 1.2.7.8/82188065/ITS Digital Archive, accessed March 26, 2019, at USHMMA.

63. Diary entry of Felix Landau, July 12, 1941, 1.2.7.8/82188065-67/ITS Digital Archive, accessed March 26, 2019, at USHMMA (emphasis in the original).

64. Diary entry of Felix Landau, July 17, 1941, 1.2.7.8/82188069/ITS Digital Archive, accessed March 26, 2019, at USHMMA.

65. Diary entries of Felix Landau, July 21–22, 1941, 1.2.7.8/82188070-71/ITS Digital Archive, accessed March 26, 2019, at USHMMA. *Sonderbehandlung* or "special handling" was the term used by the perpetrators as a euphemism for killing.

66. Testimony of Ferdinand W., 204 AR-Z 1251/1965, file 1, pp. 39–40, ZStl.

67. Quoted in Rita Gabis, *A Guest at the Shooters' Banquet: My Grandfather's SS Past, My Jewish Family, a Search for the Truth* (New York: Bloomsbury, 2015), 234.

68. Stefan Klemp, *"Aktion Erntefest"*: *Mit Musik in den Tod, Rekonstruktion eines Massenmordes* (Münster: Stadt Münster, 2013), 52.

69. "Berichte ehemaliger politischer Gefangener über das KZ Ravensbrück, 1946–8, 1963–5, 1971," NY 4178/52, pp. 80–81, BAB.

70. United Nations War Crimes Commission, Yugoslav Charges against German War Criminals, Case No. R/N/646, RG 67.041M, reel 25, p. 612, USHMMA. I would like to thank Andrew Kloes for bringing this document to my attention.

71. Letter from Karl Kretschmer, dated October 15, 1942, RG 14.101M, reel 434, folder 3517, p. 15, USHMMA.

72. Desbois, *In Broad Daylight*, 38–39.

73. Desbois, 40.

74. Svetlana Alexievich, *Secondhand Time: The Last of the Soviets*, trans. Bela Shayevich (New York: Random House, 2016), 202.

75. "Happy Man," in *The Act of Killing*, dir. Joshua Oppenheimer, Drafthouse Films, 2012, DVD.

76. Interrogation protocol of Josef Blösche, July 27, 1967, RG-14.068, fiche 65, pp. 529, 532, 535, USHMMA.

77. Dillon, *Dachau and the SS*, 245.

78. Quoted in Tomáš Vojta, "'A True Inferno Was Created There': Eradicating Traces of Mass Murder at Treblinka," in *Orte und Akteure im System der NS-Zwangslager*, ed. Michael Becker, Dennis Bock, and Henrike Illig (Berlin: Metropol Verlag, 2015), 202.

79. Quoted in Grabowski, *Hunt for the Jews*, 196. While less common because of the fear of increased escapes, some units clearly conducted nighttime executions under floodlights or using vehicle headlights to illuminate the site. See the testimony of policeman Franz J., June 17, 1962, 202 AR-Z 907/60, file 1, p. 137, ZStl.

80. Jewish Black Book Committee, *Black Book*, 364.

81. Confino, *World without Jews*, 186–87.

82. Testimony of Helmuth Schmidt's former wife, 204 AR-Z 12/61, file 1, pp. 29–30, ZStl.

83. Diary entry of Felix Landau, July 11, 1941, 1.2.7.8/82188065/ITS Digital Archive, accessed March 26, 2019, at USHMMA.

84. Quoted in Gross, *Golden Harvest*, 60. Prior to notifying the police, the villagers physically tortured and, in the case of the women, sexually assaulted the Jews in order to extort information on hidden valuables.

85. Berger, *Experten der Vernichtung*, 336.

86. Lehnstaedt, "Minsk Experience," 250.

87. Langbein, *Der Auschwitz-Prozeß*, 2:669.

88. Quoted in Burds, *Holocaust in Rovno*, 52.

89. Quoted in Alexander Victor Prusin, "'Fascist Criminals to the Gallows!': The Holocaust and Soviet War Crimes Trials, December 1945–February 1946," *Holocaust and Genocide Studies* 17, no. 1 (2003), 18.

90. Perechodnik, *Am I a Murderer?*, 114. Emphasis added.

91. Perechodnik, 17–18.

92. Transcript of the *Shoah* interview with Rudolf Vrba, RG 60.5034, p. 12, USHMMA.

93. Vasily Grossman, *A Writer at War: A Soviet Journalist with the Red Army, 1941–1945*, ed. and trans. Antony Beevor and Luba Vinogradova (New York: Vintage Books, 2005), 302.

94. Quoted in Jewish Black Book Committee, *Black Book*, 376.

95. Alexievich, *Secondhand Time*, 198.

96. Pawlicka-Nowak, *Chełmno Witnesses Speak*, 140, 154.

97. Investigation summary report, RG 14.101.M, reel 8, folder 14120, pp. 68–69, USHMMA.

98. Transcript of the *Shoah* interview with Abba Kovner, RG 60.5017, p. 35, USHMMA.

99. Testimony of Ferdinand W., 204 AR-Z 1251/1965, file 1, pp. 39–40, ZStl.

100. Testimony of Ida Scheiner, 1.2.7.8/82188272/ITS Digital Archive, accessed March 3, 2019, at USHMMA.

101. Pawlicka-Nowak, *Chelmno Witnesses Speak*, 123.

102. Jan Karski, *Story of a Secret State* (Boston: Houghton Mifflin, 1944), 333.

103. Karski, 333.

104. Quoted in Matthäus and Kerenji, *Jewish Responses to Persecution*, 179.

105. Heck, *A Child of Hitler*, 110.

106. Schneider, *"Auswärts eingesetzt,"* 469–71.

107. While Metzner's recollection of the events is detailed and accurate, his chronology of these events appears to be confused. See Martin Dean and Mel Hecker, eds., *The United States Holocaust Memorial Museum Encyclopedia of Camp and Ghettos, 1933–1945*, vol. II, *Ghettos in German-Occupied Eastern Europe*, Part B (Bloomington: Indiana University Press, 2012), 1273–76.

108. Affidavit of Alfred Metzner, September 18, 1947, RG 242, NO-5558, p. 2, NARA.

109. Affidavit of Alfred Metzner, September 18, 1947, RG 242, NO-5558, p. 3, NARA. Emphasis added. Gerhard Erren reported the number murdered as eight thousand "unnecessary hungry mouths." See Dean and Hecker, eds., *Encyclopedia of Camp and Ghettos*, vol. 2, part B, 1275.

110. Affidavit of Alfred Metzner, September 18, 1947, RG 242, NO-5558, p. 4, NARA.

111. Affidavit of Alfred Metzner, September 18, 1947, RG 242, NO-5558, p. 5, NARA.

112. Affidavit of Alfred Metzner, September 18, 1947, RG 242, NO-5558, p. 5, NARA.

113. Tec, *In the Lion's Den*, 123.

114. Dean and Hecker, *Encyclopedia of Camps and Ghettos*, part A, 797.

115. Testimony of Baruch Engler, RG 14.101M, reel 3052, p. 11, USHMMA.

116. Testimony of Baruch Engler, RG 14.101M, reel 3052, pp. 10, 12, USHMMA.

117. Mallmann, Rieß, and Pyta, *Deutscher Osten*, 52.

118. Schelvis, *Sobibor*, 112.

119. Rosenbaum, *"Und trotzdem war's 'ne schöne Zeit,"* 168.

120. Heck, *Child of Hitler*, 103. See also Wolfhilde von Königs, *Kriegstagebuch einer jungen Nationalsozialistin: Die Aufzeichnungen Wolfhilde von Königs, 1939–1946*, ed. Sven Keller (Oldenbourg, Germany: De Gruyter, 2015), 46–47, 142, 146, 158, 172, 186, 194, and Inge Myrick, *The Other Side! The Life Journey of a Young Girl through Nazi Germany* (Phoenix: Acacia, 2006), 26.

121. Georg Rauch, *Unlikely Warrior: A Jewish Soldier in Hitler's Army* (New York: Farrar, Straus and Giroux, 2006), 83.

122. Kiran Klaus Patel, *Soldiers of Labor: Labor Service in Nazi Germany and New Deal America, 1933–1945*, trans. Thomas Dunlap (Cambridge: Cambridge University Press, 2005), 254.

123. Nancy S. Love, *Trendy Fascism: White Power Music and the Future of Democracy* (Albany: SUNY Press, 2016), 2, 104, 117. Love's study, although focused on contemporary white supremacist groups, offers important and relevant insights regarding the use of song and music to generate hatred and spur acts of political or racial violence and has clear applicability to the use of both under Nazism.

124. Höss, *Death Dealer*, 63, and Von Lang, *Top Nazi*, 10–11.

125. "Report on the Sachsenhausen Concentration Camp," undated, 1.1.38.0/82152426/ITS Digital Archive, accessed May 16, 2019, at the USHMMA.

126. Mallmann, "'Mensch, ich feiere heut' den tausendsten Genickschuß,'" 119.

127. Mallmann, 119.

128. Biber, *Survivors*, 56.

129. Quoted in Musmanno, *Eichmann Kommandos*, 171.

130. Brian Murdoch, *Fighting Songs and Warring Words: Popular Lyrics of Two World Wars* (London: Routledge, 1990), 126.

131. Mosse, *Fallen Soldiers*, 22. The use of song to build camaraderie as part of a ritual of masculinity also occurred in the US West. See Moore, *Cow Boys and Cattle Men*, 129.

132. Michael H. Kater, *The Twisted Muse: Musicians and Their Music in the Third Reich* (Oxford: Oxford University Press, 1997), 141–42.

133. Reichardt, *Faschistische Kampfbünde*, 454, and Jay W. Baird, *To Die for Germany: Heroes in the Nazi Pantheon* (Bloomington: Indiana University Press, 1990), 79.

134. Walter, *Antisemitische Kriminalität und Gewalt*, 200.

135. Kühne, *Rise and Fall of Comradeship*, 33.

136. Henning Pieper, *Fegelein's Horsemen and Genocidal Warfare: The SS Cavalry Brigade in the Soviet Union* (New York: Palgrave Macmillan, 2015), 108.

137. Kühne, "Pleasure of Terror," 239–40.

138. Biber, *Survivors*, 88.

139. Schneider, *"Auswärts eingesetzt,"* 451.

140. Klemp, *"Aktion Erntefest,"* 66.

141. Yehoshua R. Büchler, "'Unworthy Behavior': The Case of SS Officer Max Täubner," *Holocaust and Genocide Studies* 17, no. 3 (2003): 413, 415.

142. Academy of Sciences of the Ukrainian SSR, Institute of Law, *Nazi Crimes in Ukraine*, 106, 212.

143. Wachsmann, *KL*, 331.

144. Schneider, *"Auswärts eingesetzt,"* 449.

145. Musmanno, *Eichmann Kommandos*, 171. In this case, SS *Standartenführer* Walter Blume organized these events for the men under his command.

146. Ingrao, *SS Dirlewanger Brigade*, 115.

147. Bartov, *Anatomy of a Genocide*, 197.

148. Miller et al., "Alcohol, Masculinity, Honour," 137.

149. Klemp, *Freispruch*, 48–49. The name Krochmalna was taken from a street in the ghetto where Jews attempted to trade goods for food with the outside world.

150. Jürgen Matthäus, "An vorderster Front: Voraussetzungen für die Beteilung der Ordnungspolizei an der Shoah," in *Die Täter der Shoah: Fanatische Nationalsozialisten oder ganz normale Deutsche?*, ed. Gerhard Paul (Göttingen: Wallstein Verlag, 2002), 157.

151. Klemp, *Freispruch*, 49.

152. For Hermann Göring's so-called shooting order see Erich Gritzbach, ed., *Hermann Göring: Reden und Aufsätze* (Munich: Zentralverlag der NSDAP, 1939), 17–18; Haynes, "Ordinary Masculinity," 170; and Dillon, *Dachau and the SS*, 185. In the case of the last, Dillon cites Himmler's order to have homosexual SS men brought to a concentration camp to "be shot while trying to escape," a situation in which the use of a weapon was intended to prove the masculinity of the shooter while at the same time emphasizing the emasculation of the intended victim.

153. Wolf Kaiser, Thomas Köhler, and Elke Gryglewski, *"Nicht durch formale Schranken gehemmt": Die deutsche Polizei im Nationalsozialismus* (Bonn: Bundeszentrale für politische Bildung, 2012), 53. This is taken from a facsimile reproduction of the *Grundsätze für die Polizei*. Emphasis added. I would like to thank Thomas Köhler for providing me with this source.

154. Ulf Mellström, "Changing Affective Economies of Masculine Machineries and Military Masculinities? From Ernst Jünger to Shannen Rossmiller," *Masculinities and Social Change* 2, no. 1 (2012): 5.

155. Kimberly Allar, "Ravensbrück's Pupils: Creating a Nazi Female Guard Force," paper presented at Lessons and Legacies XIV: The Holocaust in the 21st Century, at Claremont McKenna College, California, November 6, 2016. In a similar way, German women were lectured about the perils of alcohol use, a message that apparently had little resonance among the female SS guards at Ravensbrück. See Helm, *Ravensbrück*, 20, 26, 141, 376.

156. Mailänder, *Female SS Guards*, 253.

157. Mailänder, 252; Edith Eva Foger, *The Choice: Embrace the Possible* (New York: Scribner, 2017), 60; and Lengyel, *Five Chimneys*, 108.

158. Klemp, *Freispruch*, 52.

159. Ingrao, *SS Dirlewanger Brigade*, 78.

160. Klemp, *Freispruch*, 52.

161. Testimony of Richard N., RG 14.101M, reel 329, folder 2510, p. 97, USHMMA.

162. Kay, *Making of an SS Killer*, 68.

163. Langerbein, *Hitler's Death Squads*, 59.

164. Pawlicka-Nowak, *Chełmno Witnesses Speak*, 202, and Doris L. Bergen, *War and Genocide: A Concise History of the Holocaust*, 3rd ed. (Lanham, MD: Rowman & Littlefield, 2016), 248. This was the first closing of the camp. The same SS unit under SS captain Hans Bothmann returned to Chełmno in the spring of 1944 to reopen the camp to participate in the liquidation of the Jews of the Łódź ghetto.

165. Letter from Karl Kretschmer, October 15, 1942, RG 14.101M, reel 434, folder 3517, p. 15, USHMMA.

166. Benz, *Handlanger der SS*, 219.

167. Browning, *Ordinary Men*, 66, 72.

168. Interrogation Protocol of Hans Baumgartner, February 11, 1970, RG-14.068, fiche 17, p. 237, USHMMA. Baumgartner supported this statement by asserting that he always could still drive when he participated in executions despite his heavy drinking.

169. Testimony of Samson Greif, RG 14.101M, reel 3052, folder 20183, p. 36, USHMMA. For example, Greif notes that the Gestapo had their own bar (*Nachtlokal*) in Kolomea.

170. Interrogation Protocols of Hans Baumgartner, February 11, 1970, and June 24, 1970, RG-14.068, fiche 17, p. 237, and fiche 18, p. 314, USHMMA.

171. For example, see the oral history of the former Nazi policeman Albert Emmerich in Johnson and Reuband, *What We Knew*, 245.

172. Testimony of Aloys W., RG 14.101M, reel 329, folder 2509, pp. 4455–56, USHMMA.

173. Testimony of Tamara Petrowna Ignatenko, RG 14.101M, reel 185, folder 1264, p. 13, USHMMA.

174. Testimony of Kurt Gerstein, 1.1.0.4/82485386/ITS Digital Archive, accessed May 20, 2019, at USHMMA.

175. Matthäus, Böhler, and Mallmann, *War, Pacification, and Mass Murder*, 70.

176. Matthäus, Böhler, and Mallmann, 78.

6. Alcohol, Auxiliaries, and Mass Murder

1. For a discussion of Waffen-SS auxiliaries and their involvement in atrocity see Jochen Böhler and Robert Gerwarth, eds., *The Waffen-SS: A European History* (Oxford: Oxford University Press, 2017), and Gutmann, *Building a Nazi Europe*, 171–74.

2. Peter Black, "Foot Soldiers of the Final Solution: The Trawniki Training Camp and Operation Reinhard," *Holocaust and Genocide Studies* 25, no. 1 (2011): 1.

3. Chiari, *Alltag hinter der Front*, 188.

4. Wendy Lower, *The Diary of Samuel Golfard and the Holocaust in Galicia* (Lanham, MD: Alta Mira, 2011), 112. See also Wendy Lower, "'Anticipatory Obedience' and the Nazi Implementation of the Holocaust in the Ukraine: A Case Study of Central and Peripheral Forces in the Generalbezirk Zhytomyr, 1941–1944," *Holocaust and Genocide Studies* 16, no. 1 (2002): 6.

5. Excerpts from the Main Commission of German Crimes in Poland, 1.2.7.7/82186024/ ITS Digital Archive, accessed May 21, 2019, at USHMMA; and Dean, *Collaboration in the Holocaust*, 65, 71–72.

6. Mark Lawrence Schrad, *Vodka Politics: Alcohol, Autocracy, and the Secret History of the Russian State* (Oxford: Oxford University Press, 2014), 9–11, 235. Interestingly, some members of the Nazi Party "emphasized the profit seeking of alcohol capital as the real problem in the [German] alcohol question" and blamed the "so-called Jewish alcohol capital . . . with its strategy of injuring the German race through alcohol poison." See Fahrenkrug, "Alcohol and the State in Nazi Germany," 320.

7. Karel Berkhoff, *Harvest of Despair: Life and Death in Ukraine under Nazi Rule* (Cambridge, MA: Harvard University Press, 2004), 136.

8. Catherine Merridale, *Ivan's War: Life and Death in the Red Army, 1939–1945* (New York: Metropolitan Books, 2006), 191.

9. Glenn Dynner, *Yankel's Tavern: Jews, Liquor, and Life in the Kingdom of Poland* (Oxford: Oxford University Press, 2014), 20.

10. Dynner, 18–19, 23.

11. Jan T. Gross, *Neighbors: The Destruction of the Jewish Community in Jedwabne, Poland* (Princeton, NJ: Princeton University Press, 2001), 38, and Schrad, *Vodka Politics*, 204, 214.

12. Quoted in Bartov, *Anatomy of a Genocide*, 21.

13. Berkhoff, *Harvest of Despair*, 203. Berkhoff notes that peasant women also drank, but that they also gathered in social settings to spin, weave, sew, and to sing when doing so.

14. Dynner, *Yankel's Tavern*, 32.

15. Max Bergholz, *Violence as a Generative Force: Identity, Nationalism, and Memory in a Balkan Country* (Ithaca, NY: Cornell University Press, 2016), 237–38, 271.

16. Gerd Meyer, ed., *Wehrmachtsverbrechen: Dokumente aus sowjetischen Archiven* (Cologne: PapyRossa, 1997), 59.

17. "Der Reichsführer SS und Chef der Deutschen Polizei im Reichsministerium des Innern, O-Kd, Nr. 24/41 (g.)," July 25, 1941, RG 11.001M.15, USHMMA.

18. Richard Breitman, "Himmler's Police Auxiliaries in the Occupied Soviet Territories," *Simon Wiesenthal Center Annual* 7, no. 2 (1990): 23–39.

19. "Der Reichsführer SS und Chef der Deutschen Polizei im Reichsministerium des Innern, O-Kdo. I. g. Nr. II/41 (g.)," July 31, 1941, RG 11.001M.15, USHMMA.

20. Georg Tessin, "Die Stäbe und Truppeneinheiten der Ordnungspolizei," in *Zur Geschichte der Ordnungspolizei*, ed. Hans-Joachim Neufeldt, Jürgen Huck, and Georg Tessin (Koblenz: Schriften des Bundesarchivs, 1957), 56, and Tec, *In the Lion's Den*, 85.

21. "Der Reichsführer SS und Chef der Deutschen Polizei im Reichsministerium des Innern, O.Kdo. I O (1) Sch. Nr. 1/41," November 6, 1941, R 19, Band 281, BAB.

22. "Der Befehlshaber der Ordnungspolizei für das Ostland, o. Abt I," dated December 4, 1941, R19, Band 281, BAB.

23. Testimony of Richard S., RG 14.101M, reel 330, folder 2514, pp. 131–32, USHMMA and testimony of Walter M., RG 14.101M, reel 3052, folder 20186, p. 124, USHMMA.

24. "Der Chef der Ordnungspolizei, Vortrag über den Kräfte- und Kriegseinsatz der Ordnungspolizei im Jahre 1941," February 1942, T 580, reel 96, NARA.

25. Christopher Browning with Jürgen Matthäus, *The Origins of the Final Solution: The Evolution of Nazi Jewish Policy* (Lincoln: University of Nebraska Press, 2004), 274–75, and Dieter Pohl, "Ukrainische Hilfskräfte beim Mord an den Juden," in *Die Täter der Shoah: Fanatische Nationalsozialisten oder ganz normale Deutsche?*, ed. Gerhard Paul (Göttingen: Wallstein Verlag, 2002), 211.

26. Martin Dean, "The German Gendarmerie, the Ukrainian Schutzmannschaft, and the 'Second Wave' of Jewish Killings in Occupied Ukraine: German Policing at the Local Level in the Zhitomir Region, 1941–1944," *German History* 14, no. 2 (1996): 179, and Browning, *Origins*, 274.

27. Gross, *Neighbors*, 157, and Zygmunt Klukowski, *Diary from the Years of Occupation, 1939–44*, trans. George Klukowski (Urbana: University of Illinois Press, 1993), 132.

28. Tec, *In the Lion's Den*, 86. The trend involving widespread alcohol abuse also can be found among the Soviet and local partisan forces in the East. See Rachel Margolis, *A Partisan from Vilna*, trans. F. Jackson Piotrow (Brighton, MA: Academic Studies, 2010), 430, 467.

29. Berkhoff, *Harvest of Despair*, 221.

30. Jeffrey S. Kopstein and Jason Wittenberg, *Intimate Violence: Anti-Jewish Pogroms on the Eve of the Holocaust* (Ithaca, NY: Cornell University Press, 2018), 120–21, 151.

31. Mallmann, Rieß, and Pyta, *Deutscher Osten*, 29.

32. Sakowicz, *Ponary Diary*, 13, 36, 120.

33. Quoted in Mallmann, Rieß, and Pyta, *Deutscher Osten*, 30.

34. Transcript of the *Shoah* interview with Jan Piwonski, RG 60.5031, pp. 3, 30, USHMMA.

35. Mallmann, Rieß, and Pyta, *Deutscher Osten*, 169.

36. "Der Kommandeur der Gendarmerie, Shitomir, Kommandobefehl Nr. 8/42," March 18, 1942, RG 53.002M, fond 658, reel 5, folder 3, USHMMA.

37. International Military Tribunal, *Trial of the Major War Criminals before the International Military Tribunal*, vol. 29 (Nuremberg: Secretariat of the Military Tribunal, 1948), 146.

38. Bankier, *Expulsion and Extermination*, 145; Chiari, *Alltag hinter der Front*, 188–93; and Gabis, *Guest at the Shooters' Banquet*, 160–61, 166–70, 366–68.

39. Mark Kurzem, *The Mascot: Unraveling the Mystery of My Father's Nazi Boyhood* (New York: Plume, 2007), 74. Although some parts of Kurzem's account have been questioned, the discussion of the activities of the Latvian auxiliary policemen align with the historical examples of other German auxiliaries.

40. Chiari, *Alltag hinter der Front*, 178.

41. Margolis, *Partisan from Vilna*, 430.

42. Nechama Tec, *Defiance* (Oxford: Oxford University Press, 2009), 191.

43. Chiari, *Alltag hinter der Front*, 175.

44. Black, "Foot Soldiers of the Final Solution," 35.

45. Klukowski, *Diary from the Years of Occupation*, 308.

46. Trip no. 02L, witness No. 25, place of recording Kuršėnai, region of Šiauliai, date of recording November 30, 2011, Video Testimony Collection of Yahad-In Unum.

47. Leonid Rein, "Local Collaboration in the Execution of the 'Final Solution' in Nazi-Occupied Belorussia," *Holocaust and Genocide Studies* 20, no. 3 (2006): 390.

48. Gabis, *Guest at the Shooters' Banquet*, 145.

49. Gabis, 266.

50. Rein, "Local Collaboration," 393.

51. Testimony of Policeman Kurt M., RG 14.101M, reel 438, folder 3357, p. 24, USHMMA.

52. Gabis, *Guest at the Shooters' Banquet*, 234.

53. Gertrude Schneider, *Reise in den Tod: Deutsche Juden in Riga 1941–1944* (Berlin: Edition Hentrich, 2006), 39–41.

54. Browning, *Ordinary Men*, 93.

55. Black, "Foot Soldiers of the Final Solution," 32.

56. Yuri Radchenko, "Accomplices to Extermination: Municipal Government and the Holocaust in Kharkiv, 1941–1942," *Holocaust and Genocide Studies* 27, no. 3 (2013): 455–57. Radchenko borrows this typology from Alexander V. Prusin.

57. Klaus-Michael Mallmann et al., eds., *Die "Ereignismeldungen UdSSR" 1941: Dokumente der Einsatzgruppen in der Sowjetunion*, vol. 1 (Darmstadt: Wissenschaftliche Buchgesellschaft, 2011), 64–65.

58. Dean, "German Gendarmerie," 179.

59. Browning, *Origins of the Final Solution*, 274.

60. Browning, 274.

61. Edward B. Westermann, "Stone Cold Killers or Drunk with Murder? Alcohol and Atrocity in the Holocaust," *Holocaust and Genocide Studies* 30, no. 1 (2016): 1–19.

62. Kārlis Kangeris, "'Closed' Units of Latvian Police—*Lettische Schutzmannschafts-Bataillone*: Research Issues and Pre-History," in *The Hidden and Forbidden History of Latvia under Soviet and Nazi Occupations, 1940–1991*, ed. Valters Nollendorfs and Erwin Oberländer (Riga: Institute of the History of Latvia, 2005), 120–21. Hitler's authorization for the formation of these battalions on January 25, 1942, coincided closely with the Wannsee Conference and offers further evidence of the ways in which Hitler and Himmler sought to seek the implementation of the "Final Solution" by using auxiliary police formations as a key instrument in mass murder.

63. "Der Chef der Ordnungspolizei, Vortrag über den Kräfte- und Kriegseinsatz der Ordnungspolizei im Jahre 1941," T 580, reel 96, NARA.

64. Waitman W. Beorn, "A Calculus of Complicity: The Wehrmacht, the Anti-Partisan War, and the Final Solution in White Russia, 1941–1942," *Central European History* 44, no. 2 (2011): 316–17, 324.

65. Peter Witte, Uwe Lohalm, and Wolfgang Scheffler, eds., *Der Dienstkalender Heinrich Himmlers 1941/42* (Hamburg: Christians Verlag, 1999), 294.

66. Andrej Angrick et al., eds., *Deutsche Besatzungsherrschaft in der UdSSR 1941–1945: Dokumente der Einsatzgruppen in der Sowjetunion*, vol. 2 (Darmstadt: Wissenschaftliche Buchgesellschaft, 2013), 268–69.

67. Ruth Bettina Birn, *Die Sicherheitspolizei in Estland 1941–1944: Eine Studie zur Kollaboration im Osten* (Paderborn: Ferdinand Schöningh, 2006), 28–31.

68. Testimony of Walter M., RG 14.101M, reel 3052, folder 20186, p. 124, USHMMA.

69. Frank Golczewski, "Die Kollaboration in der Ukraine," in *Kooperation und Verbrechen: Formen der "Kooperation" im östlichen Europa 1939–1945*, ed. Christoph Dieckmann (Göttingen: Wallstein Verlag, 2003), 173.

70. Sakowicz, *Ponary Diary*, 24–28.

71. Yitzhak Arad, *The Holocaust in the Soviet Union* (Lincoln: University of Nebraska Press, 2009), 389.

72. Andrej Angrick, "Die Einsatzgruppe D und die Kollaboration," in *Täter im Vernichtungskrieg: Der Überfall auf die Sowjetunion und der Völkermord an den Juden*, ed. Wolf Kaiser (Berlin: Propyläen Verlag, 2002), 71–84.

73. Pohl, "Ukrainische Hilfskräfte," 212–13.

74. Browning, *Ordinary Men*, 78–113, and Pohl, "Ukrainische Hilfskräfte," 214–17. For a discussion on Ukrainian accomplices and their motivations see Radchenko, "Accomplices to Extermination," 443–63.

75. Jürgen Matthäus, "What about the 'Ordinary Men'? The German Order Police and the Holocaust in the Occupied Soviet Union," *Holocaust and Genocide Studies* 10, no. 2 (1996): 139.

76. Testimony of Moshe Lachowicki, accession number 2010.432, USHMMA, and "Schutzpolizei-Dienstabteilung Libau," dated March 24, 1943, RG 18.002M, reel 11, fond R-83, opis 1, folder 207, USHMMA.

77. Golczewski, "Kollaboration in der Ukraine," 173.

78. Mendel Balberyszski, *Stronger Than Iron: The Destruction of Vilna Jewry, 1941–1945; An Eyewitness Account*, trans. Abraham Cykiert and Theodore Balberyszski (Jerusalem: Gefen, 2010), 261.

79. Browning, *Ordinary Men*, 90. Emphasis added.

80. Browning, 93.

81. Oral history interview with Neonila Grigorjeva, RG 50.568.0016, USHMMA.

82. Excerpts from the Main Commission of German Crimes in Poland, 1.2.7.7/82186024/ITS Digital Archive, accessed May 21, 2019, at USHMMA; and transcript of the *Shoah* interview with Richard Glazar, RG 60.5028, pp. 38–39, USHMMA.

83. Quoted in Sereny, *Into That Darkness*, 157, 159.

84. Bankier, *Expulsion and Extermination*, 122. In this case, the testimony states that two Germans participated by filming the executions.

85. Gabis, *Guest at the Shooters' Banquet*, 130.

86. Gross, *Golden Harvest*, 35.

87. Blatt, *From the Ashes*, 43.

88. Alpert, *Destruction of the Slonim Jewry*, 38.

89. Grabowski, *Hunt for the Jews*, 129.

90. Grabowski, 38.

91. Yakov Kravchinsky, "How We Joined the Partisans," in *We Remember Lest the World Forget: Memories of the Minsk Ghetto*, ed. Hilda Bronstein and Bett Demby (New York: JewishGen, 2018), 80.

92. Tory, *Surviving the Holocaust*, 488.

93. Steven J. Zipperstein, *Pogrom: Kishinev and the Tilt of History* (New York: Liveright, 2018), 63.

94. William W. Mishell, *Kaddish for Kovno: Life and Death in a Lithuanian Ghetto, 1941–1945* (Chicago: Chicago Review, 1988), 150, 165.

95. Tory, *Surviving the Holocaust*, 492.

96. Eliach, *Hasidic Tales of the Holocaust*, 53–54.

97. Mishell, *Kaddish for Kovno*, 85, 91, 150.

98. Mishell, 50. Regular mass killings on the Jewish Sabbath also took place in Minsk. See Rubenstein and Altman, *Unknown Black Book*, 265–66.

99. Mishell, *Kaddish for Kovno*, 50.

100. Rubenstein and Altman, *Unknown Black Book*, 308, and Dean and Hecker, *Encyclopedia of Camps and Ghettos*, part B, 1131–32.

101. Quoted in Desbois, *In Broad Daylight*, 43.

102. Quoted in Desbois, 45. In retrospect, Gregory attributed this drinking as a coping mechanism among men who were not trained killers but simply individuals mobilized into the process of genocide based on their ethnic identity.

103. Bankier, *Expulsion and Extermination*, 145.

104. Sakowicz, *Ponary Diary*, 28.

105. Kurzem, *Mascot*, 326.

106. Kurzem, 76–77.

107. Quoted in Desbois, *In Broad Daylight*, 246.

108. Quoted in Burds, *Holocaust in Rovno*, 60.
109. Salton, *23rd Psalm*, 126.
110. Bankier, *Expulsion and Extermination*, 187.
111. Mishell, *Kaddish for Kovno*, 44.
112. Tory, *Surviving the Holocaust*, 168–69.
113. Quoted in Burds, *Holocaust in Rovno*, 60.
114. Situation and Activity Report for Auxiliary Battalion 21, April 30, 1942, RG 18.002M, reel 30, fond R-83, opis 1, folder 189, USHMMA.
115. Biber, *Survivors*, 103.
116. Excerpts from the Main Commission of German Crimes in Poland, 1.2.7.7/82186024/ ITS Digital Archive, accessed May 21, 2019, at USHMMA.
117. Chiari, *Alltag hinter der Front*, 192–93.
118. Affidavit of Alfred Metzner, September 18, 1947, RG 242, NO-5558, p. 5, NARA.
119. Quoted in Bankier, *Expulsion and Extermination*, 80.
120. Gabis, *Guest at the Shooter's Banquet*, 161, 169.
121. Levy, *Wiesenthal File*, 36.
122. Levy, 36–37.
123. Rubenstein and Altman, *Unknown Black Book*, 306–7.
124. Gabis, *Guest at the Shooters' Banquet*, 267–68.
125. Rubenstein and Altman, *Unknown Black Book*, 308.
126. Kahn, *No Time to Mourn*, 39.
127. Gabis, *Guest at the Shooters' Banquet*, 241.
128. Quoted in Bankier, *Extermination and Expulsion*, 187.
129. Quoted in Bankier, 187–88.
130. Bankier, 157.
131. Młynarczyk et al., "Eastern Europe," 172, 174–76.
132. "Der Chef der Ordnungspolizei, O-Kdo. G 2(01) Nr. 6II/40(g)," January 28, 1940, T 580, reel 96, NARA.
133. "Der Chef der Ordnungspolizei, O-Kdo. G 2(01) Nr. 6IX/40(g)," May 15, 1940, T 501, reel 212, frames 895, 900, NARA. In one case, a blue policeman was arrested for "singing inflammatory songs and for mocking the Führer."
134. "Der Chef der Ordnungspolizei, O-Kdo. G 2(01) Nr. 6IX/40(g)," May 15, 1940, T 501, reel 212, frames 895, 900, NARA.
135. Młynarczyk et al., "Eastern Europe," 207.
136. Grabowski, *Hunt for the Jews*, 118–19. Like their German counterparts after the war, Polish policemen tried for their wartime actions often sought to use alcohol consumption as a mitigating factor in their defense, with some asserting that they were able to kill only if they were drunk.
137. Gross, *Golden Harvest*, 54.
138. Gross, 55.
139. Klukowski, *Diary from the Years of Occupation*, 193.
140. Klukowski, 283.
141. Klukowski, 213, 229, 273, 275.
142. Yitzhak Arad, "The Holocaust of Soviet Jewry in the Occupied Territories of the Soviet Union," *Yad Vashem Studies* 21 (1991): 13.

7. Alcohol and the German Army

1. Willy Peter Reese, *A Stranger to Myself: The Inhumanity of War: Russia, 1941–1944*, trans. Michael Hofmann (New York: Farrar, Straus and Giroux, 2005), 98.

2. Quoted in George L. Mosse, *The Culture of Western Europe: The Nineteenth and Twentieth Centuries*, 3rd ed. (New York: Routledge, 1988), 301.

3. Ehrenburg, *Russia at War*, 97.

4. Klukowski, *Diary from the Years of Occupation*, 166, 287.

5. Klukowski, 163. In this case, Klukowski does not mention whether alcohol was involved in the murder.

6. Gertjejanssen, "Victims, Heroes, Survivors," 64.

7. Westermann, *Hitler's Police Battalions*, 239.

8. Isabel Hull, *Absolute Destruction: Military Culture and the Practices of War in Imperial Germany* (Ithaca, NY: Cornell University Press, 2005), 2, 333.

9. David Stahel, *The Battle for Moscow* (Cambridge: Cambridge University Press, 2015), 34.

10. Christian Hartmann, *Wehrmacht im Ostkrieg: Front und militärisches Hinterland 1941/42* (Munich: R. Oldenbourg, 2009), 637, and Römer, *Comrades*, 82, 85.

11. Kühne, *Rise and Fall of Comradeship*, 293.

12. Walter Bähr, ed., *Kriegsbriefe Gefallener Studenten, 1939–1945* (Tübingen: Rainer Wunderlich Verlag, 1952), 148.

13. Shepherd, *Hitler's Soldiers*, 57.

14. Grossman, *Writer at War*, 14, 30.

15. Alexander Werth, *Moscow War Diary* (New York: Alfred A. Knopf, 1942), 212.

16. Karl Fuchs, *Your Loyal and Loving Son: The Letters of Tank Gunner Karl Fuchs, 1937–1941*, ed. and trans. Horst Fuchs Richardson (Washington, DC: Brassey's, 1987), 120.

17. Stahel, *Battle for Moscow*, 255.

18. Frevert, *Nation in Barracks*, 172.

19. Frevert, 174, 176.

20. Stephen Fritz, *Frontsoldaten: The German Soldier in World War II* (Lexington: University Press of Kentucky, 1995), 73, 113, 120.

21. Reese, *Stranger to Myself*, 154, 156.

22. Gottlob Herbert Bidermann, *In Deadly Combat: A German Soldier's Memoir of the Eastern Front*, trans. Derek S. Zumbro (Lawrence: University Press of Kansas, 2000), 216. Bidermann frequently mentions alcohol consumption, normally home-brewed schnapps. See pp. 101, 106, 215–17, and 248.

23. Hager, *War Diaries of a Panzer Soldier*, 53. Diary entry of October 3, 1941.

24. Stahel, *Battle for Moscow*, 206.

25. Guy Sajer, *The Forgotten Soldier* (Washington, DC: Brassey's, 1990), 367.

26. Quoted in Fritz, *Frontsoldaten*, 73.

27. Quoted in Sajer, *Forgotten Soldier*, 75.

28. Merridale, *Ivan's War*, 220.

29. Hager, *War Diaries of a Panzer Soldier*, 55. Diary entry of November 2, 1941.

30. "Standortbefehl Nr. 323/43- OFK 365, Lemberg, January 23, 1943," P-23-3-2, p. 53, District Archive Lviv Oblast. I would like to thank Waitman Beorn for bringing this source to my attention.

31. Beck, *Wehrmacht und sexuelle Gewalt*, 217–18.

32. Quoted in Peter Steinkamp, "Zur Devianz-Problematik in der Wehrmacht: Alkohol- und Rauschmittelmissbrauch bei der Truppe" (PhD diss., Albert-Ludwigs-Universität, Freiburg im Breisgau, 2008), 376–77. The other three factors contributing to criminal offenses included physical overexertion or exhaustion, infectious disease, and psychological pressures related to combat or professional and personal difficulties.

33. Neitzel, *Tapping Hitler's Generals*, 192.

34. Neitzel, 193.

35. Neitzel, 193.

36. Stahel, *Battle for Moscow*, 118.

37. Shepherd, *Hitler's Soldiers*, 201.

38. Johannes Hürter, ed., *Notizen aus dem Vernichtungskrieg: Die Ostfront 1941/42 in den Aufzeichnungen des Generals Heinrici* (Darmstadt: Wissenschaftliche Buchgesellschaft, 2016), 38–39, 54.

39. Gertjejanssen, "Victims, Heroes, Survivors," 71.

40. Letter from Lieutenant Richard Wagner addressed to "SA der NSDAP, Sturm 14/101" [December 6, 1941], SA (former Berlin Document Center), 297-B, pp. 191–93, BAB.

41. Beck, *Wehrmacht und sexuelle Gewalt*, 168–69, 182, 327.

42. Hans von Luck, *Panzer Commander: The Memoirs of Colonel Hans von Luck* (New York: Dell, 1989), 59.

43. Quoted in Shepherd, *Hitler's Soldiers*, 98.

44. Julie S. Torrie, *German Soldiers and the Occupation of France, 1940–1944* (Cambridge: Cambridge University Press, 2018), 50, and Tewes, *Frankreich in der Besatzungszeit*, 204, 207–8.

45. Helmut Hörner, *A German Odyssey: The Journal of a German Prisoner of War*, trans. Allen Kent Powell (Golden, CO: Fulcrum, 1991), 18, 20.

46. Hörner, 22. Hörner's memoir is based in part on a diary that he kept between 1944 and 1946 and reflects many of the tropes of German postwar apologia, including allusions to the primitive nature of Russian society and the German loss only in the face of overwhelming Allied superiority. However, it is also clear from his journal that the consumption of brandy, cognac, or wine in heavy quantities was a frequent occurrence for occupation troops in France. See pp. 18–37, 72–75.

47. Interrogation protocol of Josef R. on July 18, 1962, 202 AR-Z 907/60 Pol. Res. Btl. 69, pp. 141–42, ZStL. Reiter (a pseudonym) denied participation in the murders.

48. Shepherd, *Hitler's Soldiers*, 352.

49. Hager, *War Diaries of a Panzer Soldier*, 81–82, 111, Diary entries of March 31, 1942, April 14, 1942, March 5, 1943. See also Anatoly Golovchansky et al., *"Ich will raus aus diesem Wahnsinn": Deutsche Briefe von der Ostfront, 1941–1945* (Wuppertal: Peter Hammer Verlag, 1991), 63.

50. Letter from Gustav Gerhardts, dated October 6, 1943. Letter in private collection of the author. I would like to thank Mrs. Charlotte Lange for providing me with copies of her father's letters.

51. Rauch, *Unlikely Warrior*, 128.

52. For a discussion of female auxiliaries in the East see Elizabeth Harvey, *Women and the Nazi East: Agents and Witnesses of Germanization* (New Haven, CT: Yale University Press, 2003), and Lower, *Hitler's Furies*.

53. Hager, *War Diaries of a Panzer Soldier*, 81–83.

54. Beorn, *Marching into Darkness*, 168–69.

55. For a discussion of the influence of these criminal orders (especially the decree on military jurisdiction) in the East on acts of sexual violence and atrocity see Beck, *Wehrmacht und sexuelle Gewalt*, 177–85.

56. Herzog, *Brutality and Desire*, 4.

57. Mühlhäuser, "'Racial Awareness' and Fantasies of Potency," 200.

58. International Military Tribunal, *Trial of the Major War Criminals before the International Military Tribunal*, vol. 7 (Nuremberg: Secretariat of the Tribunal, 1947), 349, 354; and Ehrenburg and Grossman, *Black Book*, 22, 26, 58, 69.

59. Christoph Rass, *"Menschenmaterial"*: *Deutsche Soldaten an der Ostfront, Innenansichten einer Infanteriedivision 1939–1945* (Paderborn: F. Schöningh, 2003) 271, 346. One manifestation of this trend was the dramatic increase in the number of sexual assaults in the opening phase of the invasion of the Soviet Union.

60. Beorn, *Marching into Darkness*, 172.

61. Ehrenburg and Grossman, *Black Book*, 302, and Nicholas Stargardt, *The German War: A Nation under Arms, 1939–1945* (New York: Basic Books, 2015), 172.

62. Rass, *"Menschenmaterial,"* 269.

63. Rass, 269.

64. Alexievich, *Last Witnesses*, 183–84.

65. David Raub Snyder, *Sex Crimes under the Wehrmacht* (Lincoln: University of Nebraska Press, 2007), 208.

66. Snyder, *Sex Crimes*, 206–8. Snyder states that there were "more than eighty individuals" involved, but he does not provide an exact number.

67. Mühlhäuser, "Sexual Violence and the Holocaust," 111.

68. Beck, *Wehrmacht und sexuelle Gewalt*, 193–96.

69. Jürgen Matthäus, "Georg Heuser—Routinier des sicherheitspolizeilichen Osteinsatzes," in *Karrieren der Gewalt: Nationalsozialistische Täterbiographien*, ed. Klaus-Michael Mallmann and Gerhard Paul (Darmstadt: Wissenschaftliche Buchgesellschaft, 2013), 117.

70. Neitzel and Welzer, *Soldaten*, 173.

71. Frevert, *Nation in Barracks*, 175–76.

72. Gertjejanssen, "Victims, Heroes, Survivors," 296.

73. Quoted in Gertjejanssen, 302.

74. Shepherd, *Hitler's Soldiers*, 56.

75. Alexander Rossino, *Hitler Strikes Poland: Blitzkrieg, Ideology, and Atrocity* (Lawrence: University Press of Kansas, 2003), 210.

76. Walter Manoschek, "Es gibt nur eines für das Judentum: Vernichtung": Das Judenbild in deutschen Soldatenbriefen, 1939–1944 (Hamburg: Hamburger Edition, 1995), 9.

77. United Nations War Crimes Commission, Yugoslav Charges against German War Criminals, Charge No. R/N/76, RG 67.041M, reel 24, p. 711, USHMMA.

78. Ehrenburg, *Russia at War*, 94.

79. Quoted in Rossino, *Hitler Strikes Poland*, 211.

80. United Nations War Crimes Commission, Yugoslav Charges against German War Criminals, Case No. R/N/31, RG 67.041M, reel 24, p. 461, USHMMA.

81. Ehrenburg and Grossman, *Black Book*, 83.

82. Testimony of Jakob Lew, 1.2.7.7/82183313–14/ITS Digital Archive, accessed April 30, 2019, at USHMMA.

83. Mallmann, Rieß, and Pyta, *Deutscher Osten*, 31, 42. The photograph that accompanied the letter is reproduced on page 42 of the book.

84. Stargardt, *German War*, 42, 170.

85. Rossino, *Hitler Strikes Poland*, 211.

86. Petra Bopp, *Fremde im Visier: Foto-Erinnerungen an den Zweiten Weltkrieg* (Bielefeld, Germany: Kerber Verlag, 2012), 37, 47.

87. For a discussion of Wehrmacht operations in Serbia see Ben Shepherd, *Terror in the Balkans: German Armies and Partisan Warfare* (Cambridge, MA: Harvard University Press, 2012); Christopher Browning, "Wehrmacht Reprisal Policy and the Mass Murder of the Jews of Serbia," *Militärgeschichtliche Zeitschrift* 33, no. 1 (1983): 31–47; and Walter Manoschek,

"Serbien ist Judenfrei": Militärische Besatzungspolitik und Judenvernichtung in Serbien, 1941/42 (Munich: R. Oldenbourg, 1993).

88. Golovchansky et al.,*"Ich will raus aus diesem Wahnsinn,"* 89.

89. Bopp, *Fremde im Visier,* 53–55, 70–72.

90. I would like to thank Gregg Philipson for sharing drawings from his private collection of Wehrmacht photo albums showing bedbugs and cockroaches alongside pictures of Jews.

91. Bopp, *Fremde im Visier,* 95–100. For a discussion of the German army's traditional fear of irregular warfare see John Horne and Alan Kramer, "German 'Atrocities' and Franco-German Opinion, 1914: The Evidence of German Soldiers' Diaries," *Journal of Modern History* 66, no. 1 (1994): 1–33.

92. Beck, *Wehrmacht und sexuelle Gewalt,* 225.

93. Neitzel and Welzer, *Soldaten,* 92.

94. Neitzel and Welzer, 160. One Luftwaffe member described how he and his colleagues drank "like mad" during the war. See also John C. McManus, *Deadly Sky: The American Combat Airman in World War II* (New York: NAL Caliber, 2016), 93, 120. As a group in World War II, pilots, especially fighter pilots, regardless of nationality, cultivated an image of male bravado in which heaving drinking, sexual conquests, and aerial kills provided the basis for ranking one's masculinity within the group.

95. Claude Lanzmann, *Sobibor, October 14, 1943, 4:00 pm* (Paris: Les films Aleph, 2001).

96. Heinz Knoke, *I Flew for the Führer: The Story of a German Fighter Pilot,* trans. John Ewing (New York: Henry Holt, 1953), 31, 62, 67, 70, 111, 136, 142, 151–52, and Römer, *Comrades,* 89–90.

97. Beorn, *Marching into Darkness,* 77.

98. Quoted in Beorn, 146.

99. Mallmann, Rieß, and Pyta, *Deutscher Osten,* 155.

100. Merridale, *Ivan's War,* 56.

101. Isaak Kobylyanskiy, *From Stalingrad to Pillau: A Red Army Artillery Officer Remembers the Great Patriotic War,* ed. Stuart Britton (Lawrence: University Press of Kansas, 2008), 224.

102. Werth, *Moscow War Diary,* 212. In this sense, the Royal Navy's grog ration provides another example of the integration of alcohol into military culture, as does the pejorative expression "Dutch courage" referring to drinking before battle. For a discussion of these terms see Scott C. Martin, ed., *The Sage Encyclopedia of Alcohol: Social, Cultural and Historical Perspectives* (Los Angeles: Sage, 2015).

103. Shepherd, *Hitler's Soldiers,* 247.

104. See Vojin Majstorović, "Red Army Troops Encounter the Holocaust: Transnistria, Moldavia, Romania, Bulgaria, Yugoslavia, Hungary, and Austria, 1944–1945," *Holocaust and Genocide Studies* 32, no. 2 (2018): 249–71, and Merridale, *Ivan's War,* 283, 313–14.

105. Vojin Majstorović, "Ivan Goes Abroad: The Red Army in the Balkans and Central Europe, 1944–1945" (PhD diss., University of Toronto, 2017), 90. I would like to thank Vojin Majstorović for sharing a copy of his excellent dissertation. For a graphic discussion of the effects of drinking and sexual violence by Soviet soldiers in Berlin see Anonymous, *A Woman in Berlin: Eight Weeks in a Conquered City,* trans. Philip Boehm (New York: Metropolitan Books, 2005).

106. Steinkamp, *Zur Devianz-Problematik in der Wehrmacht,* 15.

107. Steinkamp, 36, 40–42.
108. Quoted in Shepherd, *Hitler's Soldiers*, 468, 476.
109. Manoschek,*"Es gibt nur eines für das Judentum,"* 79.

Conclusion

1. Walter Manoschek, ed., *Der Fall Rechnitz: Das Massaker an Juden im März 1945* (Vienna: Wilhelm Braumüller Universitäts-Verlagsbuchhandlung, 2009), 32–41.
2. Manoschek, 247–49.
3. Sven Keller, *Volksgemeinschaft am Ende: Gesellschaft und Gewalt, 1944–45* (Munich: Oldenbourg Verlag, 2013), 265–66.
4. Testimony of Franz Fuchs, May 1945, 1.2.7.13/82193478/ITS Digital Archive, accessed April 30, 2019, at USHMMA. For a detailed examination of the death marches and examples of intoxicated SS guards participating in acts of brutality and killing see Daniel Blatman, *The Death Marches: The Final Phase of Nazi Genocide*, trans. Chaya Galai (Cambridge, MA: Belknap Press of Harvard University Press, 2011), 108, 285.
5. Testimony of Franz Fuchs, May 1945, 1.2.7.13/82193478/ITS Digital Archive, accessed April 30, 2019, at USHMMA.
6. Testimony of Willi Lenz, 1.1.30.0/82135032/ITS Digital Archive, accessed May 2, 2019, at USHMMA.
7. Testimony of Josef Händler, 1.1.30.0/82135133-34/ITS Digital Archive, accessed April 8, 2019, at USHMMA.
8. Quoted in Walter Kempowski, *Swan Song 1945*, trans. Shaun Whiteside (New York: W. W. Norton, 2014), 225.
9. Helm, *Ravensbrück*, 612.
10. Miklos Nyiszli, *Auschwitz: A Doctor's Eyewitness Account*, trans. Tibére Kremer and Richard Seaver (New York: Arcade, 1993), 201.
11. Nyiszli, 201.
12. Quoted in Matthäus and Kerenji, *Jewish Responses to Persecution*, 179.
13. Keller, *Volksgemeinschaft am Ende*, 121.
14. International Military Tribunal, vol. 12, p. 462.
15. Musmanno, *Eichmann Kommandos*, 234.
16. Angrick et al., *Deutsche Besatzungsherrschaft*, 32. Interestingly, the prohibition on excessive alcohol consumption is immediately followed by a proscription on "personal relationships" with the non-German population, especially with "racially alien women."
17. Höss, *Death Dealer*, 157.
18. Quoted in Earl, *SS-Einsatzgruppen Trial*, 165–66.
19. Musmanno, *Eichmann Kommandos*, 109.
20. Anne-Lise Stern, "Ei Warum, Ei Darum: O Why," in *Claude Lanzmann's Shoah: Key Essays*, ed. and trans. Stuart Liebman (Oxford: Oxford University Press, 2007), 97.
21. Transcript of the *Shoah* interview with Martha Michelson, RG 60.5033, p. 16, USHMMA.
22. Transcript of the *Shoah* interview with Franz Suchomel, RG 60.5046, p. 4, USHMMA.
23. Transcript of the *Shoah* interview with Martha Michelson, RG 60.5033, p. 21, and transcript of the *Shoah* interview with Franz Suchomel, RG 60.5046, pp. 98–100, USHMMA. For a more critical perspective on Bothmann see Pawlicka-Nowak, *Chełmno Witnesses Speak*, 201.
24. Testimony of Dr. Karl W, RG 14.101M, reel 3052, folder 20183, pp. 47–48, USHMMA.

25. Affidavit of Alfred Metzner, dated September 18, 1947, RG 242, NO-5558, pp. 4, 6, NARA.

26. Alpert, *Destruction of Slonim Jewry*, 46, 52.

27. Investigation of Gerhard Erren, Case number II 202 AR-Z 228/59, RG 14.101M, reel 39, folder 14527, p. 47, USHMMA.

28. Quoted in Christian Gerlach, *Kalkulierte Morde: Die deutsche Wirtschafts- und Vernichtungspolitik in Weißrußland 1941 bis 1944* (Hamburg: Hamburger Edition, 1999), 588.

29. Quoted in Gerlach, 588–89.

30. Michael Burleigh and Wolfgang Wippermann, *The Racial State: Germany 1933–1945* (Cambridge: Cambridge University Press, 1991), 98.

31. Paul Insel, R. Elaine Turner, and Don Ross, *Discovering Nutrition*, 3rd ed. (Boston: Jones and Bartlett, 2010), 379, and Timothy Roehrs and Thomas Roth, "Sleep, Alcohol, and Quality of Life," in *Sleep and Quality of Life in Clinical Medicine*, ed. Joris L. Verster, S. R. Pandi-Perumal, and David L. Streiner (Totowa, NJ: Humana, 2008), 333–40. In fact, these physiological effects of excessive alcohol consumption rather than psychosomatic responses may better explain some perpetrators' reactions to killing, whether stomach pains or difficulty in sleeping.

32. Diary of Major General Erwin Lahousen, dated October 1941, RG 242, NOKW-3146, p. 5, NARA.

33. Hilberg, *Destruction of the European Jews*, 331–32.

34. Transcript of the *Shoah* interview with Karl Kretschmer, RG 60.5018, p. 5, USHMMA.

35. Hilberg, *Destruction of the European Jews*, 334.

36. Jim G. Tobias, *"Ihr Gewissen war rein: Sie haben es nie benutzt": Die Verbrechen der Polizeikompanie Nürnberg* (Nuremberg: Antogo Verlag, 2005), 35.

37. Report from the Higher SS and Police Leader, Center Erich von dem Bach-Zelewski to Reich Leader of the SS and Chief of the German Police Heinrich Himmler, September 5, 1942, NS 19, reel 1671, frame 130, BAB.

38. Witte, Lohalm, and Scheffler, *Der Dienstkalender Heinrich Himmlers*, 229.

39. SS-WVHA authorization form, September 22, 1943, 1.2.7.7/82186418/ITS Digital Archive, accessed April 30, 2019, at USHMMA.

40. Quoted in Fahrenkrug, "Alcohol and the State in Nazi Germany," 330.

41. Quoted in Fahrenkrug, 332.

42. Fahrenkrug, 321.

43. Mark Danner, "America and the Bosnia Genocide," *New York Review of Books* 44, no. 19 (1997): 55–65, and Slavenka Drakulić, *They Would Never Hurt a Fly: War Criminals on Trial in the Hague* (New York: Viking, 2004), 59, 117–18.

44. Philip Gourevitch, *We Wish to Inform You That Tomorrow We Will Be Killed with Our Families: Stories from Rwanda* (New York: Farrar, Straus and Giroux, 1998), 18, 115, 130–36; Bill Berkeley, *The Graves Are Not Yet Full: Race, Tribe and Power in the Heart of Africa* (New York: Basic Books, 2001), 23, 252, 259: and Jean Hatzfeld, *Machete Season: The Killers in Rwanda Speak*, trans. Linda Coverdale (New York: Farrar, Straus and Giroux, 2005), 8, 13, 31, 49, 243–44.

45. Quoted in Elisa von Joeden-Forgey, "Genocidal Masculinity," in *New Directions in Genocide Research*, ed. Adam Jones (New York: Routledge, 2012), 77.

46. Hatzfeld, *Machete Season*, 15, 45–46.

47. Quoted in Gourevitch, *We Wish to Inform You*, 134.

48. Immaculée Ilibagiza with Steve Irwin, *Left to Tell: Discovering God in the Rwandan Holocaust* (Carlsbad, CA: Hay House, 2006), 33–36, 80, 92, 108–9, 139–40.

49. Berkeley, *Graves Are Not Yet Full*, 84, 93, and Ilibagiza, *Left to Tell*, 83, 92–93, 98, 100–101.

50. Quoted in Ehrenburg and Grossman, *Black Book*, 77.

51. Grossman, *Writer at War*, 301.

52. Gross, *Neighbors*, 140.

53. Bartov, *Anatomy of a Genocide*, 198–99.

54. Westermann, *Hitler's Police Battalions*, 237.

55. Langbein, *Der Auschwitz-Prozeß*, 1:459, 466.

56. Transcript of the *Shoah* interview with Ruth Elias, RG 60.5003, pp. 33–34, USHMMA.

57. Quoted in Langerbein, *Hitler's Death Squads*, 68.

BIBLIOGRAPHY

Archival Collections

Bundesarchiv, Berlin (BAB)

Die Deutsche Polizei

    NS 19   Persönlicher Stab Reichsführer-SS
    R 19   Chef der Ordnungspolizei, Hauptamt Ordnungspolizei

Central Office for the Investigation of National
Socialist Crimes (ZStl)

    202 AR-Z 907/60
    204 AR-Z 1251/65
    204 AR-Z 12/61
    503 AR-Z 9/1965

Records of the International Tracing Service (ITS)

Subcollection 1.1.0.4: Extermination Policy (Bureaucracy), ITS Digital Archive. Accessed at the USHMM, March–June 2019.

Subcollection 1.1.2.0: General Information on Auschwitz Concentration and Extermination Camp, ITS Digital Archive. Accessed at the USHMM, March–June 2019.

Subcollection 1.1.30.0: General Information on Neuengamme Concentration Camp, ITS Digital Archive. Accessed at the USHMM, March–June 2019.

Subcollection 1.1.38.0: General Information on Sachsenhausen Concentration Camp, ITS Digital Archive. Accessed at the USHMM, March–June 2019.

Subcollection 1.1.47.0: General Information on Various Camps, ITS Digital Archive. Accessed at the USHMM, March–June 2019.

Subcollection 1.2.7.4: Persecution Action of the "Occupied Eastern Territory" (Baltic States), ITS Digital Archive. Accessed at the USHMM, March–June 2019.

Subcollection 1.2.7.7: Persecution Action in the "General Government" (part of former Poland), ITS Digital Archive. Accessed at the USHMM, March–June 2019.

Subcollection 1.2.7.8: Persecution Action in the "General Government" / District of Galicia (part of former Poland), ITS Digital Archive. Accessed at the USHMM, March–June 2019.

Subcollection 1.2.7.10: Persecution Action in Reichsgau Danzig–Western Prussia, ITS Digital Archive. Accessed at the USHMM, March–June 2019.

Subcollection 1.2.7.13: Persecution Action in Austria, ITS Digital Archive. Accessed at the USHMM, March–June 2019.

Subcollection 5.1: Nazi Trials, ITS Digital Archive. Accessed at the USHMM, March–June 2019.

National Archives and Records Administration (NARA)

T 175   Records of the Reich Leader of the SS and Chief of German Police

T 501   Records of German Field Commands: Rear Areas, Occupied Territories, and Others

T 580   Captured German Records Microfilmed in Berlin, Germany

T 1119   Records of the US Nuremberg War Crimes Trials

United States Holocaust Memorial Museum Archive (USHMMA)

LM0343	Das Schwarze Korps
RG 11.001M.15	Deutsche Polizeieinrichtungen in den okkupierten Gebieten, 1936–1944
RG 14.015M	Persönlicher Stab Reichsführer-SS
RG 14.068	Selected Records of Postwar East German Investigative Court Cases and Trials to Nazi War Crimes
RG 14.101M	Records of the Central Office for the Investigation of National Socialist Crimes, 1933–1999
RG 15.011M	Records of the Kommandeur der Gendarmerie Lublin, 1939–1944
RG 18.002M	Selected Records from the Latvian Central State Historical Archives, 1941–1945
RG 22.004	Soviet War News, 1944
RG 50.568	USHMM Latvian Documentation Project, 2003–2011
RG 53.002M	Selected Records of the Belarus Central State Archive, Minsk, 1941–1949
RG 60.50XX	Claude Lanzmann Shoah Collection
RG 67.041M	United Nations War Crimes Commission Records, 1943–1949
RG 68.035M	Rasse- und Siedlungshauptamt-SS, 1934–1945

Testimony Regarding Nesvizh (Nieswiez), Poland, accession number 2010.432

Yahad-In Unum

Trip no. 02L, witness No. 25

Published Documents

International Military Tribunal. *Trial of the Major War Criminals before the International Military Tribunal.* Vol. 7. Nuremberg: Secretariat of the Tribunal, 1947.

International Military Tribunal. *Trial of the Major War Criminals before the International Military Tribunal.* Vol. 12. Nuremberg: Secretariat of the Tribunal, 1947.

International Military Tribunal. *Trials of the Major War Criminals before the International Military Tribunal.* Vol. 29. Nuremberg: Secretariat of the Military Tribunal, 1948.

State of Israel, Ministry of Justice. *The Trial of Adolf Eichmann: Recordings of Proceedings in the District Court of Jerusalem.* Vols. 3 and 4. Jerusalem: Trust for the Publication of the Proceedings of the Eichmann Trial, in cooperation with the Israel State Archives and Yad Vashem, 1993.

Newspapers

Das Schwarze Korps
Die Deutsche Polizei
Soviet War News

Motion Pictures

Hersonski, Yael, dir. *A Film Unfinished.* Oscilloscope Laboratories, 2010. DVD.
Lanzmann, Claude, dir. *Shoah.* Les films Aleph, 1985. DVD.
———, dir. *Sobibor, October 14, 1943, 4:00 pm.* Les films Aleph, 2001. DVD.
Oppenheimer, Joshua, dir. *The Act of Killing.* Drafthouse Films, 2012. DVD.
Spielberg, Steven, dir. *Schindler's List.* Universal Pictures, 1994. DVD.

Books and Articles

Abbey, Antonia. "Alcohol-Related Sexual Assault: A Common Problem among College Students." *Journal of Studies on Alcohol Supplement* 63, no. 2 (2002): 118–28.
Abel, Theodore. *Why Hitler Came into Power.* New York: Prentice-Hall, 1938; reprint, Cambridge, MA: Harvard University Press, 1986.
Academy of Sciences of the Ukrainian SSR, Institute of Law. *Nazi Crimes in Ukraine, 1941–1944.* Translated by V.I. Biley, S. I. Kaznady, and A. E. Sologubenko. Kiev: Naukova Dumka, 1987.
Alexievich, Svetlana. *Last Witnesses: An Oral History of the Children of World War II.* Translated by Richard Pevear and Larissa Volokhonsky. New York: Random House, 2019.
———. *Secondhand Time: The Last of the Soviets.* Translated by Bela Shayevich. New York: Random House, 2016.
Allar, Kimberly. "From Recruitment to Genocide: An Examination of the Recruitment of Auxiliary Guards in National Socialist Concentration Camps." In *Orte und Akteure im System der NS-Zwangslager*, edited by Michael Becker, Dennis Bock, and Henrike Illig, 169–97. Berlin: Metropol Verlag, 2015.

———. "Ravensbrück's Pupils: Creating a Nazi Female Guard Force." Paper presented at Lessons and Legacies XIV: The Holocaust in the 21st Century, Claremont-McKenna College, California, November 6, 2016.

Allen, James, Hilton Als, John Lewis, and Leon Litwak. *Without Sanctuary: Lynching Photography in America.* Santa Fe, NM: Twin Palms, 2000.

Alpert, Nachum. *The Destruction of Slonim Jewry: The Story of the Jews of Slonim during the Holocaust.* Translated by Max Rosenfeld. New York: Holocaust Library, 1989.

Angrick, Andrej. *Besatzungspolitik und Massenmord: Die Einsatzgruppe D in der südlichen Sowjetunion, 1941–1943.* Hamburg: Hamburger Edition, 2003.

———. "Die Einsatzgruppe D und die Kollaboration." In *Täter im Vernichtungskrieg: Der Überfall auf die Sowjetunion und der Völkermord an den Juden,* edited by Wolf Kaiser, 71–84. Berlin: Propyläen Verlag, 2002.

———. "The Men of *Einsatzgruppe* D: An Inside View of a State-Sanctioned Killing Unit in the 'Third Reich.'" In *Ordinary People as Mass Murderers: Perpetrators in Comparative Perspectives,* edited by Olaf Jensen and Claus-Christian Szejnmann, 78–96. New York: Palgrave Macmillan, 2008.

Angrick, Andrej, Klaus-Michael Mallmann, Jürgen Matthäus, and Martin Cüppers, eds. *Deutsche Besatzungsherrschaft in der UdSSR 1941–1945: Dokumente der Einsatzgruppen in der Sowjetunion.* Vol. 2. Darmstadt: Wissenschaftliche Buchgesellschaft, 2013.

Anonymous. *A Woman in Berlin: Eight Weeks in a Conquered City.* Translated by Philip Boehm. New York: Metropolitan Books, 2005.

Arad, Yitzhak. *The Holocaust in the Soviet Union.* Lincoln: University of Nebraska Press, 2009.

———. "The Holocaust of Soviet Jewry in the Occupied Territories of the Soviet Union." *Yad Vashem Studies* 21 (1991): 1–47.

Aronson, Shlomo. *Reinhard Heydrich und die Frühgeschichte von Gestapo und SD.* Stuttgart: Deutsche Verlags-Anstalt, 1971.

Ashe, Fidelma. "Gendering War and Peace: Militarized Masculinities in Northern Ireland." *Men and Masculinities* 15, no. 3 (2012): 230–48.

Ayçoberry, Pierre. *The Social History of the Third Reich, 1933–1945.* Translated by Janet Lloyd. New York: New Press, 1999.

Bähr, Walter, ed. *Kriegsbriefe Gefallener Studenten, 1939–1945.* Tübingen: Rainer Wunderlich Verlag, 1952.

Bahro, Berno. *Der SS-Sport: Organisation-Funktion-Bedeutung.* Paderborn: Ferdinand Schöningh, 2013.

Baird, Jay W. *To Die for Germany: Heroes in the Nazi Pantheon.* Bloomington: Indiana University Press, 1990.

Balberyszski, Mendel. *Stronger Than Iron: The Destruction of Vilna Jewry, 1941–1945; An Eyewitness Account.* Translated by Abraham Cykiert and Theodore Balberyszski. Jerusalem: Gefen, 2010.

Bankier, David. *Expulsion and Extermination: Holocaust Testimonials from Provincial Lithuania.* Jerusalem: Yad Vashem, 2011.

Baranowski, Shelly. *Strength through Joy: Consumerism and Mass Tourism in the Third Reich*. Cambridge: Cambridge University Press, 2004.

Barrett, Frank J. "The Organizational Construction of Hegemonic Masculinity: The Case of the US Navy." *Gender, Work, and Organizations* 3, no. 3 (1996): 129–42.

Barrows, Susanna, and Robin Room, eds. *Drinking: Behavior and Belief in Modern History*. Berkeley: University of California Press, 1991.

Bartov, Omer. *Anatomy of a Genocide: The Life and Death of a Town Called Buczacz*. New York: Simon & Schuster, 2018.

——. *Hitler's Army: Soldiers, Nazis, and War in the Third Reich*. Oxford: Oxford University Press, 1992.

Bazyler, Michael J., and Frank M. Tuerkheimer. *Forgotten Trials of the Holocaust*. New York: NYU Press, 2014.

Beck, Birgit. "The Military Trials of Sexual Crimes Committed by Soldiers in the Wehrmacht, 1939–1944." In *Home/Front: The Military, War, and Gender in Twentieth-Century Germany*, edited by Karen Hagemann and Stefanie Schüler-Springorum, 255–73. Oxford: Berg, 2002.

——. *Wehrmacht und sexuelle Gewalt: Sexualverbrechen vor deutschen Militärgerichten, 1939–1945*. Paderborn: Ferdinand Schöningh, 2004.

Beimler, Hans. *Four Weeks in the Hands of Hitler's Hell-Hounds: The Nazi Murder Camp of Dachau*. London: Modern Books, 1935.

Benz, Angelika. *Handlanger der SS: Die Rolle der Trawniki-Männer im Holocaust*. Berlin: Metropol, 2015.

Beorn, Waitman W. "Bodily Conquest: Sexual Violence in the Nazi East." In *Mass Violence in Nazi-Occupied Europe*, edited by Alex J. Kay and David Stahel, 195–218. Bloomington: Indiana University Press, 2018.

——. "A Calculus of Complicity: The Wehrmacht, the Anti-partisan War, and the Final Solution in White Russia, 1941–1942." *Central European History* 44, no. 2 (2011): 308–37.

——. "Last Stop in Lwów: Janowska as a Hybrid Camp." *Holocaust and Genocide Studies* 32, no. 3 (2018): 445–71.

——. *Marching into Darkness: The Wehrmacht and the Holocaust in Belarus*. Cambridge, MA: Harvard University Press, 2014.

Berg, Mary. *Warsaw Ghetto: A Diary by Mary Berg*. Edited by S. L. Shneiderman. New York: L. B. Fischer, 1945.

Bergen, Doris L. *War and Genocide: A Concise History of the Holocaust*. 3rd ed. Lanham, MD: Rowman & Littlefield, 2016.

Berger, Sara. *Experten der Vernichtung: Das T4-Reinhardt-Netzwerk in den Lagern Belzec, Sobibor und Treblinka*. Hamburg: Verlag des Hamburger Instituts für Sozialforschung, 2013.

Bergholz, Max. *Violence as a Generative Force: Identity, Nationalism, and Memory in a Balkan Country*. Ithaca, NY: Cornell University Press, 2016.

Berkeley, Bill. *The Graves Are Not Yet Full: Race, Tribe and Power in the Heart of Africa*. New York: Basic Books, 2001.

Berkhoff, Karel. *Harvest of Despair: Life and Death in Ukraine under Nazi Rule*. Cambridge, MA: Harvard University Press, 2004.

Bessel, Richard. "Violence as Propaganda: The Role of the Storm Troopers in the Rise of National Socialism." In *The Formation of the Nazi Constituency, 1919–1933*, edited by Thomas Childers, 131–46. Totowa, NJ: Barnes & Noble Books, 1986.

Biber, Jacob. *Survivors*. New London, CT: Star, 1982.

Bidermann, Gottlob Herbert. *In Deadly Combat: A German Soldier's Memoir of the Eastern Front*. Translated by Derek S. Zumbro. Lawrence: University Press of Kansas, 2000.

Birn, Ruth Bettina. *Die Sicherheitspolizei in Estland 1941–1944: Eine Studie zur Kollaboration im Osten*. Paderborn: Ferdinand Schöningh, 2006.

Black, Peter. "Foot Soldiers of the Final Solution: The Trawniki Training Camp and Operation Reinhard." *Holocaust and Genocide Studies* 25, no. 1 (2011): 1–99.

Blatman, Daniel. *The Death Marches: The Final Phase of Nazi Genocide*. Translated by Chaya Galai. Cambridge, MA: Belknap Press of Harvard University Press, 2011.

Blatt, Thomas Toivi. *From the Ashes of Sobibor: A Story of Survival*. Evanston, IL: Northwestern University Press, 1997.

Bloxham, Donald. *The Final Solution: A Genocide*. Oxford: Oxford University Press, 2009.

Boberach, Heinz, ed. *Meldungen aus dem Reich, 1938–1945*. Vol. 3. Herrsching: Pawlak Verlag, 1984.

Böhler, Jochen, and Robert Gerwarth, eds. *The Waffen-SS: A European History*. Oxford: Oxford University Press, 2017.

Boll, Bernd. "Złoczów, July 1941: The Wehrmacht and the Beginning of the Holocaust in Galicia." In *Crimes of War: Guilt and Denial in the Twentieth Century*, edited by Omer Bartov, Atina Grossmann, and Mary Nolan, 61–99. New York: New Press, 2002.

Bopp, Petra. *Fremde im Visier: Foto-Erinnerungen an den Zweiten Weltkrieg*. Bielefeld, Germany: Kerber Verlag, 2012.

Borggräffe, Henning. *Schützenvereine im Nationalsozialismus" Pfllege der "Volksgemeinschaft" und Vorbereitung auf den Krieg, 1933–1945*. Münster: Ardey-Verlag, 2010.

Borodziej, Włodzimierz. *Terror und Politik: Die Deutsche Polizei und die polnische Widerstandsbewegung im Generalgouvernement, 1939–1944*. Mainz: Verlag Philipp von Zabern, 1999.

Borowski, Tadeusz. *This Way for the Gas, Ladies and Gentlemen*. Translated by Barbara Vedder. New York: Penguin, 1967.

Brauer, Juliane. *Musik im Konzentrationslager Sachsenhausen*. Berlin: Metropol Verlag, 2009.

Breitman, Richard. *The Architect of Genocide: Himmler and the Final Solution*. New York: Alfred A. Knopf, 1991.

——. "Himmler's Police Auxiliaries in the Occupied Soviet Territories." *Simon Wiesenthal Center Annual* 7, no. 2 (1990): 23–39.

——. *Official Secrets: What the Nazis Planned, What the British and Americans Knew*. New York: Hill & Wang, 1998.

Broszat, Martin. *The Hitler State: The Foundation and Development of the Internal Structure of the Third Reich*. Translated by John W. Hiden. London: Longman, 1981.

Browning, Christopher. *Ordinary Men: Reserve Police Battalion 101 and the Final Solution in Poland*. New York, HarperCollins, 1992.

——. *Ordinary Men: Reserve Police Battalion 101 and the Final Solution in Poland*. Rev. ed. New York: Harper Perennial, 2017.

——. "Wehrmacht Reprisal Policy and the Mass Murder of the Jews of Serbia." *Militärgeschichtliche Zeitschrift* 33, no. 1 (1983): 31–47.

Browning, Christopher, with Jürgen Matthäus. *The Origins of the Final Solution: The Evolution of Nazi Jewish Policy*. Lincoln: University of Nebraska Press, 2004.

Brun, Arne Lie, with Robby Robinson. *Night and Fog: A Survivor's Story*. New York: Berkley Books, 1992.

The Buchenwald Report. Edited and translated by David Hackett. Boulder, CO: Westview, 1995.

Buchheim, Hans. *Anatomie des SS-Staates*. Vol. 1, *Die SS: Das Herrschaftsinstrument Befehl und Gehorsam*. Munich: Deutscher Taschenbuch Verlag, 1967.

Büchler, Yehoshua R. "'Unworthy Behavior': The Case of SS Officer Max Täubner." *Holocaust and Genocide Studies* 17, no. 3 (2003): 409–29.

Büge, Emil. *1470 KZ-Geheimnisse: Heimliche Aufzeichnungen aus der Politischen Abteilung des KZ Sachsenhausen*. Edited by Winfried Meyer. Berlin: Metropol Verlag, 2010.

Burds, Jeffrey. *Holocaust in Rovno: A Massacre in Ukraine, November 1941*. New York: Palgrave Macmillan, 2013.

——. "Sexual Violence in Europe in World War II, 1939–1945." *Politics and Society* 37, no. 1 (2009): 35–73.

Burkhard, Hugo. *Tanz mal Jude! Von Dachau bis Shanghai*. Nuremberg: Verlag Richard Reichenbach, 1967.

Burleigh, Michael. *The Third Reich: A New History*. New York: Hill & Wang, 2000.

Burleigh, Michael, and Wolfgang Wippermann. *The Racial State: Germany 1933–1945*. Cambridge: Cambridge University Press, 1991.

Caplan, Jane. "Gender and the Concentration Camps." In *Concentration Camps in Nazi Germany: The New Histories*, edited by Jane Caplan and Nikolaus Wachsmann, 82–107. New York: Routledge, 2012.

Carney, Amy. *Marriage and Fatherhood in the Nazi SS*. Toronto: University of Toronto Press, 2018.

Cassell's New German and English Dictionary. New York: Funk & Wagnalls, 1939.

Central Commission for Investigation of German Crimes in Poland. *German Crimes in Poland*. New York: Howard Fertig, 1982.

Ceran, Tomasz. *The History of a Forgotten German Camp: Nazi Ideology and Genocide at Szmalcówka*. London: I. B. Tauris, 2015.

Chervyakov, Valeriy Vladimir Shkolnikov, William Alex Pridemore, and Martin McKee. "The Changing Nature of Murder in Russia." *Social Science and Medicine* 55, no. 10 (2002): 1713–24.

Chiari, Bernhard. *Alltag hinter der Front: Besatzung, Kollaboration und Widerstand in Weissrussland, 1941–1944*. Düsseldorf: Droste Verlag, 1998.

Cocks, Geoffrey. *The State of Health: Illness in Nazi Germany*. Oxford: Oxford University Press, 2012.

Cohen, Dara Kay. *Rape during Civil War*. Ithaca, NY: Cornell University Press, 2016.

Cohn, Willy. *Kein Recht, nirgends: Tagebuch vom Untergang des Breslauer Judentums, 1939–1941*. Vol. 2. Cologne: Böhlau Verlag, 2007.

Collomp, Catherine, and Bruno Groppo, eds. *An American in Hitler's Berlin: Abraham Plotkin's Diary, 1932–33*. Urbana: University of Illinois Press, 2009.

Confino, Alon. *A World without Jews: The Nazi Imagination from Persecution to Genocide*. New Haven, CT: Yale University Press, 2014.

Connell, R. W., and James W. Messerschmidt. "Hegemonic Masculinity: Rethinking the Concept." *Gender and Society* 19, no. 6 (2005): 829–59.

Crew, David F. "Photography and Cinema." In *The Oxford Illustrated History of the Third Reich*, edited by Robert Gellately, 157–87. Oxford: Oxford University Press, 2018.

Curilla, Wolfgang. *Der Judenmord in Polen und die deutsche Ordnungspolizei, 1939–1945*. Paderborn: Ferdinand Schöningh, 2011.

——. *Die Deutsche Ordnungspolizei und der Holocaust im Baltikum und in Weißrussland, 1941–1944*. Paderborn: Ferdinand Schöningh, 2006.

Danner, Mark. "America and the Bosnia Genocide." *New York Review of Books* 44, no. 19 (1997): 55–65.

Dean, Martin. *Collaboration in the Holocaust: Crimes of the Local Police in Belorussia and Ukraine, 1941–44*. New York: St. Martin's, 2000.

——. "The German Gendarmerie, the Ukrainian Schutzmannschaft, and the 'Second Wave' of Jewish Killings in Occupied Ukraine: German Policing at the Local Level in the Zhitomir Region, 1941–1944." *German History* 14, no. 2 (1996): 168–92.

Dean, Martin, and Mel Hecker, eds. *Ghettos in German-Occupied Eastern Europe*. Vol. 2 of *The United States Holocaust Memorial Museum Encyclopedia of Camps and Ghettos, 1933–1945*. Part A. Bloomington: Indiana University Press, 2012.

——, eds. *Ghettos in German-Occupied Eastern Europe*. Vol. 2 of *The United States Holocaust Memorial Museum Encyclopedia of Camps and Ghettos, 1933–1945*. Part B. Bloomington: Indiana University Press, 2012.

DeLay, Brian. *War of a Thousand Deserts: Indian Raids and the US-Mexican War*. New Haven, CT: Yale University Press, 2008.

Delbo, Charlotte. *Auschwitz and After*. Translated by Rosette C. Lamont. New Haven, CT: Yale University Press, 1995.

Demianova, Genia. *Comrade Genia: The Story of a Victim of German Bestiality in Russia told by Herself*. London: Nicholson and Watson, 1941.

De Mildt, Dick. *In the Name of the People: Perpetrators of Genocide in the Reflection of Their Post-war Prosecution in West Germany*. The Hague: Martinus Nijhoff, 1996.

Desbois, Patrick. *In Broad Daylight: The Secret Procedures behind the Holocaust by Bullets*. Translated by Hilary Reyl and Calvert Barksdale. New York: Arcade, 2015.

——. *The Holocaust by Bullets: A Priest's Journey to Uncover the Truth behind the Murder of 1.5 Million Jews*. New York: Palgrave Macmillan, 2008.

Dicks, Henry V. *Licensed Mass Murder: A Socio-psychological Study of Some SS Killers*. New York: Basic Books, 1972.

Dierl, Florian. "The 'Internal Wehrmacht': German Order Police and the Transformation of State Power, 1936–1945." PhD diss., Royal Holloway College, 2007.

Dillon, Christopher. *Dachau and the SS: A Schooling in Violence.* Oxford: Oxford University Press, 2015.

Dinu, Radu Harald. "Honor, Shame, and Warrior Values: The Anthropology of Ustasha Violence." In *The Utopia of Terror: Life and Death in Wartime Croatia,* edited by Rory Yeomans, 119–41. Rochester, NY: University of Rochester Press, 2015.

Dobroszycki, Lucjan, ed. *The Chronicle of the Łódź Ghetto, 1941–1944.* Translated by Richard Lourie et al. New Haven, CT: Yale University Press, 1984.

Dombrowski, Nicole Ann. "Surviving the German Invasion of France: Women's Stories of the Exodus of 1940." In *Women and War in the Twentieth Century: Enlisted with or without Consent,* edited by Nicole Ann Dombrowski, 85–102. New York: Garland, 1999.

Dorsey, Jennifer Hull. *Hirelings: African American Workers and Free Labor in Early America.* Ithaca, NY: Cornell University Press, 2011.

Dower, John. *War without Mercy: Race and Power in the Pacific War.* New York: Pantheon, 1986.

Drakulić, Slavenka. *They Would Never Hurt a Fly: War Criminals on Trial in The Hague.* New York: Viking, 2004.

Dynner, Glenn. *Yankel's Tavern: Jews, Liquor, and Life in the Kingdom of Poland.* Oxford: Oxford University Press, 2014.

Earl, Hilary. *The Nuremberg SS-Einsatzgruppen Trial, 1945–1948.* Cambridge: Cambridge University Press, 2009.

Ehrenburg, Ilya. *Russia at War.* London: Hamish Hamilton, 1943.

Ehrenburg, Ilya, and Vasily Grossman, eds. *The Black Book.* Translated by John Glad and James S. Levine. New York: Holocaust Publications, 1981.

Eichmann, Adolf. *Götzen: Die Autobiographie von Adolf Eichmann.* Edited by Raphael Ben Nescher. Berlin: Metropol, 2016.

Eliach, Yaffa. *Hasidic Tales of the Holocaust.* New York: Oxford University Press, 1982.

Epstein, Catherine. *Model Nazi: Arthur Greiser and the Occupation of Western Poland.* Oxford: Oxford University Press, 2010.

Evans, Esther Sarah. "Neidenburg." Destroyed German Synagogues and Communities, http://germansynagogues.com/index.php/synagogues-and-communities.

Evans, Richard J. "A Crass and Dangerously Inaccurate Account." Review of *Blitzed: Drugs in the Third Reich,* by Norman Ohler. *Guardian,* November 16, 2016.

——, ed. *Kneipengespräche im Kaiserreich: Die Stimmungsberichte der Hamburger Politischen Polizei, 1892–1914.* Hamburg: Rowohlt, 1989.

Fackler, Guido. "Cultural Behavior and the Invention of Traditions: Music and Musical Practices in the Early Concentration Camps, 1933–6/7." *Journal of Contemporary History* 45, no. 3 (2010): 601–27.

Fahrenkrug, Hermann. "Alcohol and the State in Nazi Germany, 1933–1945." In *Drinking: Behavior and Belief in Modern History,* edited by Susanna Barrows and Robin Room, 315–34. Berkeley: University of California Press, 1991.

Fingarette, Herbert. *Heavy Drinking: The Myth of Alcoholism as a Disease.* Berkeley: University of California Press, 1988.

Flaschka, Monika J. "Race, Rape, and Gender in Nazi-Occupied Territories." PhD diss., Kent State University, 2009.

Flowers, R. Barri. *Murder, at the End of the Day and Night: A Study of Criminal Homicide Offenders, Victims, and Circumstances.* Springfield, IL: Charles C. Thomas, 2002.

Foger, Edith Eva. *The Choice: Embrace the Possible.* New York: Scribner, 2017.

Frei, Norbert, Thomas Grotum, Jan Parcer, Sybille Steinacher, and Bernd Wagner, eds. *Standort-und Kommandanturbefehle des Konzentrationslagers Auschwitz, 1940–1945.* Munich: K. G. Saur, 2000.

Freudenthal, Herbert. *Vereine in Hamburg: Ein Beitrag zur Geschichte und Volkskunde der Geselligkeit.* Hamburg: Museum für Hamburgische Geschichte, 1968.

Frevert, Ute. *A Nation in Barracks: Modern Germany, Military Conscription and Civil Society.* Translated by Andrew Boreham and Daniel Brückenhaus. Oxford: Berg, 2004.

Friedländer, Saul. *Memory, History, and the Extermination of the Jews of Europe.* Bloomington: Indiana University Press, 1993.

Friedman, Tuviah, ed. *Schupo-Kriegsverbrecher in Kolomea.* Vienna: Jewish Historical Documentation Center, 1990.

Fritz, Stephen. *Frontsoldaten: The German Soldier in World War II.* Lexington: University Press of Kentucky, 1995.

Fromm, Bella. *Blood and Banquets: A Berlin Social Diary.* New York: Harper and Brothers, 1942.

Fuchs, Karl. *Your Loyal and Loving Son: The Letters of Tank Gunner Karl Fuchs, 1937–1941.* Edited and translated by Horst Fuchs Richardson. Washington, DC: Brassey's, 1987.

Gangulee, N. *The Mind and Face of Nazi Germany.* London: Butler & Tanner, 1942.

Geldmacher, Thomas. *"Wir Wiener waren ja bei der Bevölkerung beliebt": Österreichische Schutzpolizisten und die Judenvernichtung in Ostgalizien, 1941–1945.* Vienna: Mandelbaum Verlag, 2002.

Gerhardt, Uta, and Thomas Karlauf, eds. *The Night of Broken Glass: Eyewitness Accounts of Kristallnacht.* Translated by Robert Simmons and Nick Somers. Cambridge: Polity, 2012.

Gerlach, Christian. *Kalkulierte Morde: Die deutsche Wirtschafts- und Vernichtungspolitik in Weißrußland 1941 bis 1944.* Hamburg: Hamburger Edition, 1999.

Gertjejanssen, Wendy Jo. "Victims, Heroes, Survivors: Sexual Survivors on the Eastern Front during World War II." PhD diss., University of Minnesota, 2004.

Gerwarth, Robert. *Hitler's Hangman: The Life of Heydrich.* New Haven, CT: Yale University Press, 2011.

Gilbert Murdock, Catherine. *Domesticating Drink: Women, Men, and Alcohol in America.* Baltimore: Johns Hopkins University Press, 1998.

Giles, Geoffrey. "The Denial of Homosexuality: Same-Sex Incidents in Himmler's SS and Police." *Journal of the History of Sexuality* 11, nos. 1–2 (2002): 256–90.

——. "Student Drinking in the Third Reich: Academic Tradition and the Nazi Revolution." In *Drinking: Behavior and Belief in Modern History,* edited by Susanna Barrows and Robin Room, 132–43. Berkeley: University of California Press, 1991.

Gisevius, Hans Bernd. *To the Bitter End.* Translated by Richard and Clara Winston. Boston: Houghton Mifflin, 1947.

Goetz, Rebecca Anne. *The Baptism of Early Virginia: How Christianity Created Race.* Baltimore: Johns Hopkins University Press, 2012.

Golczewski, Frank. "Die Kollaboration in der Ukraine." In *Kooperation und Verbrechen: Formen der "Kooperation" im östlichen Europa 1939–1945,* edited by Christoph Dieckmann, 151–82. Göttingen: Wallstein, 2003.

Golovchansky, Anatoly, Valentin Osipov, Anatoly Prokopenko, Ute Daniel, and Jürgen Reulecke, eds. *"Ich will raus aus diesem Wahnsinn": Deutsche Briefe von der Ostfront, 1941–1945.* Wuppertal: Peter Hammer Verlag, 1991.

Gordin, Aba, and M. Gelbart, eds. *Memorial (Yizkor) Book of the Jewish Community of Ostrowo Mazowiecka.* New York: JewishGen, 2013.

Gourevitch, Philip. *We Wish to Inform You That Tomorrow We Will Be Killed with Our Families: Stories from Rwanda.* New York: Farrar, Straus and Giroux, 1998.

Grabowski, Jan. *Hunt for the Jews: Betrayal and Murder in German-Occupied Poland.* Bloomington: Indiana University Press, 2013.

Gritzbach, Erich, ed. *Hermann Göring: Reden und Aufsätze.* Munich: Zentralverlag der NSDAP, 1939.

Gross, Jan Tomasz, with Irena Grudzinska Gross. *Golden Harvest: Events at the Periphery of the Holocaust.* Oxford: Oxford University Press, 2012.

——. *Neighbors: The Destruction of the Jewish Community in Jedwabne, Poland.* Princeton, NJ: Princeton University Press, 2001.

Grossman, Vasily. *A Writer at War: A Soviet Journalist with the Red Army, 1941–1945.* Edited and translated by Antony Beevor and Luba Vinogradova. New York: Vintage Books, 2005.

Grunberger, Richard. *The 12-Year Reich: A Social History of Nazi Germany.* New York: Holt, Rinehart and Winston, 1971.

Gruner, Wolf. "'Worse Than Vandals': The Mass Destruction of Jewish Homes and Jewish Responses during the 1938 Pogrom." In *New Perspectives on Kristallnacht: After 80 Years, the Nazi Pogrom in Global Comparison,* edited by Wolf Gruner, 25–49. West Lafayette, IN: Purdue University Press, 2019.

Grupe, Friedrich. *Jahrgang 1916: Die Fahne war mehr als der Tod.* Munich: Universitas Verlag, 1989.

Guderian, Heinz. *Panzer Leader.* Translated by Constantine Fitzgibbon. Boston: Da Capo, 1996.

Gumbel, Emil. *Vier Jahre politischer Mord.* Berlin: Verlag der neuen Gesellschaft, 1922.

Gutmann, Martin R. *Building a Nazi Europe: The SS's Germanic Volunteers.* Cambridge: Cambridge University Press, 2017.

Hager, Erich. *The War Diaries of a Panzer Soldier.* Edited by David Garden. Atglen, PA: Schiffer Military History, 2010.

Halbmayr, Brigitte. "Sexualized Violence against Women during Nazi 'Racial' Persecution." In *Sexual Violence against Women during the Holocaust,* edited by Sonja Hedgepeth and Rochelle Saidel, 29–44. Hanover, NH: University Press of New England, 2010.

Hämäläinen, Pekka. *The Comanche Empire.* New Haven, CT: Yale University Press, 2008.

Hamill, Pete. *A Drinking Life: A Memoir.* Boston: Little, Brown, 1994.

Harrison, Simon. *Dark Trophies: Hunting and the Enemy Body in Modern War.* New York: Berghahn, 2012.

Hartmann, Christian. *Wehrmacht im Ostkrieg: Front und militärisches Hinterland 1941/42.* Munich: R. Oldenbourg, 2009.

Harvey, Elizabeth. *Women and the Nazi East: Agents and Witnesses of Germanization.* New Haven, CT: Yale University Press, 2003.

Hatzfeld, Jean. *Machete Season: The Killers in Rwanda Speak.* Translated by Linda Coverdale. New York: Farrar, Straus and Giroux, 2005.

Haynes, Stephen R. "Ordinary Masculinity: Gender Analysis and Holocaust Scholarship." In *Genocide and Gender in the Twentieth Century: A Comparative Survey,* edited by Amy E. Randall, 165–88. London: Bloomsbury, 2015.

"Heavy Drinking Rewires Brain, Increasing Susceptibility to Anxiety Problems." *Science News,* September 2, 2012. https://www.sciencedaily.com/releases/2012/09/12090214 3143.htm.

Heck, Alfons. *A Child of Hitler: Germany in the Days When God Wore a Swastika.* Phoenix: Renaissance House, 1985.

Hedgepeth, Sonja, and Rochelle G. Saidel, eds. *Sexual Violence against Jewish Women during the Holocaust.* Hanover, NH: University Press of New England, 2010.

Helm, Sarah. *Ravensbrück: Life and Death in Hitler's Concentration Camp for Women.* New York: Doubleday, 2014.

Herzog, Dagmar. "Hitler's Little Helper: A History of Rampant Drug Use under the Nazis." Review of *Blitzed: Drugs in the Third Reich,* by Norman Ohler. *New York Times,* March 27, 2017.

——. "Hubris and Hypocrisy, Incitement and Disavowal: Sexuality and German Fascism." *Journal of the History of Sexuality* 11, nos. 1–2 (2002): 3–21.

——. *Sex after Fascism: Memory and Morality in Twentieth-Century Germany.* Princeton, NJ: Princeton University Press, 2005.

Hilberg, Raul. *The Destruction of the European Jews.* Vol. 3. 3rd ed. New Haven, CT: Yale University Press, 2003.

Hoffmann, Peter. *Hitler's Personal Security: Protecting the Führer, 1921–1945.* New York: Da Capo, 2000.

Hoffmann-Curtius, Kathrin. "Trophäen und Amulette: Die Fotografien von Wehrmachts- und SS-Verbrechen in den Brieftaschen der Soldaten." *Fotogeschichte* 20, no. 78 (2000): 63–76.

Höhne, Heinz. *The Order of the Death's Head: The Story of Hitler's SS.* Translated by Richard Barry. New York: Coward-McCann, 1969.

Horne, John, and Alan Kramer. "German 'Atrocities' and Franco-German Opinion, 1914: The Evidence of German Soldiers' Diaries." *Journal of Modern History* 66, no. 1 (1994): 1–33.

Hörner, Helmut. *A German Odyssey: The Journal of a German Prisoner of War.* Translated by Allen Kent Powell. Golden, CO: Fulcrum, 1991.

Höss, Rudolph. *Death Dealer: The Memoirs of the SS Kommandant at Auschwitz.* Edited by Steven Paskuly and translated by Andrew Pollinger. New York: Da Capo, 1996.

Hull, Isabel. *Absolute Destruction: Military Culture and the Practices of War in Imperial Germany.* Ithaca, NY: Cornell University Press, 2005.

Hunt, Geoffrey P., and Karen Joe Laidler. "Alcohol and Violence in the Lives of Gang Members." *Alcohol Research and Health* 25, no. 1 (2001): 66–71.

Hürter, Johannes, ed. *Notizen aus dem Vernichtungskrieg: Die Ostfront 1941/42 in den Aufzeichnungen des Generals Heinrici.* Darmstadt: Wissenschaftliche Buchgesellschaft, 2016.

Ilibagiza, Immaculée, with Steve Irwin. *Left to Tell: Discovering God in the Rwandan Holocaust.* Carlsbad, CA: Hay House, 2006.

Ingrao, Christian. *The SS Dirlewanger Brigade: The History of the Black Hunters.* Translated by Phoebe Green. New York: Skyhorse, 2011.

Insel, Paul, R. Elaine Turner, and Don Ross. *Discovering Nutrition.* 3rd ed. Boston: Jones and Bartlett, 2010.

Isaacson, Judith Magyar. *Seed of Sarah: Memoirs of a Survivor.* Champaign: University of Illinois Press, 1989.

Jäger, Herbert. *Verbrechen unter totalitärer Herrschaft.* Frankfurt am Main: Suhrkamp, 1982.

Jani, Emilio. *My Voice Saved Me: Auschwitz 180046.* Milan: Centauro Editrice, 1961.

Jeffords, Susan. "Performative Masculinities, or, 'After a Few Times You Won't Be Afraid of Rape at All.'" *Discourse* 13, no. 2 (1991): 102–18.

Jewish Black Book Committee. *The Black Book: The Nazi Crime against the Jewish People.* New York: Duell, Sloan and Pearce, 1946.

Johnson, Eric, and Karl-Heinz Reuband, eds. *What We Knew: Terror, Mass Murder, and Everyday Life in Nazi Germany.* Cambridge, MA: Basic Books, 2005.

Jones, Mark. *Founding Weimar: Violence and the German Revolution, 1918–1919.* Cambridge: Cambridge University Press, 2017.

Jones, Nigel H. *A Brief History of the Birth of the Nazis: How the Freikorps Blazed a Trail for Hitler.* New York: Carroll and Graf, 2004.

Joshi, Vandana. *Gender and Power in the Third Reich: Female Denouncers and the Gestapo, 1933–1945.* New York: Palgrave Macmillan, 2003.

Jünger, Ernst. *In Stahlgewittern.* E. S. Mittler und Sohn, 1920.

Kahn, Leo. *No Time to Mourn: A True Story of a Jewish Partisan Fighter.* Vancouver, Canada: Laurelton, 1978.

Kaiser, Wolf, Thomas Köhler, and Elke Gryglewski. *"Nicht durch formale Schranken gehemmt": Die deutsche Polizei im Nationalsozialismus.* Bonn: Bundeszentrale für politische Bildung, 2012.

Kangeris, Kārlis. "'Closed' Units of Latvian Police—*Lettische Schutzmannschafts-Bataillone:* Research Issues and Pre-History." In *The Hidden and Forbidden History of Latvia under Soviet and Nazi Occupations, 1940–1991,* edited by Valters Nollendorfs and Erwin Oberländer, 104–21. Riga: Institute of the History of Latvia, 2005.

Kaplan, Chaim A. *The Warsaw Diary of Chaim A. Kaplan.* Edited and translated by Abraham I. Katsh. Rev. ed. New York: Collier Books, 1973.

Karay, Felicja. *Death Comes in Yellow: Skarżysko-Kamienna Slave Labor Camp*. Translated by Sara Kitai. Amsterdam: Harwood Academic, 1996.

Karski, Jan. *Story of a Secret State*. Boston: Houghton Mifflin, 1944.

Kater, Michael H. *The Twisted Muse: Musicians and Their Music in the Third Reich*. Oxford: Oxford University Press, 1997.

Kay, Alex J. *The Making of an SS Killer: The Life of Colonel Alfred Filbert, 1905–1990*. Cambridge: Cambridge University Press, 2016.

Keller, Sven. *Volksgemeinschaft am Ende: Gesellschaft und Gewalt, 1944–45*. Munich: Oldenbourg Verlag, 2013.

Kellner, Friedrich. *My Opposition: The Diary of Friedrich Kellner—a German against the Third Reich*. Translated and edited by Robert Scott Kellner. Cambridge: Cambridge University Press, 2018.

Kempowski, Walter. *Swan Song 1945*. Translated by Shaun Whiteside. New York: W. W. Norton, 2014.

Kern, Erich. *Der große Rausch: Rußlandfeldzug 1941–1945*. Druffel & Vowinckel Verlag, 2008.

Kershaw, Ian. *Hitler: 1889–1936 Hubris*. New York: W. W. Norton, 1998.

———. *Hitler: 1936–1945, Nemesis*. New York: W. W. Norton, 2000.

Kertzer, David. *Ritual, Politics, and Power*. New Haven, CT: Yale University Press, 1988.

Kielar, Wieslaw. *Anus Mundi: 1500 Days in Auschwitz/Birkenau*. Translated by Susanne Flatauer. New York: Times Books, 1980.

Klee, Ernst, Willi Dressen, and Volker Riess, eds. *"The Good Old Days": The Holocaust as Seen by Its Perpetrators and Bystanders*. Translated by Deborah Burnstone. New York: Free Press, 1991.

Klein, Thomas, ed. *Die Lageberichte der Geheimen Staatspolizei über die Provinz Hessen Nassau, 1933–1936*. Vol 1. Cologne: Böhlau Verlag, 1986.

Klemp, Stefan. *"Aktion Erntefest": Mit Musik in den Tod, Rekonstruktion eines Massenmordes*. Münster: Stadt Münster, 2013.

———. *Freispruch für das "Mord Bataillon": Die NS-Ordnungspolizei und die Nachkriegsjustiz*. Münster: Lit Verlag, 1998.

———. *"Nicht ermittelt": Polizeibataillone und die Nachkriegsjustiz*. Essen: Klartext Verlag, 2011.

Klemperer, Victor. *I Will Bear Witness: A Diary of the Nazi Years*. Translated by Martin Chalmers. New York: Modern Library, 2001.

———. *The Language of the Third Reich: LTI-Lingua Tertii Imperii*. Translated by Martin Brady. London: Athlone, 2000.

Klukowski, Zygmunt. *Diary from the Years of Occupation, 1939–44*. Translated by George Klukowski. Urbana: University of Illinois Press, 1993.

Knoke, Heinz. *I Flew for the Führer: The Story of a German Fighter Pilot*. Translated by John Ewing. New York: Henry Holt, 1953.

Knotterus, J. David, Jean Van Delinder, and Jennifer Edwards. "Strategic Ritualization of Power: Nazi Germany, the Orange Order, and Native Americans." In *Ritual as a Missing Link: Sociology, Structural Ritualization Theory and Research*, edited by J. David Knotterus, 73–106. Boulder, CO: Paradigm, 2011.

Kobylyanskiy, Isaak. *From Stalingrad to Pillau: A Red Army Artillery Officer Remembers the Great Patriotic War*. Edited by Stuart Britton. Lawrence: University Press of Kansas, 2008.

Kogon, Eugen. *The Theory and Practice of Hell: The German Concentration Camps and the System behind Them*. Rev. ed. New York: Farrar, Straus and Giroux, 2006.

Koonz, Claudia. *Mothers in the Fatherland: Women, the Family, and Nazi Politics*. New York: St. Martin's, 1987.

Kopstein, Jeffrey S., and Jason Wittenberg. *Intimate Violence: Anti-Jewish Pogroms on the Eve of the Holocaust*. Ithaca, NY: Cornell University Press, 2018.

Kravchinsky, Yakov. "How We Joined the Partisans." In *We Remember Lest the World Forget: Memories of the Minsk Ghetto*, edited by Hilda Bronstein and Bett Demby, 76–81. New York: JewishGen, 2018.

Krebs, Albert. *The Infancy of Nazism: The Memoirs of Ex-Gauleiter Albert Krebs, 1923–1933*. Edited and translated by William Sheridan Allen. New York: New Viewpoints, 1976.

Krondorfer, Björn, and Edward Westermann. "Soldiering: Men." In *Gender: War*, edited by Andrea Petö, 19–35. New York: Macmillan, 2017.

Kühne, Thomas. *Belonging and Genocide: Hitler's Community, 1918–1945*. New Haven, CT: Yale University Press, 2013.

——. "The Pleasure of Terror." In *Pleasure and Power in Nazi Germany*, edited by Pamela Swett, Corey Ross, and Fabrice d'Almeida, 234–55. New York: Palgrave Macmillan, 2011.

——. *The Rise and Fall of Comradeship: Hitler's Soldiers, Male Bonding and Mass Violence in the Twentieth Century*. Cambridge: Cambridge University Press, 2017.

Kurzem, Mark. *The Mascot: Unraveling the Mystery of My Father's Nazi Boyhood*. New York: Plume, 2007.

Landberg, Jonas, and Thor Norstrom. "Alcohol and Homicide in Russia and the United States: A Comparative Analysis." *Journal of Studies on Alcohol and Drugs* 72, no. 5 (2011): 723–30.

Langa, Malose, and Gillian Eagle. "The Intractability of Militarised Masculinity: A Case Study of Former Self-Defence Unit Members in the Kathorus Area, South Africa." *South African Journal of Psychology* 38, no. 1 (2008): 152–75.

Langbein, Hermann. *Der Auschwitz-Prozeß: Eine Dokumentation*. Vols. 1 and 2. Frankfurt am Main: Verlag Neue Kritik, 1995.

——. *People in Auschwitz*. Chapel Hill: University of North Carolina Press, 2004.

Lange, Johannes. "The Proud Executioner: Pride and the Psychology of Genocide." In *Emotions and Mass Atrocity: Philosophical and Theoretical Explorations*, edited by Thomas Brudholm and Johannes Lange, 64–80. Cambridge: Cambridge University Press, 2018.

Langer, Lawrence. *Holocaust Testimonies: The Ruins of Memory*. New Haven, CT: Yale University Press, 1991.

Langerbein, Helmut. *Hitler's Death Squads: The Logic of Mass Murder*. College Station: Texas A&M University Press, 2004.

Large, David Clay. *Where Ghosts Walked: Munich's Road to the Third Reich*. New York: W. W. Norton, 1997.

Lehnstaedt, Stephan. "The Minsk Experience: German Occupiers and Everyday Life in the Capital of Belarus." In *Nazi Policy on the Eastern Front, 1941: Total War, Genocide, and Radicalization*, edited by Alex J. Kay, Jeff Rutherford, and David Stahel, 240–66. Rochester, NY: University of Rochester Press, 2012.

———. *Occupation in the East: The Daily Lives of German Occupiers in Warsaw and Minsk, 1939–1944*. Translated by dbmedia. New York: Berghahn, 2016.

Lemle, Russell, and Marc E. Mishkind. "Alcohol and Masculinity." *Journal of Substance Abuse Treatment* 6, no. 4 (1989): 213–22.

Lengyel, Olga. *Five Chimneys*. Chicago: Academy Chicago, 1995.

Lerner, Gerda. *The Creation of Patriarchy*. New York: Oxford University Press, 1986.

Leßmann, Peter. *Die preußische Schutzpolizei in der Weimarer Republik: Streifendienst und Straßenkampf*. Düsseldorf: Droste Verlag, 1989.

Levenkron, Nomi. "'Prostitution,' Rape, and Sexual Slavery during World War II." In *Sexual Violence against Jewish Women during the Holocaust*, edited by Sonja M. Hedgepeth and Rochelle G. Saidel, 13–28. Hanover, NH: University Press of New England, 2010.

Levi, Primo. *The Complete Works of Primo Levi*. Vol. 3, *The Drowned and the Saved*. Translated by Michael Moore. New York: Liveright, 2015.

Levy, Alan. *The Wiesenthal File*. Grand Rapids, MI: William B. Eerdmans, 1993.

Levy-Hass, Hanna. *Inside Belsen*. Translated by Ronald Taylor. Sussex, NJ: Harvester, 1982.

Lewy, Guenter. *Perpetrators: The World of the Holocaust Killers*. Oxford: Oxford University Press, 2017.

Lewy, Jonathan. "A Sober Reich? Alcohol and Tobacco Use in Nazi Germany." *Substance Use and Misuse* 41, no. 8 (2006): 1179–95.

Lieb, Peter. *Konventioneller Krieg oder NS-Weltanschauungskrieg? Kriegführung und Partisanenbekämpfung in Frankreich 1943/44*. Munich: Oldenbourg Wissenschaftsverlag 2007.

Lifton, Robert J. *The Nazi Doctors: Medical Killing and the Psychology of Genocide*. New York: Basic Books, 1986.

Longerich, Peter. *Die braunen Bataillone: Geschichte der SA*. Munich: C. H. Beck, 1989.

———. *Heinrich Himmler*. Translated by Jeremy Noakes and Lesley Sharpe. Oxford: Oxford University Press, 2011.

Love, Nancy S. *Trendy Fascism: White Power Music and the Future of Democracy*. Albany: SUNY Press, 2016.

Lower, Wendy. "'Anticipatory Obedience' and the Nazi Implementation of the Holocaust in the Ukraine: A Case Study of Central and Peripheral Forces in the Generalbezirk Zhytomyr, 1941–1944." *Holocaust and Genocide Studies* 16, no. 1 (2002): 1–21.

———. *The Diary of Samuel Golfard and the Holocaust in Galicia*. Lanham, MD: Alta Mira, 2011.

———. *Hitler's Furies: German Women in the Nazi Killing Fields*. Boston: Houghton Mifflin Harcourt, 2013.

Mailänder, Elissa. *Female SS Guards and Workaday Violence: The Majdanek Concentration Camp, 1942–1944.* Translated by Patricia Szobar. East Lansing: Michigan State University Press, 2015.

——. "Making Sense of a Rape Photograph: Sexual Violence as Social Performance on the Eastern Front, 1939–1944." *Journal of the History of Sexuality* 26, no. 3 (2017): 489–520.

Majstorović, Vojin. "Ivan Goes Abroad: The Red Army in the Balkans and Central Europe, 1944–1945." PhD diss., University of Toronto, 2017.

——. "Red Army Troops Encounter the Holocaust: Transnistria, Moldavia, Romania, Bulgaria, Yugoslavia, Hungary, and Austria, 1944–1945." *Holocaust and Genocide Studies* 32, no. 2 (2018): 249–71.

Mallmann, Klaus-Michael. "'Mensch, ich feiere heut' den tausendsten Genickschuß': Die Sicherheitspolizei und die Shoah in Westgalizien." In *Die Täter der Shoah: Fanatische Nationalsozialisten oder ganz normale Deutsche?*, edited by Gerhard Paul, 109–36. Göttingen: Wallstein Verlag, 2002.

Mallmann, Klaus-Michael, Andrej Angrick, Jürgen Matthäus, and Martin Cüppers, eds. *Die "Ereignismeldungen UdSSR" 1941: Dokumente der Einsatzgruppen in der Sowjetunion.* Vol. 1. Darmstadt: Wissenschaftliche Buchgesellschaft, 2011.

Mallmann, Klaus-Michael, Jochen Böhler, and Jürgen Matthäus. *Einsatzgruppen in Polen: Darstellung und Dokumentation.* Darmstadt: Wissenschaftliche Buchgesellschaft, 2008.

Mallmann, Klaus-Michael, Volker Rieß, and Wolfram Pyta, eds. *Deutscher Osten 1939–1945: Der Weltanschauungskrieg in Photos and Texten.* Darmstadt: Wissenschaftliche Buchgesellschaft, 2003.

Mangan, J. A., and Callum McKenzie. *Militarism, Hunting, Imperialism: "Blooding" the Martial Male.* London: Routledge, 2010.

Manoschek, Walter, ed. *Der Fall Rechnitz: Das Massaker an Juden im März 1945.* Vienna: Wilhelm Braumüller Universitäts-Verlagsbuchhandlung, 2009.

——, ed. *"Es gibt nur eines für das Judentum: Vernichtung": Das Judenbild in deutschen Soldatenbriefen, 1939–1944.* Hamburg: Hamburger Edition, 1995.

——. *"Serbien ist Judenfrei": Militärische Besatzungspolitik und Judenvernichtung in Serbien, 1941/42.* Munich: R. Oldenbourg, 1993.

Manz, Bruno. *A Mind in Prison: The Memoir of a Son and a Soldier of the Third Reich.* Washington, DC: Brassey's, 2000.

Margolis, Rachel. *A Partisan from Vilna.* Translated by F. Jackson Piotrow. Brighton, MA: Academic Studies, 2010.

Marsałek, Jósef. *Majdanek: The Concentration Camp in Lublin.* Warsaw: Interpress, 1986.

Martin, Scott C., ed. *The Sage Encyclopedia of Alcohol: Social, Cultural, and Historical Perspectives.* Los Angeles: Sage, 2015.

Maschmann, Melita. *Account Rendered: A Dossier on My Former Self.* Translated by Geoffrey Strachan. London: Abelard-Schuman, 1964.

Matthäus, Jürgen. "An vorderster Front: Voraussetzungen für die Beteiligung der Ordnungspolizei an der Shoah." In *Die Täter der Shoah: Fanatische Nationalsozialisten oder ganz normale Deutsche?*, edited by Gerhard Paul, 137–66. Göttingen: Wallstein Verlag, 2002.

———. "Georg Heuser—Routinier des sicherheitspolizeilichen Osteinsatzes." In *Karrieren der Gewalt: Nationalsozialistische Täterbiographien*, edited by Klaus-Michael Mallmann and Gerhard Paul, 115–25. Darmstadt: Wissenschaftliche Buchgesellschaft, 2013.

———. "What about the 'Ordinary Men'? The German Order Police and the Holocaust in the Occupied Soviet Union." *Holocaust and Genocide Studies* 10, no. 2 (1996): 134–50.

Matthäus, Jürgen, Jochen Böhler, and Klaus-Michael Mallmann. *War, Pacification, and Mass Murder, 1939: The Einsatzgruppen in Poland.* Lanham, MD: Rowman & Littlefield, 2014.

Matthäus, Jürgen, with Emil Kerenji, eds. *Jewish Responses to Persecution, 1933–1946: A Source Reader.* New York: Rowman & Littlefield, 2017.

Matthäus, Jürgen, Konrad Kwiet, Jürgen Förster, and Richard Breitman. *Ausbildungsziel Judenmord? "Weltanschauliche Erziehung" von SS, Polizei, Waffen-SS im Rahmen der Endlösung.* Frankfurt am Main: Fischer Taschenbuch, 2003.

Maubach, Franka. *Die Stellung halten: Kriegserfahrungen und Lebensgeschichten von Wehrmachtshelferinnen.* Göttingen: Vandenhoek und Ruprecht, 2009.

McManus, John C. *Deadly Sky: The American Combat Airman in World War II.* New York: NAL Caliber, 2016.

Megargee, Geoffrey P. *War of Annihilation: Combat and Genocide on the Eastern Front, 1941.* Lanham, MD: Rowman & Littlefield, 2006.

Mellström, Ulf. "Changing Affective Economies of Masculine Machineries and Military Masculinities? From Ernst Jünger to Shannen Rossmiller." *Masculinities and Social Change* 2, no. 1 (2012): 1–19.

Mermelstein, Mel. *By Bread Alone: The Story of A-4685.* Huntington Beach, CA: Auschwitz Study Foundation, 1979.

Merridale, Catherine. *Ivan's War: Life and Death in the Red Army, 1939–1945.* New York: Metropolitan Books, 2006.

Meyer, Gerd, ed. *Wehrmachtsverbrechen: Dokumente aus sowjetischen Archiven.* Cologne: PapyRossa, 1997.

Miller, Peter, Samantha Wells, Rhianna Hobbs, Lucy Zinkiewicz, Ashlee Curtis, and Kathryn Graham. "Alcohol, Masculinity, Honour and Male Barroom Aggression in an Australian Sample." *Drug and Alcohol Review* 33, no. 2 (2014): 136–43.

Miller, William Ian. *Humiliation: And Other Essays on Honor, Social Discomfort, and Violence.* Ithaca, NY: Cornell University Press, 1993.

Mishell, William W. *Kaddish for Kovno: Life and Death in a Lithuanian Ghetto, 1941–1945.* Chicago: Chicago Review, 1988.

Młynarczyk, Jacek Andrzej, Leonid Rein, Andrii Bolianovskyi, and Oleg Romanko. "Eastern Europe: Belarusian Auxiliaries, Ukrainian Waffen-SS Soldiers and the Special Case of the Polish 'Blue Police.'" In *The Waffen-SS: A European History*, edited by Jochen Böhler and Robert Gerwarth, 165–208. Oxford: Oxford University Press, 2017.

Moore, Jacqueline M. *Cow Boys and Cattle Men: Class and Masculinities on the Texas Frontier, 1865–1900*. New York: NYU Press, 2010.

Morris, Madeline. "By Force of Arms: Rape, War, and Military Culture." *Duke Law Journal* 45, no. 4 (1996): 651–781.

Mosse, George L. *The Culture of Western Europe: The Nineteenth and Twentieth Centuries*. 3rd ed. New York: Routledge, 1988.

——. *Fallen Soldiers: Reshaping the Memory of the World Wars*. Oxford: Oxford University Press, 1990.

——. *Nazi Culture: Intellectual, Cultural, and Social Life in the Third Reich*. New York: Grosset & Dunlap, 1966.

Mühlenberg, Jutta. *Das SS-Helferinnenkorps: Ausbildung, Einsatz und Entnazifizierung der weiblichen Angehörigen der Waffen-SS 1942–1949*. Hamburg: Hamburger Edition, 2010.

Mühlhäuser, Regina. "Between 'Racial Awarness' and Fantasies of Potency: Nazi Sexual Politics in the Occupied Territories of the Soviet Union, 1942–1945." In *Brutality and Desire: War and Sexuality in Europe's Twentieth Century*, edited by Dagmar Herzog, 197–220. New York: Palgrave Macmillan, 2009.

——. *Eroberungen: Sexuelle Gewalttaten und intime Beziehungen deutscher Soldaten in der Sowjetunion, 1941–1945*. Hamburg: Hamburger Edition, 2010.

——. "Sexual Violence and the Holocaust." In *Gender: War*, edited by Andrea Petö, 101–16. New York: Macmillan, 2017.

Mullen, Kenneth, Jonathan Watson, Jan Swift, and David Black. "Young Men, Masculinity and Alcohol." *Drugs: Education, Prevention and Policy* 14, no. 2 (2007): 151–65.

Müller, Filip. *Eyewitness Auschwitz: Three Years in the Gas Chamber*. Translated by Susanne Flatauer. Chicago: Ivan R. Dee, 1999.

Müller, Sven Oliver. *Deutsche Soldaten und ihre Feinde: Nationalismus an Front und Heimatfront im Zweiten Weltkrieg*. Frankfurt am Main: S. Fischer, 2007.

Müller, Yves. "Männlichkeit und Gewalt in der SA am Beispiel der 'Köpenicker Blutwoche.'" In *SA-Terror als Herrschaftssicherung*, edited by Stefan Hördler, 130–46. Berlin: Metropol Verlag, 2013.

Murdoch, Brian. *Fighting Songs and Warring Words: Popular Lyrics of Two World Wars*. London: Routledge, 1990.

Musmanno, Michael A. *The Eichmann Kommandos*. Philadelphia: Macrae Smith, 1961.

Myrick, Inge. *The Other Side! The Life Journey of a Young Girl through Nazi Germany*. Phoenix: Acacia, 2006.

Neitzel, Sönke, ed. *Tapping Hitler's Generals: Transcripts of Secret Conversations, 1942–1945*. Translated by Geoffrey Brooks. London: Frontline Books, 2007.

Neitzel, Sönke, and Harald Welzer. *Soldaten: On Fighting, Killing, and Dying*. Translated by Jefferson Chase. New York: Alfred A. Knopf, 2012.

Neurath, Paul M. "Social Life in the German Concentration Camps Dachau and Buchenwald." PhD diss., Columbia University, 1951.

Noakes, Jeremy, and Geoffrey Pridham, eds. *Nazism 1919–1945*. Vol. 1, *The Rise to Power, 1919–1934*. Exeter: Exeter University Press, 1998.

Nyiszli, Miklos. *Auschwitz: A Doctor's Eyewitness Account.* Translated by Tibére Kremer and Richard Seaver. New York: Arcade, 1993.

Ohler, Norman. *Blitzed: Drugs in the Third Reich.* Translated by Shaun Whitside. New York: Mariner Books, 2016.

Orth, Karin. "Egon Zill—ein typischer Vertreter der Konzentrationslager-SS." In *Karrieren der Gewalt: Nationalsozialistische Täterbiographien,* edited by Klaus-Michael Mallmann and Gerhard Paul, 264–73. Darmstadt: Wissenschaftliche Buchgesellschaft, 2004.

Padfield, Peter. *Himmler: Reichsführer-SS.* New York: Henry Holt, 1990.

Palshikar, Sanjay. "Understanding Humiliation." *Economic and Political Weekly* 40, no. 51 (2005): 5428–32.

Parrott, Dominic J., and Amos Zeichner. "Effects of Alcohol and Trait Anger on Physical Aggression in Men." *Journal of Studies on Alcohol* 63, no. 2 (2002): 196–204.

Patel, Kiran Klaus. *Soldiers of Labor: Labor Service in Nazi Germany and New Deal America, 1933–1945.* Translated by Thomas Dunlap. Cambridge: Cambridge University Press, 2005.

Pawełczyńska, Anna. *Values and Violence in Auschwitz: A Sociological Study.* Translated by Catherine S. Leach. Berkeley: University of California Press, 1979.

Pawlicka-Nowak, Łucja, ed. *Chełmno Witnesses Speak.* Translated by Juliet Golden and Arkadiusz Kamiński. Łódź: Oficyna Bibliofilów, 2004.

Pemper, Mietek. *The Road to Rescue: The Untold Story of Schindler's List.* Translated by David Dollenmayer. New York: Other, 2005.

Peralta, Robert L. "College Alcohol Use and the Embodiment of Hegemonic Masculinity among European American Men." *Sex Roles* 56, nos. 11–12 (2007): 741–56.

Peralta, Robert L., Lori A. Tuttle, and Jennifer L. Steele. "At the Intersection of Interpersonal Violence, Masculinity, and Alcohol Use: The Experiences of Heterosexual Male Perpetrators of Intimate Partner Violence." *Violence against Women* 16, no. 4 (2010): 387–409.

Perechodnik, Calel. *Am I a Murderer? Testament of a Jewish Ghetto Policeman.* Edited and translated by Frank Fox. Boulder, CO: Westview, 1996.

Peukert, Detlev. *Inside Nazi Germany: Conformity, Opposition, and Racism in Everyday Life.* Translated by Richard Deveson. New Haven, CT: Yale University Press, 1987.

——. *The Weimar Republic: The Crisis of Classical Modernity.* Translated by Richard Deveson. New York: Hill & Wang, 1989.

Pieper, Hennig. *Fegelein's Horsemen and Genocidal Warfare: The SS Cavalry Brigade in the Soviet Union.* New York: Palgrave Macmillan, 2015.

Plant, Richard. *The Pink Triangle: The Nazi War against Homosexuals.* New York: Henry Holt, 1986.

Pohl, Dieter. "Ukrainische Hilfskräfte beim Mord an den Juden." In *Die Täter der Shoah: Fanatische Nationalsozialisten oder ganz normale Deutsche?,* edited by Gerhard Paul, 205–34. Göttingen: Wallstein Verlag, 2002.

Polk, Kenneth. "Males and Honor Contest Violence." *Homicide Studies* 3, no. 1 (1999): 6–29.

Proctor, Robert N. *The Nazi War on Cancer.* Princeton, NJ: Princeton University Press, 1999.

Prusin, Alexander V. "'Fascist Criminals to the Gallows!': The Holocaust and Soviet War Crimes Trials, December 1945–February 1946," *Holocaust and Genocide Studies* 17, no. 1 (2003): 1–30.

Radchenko, Yuri. "Accomplices to Extermination: Municipal Government and the Holocaust in Kharkiv, 1941–1942." *Holocaust and Genocide Studies* 27, no. 3 (2013): 443–63.

Rass, Christoph. *"Menschenmaterial": Deutsche Soldaten an der Ostfront, Innenansichten einer Infanteriedivision 1939–1945*. Paderborn: F. Schöningh, 2003.

Rauch, Georg. *Unlikely Warrior: A Jewish Soldier in Hitler's Army*. New York: Farrar, Straus and Giroux, 2006.

Rauschning, Hermann. *The Voice of Destruction*. New York: G. P. Putnam's Sons, 1940.

Reese, Willy Peter. *"Mir selber seltsam fremd": Die Unmenschlichkeit des Krieges, Russland, 1941–44*. Edited by Stefan Schmitz. Munich: Claassen Verlag, 2003.

——. *A Stranger to Myself: The Inhumanity of War: Russia, 1941–1944*. Translated by Michael Hofmann. New York: Farrar, Straus and Giroux, 2005.

Reichardt, Sven. *Faschistische Kampfbünde: Gewalt und Gemeinschaft im italienischen Squadrismus und in der deutschen SA*. Cologne: Böhlau Verlag, 2002.

——. "Vergemeinschaft durch Gewalt: Der SA-'Mördersturm 33' in Berlin-Charlottenburg." In *SA-Terror als Herrschaftssicherung: "Köpenicker Blutwoche" und öffentliche Gewalt im Nationalsozialismus*, edited by Stefan Hördler, 110–29. Berlin: Metropol Verlag, 2013.

——. "Violence and Community: A Micro-study on Nazi Storm Troopers." *Central European History* 46, no. 2 (2013): 275–97.

Reifarth, Dieter, and Viktoria Schmidt-Linsenhoff. "Die Kamera der Henker: Fotografische Selbstzeugnisse des Naziterrors in Osteuropa." *Fotogeschichte* 3, no. 7 (1983): 57–71.

Rein, Leonid. "Local Collaboration in the Execution of the 'Final Solution' in Nazi-Occupied Belorussia." *Holocaust and Genocide Studies* 20, no. 3 (2006): 381–409.

Riedel, Dirk. "A 'Political Soldier' and 'Practitioner of Violence': The Concentration Camp Commandant Hans Loritz." *Journal of Contemporary History* 45, no. 3 (2010): 555–75.

Roberts, James S. *Drink, Temperance and the Working Class in Nineteenth-Century Germany*. Boston: George Allen & Unwin, 1984.

——. "The Tavern and Politics in the German Labor Movement, c. 1870–1914." In *Drinking: Behavior and Belief in Modern History*, edited by Susanna Barrows and Robin Room, 98–111. Berkeley: University of California Press, 1991.

Roehrs, Timothy, and Thomas Roth. "Sleep, Alcohol, and Quality of Life." In *Sleep and Quality of Life in Clinical Medicine*, edited by Joris L. Verster, S. R. Pandi-Perumal, and David L. Streiner, 333–40. Totowa, NJ: Humana, 2008.

Römer, Felix. *Comrades: The Wehrmacht from Within*. Translated by Alex J. Kay. Oxford: Oxford University Press, 2019.

Rose, Willi. *Shadows of War: A German Soldier's Lost Photographs of World War II*. Edited by Thomas Eller and Petra Bopp. New York: Harry N. Abrams, 2004.

Roseman, Mark. *The Wannsee Conference and the Final Solution: A Reconsideration.* London: Folio Society, 2012.

Rosenbaum, Heidi. *"Und trotzdem war's eine schöne Zeit": Kinderalltag im Nationalsozialismus.* Frankfurt am Main: Campus Verlag, 2014.

Rosenberg, Alfred. "Volksgesundheit und Männlichkeitsideal." *Der Schulungsbrief* 6, no. 2 (1939): 42–43.

Rossino, Alexander. *Hitler Strikes Poland: Blitzkrieg, Ideology, and Atrocity.* Lawrence: University Press of Kansas, 2003.

Roth, Markus. *Herrenmenschen: Die deutschen Kreishauptleute im besetzten Polen-Karrierewege, Herrschaftspraxis und Nachgeschichte.* Göttingen: Wallstein Verlag, 2009.

Rubenstein, Joshua, and Ilya Altman. *The Unknown Black Book: The Holocaust in the German-Occupied Soviet Territories.* Translated by Christopher Morris and Joshua Rubenstein. Bloomington: Indiana University Press in association with the United States Holocaust Memorial Museum, 2008.

Rushton, Colin. *Spectator in Hell: A British Soldier's Story of Imprisonment in Auschwitz.* Gretna, LA: Pelican, 2010.

Ryback, Timothy W. *Hitler's First Victims: The Quest for Justice.* New York: Alfred A. Knopf, 2014.

Sachslehner, Johannes. *Der Tod ist ein Meister aus Wien: Leben und Taten des Amon Leopold Göth.* Vienna: Styria, 2008.

Sajer, Guy. *The Forgotten Soldier.* Washington, DC: Brassey's, 1990.

Sakowicz, Kazimierz. *Ponary Diary, 1941–1943: A Bystander's Account of a Mass Murder.* Edited by Yitzhak Arad. New Haven, CT: Yale University Press, 2005.

Salton, George L., with Anna Salton Eisen. *The 23rd Psalm: A Holocaust Memoir.* Madison: University of Wisconsin Press, 2002.

Sanday, Peggy. *Fraternity Gang Rape: Sex, Brotherhood, and Privilege on Campus.* New York: NYU Press, 2007.

——. "Rape Free versus Rape Prone: How Culture Makes a Difference." In *Evolution, Gender, and Rape*, edited by Cheryl Brown Travis, 337–62. Cambridge, MA: MIT Press, 2003.

Sax, Boria. *Animals in the Third Reich: Pets, Scapegoats, and the Holocaust.* New York: Continuum, 2000.

Scarry, Elaine. *The Body in Pain: The Making and Unmaking of the World.* Oxford: Oxford University Press, 1985.

Schelvis, Jules. *Sobibor: A History of a Nazi Death Camp.* Translated by Karin Dixon. Oxford: Berg, 2007.

Schmorak, Dov B., ed. *Sieben sagen aus: Zeugen im Eichmann Prozess.* Berlin: Arani, 1962.

Schneider, Gertrude. *Reise in den Tod: Deutsche Juden in Riga 1941–1944.* Berlin: Edition Hentrich, 2006.

Schneider, Karl. *"Auswärts eingesetzt": Bremer Polizeibataillone und der Holocaust.* Essen: Klartext, 2011.

Schönstedt, Walter. *Auf der Flucht erschossen: Ein SA Roman 1933.* Paris: Éditions du Carrefour, 1934.

Schrad, Mark L. *Vodka Politics: Alcohol, Autocracy, and the Secret History of the Russian State.* Oxford: Oxford University Press, 2014.

Schulz, Miriam. "'Gornisht oyser verter'?! *Khurbn-shprakh* as a Mirror of the Dynamics of Violence in German-Occupied Eastern Europe." In *The Holocaust in the Borderlands: Interethnic Relations and the Dynamics of Violence in Occupied Eastern Europe*, edited by Gaëlle Fisher and Caroline Mezger, 185–210. Göttingen: Wallstein Verlag, 2019.

Schwarze, Johannes. *Die Bayerische Polizei, 1919–1933*. Munich: Kommissionsbuchhandlung R. Wöfle, 1977.

Sereny, Gitta. *Into That Darkness: An Examination of Conscience*. New York: Vintage Books, 1983.

Shepherd, Ben H. *Hitler's Soldiers: The German Army in the Third Reich*. New Haven, CT: Yale University Press, 2016.

——. *Terror in the Balkans: German Armies and Partisan Warfare*. Cambridge, MA: Harvard University Press, 2012.

Shik, Na'ama. "Sexual Abuse of Jewish Women in Auschwitz-Birkenau." In *Brutality and Desire: War and Sexuality in Europe's Twentieth Century*, edited by Dagmar Herzog, 221–46. Basingstoke, UK: Palgrave Macmillan, 2009.

Shirer, William L. *Berlin Diary: The Journal of a Foreign Correspondent, 1934–1941*. New York: Alfred A. Knopf, 1941.

Siemens, Daniel. *Stormtroopers: A New History of Hitler's Brownshirts*. New Haven, CT: Yale University Press, 2017.

Simms, Brendan. *Hitler: A Global Biography*. New York: Basic Books, 2019.

Sinnreich, Helene. "The Rape of Jewish Women during the Holocaust." In *Sexual Violence against Jewish Women during the Holocaust*, edited by Sonja M. Hedgepeth and Rochelle G. Saidel, 108–23. Hanover, NH: University Press of New England, 2010.

Smith, Bradley F., and Agnes F. Peterson, eds. *Heinrich Himmler Geheimreden 1933 bis 1945 und andere Ansprachen*. Frankfurt am Main: Propyläen Verlag, 1974.

Smith, Howard K. *Last Train from Berlin*. New York: Alfred A. Knopf, 1942.

Snyder, David R. *Sex Crimes under the Wehrmacht*. Lincoln: University of Nebraska Press, 2007.

Snyder, Timothy. *Bloodlands: Europe between Hitler and Stalin*. New York: Basic Books, 2010.

Spode, Hasso. *Die Macht der Trunkenheit: Kultur- und Sozialgeschichte des Alkohols in Deutschland*. Opladen: Leske and Budrich, 1993.

Stahel, David. *The Battle for Moscow*. Cambridge: Cambridge University Press, 2015.

Stang, Knut. *Kollaboration und Massenmord: Die Litauische Hilfspolizei, das Rollkommando Hamann und die Ermordung der litauischen Juden*. Frankfurt am Main: P. Lang, 1996.

Stangneth, Bettina. *Eichmann vor Jerusalem: Das unbehelligte Leben eines Massenmörders*. Zurich: Arche Verlag, 2011.

Stargardt, Nicholas. *The German War: A Nation under Arms, 1939–1945*. New York: Basic Books, 2015.

Steinkamp, Peter. "Zur Devianz-Problematik in der Wehrmacht: Alkohol- und Rauschmittelmissbrauch bei der Truppe." PhD diss., Albert-Ludwigs-Universität, Freiburg im Breisgau, 2008.

Steinweis, Alan E. *Kristallnacht: 1938.* Cambridge, MA: Harvard University Press, 2009.

Stern, Anne-Lise. "Ei Warum, Ei Darum: O Why." In *Claude Lanzmann's Shoah: Key Essays*, edited and translated by Stuart Liebman, 95–101. Oxford: Oxford University Press, 2007.

Stewart, Michael. "The Soldier's Life: Early Byzantine Masculinity and the Manliness of War." *Byzantina Symmeikta* 26, no. 1 (2016): 11–44.

Strasser, Robert, ed. *The Landmark Thucydides: A Comprehensive Guide to the Peloponnesian War.* New York: Free Press, 1996.

Szmajzner, Stanislaw. *Hell in Sobibor: The Tragedy of a Jewish Teenager.* Translated by Lucy de Lima Coimbra. N.p., 1979.

Tausk, Walter. *Breslauer Tagebuch, 1933–1940.* Berlin: Siedler Verlag, 1988.

Taylor, William B. *Drinking, Homicide, and Rebellion in Colonial Mexican Villages.* Stanford, CA: Stanford University Press, 1979.

Tec, Nechama. *Defiance.* Oxford: Oxford University Press, 2009.

——. *In the Lion's Den: The Life of Oswald Rufeisen.* Oxford: Oxford University Press, 1990.

Tessin, Georg, "Die Stäbe und Truppeneinheiten der Ordnungspolizei." In *Zur Geschichte der Ordnungspolizei*, edited by Hans-Joachim Neufeldt, Jürgen Huck, and Georg Tessin, 5–109. Koblenz: Schriften des Bundesarchivs, 1957.

Tewes, Ludger. *Frankreich in der Besatzungszeit 1940–1943: Die Sicht deutscher Augenzeugen.* Bonn: Bouvier Verlag, 1998.

Theweleit, Klaus. *Das Lachen der Täter: Breivik u.a. Psychogramm der Tötungslust.* St. Pölten, Austria: Residenz Verlag, 2015.

——. *Male Fantasies: Psychoanalyzing the White Terror.* Vol. 2. Translated by Erica Carter and Chris Turner. Minneapolis: University of Minnesota Press, 1989.

Timm, Annette. "Sex with a Purpose: Prostitution, Venereal Disease, and Militarized Masculinity in the Third Reich." *Journal of the History of Sexuality* 11, nos. 1–2 (2002): 223–55.

Tobias, Jim G. *"Ihr Gewissen war rein: Sie haben es nie benutzt": Die Verbrechen der Polizeikompanie Nürnberg.* Nuremberg: Antogo Verlag, 2005.

Torrie, Julie S. *German Soldiers and the Occupation of France, 1940–1944.* Cambridge: Cambridge University Press, 2018.

Tory, Avraham. *Surviving the Holocaust: The Kovno Ghetto Diary.* Translated by Jerzy Michalowicz. Cambridge, MA: Harvard University Press, 1990.

Umbach, Maiken. "Selfhood, Place, and Ideology in German Photo Albums, 1933–1945." *Central European History* 48, no. 3 (2015): 335–65.

Vigil, J. D., and J. M. Long. "Emic and Etic Perspectives on Gang Culture: The Chicano Case." In *Gangs in America*, edited by C. Ronald Huff, 55–68. Newbury Park, CA: Sage, 1990.

Vojta, Tomáš. "'A True Inferno Was Created There': Eradicating Traces of Mass Murder at Treblinka." In *Orte und Akteure im System der NS-Zwangslager*, edited by Michael Becker, Dennis Bock, and Henrike Illig, 198–222. Berlin: Metropol Verlag, 2015.

Von Joeden-Forgey, Elisa "Genocidal Masculinity." In *New Directions in Genocide Research*, edited by Adam Jones, 76–94. New York: Routledge, 2012.

Von Königs, Wolfhilde. *Kriegstagebuch einer jungen Nationalsozialistin: Die Aufzeichnungen Wolfhilde von Königs, 1939–1946*. Edited by Sven Keller. Oldenburg, Germany: De Gruyter, 2015.

Von Lang, Jochen. *Das Eichmann-Protokoll: Tonbandaufzeichnungen der israelischen Verhöre*. Munich: Severin und Siedler, 1982.

——. *Top Nazi: SS General Karl Wolff, the Man between Hitler and Himmler*. Translated by Mary Beth Friedrich. New York: Enigma, 2005.

Von Luck, Hans. *Panzer Commander: The Memoirs of Colonel Hans von Luck*. New York: Dell, 1989.

Von Salomon, Ernst. *The Outlaws*. Translated by Ian F. D. Morrow. London: Arktos, 2013.

Wachsmann, Nikolaus. *Hitler's Prisons: Legal Terror in Nazi Germany*. New Haven, CT: Yale University Press, 2004.

——. *KL: A History of the Nazi Concentration Camps*. New York: Farrar, Straus and Giroux, 2015.

Wackerfuss, Andrew. *Stormtrooper Families: Homosexuality and Community in the Early Nazi Movement*. New York: Harrington Park, 2015.

Walter, Dirk. *Antisemitische Kriminalität und Gewalt: Judenfeindschaft in der Weimarer Republik*. Bonn: J. H. W. Dietz Nachfolger, 1999.

Weigelt, Andreas, Klaus-Dieter Müller, Thomas Schaarschmidt, and Mike Schmeitzner, eds. *Todesurteile sowjetischer Militärtribunale gegen Deutsche (1944–1947): Eine historisch-biographische Studie*. Göttingen: Vandenhoeck & Ruprecht, 2015.

Weinberg, Felix. *Boy 30529: A Memoir*. London: Verso, 2013.

Weinberg, Gerhard, ed. *Hitler's Second Book: The Unpublished Sequel to Mein Kampf by Adolf Hitler*. Translated by Krista Smith. New York: Enigma, 2003.

Weliczker Wells, Leon. *The Janowska Road*. New York: Macmillan, 1963.

Werner, Frank. "'Hart müssen wir hier draussen sein': Soldatische Männlichkeit im Vernichtungskrieg, 1941–1944." *Geschichte und Gesellschaft* 34, no. 1 (2008): 5–40.

Werth, Alexander. *Moscow War Diary*. New York: Alfred A. Knopf, 1942.

Westermann, Edward B. "Drinking Rituals, Masculinity, and Mass Murder in Nazi Germany." *Central European History* 51, no. 3 (2018): 367–89.

——. *Hitler's Ostkrieg and the Indian Wars: Comparing Genocide and Conquest*. Norman: University of Oklahoma Press, 2016.

——. *Hitler's Police Battalions: Enforcing Racial Policy in the East*. Lawrence: University Press of Kansas, 2005.

——. "'Ordinary Men' or 'Ideological Soldiers'? Police Battalion 310 in Russia, 1942." *German Studies Review* 21, no. 1 (1998): 41–68.

——. "Stone Cold Killers or Drunk with Murder? Alcohol and Atrocity in the Holocaust." *Holocaust and Genocide Studies* 30, no. 1 (2016): 1–19.

——. "Tests of Manhood: Alcohol, Sexual Violence, and Killing in the Holocaust." In *The Holocaust and Masculinities: Critical Inquiries into the Presence and Absence of Men*, edited by Björn Krondorfer and Ovidiu Creanga, 147–69. Albany: SUNY Press, 2020.

Wette, Wolfram. *Karl Jäger: Mörder der litauischen Juden*. Frankfurt am Main: Fischer Taschenbuch Verlag, 2011.

Wieland, Christina. *The Fascist State of Mind and the Manufacturing of Masculinity: A Psychoanalytic Approach*. London: Routledge, 2015.

Wildt, Michael. *An Uncompromising Generation: The Nazi Leadership of the Reich Security Main Office*. Translated by Tom Lampert. Madison: University of Wisconsin Press, 2010.

Witte, Peter, Uwe Lohalm, and Wolfgang Scheffler, eds. *Der Dienstkalender Heinrich Himmlers 1941/42*. Hamburg: Christians Verlag, 1999.

Woods, Amy Louise. *Lynching and Spectacle: Witnessing Racial Violence in America, 1890–1940*. Chapel Hill: University of North Carolina Press, 2009.

Wygoda, Hermann. *In the Shadow of the Swastika*. Edited by Mark Wygoda. Urbana: University of Illinois Press, 1998.

Zipperstein, Steven J. *Pogrom: Kishinev and the Tilt of History*. New York: Liveright, 2018.

INDEX

Photographs are indicated by page numbers in italics.